Religion and the Morality of the Market

Since the collapse of the Berlin Wall, there has been a widespread affirmation of economic ideologies that conceive of the market as an autonomous sphere of human practice, holding that market principles should be applied to human action at large. In the wake of the 2008 financial crisis, the ascendance of market reason has been countered by calls for reforms of financial markets and for the consideration of moral values in economic practice. This book intervenes in these debates by showing how neoliberal market practices engender new forms of religiosity, and how religiosity shapes economic actions. It reveals how religious movements and organizations have reacted to the increasing prominence of market reason in unpredictable, and sometimes counterintuitive, ways. Using a range of examples from different countries and religious traditions, the book illustrates the myriad ways in which religious and market moralities are closely imbricated in diverse global contexts.

DAROMIR RUDNYCKYJ is Associate Professor in the Department of Anthropology at the University of Victoria, Canada. His research addresses globalization, religion, development, Islam, and the state in Southeast Asia, focusing on Indonesia and Malaysia. His current research examines the globalization of Islamic finance and analyzes efforts to make Kuala Lumpur the "New York of the Muslim World" by transforming it into the central node in a transnational Islamic financial system. His book, *Spiritual Economies: Islam, Globalization, and the Afterlife of Development* (2010), was awarded a Sharon Stephens Prize from the American Ethnological Society. His research has been supported by the American Council for Learned Societies, the Social Sciences and Humanities Research Council of Canada (SSHRC), the Social Science Research Council, the Wenner-Gren Foundation for Anthropological Research, and other scholarly foundations.

FILIPPO OSELLA is Professor of Anthropology and South Asian Studies at the University of Sussex, UK. He has conducted research in Kerala, South India, since 1989 and published two joint monographs, one on issues of stratification, identity and social mobility among an "ex-untouchable" community and another on masculinities. Based on fieldwork in Kerala and a number of Gulf countries, his more recent research has examined contemporary transformations of South Indian Muslims communities resulting from economic liberalization and the popularization of Islamic reformism. Recently he has concluded a research project on Muslim practices of charity and philanthropy in Sri Lanka.

Religion and the Morality of the Market

Edited by

Daromir Rudnyckyj
University of Victoria

Filippo Osella
University of Sussex

CAMBRIDGE
UNIVERSITY PRESS

CAMBRIDGE
UNIVERSITY PRESS

University Printing House, Cambridge CB2 8BS, United Kingdom
One Liberty Plaza, 20th Floor, New York, NY 10006, USA
477 Williamstown Road, Port Melbourne, VIC 3207, Australia
4843/24, 2nd Floor, Ansari Road, Daryaganj, Delhi – 110002, India
79 Anson Road, #06-04/06, Singapore 079906

Cambridge University Press is part of the University of Cambridge.

It furthers the University's mission by disseminating knowledge in the pursuit of education, learning, and research at the highest international levels of excellence.

www.cambridge.org
Information on this title: www.cambridge.org/9781316636961
10.1017/9781316888704

First published 2017

A catalogue record for this publication is available from the British Library.

Library of Congress Cataloging-in-Publication Data
Names: Rudnyckyj, Daromir and Osella, Filippo 1972– editors.
Title: Religion and the morality of the market / edited by Daromir Rudnyckyj, University of Victoria, Filippo Osella, University of Sussex.
Description: New York: Cambridge University Press, 2017. |
Includes bibliographical references and index.
Identifiers: LCCN 2016041864| ISBN 9781107186057 (hard back) |
ISBN 9781316636961 (paper back)
Subjects: LCSH: Economics – Religious aspects. | Economics –
Moral and ethical aspects.
Classification: LCC HB72.R45133 2016 | DDC 201/.73–dc23
LC record available at https://lccn.loc.gov/2016041864

ISBN 978-1-107-18605-7 Hardback
ISBN 978-1-316-63696-1 Paperback

To Jill, Jos, Robbin, and Zhdan. – DR
To Anna, Gabriele. – FO

Contents

Figures

Contributors

JULIE Y. CHU is a sociocultural anthropologist at the University of Chicago with interests in mobility and migration, economy and value, ritual life, material culture, media and technology, and state regulatory regimes. Her book, *Cosmologies of Credit: Transnational Mobility and the Politics of Destination in China* (2010), received the 2011 Sharon Stephens Prize from the American Ethnological Society and the 2012 Clifford Geertz Prize from the Society for the Anthropology of Religion. Her current writing project is entitled *The Hinge of Time: Infrastructure and Chronopolitics at China's Global Edge*. Based on three years of fieldwork largely among Chinese customs inspectors and transnational migrant couriers, this work will analyze the various infrastructures in place (legal-rational, financial, cosmic, piratical) for managing the temporal intensities and rhythms of people and things on the move between southern China and the United States.

SIMON COLEMAN is Chancellor Jackman Professor of the Study of Religion at the University of Toronto. He has been editor of the *Journal of the Royal Anthropological Institute* and is now coeditor of *Religion and Society: Advances in Research*. His research interests include Pentecostal and charismatic Christianity, pilgrimage, hospital chaplaincies, and cathedrals. He has conducted research in Sweden, the United Kingdom, and Nigeria. Publications include *The Globalisation of Charismatic Christianity: Spreading the Gospel of Prosperity* (Cambridge University Press, 2000) and *Reframing Pilgrimage: Cultures in Motion* (edited with John Eade, 2004). His publications on the economics of the prosperity gospel include "The Charismatic Gift" (*Journal of the Royal Anthropological Institute* 2004, 10(2): 421–442) and "Prosperity Unbound? Debating the 'Sacrificial Economy'" (*Research in Economic Anthropology* 2011, 31: 23–45). With Rosalind Hackett, he has edited *The Anthropology of Global Pentecostalism and Evangelicalism* (2015).

NANDINI GOOPTU is head of the Oxford Department of International Development and fellow of St Antony's College, Oxford. Educated in Calcutta and at Cambridge, and trained as a social historian, she is the author of *The*

Politics of the Urban Poor in Early-Twentieth Century India (Cambridge University Press, 2001), editor of *Enterprise Culture in Neoliberal India* (2013), and coeditor of *India and the British Empire* (Oxford History of the British Empire series, 2012) and *The Persistence of Poverty in India* (2014). She has taught at Cambridge and Oxford. While her past research has been on late colonial India, her current research is concerned with social and political transformation and cultural change in contemporary India in the wake of economic liberalization.

FARZANA HANIFFA obtained her PhD in Anthropology from Columbia University in New York in 2007 and is currently a senior lecturer in the Sociology Department of the University of Colombo. Her research and activist interests for the past fifteen years have concentrated on minority politics in Sri Lanka with an emphasis on the country's Muslim communities. She has published on Islamic reform movements in Sri Lanka, the history of Muslims' involvement in electoral politics, and the ethnic conflict. More recently Haniffa has written on problems of postwar resettlement in northern Sri Lanka, and the mobilizing of anti-Muslim sentiment after the war. In 2009 she initiated – through the Law and Society Trust – a Citizens' Commission to inquire into and report on the expulsion of Muslims from the Northern Province of Sri Lanka by the Liberation Tigers of Tamil Eelam. The final report, titled *A Quest for Redemption: The Story of the Northern Muslims*, was released in 2011 and translated into Tamil and Sinhala. Dr. Haniffa has also written on issues of women and conflict, transitional justice, militarization, and child rights in Sri Lanka. She is a member of the management council of the Social Scientists' Association and chair of the board of directors of the Secretariat for Muslims.

HILMAN LATIEF is Assistant Professor at the Faculty of Islamic Studies, Muhammadiyah University of Yogyakarta (UMY). He was trained in cross cultural studies and comparative religion at Gadjah Mada University (Indonesia) and Western Michigan University (USA), where he obtained MA degrees in 2003 and 2005 respectively. He was awarded a PhD degree in Islamic Studies from Universiteit Utrecht, the Netherlands in 2012 and was appointed as a research fellow in KITLV-Leiden in 2013. His research interests include Islamic charities, modern Muslim social and intellectual history, and religion and development in Southeast Asia. His current research projects include philanthropy and Muslim citizenship; faith-based philanthropy and minority groups; and Gulf charities, social engagement, and Islamic renewal in Southeast Asia.

VALENTINA NAPOLITANO is Associate Professor of Anthropology at the University of Toronto. She works on critical Catholic studies as well as on the anthropology of traces, borderlands, and migration. Her most recent works are *Migrant Hearts and the Atlantic Return: Transnationalism and the Roman Catholic Church* (2016), and, coedited with K. Norget and M. Mayblin, *The Anthropology of Catholicism: A Compendium Reader* (in press). She is also the co-editor, with N. Stadler and N. Luz, of *Borderlands and Religion: Materialities, Ontologies and the Transformation of Sovereignty.* (Religion and Society: Advances in Research, 2015), and she is currently working on a book on Francis as the first Jesuit pope from the Americas.

FILIPPO OSELLA is Professor of Anthropology and South Asian studies at the University of Sussex. He has conducted research in Kerala, South India, since 1989 and co-authored two monographs with Caroline Osella: one on issues of stratification, identity and social mobility among an "ex-untouchable" community (*Social Mobility in Kerala*, 2000) and another on masculinities (*Men and Masculinity in South India*, 2007). His recent research examines contemporary transformations of South Indian Muslim communities, with fieldwork in Kozhikode (Calicut) and a number of Gulf countries. He has coedited a special issue of *Modern Asian Studies* on "Islamic Reform Movements in South Asia" (with C. Osella), a special issue of *South Asia: Journal of South Asian Studies* on "The Politics of Food in South Asia" (with C. Osella), and a special issue of *Journal of the Royal Anthropological Institute* on "Islam, Politics and Modernity" (with B. Soares). He has recently concluded a joint Economic & Social Research Council–Department for International Development–funded research project (with R. Stirrat and T. Widger) on charity, philanthropy, and development in Colombo, Sri Lanka. He is currently coediting a special issue of *Modern Asian Studies* on traditions and practices of charity and philanthropy in South Asia.

DAROMIR RUDNYCKYJ is Associate Professor in the Department of Anthropology at the University of Victoria, Canada. His research addresses globalization, religion, development, Islam, and the state in Southeast Asia, focusing on Indonesia and Malaysia. His current research examines the globalization of Islamic finance and analyzes efforts to make Kuala Lumpur the "New York of the Muslim World" by transforming it into the central node in a transnational Islamic financial system. His book, *Spiritual Economies: Islam, Globalization, and the Afterlife of Development* (2010), was awarded a Sharon Stephens Prize from the American Ethnological Society. Dr. Rudnyckyj has published articles in *Journal of Asian Studies, American Ethnologist, Cultural Anthropology, Social Text, Anthropological Theory, Journal of the Royal Anthropological Institute, Political and Legal Anthropology Review*, and elsewhere. His research has been supported by the American Council for Learned Societies, the Social Sciences and Humanities Research Council of Canada (SSHRC), the Social Science Research Council, the Wenner–Gren Foundation for Anthropological Research, and other scholarly foundations.

CHINA SCHERZ is Assistant Professor of Anthropology at the University of Virginia. She received her PhD in Medical Anthropology from the Universities of California at San Francisco and Berkeley. She is the author of *Having People, Having Heart: Charity, Sustainable Development, and Problems of Dependence in Central Uganda* (2014) and has published articles in *American Ethnologist*, *Political and Legal Anthropology Review*, and *Anthropological Theory*. She is presently engaging a new set of questions related to ethics, religion, and agency in relation to alcohol use and rehabilitation in Uganda.

BENJAMIN SOARES is Professor of Religion and African Studies at the University of Florida, Gainesville, and Professor of Anthropology at the University of Amsterdam. He is a scholar of Islam and Muslim societies in Africa, having conducted research in Mali, Mauritania, Nigeria, Senegal, and Sudan, as well as among African Muslims in Europe and Asia. He is the author of *Islam and the Prayer Economy* (2005); editor of *Muslim-Christian Encounters in Africa* (2006); and co-editor of a series of interrelated books, *Islam, Politics, Anthropology* (2010); *Islam, état et société en Afrique* (2009), *Islam and Muslim Politics in Africa* (2007); *New Media and Religious Transformations in Africa* (2015); and *Muslim Youth and the 9/11 Generation* (2016). He also coedits the International African Institute's book series, the International African Library (Cambridge University Press).

SANJAY SRIVASTAVA is Professor of Sociology at Institute of Economic Growth, Delhi University. His publications include *Constructing Post-Colonial India: National Character and the Doon School* (1998); *Asia: Cultural Politics in the Global Age* (coauthor, 2001); *Sexual Sites, Seminal Attitudes: Sexualities, Masculinities and Culture in South Asia* (contributing editor, 2004); *Passionate Modernity. Sexuality, Class and Consumption in India* (2007); and *Sexuality Studies* (contributing editor, 2013). Most recently, he has published *Entangled Urbanism: Slum, Gated Community and Shopping Mall in Delhi and Gurgaon* (2015). He is coeditor of the journal *Contributions to Indian Sociology*.

V. J. VARGHESE teaches at the Department of History, University of Hyderabad, India. His areas of interest include modern South Asian history, transnational migrations, and the making of regional modernities in South Asia, with a focus on Kerala in South India and Punjab in North India. He has coauthored *Dreaming Mobility and Buying Vulnerability: Overseas Recruitment Practices in India* (2011) and coedited *Anjuru Varshathe Keralam: Chila Arivadayalangal* in Malayalam (1999/2011), and *Migration, Mobility and Multiple Affiliations: Punjabis in a Transnational World* (Cambridge University Press, 2015).

Acknowledgments

We extend our utmost gratitude to all those who helped bring this volume to fruition. The conception for this volume began in June 2013 with a two-day workshop at King's College, London that generated a conversation among many of the contributors to the volume. The workshop was generously supported by funds from King's College London, Sussex University, Quaid-i-Azam University Islamabad, the British Council, and the Higher Education Council of Pakistan. Daromir Rudnyckyj would like to acknowledge the support of the Social Sciences and Humanities Research Council of Canada and the American Council of Learned Societies, both of which provided material support to enable this project. The initial workshop would not have taken place without the intellectual contribution and practical efforts of Humeira Iqtidar and Ammara Maqsood. We are truly indebted to them, as well as to all of those who attended the workshop but were not able to contribute to this volume. We would also like to express our gratitude to our respective departments at the University of Victoria and Sussex University for allowing us precious time away from our teaching and administrative duties to write and complete the editing. A number of colleagues, doctoral students, and friends commented on the formulation of the volume and/or the writing in the Introduction, pushing us to refine our thinking and analyses. In particular, we would like to thank Roderick (Jock) Stirrat, Magnus Marsden, Jon Mitchell, Dinah Rajak, Ben Soares, Maria Teresa Silvestrini, and Syed Mohammed Faisal for their valuable insights and stimulating criticisms. Basit Karim Iqbal diligently read through the entire volume and gave us detailed editorial suggestions. Two anonymous reviewers encouraged us to tighten the framing of the project and rightfully challenged us to enhance the specificity of the insights we sought to make. Lucy Rhymer and Andrew Winnard at Cambridge University Press guided and supported our project throughout. We are thankful for their generosity and forbearance. Finally, a big thank you to our respective families, who stalwartly coped with our distractions throughout the production of this volume.

Introduction: Assembling Market and Religious Moralities

Filippo Osella, University of Sussex,
Daromir Rudnyckyj, University of Victoria

At the end of 2013, the director of mission and public affairs for the Church of England, Malcolm Brown, wrote in the pages of the widely read British liberal newspaper *The Observer*, "For the first time in a century, the Church of England is speaking about the morality of the marketplace and is not being told that 'theology has nothing to say to economics, so shut up' " (Brown 2013: 29). Five years after the start of global economic recession, the Church's public intervention is not, however, simply posing religious ethics against the apparent a/immoral working of markets. Rather, "it's the recognition that the market is a brilliant distributional mechanism with great power to adapt and self-correct, provided there is enough moral awareness among the players to prevent the accumulation of overweening monopoly power." Condemning the tendency of current markets to produce uncompetitive monopolies, Brown suggests that

> A better economy need not mean jettisoning the disciplines of the market economy. It does mean recognizing that the market's inbuilt tendency to erode competition damages us all unless held in check. Regulation may be part of a solution, but it contains the ever-present spectre of distributing too much power in the hands of the state. The missing link is one which Adam Smith would have understood – the rediscovery of a moral consensus (he called it mutual sympathy) to mark the limits to markets so that, paradoxically, the market can deliver what people – including those too poor to interest an uncompetitive market – want and need. (ibid.)

Some months before Brown's comments, in a fundraising event organized in 2012 by the Islamic Education and Research Academy, Mr Amir delivered a lecture in Birmingham to a gathering of more than 3,000 people, mostly of Pakistani origin. An Egyptian-Canadian, Mr Amir is a well-known Muslim charity fundraiser, regularly invited by mosques, community organizations and charities to motivate and mobilize potential Muslim donors. To a rapt audience he intoned:

> Doing *sadaqa* [voluntary charity] is like opening a savings account in the bank of Allah. As you open a savings account in any British bank, you get a fixed amount of money as profit at the end of every month. But the bank of Allah is neither a miser nor mean, and unlike worldly banks it does not operate on the principles of greed and exploitation.

> My friends, no bank is richer than the bank of Allah as nothing is wealthier than Him. Likewise, nobody can give you more profit that Allah himself. If you invest one pound as sadaqa in your savings account in the bank of Allah, He will give you profit of seven pounds. If you invest ten pounds, He will give you a profit of seventy pounds...The profit money will come to you in this world in mysterious ways and there will be an equal reward of merits in the after world for you. Isn't this a fair trade with Allah? (Abid 2015: 164)

Mr Amir's comparison of the rewards for pious acts to the returns on a financial investment might be read as indicating that, in the context of globalization and neoliberal reforms, the hidden hand of the market has extended its reach as far as colonizing the hitherto discrete life-world of religion (cf. Habermas 1992). Yet at the same time, as shown in Brown's account, organized religion suggests that an appropriately moralized market could (and should) become the means for the realization of ethical values compatible with religious injunctions for social justice. Here, religion extends its sacred touch to redress (moral) failings of the market economy.

This volume takes up the modalities of economic action and religious practice delineated in Brown and Amir's appeals to the role of faith in the market to address two central questions. First, how are economic practices and market forms eliciting new moral dispositions and religious configurations? Second, how do religious moralities frame contemporary economic practices? Indeed, as far back as the work of Marcel Mauss and Karl Polanyi, the presumption has been that modernity is characterized by the "disembedding" of the market and its moral claims from society and religion (Mauss 1925; Polanyi 1944). Rather than presuming a progressive secular separation of economy from society, we suggest that market moralities are playing a key role in creating contemporary religious forms and social relationships. In this sense, *Religion and the Morality of Markets* highlights how religious forms in both the global South and the global North, are being reembedded in market actions and, on occasion, framing those actions.

Modernity has long presumed that religiosity is proper to the private domain and that the progressive disenchantment of the world is inevitable. The assumption is that "religion" would provide a remedy to the moral deficiencies of a self-regulating market, which, more often than not, appears unable to turn self-interest and self-love into means for fostering social good.[1] Inevitably, then, the discourse of modernity leads us to pause over the apparent blurring of boundaries between market and religion in Amir and Brown's public interventions. Indeed, market practices diverging from the logic of rational calculation, or expressions of religiosity dangerously close to market ideologies, have drawn considerable academic attention beyond anthropology's time-honoured concern with the operation and transformation of premodern or precapitalist societies. Taking for granted the ontological premises of modernity, much social scientific research has sought either to establish the compatibility of market rationality with religion or to find lines of causation to processes through which the market appears to mobilize/colonize religion and religiosity for the purpose of capital accumulation.

One strand of work has suggested that modern capitalism and the forms of rationality it engenders do not lead inevitably to a progressive disenchantment or secularization of life-worlds. Under certain circumstances and in specific locales, the logic and ideology of the market might enable the persistence, if not proliferation of different modalities of religiosity (for a review, see Obadia and Wood 2011; Obadia 2013; see also Rey 2004), leading some scholars to employ the analytical tools of economics – rational choice theory, for instance – to explain renewed participation in religious life (see, e.g., Stark and Bainbridge 1985; Stark and Finke 2000; Stolz 2006; Blasi 2009). In the United States, research suggests that competition between churches and the marketing of religiosity has fostered the development of vigorous and assertive religious communities, shoring up Christianity from the apparent decline observed in Western Europe. The emergence of a buoyant market in religion resonates with and gives expression to neoliberal principles of market competition and consumer choice, shot through with American modalities of individual self-realization, community building and entrepreneurship (Harding 2000; Casanova 2003; Moreton 2009; Elisha 2011).

Although it might be difficult to identify comparable markets in religion beyond North America (see Turner 2004; Csordas 2009; Van der Veer 2012), religiosity appears as the object of market competition and consumerism well outside both the United States and the Christian tradition. In India, for instance, rapid economic development has been accompanied by the proliferation of religious specialists across the religious spectrum, including *poojaris*, *mullahs*, gurus, astrologers, priests, healers and more, who can be approached or sponsored in an effort to shore up chances of success in everything from university entrance exams to stock market tips, in an increasingly competitive economy and expanding culture of aggressive entrepreneurship (see, e.g., Osella and Osella 2003). Often advertised in newspapers or popularized through television programs, religious specialists have in some cases become successful entrepreneurs who compete for customers-cum-followers in a vibrant and crowded religious market. In Taiwan, the new rich travel to shrines honouring ghosts like the Eighteen Lords Temple to receive insight on lucky lottery numbers from beyond the grave (Weller 2009), while urban professionals seeking success in a neoliberal economy attend Heqi sessions that contain elements of both self-help theory and New Age philosophy. In Thailand, traditional Buddhist practices, such as meditation and merit-making, are mobilized to achieve personal prosperity in new institutions such as the Dhammakāya Temple (Scott 2009). From its founding in the Philippines, the El Shaddai movement has expanded to 10 million followers worldwide who subscribe to a charismatic Catholic version of the American evangelical "prosperity gospel" (Wiegele 2005). The demise of socialism has precipitated a host of New Age movements and reengineered religious practices attuned to making sense of new market realities (Chu 2010; Luehrmann 2011; Matza 2012). Researchers have also noted that the global spread of Pentecostalism from Africa to Oceania illuminates the profound synergy of this strand of Christianity with market morality, a resonance due to its focus on individual responsibility for salvation (Newell 2007; Pfeiffer, Gimbel-Sherr and Augusto 2007; Schram 2010; Haynes 2012). Across the Muslim world from Turkey to Indonesia a new strand of moderate religious figures are creating practices of Islamic piety conducive to business success (Soares 2005; Marsden 2014; Isik 2010; Jones 2010; Howell 2013).

Sudden economic transformations appear, then, to have intensified the search for the means to tame the inevitable uncertainties that the future holds, if not to bring forward miraculous life-changing transformations (see, e.g. Ewing 1997; Werbner 2003). And yet, in India the commodification of religious practices and rituals cannot be reduced to economic liberalization and consequent "consumer citizenship" (see, e.g., Srivastava 2007; Lukose 2009). Intense competition between religious specialists to attract wealthy and powerful devotees-cum-customers has been observed across different religious traditions and historical periods (Appadurai and Breckenridge 1976; Parry 1980; Fuller 1984; Green 2011). The selling of spiritual indulgences across the pre-Reformation Christian world (for an excellent discussion, see Swanson 2007) or the commerce in relics imbued with spiritual power well beyond the confines of European Christianity (see, e.g., Burns 1982; Tambiah 1984; Geary 1986; Wheeler 2006; for an overview, see Walsham 2010) all indicate a longer history of reciprocity between religion and market moralities.

Religion and the Market after False Consciousness

Regardless of historical antecedents and continuities, it is the global spread of market capitalism and neoliberal techniques that has been attributed the power to colonize the language and organization of religion, turning religiosity into a means of capital accumulation. Religion, here, has become inextricably bound to the (neoliberal) market, either by fostering the development of novel forms of consumption and securing the allegiance of consumers, or by producing specific dispositions towards competition, entrepreneurship and flexibility that resonate with the demands of production and market participation in globalized capitalism. Research has moved beyond a narrow focus on the circulation of and market for religious objects, and of the politics of piety they engender and materialize (see e.g., Jackson 1999; Simpson 2007; Soares 2005), to examine the emergence of markets simultaneously fostering and catering to the tastes and needs of specific bodies of religious-oriented consumers (see, for instance, debates concerning the emergence of Islamic forms of consumerism, from fashion to food: Kandiyoti and Saktanber 2002; Meneley 2007; Moors and Tarlo 2007; Fischer 2008, 2011; Jones 2010). In the meantime, a number of studies have charted the emergence of management practices that mobilize the discourse of religious duty and piety to secure labour practices commensurable with the demands of market competition. Studies of Japanese (Kondo 1990), Turkish (Buğra 1998, 2002), South Indian (Osella and Osella 2009), Malaysian (Sloane 1999) or Indonesian (Watson 2005) industrialists and entrepreneurs, for instance, have explored ways through which novel forms of production and work discipline are elicited and reproduced through religious discourses that reconfigure labour as an ethical duty. Whilst we will return later to these studies, for the moment we notice that many a time these debates have evoked the ghost of Max Weber not only to claim the compatibility of certain forms of religious reformism with modernity (see, e.g., Geertz 1968; Singer 1972; Gellner 1981; Eickelman and Piscatori 1996; Meyer 1999), but also to establish degrees of elective affinity between processes of rationalization of religious life and the adoption of "modern" market practices (Geertz 1963; Adas 2006; Baldacchino 2012). Read through the lens of Weber's *Protestant Ethic*, "reformist" Hinduism (Van der Veer 1994), Buddhism (Gombrich and Obeyesekere 1988) and Islam (Robinson 2008) have been linked with the development of particular subjectivities and dispositions that resonate with, and eventually foster, novel political and economic orientation among emerging middle classes (see, e.g., Joshi 2001; Birla 2008).

It is the prosperity gospel preached by an array of fast-expanding Christian evangelical churches across the world that has generated some of the most engaging debates on the affinity between market and religion. Followers of prosperity movements believe that enhanced religious devotion will net them economic success through divine intervention (Coleman 2000). Especially popular in these movements is the "seed-faith principle" in which adherents are encouraged, to use Wiegele's words, to "invest in miracles" by making donations to religious groups as a means of "eliciting miracles from God" (2005: 21). Addressing the rapid expansion of charismatic and evangelical Christian churches in the global South, research, on the one hand, has connected the spread of the prosperity gospel to the global expansion of either (neoliberal) capitalism (see, e.g., Brouwer, Gifford and Rose 1996) or modernity (see, e.g., Maxwell 1998; Meyer 1998, 1999, 2004; Keane 2008). On the other hand, research has also explained away the success of charismatic churches as a means of appropriating the modern, and to engage with an apparent sense of marginalization and hopelessness generated by policies of structural adjustment in the postcolony. Jean and John Comaroff (2000) have offered a more nuanced version of "deprivation" approaches

(Coleman 2011: 31) to the study of the prosperity gospel, focusing on the dialectical relations between two different expressions or understandings of "occult forces" animating millennial capitalism in the southern African post-colony. Fostering individualism/individualization, an ethics of entrepreneurship and orientations towards novel forms of consumerism, the Comaroffs argue that the "health and wealth" gospel produces the illusion that economic prosperity can be achieved through the magical intervention of the hidden hand of both the market and God. At the same time, witchcraft accusations and rumours of blood-stealing vampires or of zombified workers mobilized to toil for the wealthy and powerful are presented as a demotic means through which the apparently inscrutable processes of capital accumulation under global capitalism are apprehended and evaluated (see also Weiss 1998; White 2000).

Although the Comaroffs (2000) struggle to negotiate a narrow path between economic determinism and looser notions of elective affinity, in their account new forms of religiosity are eventually reduced to instances of false consciousness: ideological props that propel the expansion of a hegemonic global capitalism (Marshall 2009; Rudnyckyj 2010). The prosperity gospel, and born-again churches more generally, are a means to propagate the "spirit of neoliberalism," supporting along the way the structural reorganization of economic and political processes. Jean Comaroff (2009) warns that neo-Protestantism's theocratic orientation and unreflexive penchant for the coherence of absolute truths (and, we guess, of other expressions of so-called "religious fundamentalism") undermine the core principles of secular modernity. If under modernity, to use Habermas's words, "the social integrative powers of the religious tradition shaken by enlightenment" are replaced by "the unifying, consensus-creating power of reason" (1985: 197; see also Tawney 1926), then the continued or re-merging role of religion and religiosity needs explaining, and is eventually reduced, as in the Comaroffs' interventions, to an epiphenomenon of the secular functioning of the social totality. In other words, the specific political and intellectual genealogies of European and North American Christian-secular representations of "economy" and "religion" as separate ontological categories of thought and practice are attributed universal value (cf. Asad 2003; Marshall 2009; Agamben 2011). As a result of this process of disembedding and autonomization, religion, Zizek argues, can be attributed only two possible roles, "therapeutic or critical. It either helps individuals to function better in the existing order, or it tries to assert itself as a critical agency articulating what is wrong with this order as such, a space for the voices of discontent" (2003: 3). What goes amiss here is Weber's insight that while capitalism (Western, and to be more precise, Northern European and American) presents itself as necessarily secular, it is in fact profoundly Protestant in the forms of ethical comportment that it entails and fosters. It is the normalization of the latter that, in turn, allows modern capitalism to justify claims of secularity.

Moving from the determinations of capitalism to those of globalization at large, Csordas (2009) addresses the problem of religion and the market by examining the articulation of globalization and religion, addressing both the globalization of religion and what he calls the religion of globalization. On the one hand, by the globalization of religion, Csordas refers to the ways in which religion "travels." He identifies easily learned and quickly disseminated "portable practices," such as yoga and feng shui, as marking one manifestation of the way in which religious practices spread transnationally. "Transposable messages," such as prosperity gospels, which capture how particular religious tenets gain traction in a range of cultural settings, demonstrate another manifestation of the globalization of religion. In a parallel move, Olivier Roy argues that globalization has acted as a catalyst for various instances and expressions of religious revivalism. For Roy (2004), expanding forms of religiosity are those that travel well, that is, those that can mirror the disembedding and dislocation of cultural and social practices engendered by globalization itself as found, for instance, in certain forms of Islamism propagated through electronic media. On the other hand, echoing the Comaroffs' claims regarding millennial capitalism and the culture of neoliberalism, Csordas (2009) draws attention to "globalization as religion", which refers to how the ideology of an integrated global market has become a universal economic orthodoxy. To these ways of conceptualizing the articulation of religion and the market, this volume adds a third: the ways in which religious practices are themselves mobilized to facilitate economic integration and action commensurate with the logic of the market (see also Osella and Osella 2009; Muehlebach 2012; O'Neill 2013). Thus, we draw attention to new ways of conceiving of religious expression and organizing religious communities enabled by the language and logic of the market.

Pious Modernity

Departing from understandings of religion as derivative of economic or political relations connecting the local with the global – and also from the recovery of religiosity characteristic of the so-called "post-secular turn" in social theory[2] – we note that the genealogies of the modern are inflected by specific religious traditions (see, e.g., Asad 1993; Chatterjee 1993; Salvatore 1997; Prakash 1999; Agamben 2011: 261ff). The historical, cultural and geographic specificities of the modern lead to the articulation of diverse, albeit at times parallel and overlapping, categorizations and definitions of both secularity and religiosity that cannot easily be subsumed into the universalist models of Western social theory. While the historical contingency of categories such as "religion" and "economy" makes us skeptical of their analytical or heuristic value, we take stock of the fact that it is not social theory alone that produces essentialist and dichotomizing understandings of social practice, nor is such a work of purification exclusive to modernity. Social actors themselves frequently objectify economic action and religiosity as separate social and moral domains whose interaction is of wider concern. Yet, in other historical contexts, such an opposition is softened or dissolved altogether. Iqtidar (2011) and Haenni (2005), for instance, have argued that, following the introduction of economic liberalization in Pakistan and Egypt respectively, the market is increasingly perceived to be expanding its influence to the point of replacing the role of state in normalizing social life and political relations. As a consequence, in both Pakistan and Egypt the market has drawn the attention of Islamist organizations and sympathizers, becoming the target of "conquest" in the similar way as the state had been in earlier times (see also Kuran 2004; Tripp 2006; cf. Ahmad 2009).

However, the complexities, tensions, and heterogeneity of religious orthopraxy make it implausible to generalize about the orientations of specific religious traditions towards accumulation of wealth, consumption or capitalism as whole. Consider, for example, Pope Francis's recent calls for a reintroduction of ethics into economic life. In his public interventions we can detect the (re)emergence of a theology that objectifies the "market" as the realm of self-interest and profit alone. Represented as able to generate but a weak sense of moral engagement and responsibility, the market requires external moral disciplining and policing (see Napolitano, Chapter 12). The history of Catholic theology and practice, though, reveals tensions – and eventual mediation and coexistence – between significantly different orientations towards economic action and the management of property. In medieval monastic orders, for instance, "wealth could be handled in a variety of ways – either in glorified Cluniac-style, maximized and de-aestheticized the Cistercian way, or radically attacked as in the movements calling for a return to true apostolic poverty" (Silber 1993: 116; see also Muehlebach 2009).[3] The capacity to encompass opposites and to maintain them in an unresolved productive tension is not the prerogative of medieval Catholic theology alone. Liberal and neoliberal subjectivities emerge, Muehlebach (2009, 2012) argues in her study of contemporary voluntarism in Italy, precisely at the intersection of market-driven self-interested instrumentality and altruistic humanitarian compassion and benevolence (see also Mauss 1925). More importantly, common to medieval monastic understandings of wealth is "the principle of distinction between personal and collective or corporate wealth", the precursor, Silber argues, of the rhetoric of "de-personification and autonomization of economic activity" (1993: 116) underpinning the modern market economy (cf. Hirschman 1997). The progressive disembedding and aestheticization of the economy, then, has a genealogy that arches back well beyond the modern (Foucault 2008) or the Protestant reformation (Weber 2002).[4]

Although anthropology has been particularly adept at charting out and theorizing the moral economies of non-capitalist societies, it has sometimes been complicit in naturalizing and universalizing, and thus conferring reality to the disembeddedness and amorality of market capitalism. The notion of "moral economy" deployed by anthropologists is used in two distinct, but related, ways – one stressing its economic aspect, the other its moral content (Fassin 2009). In the first, moral *economy* refers to the embeddedness of economic practice, that is, to the degree to which economic activity is shaped by and carried out in the context of basic social and cultural relations that are found everywhere in the society (Mauss 1925; Polanyi 1944; Gregory 1982; Granovetter 1985; Carrier 1995). In the second meaning, *moral* economy draws attention to relationships between social actors based on mutual obligations and expectations of reciprocity – a pre-modern social contract, that is – that might provide subaltern groups with the means to engage critically with, or resist the penetration of capitalist relations and state power (Thompson 1971; Scott 1976). Although Carrier (1995) and Keane (2008) have warned that neither economy nor market can ever achieve total autonomy from the social, the fact that anthropologists have restricted empirical research to the working of moral economies in traditional or pre-capitalist contexts and to the articulation of the latter with market economies suggests implicitly that capitalism might be driven by self-interest and calculation alone, standing outside the wider sociocultural realm of ethics and morality. That is, "self-love" alone is considered to be insufficient to bind society together, leading Parry and Bloch (1989) to theorize tensions between different cycles of social reproduction. Here, individual gains made through market exchange in the capitalist economy need to be harnessed and socialized to become socially productive. From this perspective, capitalism and market economy might constitute a moral *economy*, but not a full-fledged *moral* economy, limiting, then, the possibility of an engagement with and theorization of the working of contemporary economies of morality.

To reveal the moral underpinnings of the market, then, we have to turn elsewhere, to research by economic sociologists who, in the steps of Polanyi and Granovetter, have explored processes through which "the market" is produced as an effect of the cumulative interventions of a heterogeneous assemblage, involving both human and nonhuman actors: market traders, economists, mathematicians, state apparatuses, legislations, educational institutions, economic theories, information technology, algorithms, electronic trading and more (Callon 1998; Mitchell 2005; MacKenzie, Muniesa and Siu 2007; MacKenzie 2008; Çalişkan 2010; Lépinay 2011). Critiques notwithstanding,[5] this body of research has underscored the sociality of processes leading to the production and reproduction of markets, but also the economy of affects, values, dispositions and habituations enabling everyday market practices and subjectivities (Thrift 2001; Richard and Rudnyckyj 2009). Ethnographic studies of stock markets and financial institutions have revealed the role of personal connections, life-styles, corporate fashions, creative intuitions, blind faith and plain luck in the working of financial markets (Zaloom 2006; Ho 2009; Miyazaki 2013). Here, the enchantment of actual market practice is teased out from the hegemonic rhetoric of economic rationality – from "quasimagical" reverence for esoteric mathematical models and statistics (LiPuma and Lee 2012), to strategies of divination and games of chance informing attempts to exploit or tame the uncertainties of financial markets (Appadurai 2011; see also Zaloom 2009). To date, however, discussions of "market cultures" have scantly engaged with religion and religiosity. An exception here is Guyer's (2007) analysis of correspondences and overlaps between notions of temporality articulated in macroeconomic theories and evangelical Christian theology – concerned with the consequences that actions in the present have on the distant future, they both "evacuate" the near future (see also Scherz 2013; Lazzarato 2012).[6]

Moral Claims and Neoliberal Religiosity

Since the 1970s there has been a significant shift in economic thought and practice, from a regime broadly dominated by Keynesian approaches in which the state is conferred a major role in economic management, to one that emphasizes neoliberal principles of market freedom and individual entrepreneurship. We argue that this transformation in economic thought and practice has inspired changing forms of religious practice, just as religious moralities have been deployed in new ways in the market. Thus, the goal of this volume is to demonstrate the diversity of forms of religious practice that emerge in this new landscape. This should not be taken to imply that new religious forms are the necessary outcome of changing material relationships. Rather, the empirical studies featured herein demonstrate that specific economic forms have affinities with particular religious practices. Thus, modern life is characterized as much as the convergence between religious and market moralities as by secularization and their increasing separation.

The notion of assemblage can be mobilized to analyse the complex production of markets and market cultures, to delineate the contours of what has been commonly referred to as neoliberalism (Callon 1998; see also Collier and Ong 2005), which is sometimes identified as the driving force of recent transformations of religiosity. We consider neoliberalism to be a heterogeneous assemblage of intellectual orientations, ideologies, social practices, institutional arrangements and policy experimentations seeking not only to foster and shore up novel forms of capital accumulation – from the introduction of flexible labour practices to the financialization of the economy – but also as the extension of economic rationality as a technology for the government of both individuals and populations (Ong 2007; Rudnyckyj 2010, 2014). Although supported and promoted by a variety of international organizations, think tanks, academic institutions and more, neoliberalism, as such, is neither coherent and monolithic, nor does it live up, in practice, to its ideological orthodoxy concerning the shape, working and effects of an autonomous and self-regulating market (Collier and Ong 2005; Ong 2006; Goldstein 2012; Hilgers 2012). We have to differentiate, then, between the representations free-marketeers make of themselves and of the outcomes of regulatory practices they promote, and the way the latter unfold in everyday life.

Indeed, processes of economic liberalization underpinning neoliberal-inspired reorganizations of the economy and market have had diverse outcomes in different locales, countries and continents. Compared to the United Kingdom, for instance, in India processes leading to the informalization of labour – the outcome of post-1991 economic liberalization – have taken place in a context in which the formal economy has been traditionally overshadowed by the vitality of an expansive informal sector (Gooptu 2001; De Neve 2005), and where the postcolonial developmental state had struggled historically to provide services for its citizens. Although we can neither lend homogeneity to neoliberalism and anticipate its outcomes nor extend the term to indiscriminately describe processes that have specific long-term histories and determinations (Yang 2000; Kipnis 2008; Nonini 2008; Ferguson 2010; cf. Cross 2010; Hilgers 2013), we should be mindful of social practices and cultural orientations that have emerged alongside the long march of economic liberalization and might have impacts beyond the local. We are not delineating a global neoliberal subjectivity drawn from ethnocentric readings of specifically European or North American historical contingencies, nor are we rushing to identify singular characteristics or orientations to processes of subjectivation – both of which are shortcomings of notions of consumer citizenship deployed to characterize the pre-2008 apex of economic liberalization. Rather, we suggest that certain core principles of neoliberalism – competition, meritocracy, individual autonomy, market calculation, entrepreneurship – might have acquired ethical and aesthetic value beyond the realm of economic action, becoming the means through which the social is apprehended, experienced and disciplined (Lazzarato 2012; Dardot and Laval 2014; see also Elyachar 2005, 2010; Roy 2012). Lazzarato, for instance, suggests that the economy of credit/debt underpinning both the neoliberal-driven expansion of the market, and the management of the aftermath of the 2008 economic crisis, "is inseparable from the production of the debtor subject and his [sic] 'morality'" (2012: 11; cf. Zelizer 2010). The work-on-the-self elicited and expected from the "indebted man" (sic) – the bearer of personal as well as collective/national debt – entails the cultivation of individual dispositions towards self-entrepreneurship, guaranteeing that he will take upon himself the full costs of the economic crisis.

Whilst we remain agnostic as to whether notions such as that of the "indebted man" might have purchase beyond European or North American modalities of capitalism (cf. Chua 2014), we find it useful to consider ways through which, to use Lazzarato's words, "the notion of 'economy'" has extended its reach so as to cover "both economic production and the production of subjectivity" (Lazzarato 2012: 11; see also Foucault 1991; Mitchell 2002: 80–119; Mitchell 2005). We are suggesting, then, that specific forms of material exchange and economic engagement are not only central to objectification of religious experience and piety (Coleman 2004; Keane 2008), but become also the means through which to imagine and experience novel forms of religiosity and religious organization. Members of Coleman's Word of Life Church, a globalizing Swedish Christian charismatic church, use the gift of words and money as a means to expand and transfer the power of the Holy Spirit to others, the eventual goal being "to promote divine influence without concern for boundaries between the material, the social and the spiritual" (Coleman 2004: 236). Similarly, Bielo (2007) argues that for evangelical Christians in the North American Midwest, financial success is both embedded in and enables the expression of a novel, born-again personhood (see also Harding 2000; Bialecki 2008). Beyond the world of churches preaching the prosperity gospel, charitable giving (of money, goods or time) remains one of the most obvious modes for the objectification and enactment of modalities of religious piety (see, e.g., Osella and Osella 2009; Bornstein 2013; Muehlebach 2012; Atia 2013).

The materiality of religiosity and of morality, and the affective underpinnings of the market lead us to consider relationships among dispositions, habituations, aesthetics and affects, that is, economies of morality, that are produced – contingently and haphazardly – by particular modalities of economic and religious practice under regimes of neoliberal reform. Unsurprisingly, divergences and convergences appear with equal frequency. In a study of Nigerian Pentecostalism, Marshall (2009) argues that the practices of Born Again Christian churches elicit particular moral dispositions that enable critical engagements with political life, allowing for the imagination of novel political relationships. A productive tension between individuation and social engagement informs, in different ways, the orientations and practices of North American Megachurches (Elisha 2011) or Pentecostal Christians in the Zambian Copperbelt (Haynes 2012). Here religiosity engenders not only economic and social integration, but also the (re)production of forms of sociality that compensate for or address the shortcomings of the market (see also Wiegele 2005). In other contexts, though, religious and market ethics might come together either to foster participation in economic activities (see, e.g., Van Dijk 2004) or to sustain neoliberal restructuring of the economy (see, e.g.,

Buğra 1998, 2002; Sloane 1999, 2011; Haenni 2005; Watson 2005; Adas 2006; Osella and Osella 2009; Baldacchino 2012). The introduction of Islamized human resources management techniques in an Indonesian steel plant planned for privatization is Rudnyckyj's entry point to elucidate the assemblage of Islam and neoliberal capitalism. Suggesting that "the hallmark of contemporary neoliberalism is that it seems to enable assemblages of religion and economics that certain strands of the social science have kept apart" (2009: 108), he develops the notion of "spiritual economies" to characterize "projects that seek to simultaneously transform workers into more pious subjects and more productive economic subjects" (ibid.: 106; see also 2010; cf. Marshall's 2009 notion of "political spiritualities").

The reciprocal process of neoliberalization of Islam and Islamization of neoliberalism identified by Rudnyckyj brings us back to the vexed question of the relation between religion and market. In discussing ways through which the hidden hand of God and of the market might often work together, we have emphasized the unhelpfulness of analyses that, in seeking to demonstrate lines of causality or structural determinations collapse, reduce religiosity to an epiphenomenon of economic thought and practice. Although it would be naïve to suggest that modernity alone objectifies religion and economy as discrete ontological and epistemological domains (Marshall 2009; Agamben 2011), it is the modernist teleology of rationalization and secularization that leads us to an apparently unresolvable causality dilemma. Modern capitalism, as Weber observed, goes alongside an ethicalization of labour as a duty and of capital accumulation as a virtue. That is, it entails the mobilization of values and dispositions that are beyond a strict logic of rational calculation, the apparent sole driving force of the modern market. In narratives of the modern – from Adam Smith, Weber, and Tawney to the current proponents of notions of post-secularism – religion, once it had been expelled through the door by rationality and secularism, is brought back in through the window to shore up capitalist development, to make it work for the good of society as a whole. Modernity's premises concerning the progressive secularization and autonomization of the social, then, set the stage for questions about the direction and intensity of the relationship between religion and market.

To move away from such an epistemological impasse, we suggest, following Marshall (2009), that congruencies, articulations and intersections between religion and market are, quite simply, the result of the common contingent historical milieu in which particular intellectual traditions and practices develop and gain wider plausibility. We have to consider, then, the role of institutions and networks that allow for the reproduction and circulation of specific knowledges, ideologies, aesthetics and practices at particular historical junctures (see Thrift 2005). Pope Francis's critical interventions on the immorality of unbridled capitalism, then, are as much the reflection of a specific Catholic theology as they are of his experience of hailing from a continent where neoliberal reforms were initially piloted and met with widespread refusal amidst widespread social dislocation. The pope's exhortations have gained traction within the Catholic Church and beyond because they resonate with wider disillusions in the aftermath of the post-2008 financial upheaval about the capacity of the market to foster the common good.

That in the last twenty-five years Gordon Gekko's flamboyant Wall Street excesses have morphed into Jordan Belfort's wolfish frauds and corruption underscores not only the contingency of moral evaluations of the market, but also that the ethics of market and religion might get the best of each other in unforeseen ways (see, e.g., Tuğal 2009: 124ff). The logic of the market and the exchanges it engenders might enable the articulation of novel religious theologies and practices, but in other circumstances it might be deemed to stand in the way of piety and salvation. In the same way, whether specific forms of religiosity might foster dispositions facilitating various modalities of engagement with the market or not, all depends on particular historical configurations that shape religion and market alike. In other words, elective affinities emerge, or unravel, not within a teleology of rationalization, secularization or abstraction, but in the midst of debates and practices whose reach, longevity and (both intended and unintended) consequences are contingent on the unfolding of history itself (Gregory 2012: 235ff). The question to address, then, is not the relation between formally defined domains of thought and practice (see Agamben 2013: 91). Rather we should discover, as the contributors of this volume do, how and by whom, and in what historical circumstances, religion and market might be produced as discrete categories whose relation might entail various degrees of overlap, assemblage, articulation and (in)compatibility.

Religion and the Morality of Markets

This volume includes twelve contributions that document both how market forms produce new religious dispositions and how religious moralities frame contemporary economic practices. Taken as a whole, the volume shows that the modernist conceit by which these two domains could be neatly cleaved from one another is untenable, a problem that is global in scope rather than confined to a discrete world region. In highlighting the global nature of this configuration, we argue that the transformation in the relationship between religiosity and economy that we seek to highlight is not located to a specific country or region, but rather illuminates a set of processes occurring simultaneously with distinct affinities in various parts of the world. Including evidence from East Asia, Southeast Asia, South Asia, sub-Saharan Africa, the Middle East, Europe, North America and Latin America, the chapters demonstrate the myriad ways in which religious and market moralities intersect in domains from Chinese fortune telling to Islamic revivalism to Catholic charity. In so doing, we seek to underscore the articulation of religious and market moralities through the lens of thc global.

Julie Chu's chapter examines the way in which customs officials at China's booming port of Xiamen simultaneously engage in sophisticated techniques of risk management and esoteric fortune telling practices, which have long been part of Chinese vernacular religious traditions. In so doing, she reveals a distinct chronopolitics in the apparently paradoxical fact that at the precise moment that techniques of increasingly sophisticated risk management have emerged to manage smuggling, customs workers are engaging in the ritualistic uncertainty of fortune-telling. Thus, occult practices such as fortune-telling frame the risk calculations of customs officials and Chu obliquely suggesting that occult practices are not as distinguishable from rational calculation as is often presumed. Chu shows how alongside the imperative toward a bureaucratic rationality premised on a moral order in which the sovereignty of the state is unquestioned, customs workers appeal to other moralities that cannot be reduced to the calculus of risk management.

Similarly, Simon Coleman's contribution addresses how risk and uncertainty are handled in Western prosperity gospels in the United Kingdom and North America. In so doing, he seeks to excavate an alternative approach to prosperity religions that have become overdetermined by the "occult economies" approach pioneered by Jean and John Comaroff. Whereas the latter see religious practice as an emotional response to social dislocation, Coleman reveals the latent functionalism in such approaches. By focusing on decidedly first-world locales, such as prosperous airport bookstores, rather than shantytown storefront churches, Coleman turns the anthropological gaze on the Western self to suggest that the prosperity gospel produces vigorous entrepreneurs with as much acumen as it does the listless zombies invoked by the Comaroffs. In analysing the prosperity gospel in Western contexts, Coleman shows that prosperity gospels are always already in a complex, dynamic relationship with neoliberal logic and moralities. Thus, participants in the prosperity economy must engage with the morality of market exchange.

Nandini Gooptu likewise picks up the convergence of market morals and religious logics in her analysis of a burgeoning literary market in India where self-styled self-help gurus, some of whom are CEOs of large corporations, integrate stories from Hindu folklore into corporate practice and human resources management. In this context, religious myths are reinterpreted to construct a moral order conducive to a globalized economy. Myths thus serve as techniques through which elites draw on a familiar repertoire of cultural knowledge to act on the actions of employees and workers. Gooptu shows how the mythical figure Hanuman, who figures prominently in the Indian epic the *Ramayana*, is invoked as an ideal worker with an extraordinary work ethic and capacity for self-management and individual responsibility. She quotes Devdutta Pattanaik

(Chief Belief Officer at a prominent Indian supermarket chain) echoing the sentiments of an earlier anthropology in asserting that a myth is "a cultural construct…that binds individuals and communities together." In this sense some of the analytical tools that anthropologists have made use of to comprehend religious morality are being redeployed in the construction of a moral order conducive to neoliberal development.

Also focusing on the post-liberalization period, Sanjay Srivastava details the emergence of what he calls "moral consumption" in India today. Citing ethnographic examples such as gated communities and private, profit-generating universities, he shows how India's emergent middle class creates a new configuration of capitalism that, as in Gooptu's case, makes recurrent reference to Hindu doctrine and practice. In both sites, Srivastava detects an effort to configure a Hindu subject capable of acting and competing in a neoliberal economic environment. Nonetheless, he argues, the neoliberalism in this configuration is profoundly "informed by the requirements of religious belief." Moral consumption, in turn, constitutes India's contemporary "divine market" where commodities are spiritualized and spirituality is subjected to a logic of commodification.

Whereas Srivastava's chapter shows how economic liberalization has coincided with a resurgence of Hindu practice in India, across the Palk Strait Farzana Haniffa shows how the convergence of religious discrimination and a state-supported project of liberalization has led members of Sri Lanka's Muslim minority to embrace a neoliberal outlook. As Muslim businesses have flourished in the export-oriented economy, so has Sinahala Buddhist ethno-nationalism. Thus, Haniffa shows how what on the surface appears to be a religious or ethnic conflict, in fact is a concrete outcome of the spread of market relationships. In this tense political environment, supercharged rhetoric about religion, income and commercial success flies thick and fast, a context in which some Sinhala nationalists use the very language of neoliberalism to denigrate efforts to establish *halal* labelling. Haniffa astutely observes that Sri Lankan Muslims cast their lot with neoliberalism, which guarantees their rights to practice their religion through access to halal-certified goods. The Sinhala-dominated state benefits doubly, as production of halal goods supports the Sinhala-dominated state's economic export-oriented development paradigm, but also marks the Muslim community as an internal Other whose presence can fan the flames of an ethno-nationalist political mobilization that the state can use to enhance its political power.

Benjamin Soares addresses the articulation of Islam and liberalization in his study of the "religious economy" in contemporary Mali. Alongside economic deregulation, the privatization of state functions, the end of the providential state, and a growing emphasis on entrepreneurship, he notes the contemporaneous emergence of what one of his research participants identifies as "structural adjustment Islam." This is a new configuration of Islamic piety characterized by charismatic religious authorities immersed in fee-for-service religious practices, a configuration that emerged concurrently with International Monetary Fund and World Bank targets for government reforms. The emblematic figure for structural adjustment Islam is the "religious entrepreneur," who promises health, wealth and success through esoteric interventions in exchange for either money or commodities. This can be seen as the other side of Srivastava's "moral consumption," where it is the producers of religious knowledge who modulate their expertise along these new economic lines.

The chapter by Daromir Rudnyckyj addresses the assemblage of Islam and liberalism in the context of Malaysia's ambitious, state-led Islamic finance project. Rudnyckyj documents the debates that emerge among experts as they seek to make Kuala Lumpur, Malaysia's capital, the "New York of the Muslim world". The chapter finds that amidst this project, experts recurrently question themselves and each other about the Islamicity of Islamic finance. These debates are often organized by the problem of whether Malaysia's Islamic finance should (or can) be a moral project intended to improve human life by implementing Islamic values such as justice and social well-being for all citizens, or whether it conforms to the same economic logics as its conventional counterpart. The chapter shows that this debate is unavoidably framed by a liberal conception of the economy and economics.

China Scherz's contribution also addresses the limits of neoliberal logics, offering a counterpoint to Andrea Muehlebach's germinal work on the "moral neoliberal" (Muehlebach 2012). Her study of the Ugandan Catholic charity Mercy House shows how this institution has not conformed to the audit culture that increasingly characterizes charitable giving (for instance, as documented in the contributions by Hilman Latief and Filippo Osella). Mercy House has instead maintained a "commitment to an ethic of virtue over an ethic of audit". Thus, Scherz observes that while transnational donors increasingly expect their grantees to conform to the forms that characterize neoliberal philanthropy, such as branding, audit and volunteerism, the sisters at Mercy House obstinately refuse to embrace these techniques. This choice is not without its hazards. Scherz notes that the "the sisters' lack of interest in producing public accountings and reports has left them unable to effectively participate in a funding market that has become increasingly reliant on such reports as indicators of future organizational effectiveness". Finding limits to neoliberal morality at remote sites such as far-flung missions in rural Uganda, is perhaps not surprising, but Scherz's ethnographically rich chapter raises the question as to the frequency of such resistances and what their time horizon might be.

The chapter by Hilman Latief offers a compelling counterpoint to Scherz's essay. He likewise directs his analysis toward the articulation of religious charity and market reason; however, he looks at Islamic-inspired charity in

Indonesia, where a middle-class religious movement seeks to equip relatively low-skilled, young rural women with the tools to become domestic workers. Latief develops the concept "the marketization of piety" to show how Islamic faith is mobilized toward eliciting contributions from pious middle-class Muslims to fund the training of young rural women. A critical dimension of this indoctrination entails equipping these women not only with the technical skills required of infant care workers but also with a considerable amount of Islamic expertise. Thus, the value of the young women's labour is enhanced through the acquisition of Islamic knowledge that they can then pass on to the children in their care. Latief shows how the enhanced display of Islamic piety by middle-class Muslims is instrumental to an emerging spiritual economy in Indonesia today.

Fillippo Osella extends Latief's analysis by demonstrating that whereas charity is commonly understood as transforming its objects (the recipients of charity), it can also be a means for the religious and moral transformation of its subjects. Thus, his analysis shows that in a context of economic liberalization, it is those who provide charity who are expected to be transformed by it. Evoking arguments that Saba Mahmood has made about the relationship between religious dispositions and moral states (Mahmood 2005), Osella shows how acts of charity are a means of inculcating specific types of moral dispositions among the charitable. In Osella's case, well-off donors turn the individual religious obligation of *zakat* (almsgiving), which is one of the five core principles of Islamic practice, into a technique for the "spiritual and economic renewal of the Muslim community as a whole". Thus, as in Latief's analysis, the relatively well-to-do demonstrate their piety and membership in the minority religious community through the act of charitable giving.

V. J. Varghese and Valentina Napolitano conclude this volume by exploring ways through which Christian theologies engage with global capitalism, both chapters focusing on migration. Varghese brings us to 1920s Kerala, in south India, a time of political turmoil and economic stagnation that marks the beginning of the exodus of Syrian Christian farmers and petty traders to virgin hills and forests in the north of the state. Over the following forty years, tens of thousands of Syrian Christian settlers turned inhospitable land into fertile farms and plantations, becoming one of the most wealthy and entrepreneurial communities in the state. Lending theological impetus to community endeavours, Church leaders rationalize migration and settlement in fallow forest land as a divinely ordained mission to transform the environment according to God's plans, and to deliver the Syrian Christians into a biblical land of milk and honey. Sustained by an ethic of hard work, ingenuity and sheer determination, Christian farmers struggle in God's name to bring prosperity and wealth to themselves, their community and the state as a whole. At the same time, the Church leads the struggle against evictions and repossessions of land orchestrated by the state government against the migrant farmers, developing alliances along the way with their historical ideological foes, the Communist Party and its trade unions. In Weberian fashion, Varghese argues that in south India it is the Church and its novel theologies that sustain the emergence of modern political and economic rationalities, turning the Syrian Christian community into shrewd and successful capitalists.

The ethnographic focus of Valentina Napolitano's chapter is the migration of Latin American men and women to Rome, where many of them take on employment in the care industry. The Catholic Church is prominent in the lives of these migrants: it provides spiritual guidance, spaces for sociality, contacts with perspective employers, mediation in case of labour disputes and more. Importantly, the Church under the leadership of Pope Francis has mounted a public campaign to give theological as well as political centrality and attention to those who have been marginalized by global capitalism. Here Napolitano traces the history of papal interventions on poverty and its causes, suggesting both continuities and theological breaks. She argues that Pope Francis's statements on the sin of ignoring the plight of those who have been turned into "the jetsam and flotsam" of global capitalism draw from the theological tradition of medieval monasticism, in particular concerns about the sin of *acedia* (lack of attention, which leads to the breach of monastic rules). Pope Francis and the Catholic Church's attempts face a public that has become numb to the suffering of others, while running against the everyday tactics of Latin American care workers in Rome. These migrants often deploy their social invisibility to navigate the quagmire of Italian immigration laws and the predicaments of (often precarious) employment. In both Varghese and Napolitano's chapters the Church, through its theologies and structures, simultaneously reproduces and undermines the economies of global capitalism, underscoring the working of a *complexio oppositorum* – keeping together apparently incommensurable opposites – which Carl Schmitt identified as a foundational characteristic of Catholic theological reasoning and practice (Muehlebach 2009).

The volume as a whole demonstrates the myriad ways in which religious and economic logics variously inflect each other, in some cases appearing to be indistinguishable, at least in the eyes of proponents of such spiritual economies. One dominant tendency in social science has been to see religion as either a realm of refuge or a domain of resistance against capitalism. Another has been to point out how capitalist representations resemble religious ones. Taken together, the studies in this volume develop a third approach to the assemblage of religion and the economy by demonstrating how religious practices are mobilized towards economic ends and can be deployed to elicit practices commensurate with neoliberalism. The ethnographic approach taken by all contributors seeks to understand how the actors under observation comprehend and enact the assemblage of market and religious reason. This should not be taken to suggest that religion is used only in instrumental fashion. Indeed, another feature of the volume as a whole is that all contributors take religion seriously as an ethnographic object. That is to say, the chapters do not treat religion as a form of false consciousness but rather understand it as a powerful means for motivating human action that must be approached on its own terms. Thus, collectively the studies take religious practice as a means of both making sense of the world and providing instruction on how to act ethically within it. Religion in this sense is understood as a flexible means of moral action that can be assembled with market logics, but such assemblages are neither necessary nor preordained.

Notes

1 See, for instance, Adam Smith's pessimism in *The Wealth of Nations* (Paganelli 2008) or Tawney's stress on the necessity of moral education (1926).
2 A return of religiosity opening the space for the emergence of either uncivil (Mandaville 2007; Comaroff 2009) or civil religion (Braidotti 2008; Habermas 2008; McLennan 2010; Beiner 2011; Hefner 2011).
3 China Scherz's recent study of the charitable activities of a community of East African nuns in Central Uganda suggests that the Franciscan Sisters of Africa's work in a charity home focuses "on the intrinsic good of individual actions" (2013: 625) mediated and enabled by the working of Divine Providence, rather than the logic of humanitarianism and socioeconomic development (cf. Bornstein 2003).
4 Similarly, Agamben (2011) locates the roots of the dialectics between sovereignty and biopolitics in the first centuries of Christian theological debates concerning the Trinity.
5 Critics of the Callon circle have argued, for instance, that the performativity or agencement of these (discursive and non-discursive) interventions might not actually produce an actual progressive disembedding of market and economy, but simply give the impression that there is a substantial reality in what is alluded to in the performance itself (see, e.g., Miller 2002; cf. Butler 1993).
6 This line of enquiry opens up the possibility of exploring simultaneously, for instance, the destructive/productive logic of both sacrifice and market, or ways through which Judeo-Christian notions of sacrifice might underpin theoretical understandings of neoliberal capitalism (see, e.g., Harvey 2007).

References

Abid, S. 2015. "Islamic Reform, Piety and Charity among Muslim Businessmen and Entrepreneurs in Birmingham." Unpublished PhD thesis, Sussex University.
Adas, E. B. 2006. "The Making of Entrepreneurial Islam and the Islamic Spirit of Capitalism." *Journal for Cultural Research* 10(2): 113–137.
Agamben, G. 2011. *The Kingdom and the Glory: For a Theological Genealogy of Economy and Government*. Stanford, CA: Stanford University Press.
2013. *Opus Dei: An Archaeology of Duty*. Stanford, CA: Stanford University Press.

Ahmad, I. 2009. *Islamism and Democracy in India: The Transformation of Jamaat-e-Islami*. Princeton, NJ: Princeton University Press.
Appadurai, A. 2011. "The Ghost in the Financial Machine." *Public Culture* 23(3): 517–539.
Appadurai, A., and C. A. Breckenridge. 1976. "The South Indian Temple: Authority, Honor and Redistribution." *Contributions to Indian Sociology* 10(2): 187–211.
Asad, T. 1993. *Genealogies of Religion: Discipline and Reasons of Power in Christianity and Islam*. Baltimore: Johns Hopkins University Press.
2003. *Formations of the Secular: Christianity, Islam, Modernity*. Stanford, CA: Stanford University Press.
Atia, M. A. 2013. *Building a House in Heaven: Islamic Charity in Neoliberal Egypt*. Minneapolis: University of Minnesota Press.
Baldacchino, J. P. 2012. "Markets of Piety and Pious Markets: The Protestant Ethic and the Spirit of Korean Capitalism." *Social Compass* 59(3): 367–385.
Beiner, R. 2011. *Civil Religion: A Dialogue in the History of Political Philosophy*. Cambridge: Cambridge University Press.
Bialecki, J. 2008. "Between Stewardship and Sacrifice: Agency and Economy in a Southern California Charismatic Church." *Journal for the Royal Anthropological Institute* 14(2): 372–390.
Bielo, J. 2007. "'The Mind of Christ': Financial Success, Born-Again Personhood, and the Anthropology of Christianity." *Ethnos* 72(3): 315–338.
Birla, R. 2008. *Stages of Capital: Law, Culture, and Market Governance in Late Colonial India*. Durham, NC: Duke University Press.
Blasi, A. J. 2009. "A Market Theory of Religion." *Social Compass* 56(2): 263–272.
Bornstein, E. 2003. *The Spirit of Development: Protestant NGOs, Morality, and Economics in Zimbabwe*. Stanford, CA: Stanford University Press.
Braidotti, R. 2008. "In Spite of the Times: The Postsecular Turn in Feminism." *Theory, Culture & Society* 25(6): 1–24.
Brouwer, S., P. Gifford, and S. D. Rose. 1996. *Exporting the American Gospel: Global Christian Fundamentalism*. London: Routledge.
Brown, M. 2013. "Without Morality, the Market Economy Will Destroy Itself." *The Observer* (December 22), 29.
Buğra, A. 1998. "Class, Culture, and State: An Analysis of Interest Representation by Two Turkish Business Associations." *International Journal of Middle East Studies* 30(4): 521–539.
2002. "Labour, Capital, and Religion: Harmony and Conflict among the Constituency of Political Islam in Turkey." *Middle Eastern Studies* 38(2): 187–204.
Burns, R. I. 1982. "Relic Vendors, Barefoot Friars, and Spanish Muslims: Reflections on Medieval Economic and Religious History." *Comparative Studies in Society and History* 24(1): 153–163.
Butler, J. 1993. *Bodies That Matter: On the Discursive Limits of "Sex"*. New York: Routledge.
Çalişkan, K. 2010. *Market Threads: How Cotton Farmers and Traders Create a Global Commodity*. Princeton, NJ: Princeton University Press.
Callon, M. (ed.). 1998. *The Laws of the Markets*. Oxford: Blackwell.
Carrier, J. G. 1995. *Gifts and Commodities: Exchange and Western Capitalism since 1700*. London: Taylor & Francis.

Casanova, J. 2003. "Beyond European and American Exceptionalisms: Towards a Global Perspective." In *Predicting Religion*, edited by G. Davie, P. Heelas, and L. Woodhead, 17–29. Aldershot: Ashgate.
Chakrabarty, D. 2000. *Provincialising Europe: Post-colonial Thought and Colonial Difference*. Princeton, NJ: Princeton University Press.
Chatterjee, P. 1993. *The Nation and Its Fragments: Colonial and Postcolonial Histories*. Princeton, NJ: Princeton University Press.
Chu, J. Y. 2010. *Cosmologies of Credit: Transnational Mobility and the Politics of Destination in China*. Durham, NC: Duke University Press.
Chua, J. L. 2014. *In Pursuit of the Good Life: Aspiration and Suicide in Globalizing South India*. Berkeley: University of California Press.
Coleman, S. 2000. *The Globalisation of Charismatic Christianity*. Cambridge: Cambridge University Press.
2004. "The Charismatic Gift." *Journal of the Royal Anthropological Institute* 10(2): 421–442.
2011. "Prosperity Unbound? Debating the 'Sacrificial Economy.'" *Research in Economic Anthropology* 31: 23–45.
Collier, S. J. 2012. "Neoliberalism as Big Leviathan, or…? A Response to Wacquant and Hilgers." *Social Anthropology* 20(2): 186–195.
Collier, S. J., and A. Ong. 2005. "Global Assemblages, Anthropological Problems." In A. Ong and S. J. Collier (eds.), *Global Assemblages: Technology, Politics, and Ethics as Anthropological Problems*, 3–21. London and New York: Blackwell.
Comaroff, J. 2009. "The Politics of Conviction: Faith on the Neo-liberal Frontier." *Social Analysis* 53(1): 17–38.
Comaroff, J., and J. L. Comaroff. 2000. "Millennial Capitalism: First Thoughts on a Second Coming." *Public Culture* 12(2): 291–343.
Cross, J. 2010. "Neoliberalism as Unexceptional: Economic Zones and the Everyday Precariousness of Working Life in South India." *Critique of Anthropology* 30(4): 355–373.
Csordas, T. J. 2009. "Modalities of Transnational Transcendence." In T. J. Csordas (ed.), *Transnational Transcendence: Essays on Religion and Globalization*, 1–30. Berkeley: University of California Press.
Dardot, P., and C. Laval. 2014. *The New Way of the World: On Neoliberal Society*. London: Verso.
De Neve, G. 2005. *The Everyday Politics of Labour: Working Lives in India's Informal Economy*. New York: Berghahn Books.
Eickelman, D. F., and J. Piscatori. 1996. *Muslim Politics*. Princeton, NJ: Princeton University Press.
Elisha, O. 2011. *Moral Ambition: Mobilization and Social Outreach in Evangelical Megachurches*. Berkeley: University of California Press.
Elyachar, J. 2005. *Markets of Dispossession: NGOs, Economic Development, and the State in Cairo*. Durham, NC: Duke University Press.
2010. "Phatic Labor, Infrastructure, and the Question of Empowerment in Cairo." *American Ethnologist* 37(3): 452–464.
Ewing, K. P. 1997. *Arguing Sainthood: Modernity, Psychoanalysis, and Islam*. Durham, NC: Duke University Press.
Fassin, D. 2009. "Les économies morales revisitées." *Annales: Histoire, Sciences Sociales* 64(6): 1237–1266.

Ferguson, J. 2010. "The Uses of Neoliberalism." *Antipode* 41: 166–184.
Fischer, J. 2008. *Proper Islamic Consumption: Shopping among the Malays in Modern Malaysia*. Copenhagen: NIAS Press.
2011. *The Halal Frontier: Muslim Consumers in a Globalized Market*. New York: Palgrave Macmillan.
Foucault, M. 1991. "Governmentality." In *The Foucault Effect: Studies in Governmentality*, edited by G. Burchall, C. Gordon, and P. Miller, 87–104. Chicago: University of Chicago Press.
2000. "'Omnes et Singulatim': Toward a Critique of Political Reason." In *Power: Essential Works of Michel Foucault, 1954–1984*, Vol. 3, edited by J. D. Faubion, 298–325. New York: New Press.
2008. *The Birth of Biopolitics: Lectures at the College de France, 1978–79*. London: Palgrave Macmillan.
Fuller, C. J. 1984. *Servants of the Goddess: The Priests of a South Indian Temple*. Cambridge: Cambridge University Press.
Geary, P. 1986. "Sacred Commodities: The Circulation of Medieval Relics." In *The Social Life of Things: Commodities in Cultural Perspective*, edited by A. Appadurai, 169–191. Cambridge: Cambridge University Press.
Geertz, C. 1963. *Peddlers and Princes: Social Development and Economic Change in Two Indonesian Towns*. Chicago: University of Chicago Press.
1968. *Islam Observed*. Chicago: University of Chicago Press.
Gellner, E. 1981. *Muslim Society*. Cambridge: Cambridge University Press.
Goldstein, D. M. 2012. "Decolonialising 'Actually Existing Neoliberalism'." *Social Anthropology* 20(3): 304–309.
Gombrich, R., and Obeyesekere, G. 1988. *Buddhism Transformed: Religious Change in Sri Lanka*. Princeton, NJ: Princeton University Press.
Gooptu, N. 2001. *The Politics of the Urban Poor in Early Twentieth-Century India*. Cambridge: Cambridge University Press.
Granovetter, M. 1985. "Economic Action and Social Structure: The Problem of Embeddedness." *American Journal of Sociology* 91(3): 481–510.
Green, N. 2011. *Bombay Islam: The Religious Economy of the West Indian Ocean, 1840–1915*. Cambridge: Cambridge University Press.
Gregory, B. S. 2012. *The Unintended Reformation: How a Religious Revolution Secularized Society*. Cambridge, MA: Belknap Press of Harvard University Press.
Gregory, C. A. 1982. *Gifts and Commodities*. London: Academic Press.
Guyer, J. I. 2007. "Prophecy and the Near Future: Thoughts on Macroeconomic, Evangelical, and Punctuated Time." *American Ethnologist* 34(3): 409–421.
Habermas, J. 1985. *The Philosophical Discourse of modernity*. Cambridge, MA: Polity Press.
1992. "Modernity: An Incomplete Project." In *Modernism/Postmodernism*, edited by P. Brooker, 125–138. London: Longman.
2008. "Notes on a Post-Secular Society." *New Perspectives Quarterly* 25(4): 17–29.
Haenni, P. 2005. *L'islam de marché: L'autre révolution conservatrice*. Paris: Seuil.
Harding, S. 2000. *The Book of Jerry Falwell: Fundamentalist Language and Politics*. Princeton, NJ: Princeton University Press.
Harvey, D. 2007. "Neoliberalism as Creative Destruction." *The Annals of the American Academy of Political and Social Science* 610(1): 21–44.

Haynes, N. 2012. "Pentecostalism and the Morality of Money: Prosperity, Inequality, and Religious Sociality on the Zambian Copperbelt." *Journal of the Royal Anthropological Institute* 18(1): 123–139.

Hefner, R. W. 2011. *Civil Islam: Muslims and Democratization in Indonesia*. Princeton, NJ: Princeton University Press.

Hilgers, M. 2012. "The Historicity of the Neoliberal State." *Social Anthropology* 20(1): 80–94.

2013. "Embodying Neoliberalism: Thoughts and Responses to Critics." *Social Anthropology* 21(1): 75–89.

Hirschman, A. O. 1997. *The Passions and the Interests: Political Arguments for Capitalism Before Its Triumph*. Princeton, NJ: Princeton University Press.

Ho, K. 2009. *Liquidated: An Ethnography of Wall Street*. Durham, NC: Duke University Press.

Howell, J. D. 2013. "'Calling' and 'Training': Role Innovation and Religious De-differentiation in Commercialised Indonesian Islam." *Journal of Contemporary Religion* 28(3): 401–419.

Iqtidar, H. 2011. "Secularism beyond the State: the 'State' and the 'Market' in Islamist Imagination." *Modern Asian Studies* 45(3): 535–564.

Isik, D. 2010. "Personal and Global Economies: Male Carpet Manufacturers as Entrepreneurs in the Weaving Neighborhoods of Konya, Turkey." *American Ethnologist* 37(1): 53–68.

Jackson, P. A. 1999. "The Enchanting Spirit of Thai Capitalism: The Cult of Luang Phor Khoon and the Post-modernization of Thai Buddhism." *South East Asia Research* 7(1): 5–60.

Jones, C. 2010. "Materializing Piety: Gendered Anxieties about Faithful Consumption in Contemporary Urban Indonesia." *American Ethnologist* 37(4): 617–637.

Joshi, S. 2001. *Fractured Modernity: Making of a Middle Class in Colonial North India*. New Delhi: Oxford University Press.

Kandiyoti, D., and Saktanber, A. (eds.). 2002. *Fragments of Culture: The Everyday of Modern Turkey*. New Brunswick, NJ: Rutgers University Press.

Keane, W. 2008. "Market, Materiality and Moral Metalanguage." *Anthropological Theory* 8(1): 27–42.

Kipnis, A. B. 2008. "Audit Cultures: Neoliberal Governmentality, Socialist Legacy, or Technologies of Governing?" *American Ethnologist* 35(2): 275–289.

Kondo, D. K. 1990. *Crafting Selves: Power, Gender, and Discourses of Identity in a Japanese Workplace*. Chicago: University of Chicago Press.

Kuran, T. 2004. *Islam and Mammon: The Economic Predicaments of Islamism*. Princeton, NJ: Princeton University Press.

Lazzarato, M. 2012. *The Making of the Indebted Man: Essay on the Neoliberal Condition*. Los Angeles: Semiotext(e).

Lépinay, V. A. 2011. *Codes of Finance: Engineering Derivatives in a Global Bank*. Princeton, NJ: Princeton University Press.

LiPuma, E., and B. Lee. 2012. "A Social Approach to the Financial Derivatives Markets." *South Atlantic Quarterly* 111(2): 289–316.

Luehrmann, S. 2011. *Secularism Soviet Style: Teaching Atheism and Religion in a Volga Republic*. Bloomington: Indiana University Press.

Lukose, R. A. 2009. *Liberalization's Children: Gender, Youth, and Consumer Citizenship in Globalizing India*. Durham, NC: Duke University Press.

MacKenzie, D. 2008. *An Engine, Not a Camera: How Financial Models Shape Markets.* Cambridge, MA: MIT Press.

MacKenzie, D. A., F. Muniesa, and L. Siu (eds.). 2007. *Do Economists Make Markets? On the Performativity of Economics.* Princeton, NJ: Princeton University Press.

Mahmood, S. 2005. *Politics of Piety: The Islamic Revival and the Feminist Subject.* Princeton, NJ: Princeton University Press.

Mandaville, P. 2007. *Global Political Islam.* London: Routledge.

Marsden, M., 2014. *Trading Worlds: Afghan Merchants across Modern Frontiers.* London: Hurst.

Marshall, R. 2009. *Political Spiritualities: The Pentecostal Revolution in Nigeria.* Chicago: University of Chicago Press.

Matza, T. 2012. "Good Individualism"? Psychology, Ethics, and Neoliberalism in Postsocialist Russia." *American Ethnologist* 39(4): 804–818.

Mauss, M. 1925. *The Gift: Forms and Functions of Exchange in Archaic Societies.* New York: W. W. Norton.

Maxwell, D. 1998. "'Delivered from the Spirit of Poverty?': Pentecostalism, Prosperity and Modernity in Zimbabwe." *Journal of Religion in Africa* 28(3): 350–373.

McLennan, G. 2010. "The Postsecular Turn." *Theory, Culture & Society* 27(4): 3–20.

Meneley A. 2007. "Fashions and Fundamentalisms in Fin-de-siècle Yemen: Chador Barbie and Islamic Socks." *Cultural Anthropology* 22(2): 214–243

Meyer, B. 1998. "'Make a Complete Break with the Past': Memory and Post-Colonial Modernity in Ghanaian Pentecostalist Discourse." *Journal of Religion in Africa* 28(3): 316–349.

1999. *Translating the Devil: Religion and Modernity among the Ewe in Ghana.* Oxford: Oxford University Press.

2004. "Christianity in Africa: From African Independent to Pentecostal-Charismatic Churches." *Annual Review of Anthropology* 33: 447–474.

Miller, D. 2002. "Turning Callon the Right Way Up." *Economy and Society* 31(2): 218–233.

Mitchell, T. 2002. *Rule of Experts: Egypt, Techno-politics, Modernity.* Berkeley: University of California Press.

2005. "The Work of Economics: How a Discipline Makes Its World." *European Journal of Sociology* 46(2): 297–320.

Miyazaki, H. 2013. *Arbitraging Japan: Dreams of Capitalism at the End of Finance.* Berkeley: University of California Press.

Moors, A., and E. Tarlo. 2007. "Introduction to Muslim Fashions." *Fashion Theory* 11(2/3): 133–142.

Moreton, B. 2009. *To Serve God and Wal-Mart: The Making of Christian Free Enterprise.* Cambridge, MA: Harvard University Press.

Muehlebach, A. 2009. "Complexio Oppositorum: Notes on the Left in Neoliberal Italy." *Public Culture* 21(3): 495–515.

2012. *The Moral Neoliberal: Welfare and Citizenship in Italy.* Chicago: University of Chicago Press.

Newell, S. 2007. "Pentecostal Witchcraft: Neoliberal Possession and Demonic Discourse in Ivoirian Pentecostal Churches." *Journal of Religion in Africa* 37(4): 461–490.

Nonini, D. M. 2008. "Is China Becoming Neoliberal?" *Critique of Anthropology* 28(2): 145–176.

Obadia, L. 2013. *La marchandisation de Dieu*. Paris: CNRS Editions.

Obadia, L., and D. C. Wood (eds.). 2011. "Economics *and* religion, economics *in* religion, economics *of* religion: reopening the grounds for anthropology?" In *The Economics of Religion: Anthropological Approaches* (pp. xiii–xxxvii). Bradford: Emerald Group.

Olivier, R. 2010. "Religious Revivals as a Product and Tool of Globalization." *Quaderni di Relazioni Internazionali* 12(2): 22–34.

O'Neill, K. "Left Behind: Security, Salvation, and the Subject of Prevention." *Cultural Anthropology* 28(2): 204–226.

Ong, A. 2006. *Neoliberalism as Exception: Mutations in Citizenship and Sovereignty*. Durham, NC: Duke University Press.

2007. "Neoliberalism as a Mobile Technology." *Transactions of the Institute of British Geographers* 32(1): 3–8.

Osella, F., and C. Osella. 2003. "Migration and the Commoditisation of Ritual: Sacrifice, Spectacle and Contestations in Kerala, India." *Contributions to Indian Sociology* 37(1–2): 109–139.

2009. "Muslim Entrepreneurs in Public Life between India and the Gulf: Making Good and Doing Good." *Journal of the Royal Anthropological Institute* 15(s1): S202–S221.

Paganelli, M. P. 2008. "The Adam Smith Problem in Reverse: Self-interest in Adam Smith's *Wealth of Nations* and *Theory of Moral Sentiments*." *History of Political Economy* 40(2): 365–382.

Parry, J. 1980. "Ghosts, Greed and Sin: The Occupational Identity of the Benares Funeral Priests." *Man* 15(1): 88–111.

1986. "The Gift, the Indian Gift and the 'Indian Gift.' " *Man* 21(3): 453–473.

Parry, J., and M. Bloch. 1989. "Introduction: Money and the Morality of Exchange." In *Money and the Morality of Exchange*, edited by J. Parry and M. Bloch, 1–32. Cambridge: Cambridge University Press.

Pfeiffer, J., K. Gimbel-Sherr, and O. J. Augusto. 2007. "The Holy Spirit in the Household: Pentecostalism, Gender, and Neoliberalism in Mozambique." *American Anthropologist* 109(4): 688–700.

Polanyi, K. 1944. *The Great Transformation: The Political and Economic Origins of Our Time*. New York: Beacon Press.

Prakash, G. 1999. *Another Reason: Science and the Imagination of Modern India*. Princeton: Princeton University Press.

Rey, T. 2004. "Marketing the Goods of Salvation: Bourdieu on Religion." *Religion* 34(4): 331–343.

Richard, A., and D. Rudnyckyj. 2009. "Economies of Affect." *Journal of the Royal Anthropological Institute* 15(1): 57–77.

Robinson, F. 2008. "Islamic Reform and Modernities in South Asia." *Modern Asian Studies* 42(2–3): 259–281.

Roy, A. 2012. "Ethical Subjects: Market Rule in an Age of Poverty." *Public Culture* 24(1): 105–108.

Roy, O. 2004. *Globalized Islam: The Search for a New Ummah*. London: Hurst.

Rudnyckyj, D. 2009. "Spiritual Economies: Islam and Neoliberalism in Contemporary Indonesia." *Cultural Anthropology* 24(1): 104–141.

2010. *Spiritual Economies: Islam, Globalization, and the Afterlife of Development.* Ithaca, NY: Cornell University Press.

2014. "Regimes of Self-Improvement Globalization and the Will to Work." *Social Text* 32(3 120): 109–127.

Salvatore, A. 1997. *Islam and the Political Discourse of Modernity.* Reading: Ithaca Press.

Scherz, C. 2013. "'Let Us Make God Our Banker': Ethics, Temporality, and Agency in a Ugandan Charity Home." *American Ethnologist* 40(4): 624–636.

Schram, R., 2010. "Finding money: Business and charity in Auhelawa, Papua New Guinea." *Ethnos* 75(4): 447–470.

Scott, J. C. 1977. *The Moral Economy of the Peasant: Rebellion and Subsistence in Southeast Asia.* New Haven, CT: Yale University Press.

Scott, R. M. 2009. *Nirvana for Sale? Buddhism, Wealth, and the Dhammakaya Temple in Contemporary Thailand.* Albany: SUNY Press.

Silber, I. F. 1993. "Monasticism and the 'Protestant Ethic': Asceticism, Rationality and Wealth in the Medieval West." *British Journal of Sociology* 44(1): 103–123.

Simpson, E. 2007. *Muslim Society and the Western Indian Ocean: The Seafarers of Kachchh.* London: Routledge.

Singer, M. 1972. *When a Great Tradition Modernizes: An Anthropological Approach to Indian Civilization.* Chicago: University of Chicago Press.

Sloane, P. 1999. *Islam, Modernity, and Entrepreneurship among the Malays.* London: St. Martin's Press.

Sloane-White, P. 2011. "Working in the Islamic Economy: Sharia-ization and the Malaysian Workplace." *Sojourn: Journal of Social Issues in Southeast Asia* 26(2): 304–334.

Soares, B. F. 2005. *Islam and the Prayer Economy: History and Authority in a Malian Town.* Edinburgh: Edinburgh University Press.

Srivastava, S. 2007. *Passionate Modernity: Sexuality, Consumption, and Class in India.* New Delhi: Routledge.

Stark, R., and W. S. Bainbridge. 1985. *The Future of Religion: Secularization, Revival, and Cult Formation.* Berkeley: University of California Press.

Stark, R., and R. Finke. 2000. *Acts of Faith: Explaining the Human Side of Religion.* Berkeley: University of California Press.

Stolz, J. 2006. "Salvation Goods and Religious Markets: Integrating Rational Choice and Weberian Perspectives." *Social Compass* 53(1): 13–32.

Swanson, R. N. 2007. *Indulgences in Late Medieval England: Passports to Paradise?* Cambridge: Cambridge University Press.

Tambiah, S. J. 1984. *The Buddhist Saints of the Forest and the Cult of Amulets.* Cambridge: Cambridge University Press.

Tawney, R. 1926. *Religion and the Rise of Capitalism.* New York: Harcourt Brace.

Thompson, E. P. 1971. "The Moral Economy of the English Crowd in the Eighteenth Century." *Past and Present* 50(1): 76–136.

Thrift, N. 2001. "'It's the Romance, Not the Finance, That Makes the Business Worth Pursuing': Disclosing a New Market Culture." *Economy and Society* 30(4): 412–432.

2005. *Knowing Capitalism.* London: SAGE.

Tripp, C. 2006. *Islam and the Moral Economy: The Challenge of Capitalism.* Cambridge: Cambridge University Press.

Tuğal, C. 2009. *Passive Revolution: Absorbing the Islamic Challenge to Capitalism*. Stanford, CA: Stanford University Press.

Turner, B. 2004. "Fundamentalism, Spiritual Markets and Modernity." *Sociology* 38(1): 195–202.

Van der Veer, P. 1994. *Religious Nationalism: Hindus and Muslims in India*. Berkeley: University of California Press.

2012. "Market and Money: A Critique of Rational Choice Theory." *Social Compass* 59(2): 183–192.

Van Dijk, R. 2004. "Negotiating Marriage: Questions of Morality and Legitimacy in the Ghanaian Pentecostal Diaspora." *Journal of Religion in Africa* 34(4): 438–467.

Walsham, A. 2010. "Introduction: Relics and Remains." *Past & Present* 206(s5): 9–36.

Watson, C. W. 2005. "A Popular Indonesian Preacher: The Significance of AA Gymnastiar." *Journal of the Royal Anthropological Institute* 11(4): 773–792.

Weber, M. 2002 [1904]. *The Protestant Ethic and the Spirit of Capitalism: and Other Writings*. London: Penguin.

Weiss, B. 1998. "Electric Vampires: Haya Rumors of the Commodified Dody. In *Bodies and Persons: Comparative Perspectives from Africa and Melanesia*, edited by M. Lambek and A. Strathern, 172–196. Cambridge: Cambridge University Press.

Weller, R. 2009. "Asia and the Global Economies of Charisma." In *Religious Commodifications in Asia: Marketing Gods*, edited by P. Kitiarsa, 15–30. London: Routledge.

Werbner, P. 2003. *Pilgrims of Love: The Anthropology of a Global Sufi Cult*. Bloomington: Indiana University Press.

Wheeler, B. 2006. *Mecca and Eden: Ritual, Relics, and Territory in Islam*. Chicago: University of Chicago Press.

White, L. 2000. *Speaking with Vampires: Rumor and History in Colonial Africa*. Berkeley: University of California Press.

Wiegele, K. L. 2005. *Investing in Miracles: El Shaddai and the Transformation of Popular Catholicism in the Philippines*. Honolulu: University of Hawaii Press.

Yang, M. M. H. 2000. "Putting Global Capitalism in its Place." *Current Anthropology* 41(4): 477–509.

Zaloom, C. 2006. *Out of the Pits: Traders and Technology from Chicago to London*. Chicago: University of Chicago Press.

2009. "How to Read the Future: The Yield Curve, Affect, and Financial Prediction." *Public Culture* 21(2): 245–268.

Zelizer, V. A. 2010. *Economic Lives: How Culture Shapes the Economy*." Princeton, NJ: Princeton University Press.

Žižek, S. 2003. *The Puppet and the Dwarf: The Perverse Core of Christianity*. Cambridge, MA: MIT Press.

1 Risk, Fate, Fortune: The Lives and Times of Customs Inspectors in Southern China

Julie Y. Chu, University of Chicago

On the day that two Chinese bullet trains collided just south of Wenzhou en route to their final destination in Fujian Province in July 2011, it just so happened that China's most wanted fugitive – the Fujian-based smuggler Lai Changxing – was also finally extradited back to China from Canada to face charges for one of the nation's biggest smuggling and corruption scandals in the post-Mao era. Once anticipated as the headline-making event of the day, Lai's return to Beijing on the afternoon of July 23 all but disappeared from state media overnight when the tragedy of the Wenzhou crash and its subsequent botched rescue efforts came to dominate news channels and public attention. Although the date 7/23 quickly became synonymous with the disastrous event of Wenzhou's rail collision, Lai's uneventful return nonetheless developed its own spectral life as part of a growing conspiracy theory of fateful coincidences.

Infamous as the "shadow customs chief" in the port city of Xiamen, where he based his operations from 1996 to 1999, Lai at one point had controlled entire local departments of the Fujian Customs, with an estimated 160 customs staff, including Fujian's top bureau director and deputy director, all working with him to smuggle in more than 53 billion RMB (7.8 billion USD) worth of contraband across China's southeastern border (Shieh 2005). His political influence was rumored to extend beyond provincial leaders in Fujian all the way to Beijing's central government. Seeking political asylum in Canada, where he had fled in 1999 amid a sweeping anti-smuggling campaign against his operation, Lai claimed to be a victim of a political power struggle among China's top leaders in Beijing. Moreover, as an archetypical man who knew too much, he argued that in his exile, he had become a political threat to many still in power in China whom he could implicate in corruption from afar and who he said "want to get me back so they can shut me up for good" (Beech 2002).

Returned in handcuffs to China on the same day that the two bullet trains crashed, Lai soon became the center of a popular "wag the dog" conspiracy theory linking corruption in the Railway Ministry to the not-so-distant failings of Fujian Customs. Could the spectacle of the crash be a ploy of mass distraction to divert public attention from the scandalous implications and political accusations posed by a man who knows too much? Was it just coincidence that the colliding bullet trains were heading to Fujian Province – the very site of Lai's most widespread political influence and where a crop of China's current leaders made their careers in the 1990s? The Chinese blogosphere was especially abuzz with sinister questions about the current Railway Ministry's head Sheng Guangzu, who had only recently been transferred over from his post as customs director and who subsequently was caught in scandalous photographs wearing different extravagant foreign watches – including a gold Rolex valued at 73,000 RMB (about US$12,000) and considered well beyond a civil servant's means – while making various public appearances around the time of the Wenzhou crash.

In Fujian's capital, Fuzhou, where I had been conducting field research on customs inspection since 2009, these insinuations of linked corruption became a common catalyst for many self-deprecating jokes as well as serious reflection among local customs officers grappling with the persistent challenges and pitfalls of their work. Already overburdened by a decade of political scrutiny since Lai's Xiamen smuggling scandal broke in 2000, no one in Fuzhou Customs I talked to after the crash seemed particularly surprised that their regional notoriety as state gatekeepers would be merged with another infamous case of massive failure in the state control of proper flows. When images of a Rolex-wearing Sheng Guangzu became the talk of the town, for instance, customs officer Chen Yongming only worried how such news might intensify the already embattled atmosphere at his workplace, where he complained people had become so accustomed to the threats of recurring scandals and sting operations that "you're lucky to exchange three genuine sentences [with your coworkers] in a day." Conspiracies about customs were not only a fixation of public imagination, Chen suggested; they also pervaded the bureau itself from the inside out, spreading doubt and distrust among a workforce constantly bracing for the next big corruption charge or internal shakeup of its organization.

This chapter examines how customs inspectors at the global edge of contemporary China manage the ongoing suspicions and ambiguous fortunes of their bureau and their own moral careers through two distinct models for dealing with uncertainty: risk management and fortune-telling. While risk management has become a key sign of the "modernizing" professional ethos of the Chinese Customs Administration, which has been undergoing "reform" since the outbreak of Lai's Xiamen smuggling scandal in 2000, curiously fortune-telling has also emerged as a popular pastime among many officials eager to get a grip on the cosmic variables for managing the future and the possible surprise of mis/fortunes in their midst. This chapter analyzes the tensions and resonances between worlds of statistical risk and of cosmic fate that govern the professional and personal lives of street-level inspectors and other customs officials during a time of significant institutional change in the bureau, along with widespread moral questioning about public goods and public service in China. By attending to the temporal sensibilities and calculative logics at play in models of risk management and of fortune-telling, I will highlight a distinct "chronopolitics" at stake in the shifting political landscape of agency and accountability among Chinese customs workers. Paul Virilio (1998) most famously described chronopolitics as the emergent modality of contemporary struggles through which the old geopolitics of territorial dominance and spatial extension had been supplanted by new concerns over the global management of time and its intensities. But while Virilio mostly fixated on the implications of speed, I want to offer a more nuanced reading of chronopolitics as a globalized struggle over *pace* and *rhythm*, that is, as a problem of *tempo* rather than simply of time's brute compression in a world of "fast capitalism." Specifically in relation to recent customs reforms, my aim is to examine the ways in which risk and fate offer distinct yet resonant modalities for honing an ethics of *timely response* to the emergent occupational and moral hazards facing state actors at the front lines of global trade and security concerns in a post-millennial China.

"Control" and "Flow": From Risk Manager to Risk Factor

Once considered the backwaters of state civil service, China's Customs Administration had grown in both national importance and public scrutiny since the 1990s as its workers came to be seen as the key managers of expanding international trade and accumulating national wealth in an export-oriented post-Mao economy. The Xiamen smuggling scandal only confirmed the extent to which customs had become both an essential gatekeeper and problematic bottleneck in the distribution of flows, as China increasingly organized its material resources and social energies according to the global market rhythms of just-in-time production (cf. Harvey 2010; Dicken 2011). In Fuzhou, most officers viewed their rising standing and visibility with decidedly mixed feelings. On the one hand, the influx of customs revenues with expanding global trade has enabled the bureau to become one of the best endowed and crucial state units in the post-Mao era.[1] On the other hand, as a key agent in facilitating foreign trade, and by extension in attracting ongoing foreign direct investment to China's shores, customs has also been subjected to escalating state pressure for "harmonizing" its practices with certain globalizing signs of "modernization" and "good governance."[2] This odd combination of increasing wealth and intensifying scrutiny has dramatically transformed customs from a marginal bureau of last resort, where the least competent state workers often ended up, to one of the most prominent and selective departments, where increasingly large pools of highly skilled and professionalized applicants compete for coveted positions. In 2009, for instance, one entry-level position in Xiamen sparked what newspapers dubbed as "customs fever" (*haiguan re*) by attracting nearly

3,000 applicants (Yang 2009). Between 2000 and 2007, customs personnel grew by 25 percent to a total of more than 50,000 staff nationwide (Zhang and Zhao 2009: 125).[3] This new desirability and growth of the bureau has been a shock to older staff like Yang Juan, a midlevel manager in custom's personnel department who still remembered how disappointed she was in the early 1980s when she ended up in Fuzhou Customs instead of being placed in one of the coveted state factories in the region, many of which are now defunct or in serious decline.

Customs' growing staff numbers have been dwarfed by an even more astronomical expansion in the total volume of imports and exports, which increased by 358 percent, compared to 25 percent for staff, over the same period (Zhang and Zhao 2009: 125). Outmanned by the sheer flood of commodities moving in and out of the country, China's Customs Administration responded to these flows by adopting a set of WTO-approved strategies for "Customs Modernization." Specifically, like many of its global trading partners and competitors such as the United States and Japan, China's customs reorganized its operation around new automated and computerized systems of data clearance and risk management. The first phase of these changes, roughly from 1998 to 2003, seemed mostly to involve the introduction of IT into the occupational culture of customs, a time when most officers fondly recall learning to use their first desktop computers and to relay information through the bureau's intranet. The second phase, from 2004 to 2010, most dramatically affected the daily workflow and interactions among the staff through the integration of a comprehensive risk management platform into the system of inspection and clearance through the installment of new computer monitoring programs, recurring staff training seminars on the concept of "risk," and the reorganization of the bureau's personnel via the hiring of more risks analysts and the establishment of a standalone risk management unit.

Although some techniques of risk analysis had been part of Chinese customs at least since the 1980s,[4] at some time during the installation of the new computerized models in the mid-2000s customs officers in Fuzhou began to realize that they were no longer just being trained to analyze risks in the flow of commodities across their checkpoints; they themselves had become one of the key "risk factors" requiring constant monitoring in the emerging regulatory system of control. Take, for instance, the changing practice of physical inspection at cargo ports. It used to be that frontline workers would aspire for 100 percent inspection of all shipments passing through their ports. Now customs officers can be penalized, or at least be forced to justify themselves administratively, if they exceed more than 3–5 percent inspection for certain low-risk categories of goods. In contrast to the relatively straightforward flow of all cargo through the same line of inspection, customs clearance now operated as a multichannel system of priority queuing through which only select goods were targeted for hands-on examination based on calculations of probable risk. Describing the shifting orientation and rhythms of clearance, one midlevel official recalled how holding shipments for inspection used to be a sign of agency and authority among workers embracing the bureau's mission for "protecting the nation's gateways" (*baohu guomen*). He noted that now, however, "the key words are 'trade facilitation' (*maoyi bianlihua*) and the most important measure [of performance] is the quick release of goods."[5] As another seasoned customs official put it, "before it was all about *jin* ('entry'control) and now it's all about *dong* (ensuring 'flow')."

This new orientation to flows, however, was not just about speed so much as it was about honing the timeliness of response to the fluctuating rhythms of global supply chains. Nowhere was this new emphasis on timeliness more evident than in the overhaul of working hours for all frontline staff – that is, those who most closely interacted with the public in divisions such as port inspection, customer service, and IT. In the past decade, all these frontline divisions saw their schedules transformed from standard 9 to 5 workdays into rotating overnight and on-call shifts on a 24/7 cycle to promote the bureau's timely response to the needs of "trade facilitation." This shift to 24/7 demanded not just an acceleration of pace but rather a constant modulation of the workflow according to the lurching rhythms of just-in-time production, with its short bursts of intensified flows as commodity components were merged transnationally into finished products according to specific peaks in consumer demands followed by periods of dormancy and strategic delays along the global assembly line amid lulls in sales and in other market triggers for moving inventory (Levesque 2011). Whereas customs inspectors used to take pride in disciplining shippers according to the bureau's own regulatory pace, now they were expected to rush and to wait on a 24/7 basis according to the shifting tempo of global supply chains.

Moreover, just as backed up queues invoked critiques of inefficiency and disorder, in the aftermath of the Xiamen scandal, a clearance process that appeared too fast and frictionless in China could also conjure the specter of greased hands and backdoors (*zou houmen*). In the new workflow of clearance, for instance, the first pass of inspection no longer moved through the hands of locally embedded actors; it now belonged to computer-mediated programs that sorted shipments into queues of variable risk and speeds, and in turn randomly assigned workers to the goods flagged by risk models for additional physical inspection. Inciting "quality" as much as speed in its operations, these new programs tracked not only the flow of goods through clearance but also the inspectors assigned to mediate these flows, who, like the cargo they intercepted, now accrued records in the computer system that then fed back into various performance measures of worker efficiency and risk. One frontline inspector told me that the computers at some cargo ports even monitored the time workers spent away from their assigned stations, forcing anyone gone for longer than fifteen minutes to log a formal explanation of his or her absence into the system. Noting the pervasive nature of such monitoring, another deputy officer complained, "it's now supervision all the way, all the time."

Once the primary risk managers at China's borders, frontline inspectors in customs now found themselves to be as much targets of risk analysis as they were the agents of such controls. Not only were they being randomly assigned to inspect cargo by a computer program; when it came to the inspection of containers, the computer system even designated the specific portion of the container for them to spot check. People's sense of diminishing control over their assignments in customs was further exacerbated by new reforms since the Xiamen scandal that required all frontline staff to rotate out of their positions every two to three years. While such reforms were meant to prevent workers from getting too entangled in personalistic networks in any one place, many customs staff complained not only of the disruption such constant rotation caused to their work lives, but moreover of the difficulties for them to build up and hone their expertise in any one position. Expert knowledge now accrued in the computerized network rather than in the individualized bodies of workers, whose task was to blend into the calculative background as part of a larger cybernetic system of regulation.

This is not to suggest that such regimes of risk management had become totalizing in their control. In fact, one of the most striking things about workers' complaints of risk management was how often they veered from detailed description of the system's widespread impact into confessional shrugs or peevish disavowals of the new technology's actual importance. As Chen Yongming put it at the end of a long discussion of expanding computerization and risk analysis at his workplace, "Risk, risk…Yeah, we all know how to talk 'risk' now. But let's face it: it's still a society of *renqing* (human feelings)." In pointing to a traditional Confucian term such as *renqing*, Chen meant to gesture to a more longstanding Chinese moral economy underlying or better yet, still entangled with the work of customs and that he argued no expansion of a risk management platform could ever fully replace or obliterate. As a basic gloss for social connectedness, the term *renqing*, as Chen knew well, had both positive and negative valences. On the one hand, *renqing* referred to a world of thick sociality and proper exchange based on a sense of indebtedness, loyalty, and sentiment with others; these were features that went into the making of moral personhood (*zuoren*). On the other, it also pointed to the unseemly burdens and instrumentality that could come with affective attachments – a kind of intimacy that easily veered into corruption and that people sometimes described as a form of emotional blackmail or polluting conviviality that harnessed "feelings" for dubious personal gains (Hsu 1971; Chang and Holt 1994).

Despite the attempts of new risk management systems to reorganize the workflow of customs to "harmonize" with global market rhythms and international standards of performance, ultimately Chen's point was that no regime of control could ever completely disembed workers from their localized attachments to a moral economy revolving around these claims on "human feeling" – in both the positive and negative senses of the term. As another customs official argued, it was not that risk management could truly dislodge workers from their entanglements in local regimes of value, including from entreaties to personal favors and private patronage that come with occupying a position of state authority. What the new customs reforms did, however, was redistribute the opportunities for corruption from the frontline zones of port inspection to the new calculative centers of internal control such as IT and the new risk management division itself. For instance, one department head cited a 2011 corruption case in which an IT programmer conspired with smugglers to "hack" the bureau's own electronic clearance system so that certain shipments of goods could automatically pass through customs without paying duties. Others pointed to China's history of unreliable data collection to cast doubt on the efficacy of the new risk models, with one deputy even confessing how his department's own celebratory report of annual economic growth and other performance indicators had been based on the creative manipulation of in-house number crunchers (cf. Liu 2012).

While it was true that risk management had gone to some lengths to break up the discretionary power of frontline workers, it did so only by redistributing the capacity for decidability, and hence accountability up the career ladder through what Michael Power (2007) has described as the increasing "responsibilization" of senior management. Not unlike social claims to "human feelings," risk management can also be seen, as Power argued, as a distinctive "moral technology" for promoting "organizational virtue and virtuosity." One way it did this was by recalibrating the institutional terms of "actorhood" through a new cosmology of manageable "risk" (Power 2007: 69) whereby previously incalculable hazards were brought under the administrative duties of those assigned to the internal measure and supervision of others (Dean 1998; cf. Beck 1992). As Power notes, this was not just a matter of introducing statistical instruments of probability, that is, the technologies of risk analysis; it was as much about the nonquantitative arts of "reform" through organizational restructuring and through new rituals of "training" for shaping workers' orientations toward a future of lurking hazards and incalculable chance. That is to say, attuning customs officers to the concept of "risk" was a pedagogical, moralizing practice anchored to more than just technologies of rational calculation.[6] In the text that follows I examine how the redistribution of agency within the bureau – particularly with its new emphasis on managerial responsibilities – generated new uncertainties for customs workers trying to find their moral footing amid a shifting landscape of professional hazards and rewards.

The Ethics of Work and Play

Customs officer Chen Yongming and his friend Wang Ping, a recently retired judge, were having one of their usual debates over which civil service department was *worse* – customs administration or the judicial courts – over dinner with me one evening in early September 2011. Over the preceding three years I had come to appreciate the black humor pervading these common rituals of one-upmanship in which these mostly male officials would rib each other for living the high life as state workers while complaining about their own demoralizing career woes. On this occasion, Chen had just finished a rant about his terribly paranoid and self-protective coworkers when Wang brought up the growing conspiracy theory linking the recent Wenzhou crash to the extradition of Lai Changxing and customs' scandalous past. "So tell me, my friend," Wang playfully addressed the customs officer. "What's with your old boss wearing a fancy Rolex at Wenzhou?" Chen sighed and repeated something he had already told us on many occasions. "Ah, well…what can you do? There are both the good and the bad [among the staff] at Customs," he shrugged. "Although the very worst," he admitted for the first time that night, "are often the leaders at the top."

Currently a midlevel officer with a desk job in a 9-to-5 department of customs, Chen had entered the bureau at the beginning of major civil service reform in the late 1990s when workers began to compete openly for state positions through a new system of standardized entrance exams rather than simply assigned to jobs through the opaque deliberations and bureaucratic maneuverings of their work units. As his friend Wang and I both knew, Chen had been on the cusp for promotion to a more prominent leadership position for quite some time. In turn, his confession of disaffection with those "at the top" of customs was a telling reminder of his own career anxieties as a middle manager stuck in a lackluster holding pattern in the bureau.

In fact, after noting how corruption was worst among officials at the top, Chen Yongming confessed that he had come to dread the possibility of promotion altogether because, as he saw it, the more one moved up the career ladder in Customs the more one became a visible target for both those seeking personal favors and those aiming to unearth political scandals. Recalling his father's career as a civil servant in the late 1970s and early 1980s, Chen admitted that it had always been hard for those in public office to disentangle their personal ties from their professional duties. Yet however dysfunctional officialdom had seemed in the past, "conscientious" (*renzhen*) people like his father, he argued, used to be able to climb the career ladder with some sense of integrity intact. "Things just seemed less complicated," Chen suggested, before the Maoist ethos of "serving the people" gave way to a new emphasis on "getting rich first." This nostalgic sense of simpler times was echoed by many other customs workers including two retirees who had been at the bureau during the 1970s, one of whom suggested that there was less temptations for graft in the past, when state resources were both more meager and more evenly distributed among the population. Retired in 1979 on the cusp of economic reforms, this former customs inspector recalled how workers used to be grateful just to have more than one pair of shoes and a nice uniform allocated to them by their work unit. In contrast, with the rise of massive trade surpluses in China, the possibilities for personal enrichment and, by extension, for corruption were now dizzying in customs.

Like his friend Wang, the recently retired judge, the forty-two-year-old Chen Yongming belonged to the post-'70s generation of officials who entered public service during the growing pains of transition from a Maoist economy of state command and comradeship to a post-Mao world emphasizing market liberalization and a more competitive entrepreneurial spirit. This was a transition replete with the promise not only of a more "well-off society" (*xiaokang shehui*) of increasing personal wealth but also of a more meritocratic and professionalized civil service in which state workers were being called on to meet new standards of productivity and public trust. Recurring post-Mao campaigns against corruption, for instance, typically cited Deng Xiaoping's call for working with "two hands": to advance economic growth on one hand while fighting rising economic crimes among officials on the other (van Rooij 2005: 296).

Chen had barely arrived at customs when the bureau was hit with its most intensive wave of anti-smuggling investigations ever – a nationwide campaign beginning in 1998 that shook up many regional divisions of customs and that ultimately led to the bureau's definitive scandal in 2000 over Lai Changxing's illicit operations. Far from a clear victory for state reformers, however, there was something always double-edged about these campaigns, which often confirmed existing public suspicions of the extensive nature of corruption as much as they pointed to new enforcement successes. For instance, the fact that Lai had managed to evade arrest in 1999 because of internal leaks from the investigative team revealed the extent of actually existing conspiracy between some top law enforcement agents and the criminal elements they were supposed to be stamping out. In addition, the uneven field of convictions in the aftermath of this scandal – with some officials seemingly toppled by the barest connections to Lai while other powerful figures with clear ties escaping legal punishment altogether – furthered suspicions that campaigns against corruption were less about law and justice than about unlucky officials caught with the wrong alliances or lacking favors amid escalating political battles and convenient witch hunts.

For customs agents in Fuzhou, these crackdowns had a way of spreading disillusion and paranoia at the workplace, with the proliferation of scandal intensifying public scrutiny on the one hand and prompting more internal reflexivity and anxious self-regulation on the other. For instance, when the Xiamen scandal broke and spread across Fujian into wider interrogations throughout customs, one deputy officer recalled how everyone from top to bottom of the organization not only felt the escalation of external surveillance; they also began to eye one another with increasing suspicion as either possible criminal conspirators or hidden state informants. The spread of internal distrust and monitoring would culminate with the installation of custom's risk management system in 2004, which worked to formalize the kind of managerial reflexivity and calculative orientation already in play at the bureau, in which workers appear as probable patterns of "risk" to be variously screened, processed, and controlled.

In a milieu in which one was constantly in danger of being swept up in public scandals or triggering internal alarms, the only way Chen said many civil servants now could maintain some dignity was to give up on the idea of having a distinguished *hangye* or career altogether. Having cycled through his share of frontline positions as a constant target of external audits and internal risk management, Chen had come to take refuge in an obscure but stable midlevel job, a position that he had held for an unprecedented seven years by studiously avoiding all further advancement despite mounting pressures from his superiors to move up the career ladder and make a more prominent name for himself. Moreover, he argued that he was not the only one taking shelter in the undistinguished middle of the career ladder in customs. From the massive pools of job applicants for entry-level positions, it certainly looked as if customs had become a highly sought after career. Yet Chen argued that once inside the bureau, there was a sharp decline in internal candidates for promotions, especially for the most prominent managerial and leadership positions. For instance, when a slew of top customs positions in Beijing became available in 2011 after the bureau director Sheng Guangzu left to head the Railway Ministry, Chen noted that no more than fifty people out of the entire national staff of 50,000 bothered to apply for any of these jobs. In fact, the pool for leadership positions was often so lackluster within the bureau that Chen said that he had been pressured by his superiors to apply for promotion on several occasions. In these circumstances, Chen admitted that he often had to do enough to "give face" to his bosses, whose authority as senior officials in the bureau was often tied to their charismatic capacity to groom their subordinates to advance into more prominent positions of power and of continual loyal support.

Much of this cultivation of loyalty and charisma actually took place outside of the workplace through the common social practice of *yingchou* – the art of entertaining and banqueting through which coworkers gathered in the name of convivial "fun" (*hao wan*) and "human feeling" (*renqing*) (cf. Osburg 2013). While appearing to be a voluntary activity of leisure, banqueting among officials was actually more like a necessary chore that everyone had to do to nurture collegiality and connections for work. Such playful activity was so crucial in customs that those particularly adept at entertaining and drinking to excess with their superiors and with other private sector "friends" were often expected to rise more quickly up the career ladder because they could be counted on to stimulate the kind of exuberance of "human feeling" essential to drawing people together into personalized networks of reciprocity and trust. Yet it was also these entangling aspects of such obligatory "fun" that many officials such as Chen Yongming dreaded for luring them down a slippery slope of ever more corrupting and incriminating relations.

This gray zone of entertainment and commensality was, after all, what made the Lai smuggling scandal such a lightning rod for public debates about *renqing* (human feeling). While infamous for lavishly wining, dining, and providing female escorts for officials at his entertainment complex, the "Red Mansion," Lai also seemed to have cultivated an admirable local reputation for civic-minded and thoughtful generosity during his heydays in Xiamen in the 1990s. Respected for his impeccable timing in extending friendship and support to others, Lai was known for winning over those who usually turned down crass appeals for favors by cultivating people's ethical sense of long-term loyalty and reciprocity. Through personal and spontaneous gestures of "human feeling," he often seemed to anticipate people's most intimate needs before they even knew these needs existed, such as by preempting an official's concern for a child heading overseas for school by paying for that child's foreign residence and tuition well in advance. His history of charitable work in and around his hometown especially made him into something of a local folk hero, including garnering official recognition and praise in the media. In turn, his public downfall was a reminder of the fine line between honorable giving and illicit bribery. Did Lai fall out of political favor because he proved to be corrupt? Or did he turn out to be "corrupt" because he had lost his political favors? As Bourdieu (1990) once noted about the moral hazards of gifts and return-gifts, so much hinged on the politics of timing.[7]

As a gesture of "human feeling" and ethical commitment to his superiors, Chen noted that he sometimes had to demonstrate some minimum ambition to satisfy their calls for him to move up the career ladder, where he could better support their agendas from a position of greater influence. Yet because the actual application process was ultimately out of his bosses' control, Chen said he had thus far managed to avoid promotion by simply playing dumb and flubbing his various placement exams and interviews for higher positions. In this way, he tried to play the pressing personal demands for *renqing* reciprocity against the new depersonalized rhythms for professional advancement in the reforming bureaucratic regime. Anticipating only more corrupting temptations and public scrutiny up the chain of command, he said he had learned to let go of any grand ambitions and see Customs as "just a job" where "it's best if you work like just part of this machine." Caught between the defunct order of his father's civil service past and a still cloudy future as a subject of risk, Chen ultimately settled for just blending into the background of the new cybernetic system of regulation. This was his stop-gap solution – to lay low as a machinic part of an otherwise "risky" order at a time of ongoing institutional and moral uncertainty, especially for those rising into the responsibilized ranks of senior management in the bureau.

In embracing his cybernetic positioning as a machinic component of the state apparatus, Chen learned to take comfort in the deferral of agency and authority from his own person. In fact, as a strategy of self-protection, Chen had developed a real knack for playing dumb and coming across as a distinctly dull and wooden bureaucrat. Acting *daidai* (dim-witted), he noted, seemed to work equally well for warding off personal entreaties from cunning outsiders and for buffering internal pressures for promotion. His studied lack of personality made him especially poor company for his bosses, and in turn enabled him to beg off from many banqueting obligations without causing serious offense, or even better, to be nixed from such social gatherings altogether. Divested of ambition and charisma as a worker, Chen found a way to remain relatively unimportant and to have "just a job" instead of worrying about all the entangling hazards that came with a rising career in customs.

With the time freed from vexing about professional advancement and hence from spending "off" hours entertaining his superiors, Chen said he was able to invest in the personal hobbies and self-cultivating practices he truly cared about. This included honing his love of gaming and statistics as a basketball fan online, where he maintained an active blog analyzing the performance of his favorite American NBA players and where he constantly competed with others to assemble a virtual team of superior free-throw percentages and points scored in his internet NBA fantasy league. Chen's enumerative interest also extended to the popular mantic arts of *suan ming* – literally translated as the "computation" of "life-cum-fate." He was especially keen to consult with masters in the more technically complex and esoteric forms of divination drawing from the Daoist classic, *The Book of Changes* (I-ching or *Yijing*). These learned forms included the geomantic practice of *feng shui*, the numerological readings of the "eight trigrams" (*bagua*), and the astrological chartings of the "eight characters" (*bazi*). Through such consultations, he hoped to grasp the elusive sign of the times for planning and making his next auspicious move amid the ongoing hazards of *renqing* exchange and risk management.

One of the most surprising things about my research with the customs bureau was finding out how common it was for officials to embrace fortune-telling as a common source of "good fun" (*hao wan*) and even serious interest. When some civil servants like Chen found out that a local research partner and I had done prior fieldwork on popular religion in the Fuzhou area, they were often quick to express their brimming curiosity and confessed enjoyment in consulting various experts of "fate calculation" – a pleasure they typically framed as a "cultural" interest in China's more esoteric "folk customs" or as a therapeutic pastime for airing problems to an experienced, if not always reliable, adviser who might lend a different perspective. Sometimes officials would even ask us where to find the best fortune-tellers in the area and how to tell the genuinely skilled and efficacious diviners from the dubious tricks of quackery. One department head and his deputy officer were especially eager to get recommendations for good diviners so that they could impress their superiors and other visiting delegates of officials as part of their *yingchou* (entertaining/hosting) duties. The latter, they said, often liked to tour local temples and consult fortune-tellers "for fun" on their trips, especially in a region like Fujian known for its excessively varied and lively traditions of popular religious practices.

While often couched as merely "good fun," fortune-telling's incorporation into the activities of *yingchou* (hosting/entertaining) also suggested how easily it could blur the boundaries of work and play in the lives of officials. At the very least, its seriousness as "play" among certain stressed out and disaffected civil servants has become a topic of increasing public and state concern. In fact, the extent of official engagement with fortune-telling came to be something of a public shock in 2007 when a survey by the Chinese Academy of Governance revealed that 52 percent of county-level civil servants admitted belief in some form of popular divination ranging from face reading and dream interpretations to casting lots and astrological charts (Guo 2007; Levin 2013). That same year the State Council also publicly highlighted "superstitious gatherings" among officials as one of the punishable offenses in new civil service regulation against "disreputable conduct." Government crackdowns on "superstitious" officials culminated most recently in the infamous corruption case of the former Railway Ministry head, Liu Zhijun, who was convicted in 2011 not only for taking bribes and engaging in sexual misconduct but also for consulting a feng shui master on auspicious dates for breaking ground on major construction projects (Levin 2013).

It is tempting to read these crackdowns on "superstitious" officials as simply a sign of the secularizing failures of the Chinese party-state in making rational-calculative subjects out of its most technocratic members. After all, officials' enchantment with certain human agencies for divining the future seemed to be surfacing at a time when those calculative powers were being diverted to posthuman systems of risk management largely out of people's own personal control. Such a reading, however, would hardly do justice to the Chinese moral imaginary of "fate" or *mingyun* (literally, life's flow of fortune), which cannot easily be positioned in binary opposition to a cosmology of "risk." Instead of presuming a clash between these forms for managing uncertainty, as scholars arguing for the singularity of modern "risk societies" are apt to do (e.g., Beck 1992; Giddens 1998; Lash 2000), in the last section of this chapter I demonstrate some of ways risk and fate can resonate and even interpenetrate as "hopeful" technologies of speculation (Miyazaki 2004).

Account-abilities: Dividual and Deferential Agencies

Although risk management and fortune-telling are often juxtaposed as contrasting modalities of pattern recognition (cf. Giddens 1998), they actually share a certain optimism in the computational capacity of experts and their specialized technologies to manage uncertainty and the surprises of mis/fortune. Customs officials with interests in fortune-telling often took much pleasure in discussing the esoteric instruments and embodied technical virtuosity of their past diviners. Even those who proved to be frauds were often admired for their cunning tricks and actual sociological know-how for grasping people's circumstances and state of mind: to guess the appropriate life cycle issue at stake from a client's gender and age (read: twenty-four-year-old woman = problem of marriageability), to feel out class status, literally, by the coarseness of the client's handshake (read: rough hand = manual labor). Yet while officials enjoyed swapping stories about the skillful ploys of "fake" diviners, they almost always had at least one tale of some awe-inspiring diviner whose precise foreknowledge and uncanny predictions defied any rational debunking or clear insight. How did one fortune-teller tossing coins to read the randomized, opaque patterns of the eight trigrams (*bagua*) come to the correct conclusion that one Customs officer's pregnant wife not only would give birth two days later around 1 in the afternoon but also that the baby would come out feet first in the uncommon breech position? While the Customs officer who shared this example had spent most of an evening with another coworker gamely showing how much "fun" could be had from engaging and later dissecting the various tricks of the fortune-telling trade, he also confessed to being captivated by the one diviner whose predictions turned out to be spot on and un-debunkable. Without admitting to "belief" in cosmic powers per se, this officer went on to explain how he had found renewed admiration for the mysterious craft of divination after this experience, which proved to be truly "magical" in the technically efficacious, if not otherworldly, sense of the term (Gell 1992). At the very least, such cases of inscrutable yet accurate prescience held open the possibility that amid all the quacks in the business, some fortune-tellers were "real" experts capable of providing helpful insights into their clients' future.

In fact, as a highly opaque form of pattern recognition and prognostication, the "real" craft of fortune-telling was not so different from the computational magic of risk analysis – a world full of references to the technical virtuosity of programming "wizards" and tech "gurus" (cf. Appadurai 2011 Mackenzie and Spears 2012). Moreover, as an inspiration for Leibniz's development of binary calculus – the roots of our contemporary computer architecture – the eight trigrams in the *Book of Changes* (*Yi Jing* or *I-Ching*), with its flexible code for divining fate, have even been claimed by some mathematicians and computer scientists as exemplifying the world's "first primitive computer" or low-tech "database."[8] Similarly, the somewhat simplified calculative practice of *bazi* (eight characters) has been celebrated as a divining "algorithm" or cosmic information technology by some contemporary fortune-tellers in places like Singapore, Hong Kong, Taiwan as well as in Fujian, where I encountered one *bazi* expert entering his clients' personal data into a computer program designed to process and print out their astrological charts for his readings. The growing institutionalization of feng shui as a marketable form of expertise in China likewise points to its "modern" value as a legitimate technical skill as opposed to being simply "superstitious belief."

There are good reasons to take seriously these arguments of affinity between Chinese divination and more "modern" modes of prognostication rather them seeing than as mere moves to "scientize" religion. If anything, contemporary risk management, with renewed interest in complexity theory and incalculable events or "black swans" (cf. Taleb 2007; Amoore 2013), appear to be moving closer in orientation and practice to Chinese fortune-telling rather than the other way around. This is particularly true when it comes to thinking about how they handle uncertainty and in turn, set up the terms of agency and accountability. Not unlike programs of risk management, Chinese practices for the "computation" of "fate" (*suanming*) are centrally concerned with enabling timely response at the crossroads of two kinds of uncertainties – what statisticians refer to as the problem of non-knowledge (epistemic uncertainty) and that of irreducible surprise (aleatory uncertainty). Far from being a deterministic concept akin to fatalism, the Chinese term that is usually translated as "fate" (*mingyun*) actually points to the contingent flow (*yun*) of life's fortune (*ming*) through a world of ongoing epistemic and aleatory murk.

Ming, meaning "life-cum-fate," carries both determinate and indeterminate meanings. On the one hand, it gestures to the given conditions inherited at birth and also to life's inexorable movement from vitality toward death. On the other hand, from the karmic perspective of rebirth, it also indexes a complex field of moral transactions linking invisible demerits accrued from past lives to the unfolding of this-worldly fortunes for the reincarnated person. It is through this latter sense of *ming* as a shifting cosmic accounting of de/merits that diviners and their clients point to the epistemic uncertainty of life's prospects. Since every human action inherently produces karmic merit or demerit, one's cosmic balance of fortune is always in flux; its bottom line is impossibly obscured through a process of accumulation spread across not only one lifetime of immoral action, but moreover across the blinders of multiple lives through which one has no recourse of memory. To scramble the equation of karmic debt and repayment further, every cosmic account is also subject to unknown and unpredictable transfers of demerit from particularly wicked ancestors and living kin over the many cycles of one's life and rebirth.

Not unlike the subject of risk made visible through data traces and profiles, a person's fortunes appear here as a shifting portfolio of innumerable transactions accrued across many lives. Less a self-possessing individual than the informationalized "dividual" (Deleuze 1992),[9] the subject of cosmic accounting –like that of risk management – cannot be analyzed and grasped as a "whole." It is always a composite pattern and interpretive artifact of incomplete and anticipatory knowledge – a temporal mode of being open to the dynamic resonance of obscured past lives and uncertain future living.

Besides recognizing the always partial knowledge on which their forecasts are based, both risk management and fortune-telling also share a central focus on the problem of chance or aleatory uncertainty in the unfolding of mis/fortunes. If *ming* indexes the ongoing difficulties of epistemic murk, the other part of the common term for "fate" – the *yun* in *mingyun* – points to the anticipatory challenges of life's irreducible surprises. Literally meaning "transit" or "luck," *yun* is the short game to *ming*'s long game of fate calculation. While *ming* in its most rigid sense points to the inevitable movement from birth to death, *yun* gestures to the contingent openings for creative response along the unknown twists and turns of life's path. Although *ming*'s conclusion may be a given, *yun* promises tactical opportunities for optimizing fortune in the short run and moreover, for extending – or better yet, karmically refinancing – one's temporary purchase on this-worldly life.

Both risk management and fortune-telling require attunement to an endemic logic of chance. They encourage an alert passivity to the possibility of immanent surprise. The main difference, however, is that chance appears only as a "problem" in risk management systems while it is viewed as more of an "opportunity" for those consulting Chinese diviners about their futures. Successful risk management renders chance uneventful – it celebrates "near misses" and "risk incubation" (Power 2007); it works to preempt the upheavals of phase transitions in favor of the regularities of existing order (Amoore 2013). In contrast, fortune-telling often frames surprise as eventful opportunities for changing the current patterning of life's fortune. Here the goal is not to smooth over the twists and turns of seasonality but to cultivate a breakout moment by learning how to pace oneself – at times waiting out dangers and at other times pouncing on fleeting opportunities – according to the expert calculations of a life's momentary cosmic resonance with other social rhythms: the just-in-time global economy, the tempo of *renqing* gifts, the uneventful politics of risk preemption.

Ultimately, as moral technologies, what both calculations of risk and of fate have in common is the cultivation of deferential subjects who are oriented less toward transcendent ideals of autonomous action and mastery than to the interdependent promise for meeting surprise with timely response in a polyrhythmic world. Here it is not action per se as but an ethics of *reaction* – a yielding to the irreducible play of chance – that comes to define both risky and fateful situations. Customs officer Chen perhaps best captured this deferential sensibility by blending into the "machine" of risk management at work while also yielding in his free time to experts in fate calculation for dealing with uncertainty. On both fronts, Chen learned to give in to more distributed and remote forms of agency and accountability. He came to take comfort in the opacity of expert technologies for managing mis/fortunes, where the methods of calculation – whether as risk algorithm or numerological forecasting – always seemed to be in the process of involution and in receding from full comprehension and control. Far from common modern descriptions of the "risk-bearing" entrepreneurial subject boldly pursuing the possibilities offered by the volatility of chance, Chen learned to hone a distinctly passive and patient posture toward future hazards and opportunities in which, as he saw it, the most ethical stance was not one of self-assertion and -control but premised on a nonsovereign and heteronomous sense of one's position in fields of shifting moral complexity. By playing dumb in a system of risk management while also playing with fate and its arcane computations on the side, Chen came to find hope through the deferral of his own personal agency. This way of dealing with uncertainty resonates with Robert Weller's observation more than a decade earlier about Chinese sensibilities of chaos and control. As Weller noted, "This idea that truer and better knowledge always lies just out of reach recurs in many areas of China...It is enough to feel confident that explanation exists somewhere, even if expert knowledge follows the same kind of infinite recession into unresolved detail..." (1994: 123). There is also something hopeful in both of these ways of dealing with uncertainty in Hirozaku Miyazaki's sense of "hope as method." As models oriented toward the efficacies and entailments of anticipatory knowledge rather than the retrospective problems of causality and redress, risk and fate are ultimately methods for ensuring prospective momentum through the "abeyance of human agency" and through "acts of delegation" that forestall closure (Miyazaki 2004). In this way, they enable officials like Chen, otherwise feeling caught in a hazardous web of ever growing complexity, to cultivate an anticipatory posture toward indeterminancy and in turn, to continually proliferate the hopeful questions: What might happen *next*?[10] And how might one be primed for timely response?

Notes

1 In fact, in Fuzhou the local customs bureau was widely seen as one of the wealthiest civil service departments – a perception bolstered by its relocation into luxurious new headquarters as well as by a nationwide public expenditure report in 2011 that placed Chinese Customs Administration at no. 2 in the use of state resources.

2 This was evident by the kinds of anti-corruption operations that culminated in the Xiamen smuggling case as well as by a growing system of external audit involving not only higher state authorities but also international organizations such as the World Trade Organization (WTO) and the World Bank interested in the performance of Chinese Customs vis-à-vis its counterparts in other countries. For instance, see the World Bank's report "Connecting to Compete" on the "logistics performance index" for comparing customs agencies (Arvis et al. 2010).

3 Fuzhou Customs itself has grown tenfold since the launch of post-Mao reforms, from fewer than a hundred workers to more than a thousand strong.

4 For instance, risk management techniques can be traced back to 1986, when the bureau adopted the now standard system of red and green channels for the self-declaration of dutiable goods. However, it was not until 1999 that the concept of risk management was formally adopted by the World Customs Organization (WCO) with its passage of the Kyoto Convention, which required all contracting parties of the WCO, including China, to integrate the principle of risk management into all their customs control programs.

5 The release time of goods is a standard customs performance indicator, which the WCO has promoted and provided technical consultation for its members since 1994 (Zhang 2009; WCO 2011).

6 The fact that risk management exceeds rational calculation and the technologies of statistical intervention has been noted in several fields such as finance and security in recent years (Taleb 2007; Appadurai 2011; Ewald 2011; Amoore 2013), not to mention by sociologists of modernity arguing for the runaway incalculable hazards of risk technologies themselves (Beck 1992). Also see Daston (1995) on the moral relationship of probability to risk, which she argues stabilized only with the rise of Western bourgeois arguments for distinguishing the sober rational ethos of insurance from the immoral passions of gambling.

7 On timing of the gift versus bribery in China, see Smart 1993; Yang 1994; and Hsing 1996.

8 In addition to computer science and mathematics, the I-Ching has been variously claimed in both China and overseas as a scientific forerunner or resonant form of technical expertise in such fields as physics (Capra 2010), medicine (Farquhar 1996; Zhang 2007), psychotherapy (Jung 2010), operations research and systems theory (Churchman 1971), and business management (Cheng 2013). Also see Smith 2012 for a discussion of "*Yijing* fever" and its "scientific" emphasis in China in the 1980s and 1990s.

9 Anthropologists such as Marriot (1976), Strathern (1990), Gell (1998), and Sahlins (2013) have also discussed "dividual" or "distributive" forms of personhood, although not directly in relation to the logics of information.

10 I borrow this question from Charles Stafford's insightful work on fortune-telling in Taiwan and China.

References

Amoore, Louise. 2013. *The Politics of Possibility: Risk and Security Beyond Probability*. Durham, NC: Duke University Press.

Appadurai, Arjun. 2011. "The Ghost in the Financial Machine." *Public Culture* 23 (3): 517–539.

Arvis, Jean-Francois, Monica Alina Mustra, Lauri Ojala, Ben Shepherd, and Daniel Saslavsky. 2010. *Connecting to Compete: Trade Logistics in the Global Economy*. Washington, DC: The World Bank.

Beck, Ulrich. 1992. *Risk Society: Towards a New Modernity*. London: SAGE.

Beech, Hannah. 2002. "Smuggler's Blues." *Time*, October 14. http://content.time.com/time/world/article/0,8599,2056114,00.html.

Bourdieu, Pierre. 1990. "The Work of Time." In *The Logic of Practice*, 98–111. Stanford, CA: Stanford University Press.

Capra, Fritjof. 2010. *The Tao of Physics: An Exploration of the Parallels between Modern Physics and Eastern Mysticism*. Boston: Shambhala Publications.

Chang, Hui-Ching, and G. Richard Holt. 1994. "Debt-Repaying Mechanism in Chinese Relationships: An Exploration of the Folk Concepts of Pao and Human Emotional Debt." *Research on Language & Social Interaction* 27(4): 351–387.

Cheng, Chung-Ying. 2013. "On Yijing as Basis of Chinese Business Ethics and Management." In *Handbook of the Philosophical Foundations of Business Ethics*, edited by Christoph Luetge, 1027–1049. Dordrecht, the Netherlands: Springer. http://link.springer.com/referenceworkentry/10.1007/978-94-007-1494-6_8.

Churchman, Charles West. 1971. *The Design of Inquiring Systems: Basic Concepts of Systems and Organization*. New York: Basic Books.

Daston, Lorraine. 1995. *Classical Probability in the Enlightenment*. Princeton, NJ: Princeton University Press.

Dean, Mitchell. 1998. "Risk, Calculable and Incalculable." *Soziale Welt* 49(1): 25–42.

Deleuze, Gilles. 1992. "Postscript on the Societies of Control." *October* 59 (January): 3–7.

Dicken, Peter. 2011. *Global Shift: Mapping the Changing Contours of the World Economy*, 6th ed. New York: The Guilford Press.

Ewald, Francois. 2011. "Omnes Et Singulatim. After Risk." *Carceral Notebooks* 7: 77-107.

Farquhar, Judith. 1996. "'Medicine and the Changes Are One': An Essay on Divination Healing with Commentary." *Chinese Science* 13: 107–134.

Gell, Alfred. 1992. "The Technology of Enchantment and the Enchantment of Technology." In *Art and Agency: An Anthropological Theory*, edited by Jeremy Coote and Anthony Shelton, 40–63. Oxford: Oxford University Press.

1998. *Art and Agency: An Anthropological Theory*. Oxford: Oxford University Press.

Giddens, Anthony. 1998. "Risk Society: The Contest of British Politics." In *The Politics of Risk Society*, edited by Jane Franklin, 23–34. Cambridge, MA: Polity Press.

Guo, Li. 2007. "These Government Officials Belief in Fenshui, Gods and Ghosts, but Not Marxism-Leninism (Zheixie Guanyuan Mi Fengshui Buxin Ma-Lie Xin Guishen)." *Southern Weekend (Nanfang Zhoumo)*, May 17.

Harvey, David. 2010. *The Enigma of Capital: And the Crises of Capitalism*, Oxford: Oxford University Press.

Hsing, You-chien. 1996. "Building Guanxi Across the Straits: Taiwanese Capital and Local Chinese Bureaucrats." In *Ungrounded Empires: The Cultural Politics of Modern Chinese Transnationalism*, edited by Aihwa Ong and Donald Nonini, 143–166. New York: Routledge.

Hsu, Francis L. K. 1971. "Eros, Affect, and Pao." In *Kinship and Culture*, 439–475. Chicago: Aldine.

Jung, Carl G. 2010. *Synchronicity: An Acausal Connecting Principle*. Translated by R. F. C. Hull. Princeton, NJ: Princeton University Press.

Lash, Scott. 2000. "Risk Culture." In *The Risk Society and Beyond: Critical Issues for Social Theory*, edited by Barbara Adam, Ulrich Beck, and Joost Van Loon, 47–62. London: SAGE.

Levesque, Peter J. 2011. *The Shipping Point: The Rise of China and the Future of Retail Supply Chain Management*. New York: John Wiley & Sons.

Levin, Dan. 2013. "Feng Shui Grows in China as Officials Seek Success." *New York Times*, May 10, sec. World / Asia Pacific. www.nytimes.com/2013/05/11/world/asia/feng-shui-grows-in-china-as-officials-seek-success.html.

Liu, Xin. 2012. *The Mirage of China*. New York: Berghahn Books.

MacKenzie, Douglas, and Taylor Spears. 2012. "'The Formula That Killed Wall Street': The Gaussian Copula and the Material Cultures of Modelling." www.sps.ed.ac.uk/__data/assets/pdf_file/0003/84243/Gaussian14.pdf.

Marriot, McKim. 1976. "Hindu Transactions: Diversity without Dualism." In *Transaction and Meaning: Directions in the Anthropology of Exchange and Symbolic Behavior*, 109–142. Philadelphia: ISHI Publications.

Miyazaki, Hirokazu. 2004. *The Method of Hope: Anthropology, Philosophy, and Fijian Knowledge*. Stanford, CA: Stanford University Press.

Osburg, John. 2013. *Anxious Wealth: Money and Morality Among China's New Rich*. Stanford, CA: Stanford University Press.

Power, Michael. 2007. *Organized Uncertainty: Designing a World of Risk Management*. Oxford: Oxford University Press.

Sahlins, Marshall. 2013. *What Kinship Is – And Is Not*. Chicago: University of Chicago Press.

Shieh, Shawn. 2005. "The Rise of Collective Corruption in China: The Xiamen Smuggling Case." *Journal of Contemporary China* 14(42): 67–91.

Smart, Alan. 1993. "Gifts, Bribes, and Guanxi: A Reconsideration of Bourdieu's Social Capital." *Cultural Anthropology* 8(3): 388–408.

Smith, Richard J. 2012. *The I Ching: A Biography*. Princeton, NJ: Princeton University Press.

Stafford, Charles. 2007. "What Is Going to Happen Next?" In *Questions of Anthropology*, edited by Rita Astuti, Jonathan Parry, and Charles Stafford, 55–75. Oxford: Berg.

Strathern, Marilyn. 1990. *The Gender of the Gift: Problems with Women and Problems with Society in Melanesia*. Berkeley: University of California Press.

Taleb, Nassim Nicholas. 2007. *The Black Swan: The Impact of the Highly Improbable*. New York: Random House.

Van Rooij, Benjamin. 2005. "China's War on Graft: Political-Legal Campaigns against Corruption in China and Their Similarities to the Legal Reactions to Crisis in the U.S." *Pacific Rim Law & Political Journal* 14(2): 289–336.

Virilio, Paul. 1998. *The Virilio Reader*. New York: John Wiley & Sons.

Weller, Robert P. 1994. *Resistance, Chaos and Control in China: Taiping Rebels, Taiwanese Ghosts and Tianmen*. London: Macmillian.

Willmot, William. 1972. "Marketing and Credit in a Hong Kong Wholesale Market." In *Economic Organization in Chinese Society*, 327–352. Stanford, CA: Stanford University Press.

World Customs Organization. 2011. *Guide to Measure the Time Required for the Release of Goods, Version 2*. Brussels: World Customs Organization.

Yang, Mayfair Mei-hui. 1994. *Gifts, Favors, and Banquets: The Art of Social Relationships in China*. Ithaca, NY: Cornell University Press.

Yang, Ziwang. 2009. "National Civil Servant Exam: Over 3000 People Apply for Xiamen Haiguan Position (Guojia Gongwuyuan Kaoshi: Xiamen Haiguan Gangwei Baomingzhe Jin 3000 Ren)." *Xinhua News*, October 18, Online edition. http://news.xinhuanet.com/employment/2009–10/18/content_12258899.htm.

Zhang, Qicheng. 2007. *Yi Studies and Chinese Medicine (Yixue Yu Zhongyi)*. Guangxi, China: Guangxi Science and Technology Press.

Zhang, Shujie. 2009. "TRS as a Measurement of Trade Facilitation: Customs' Experience in the Asia-Pacific Region." *World Customs Journal* 3(2): 125–134.

Zhang, Shujie, and Shilu Zhao. 2009. *The Implication of Customs Modernization on Export Competitiveness in China*. Studies in Trade and Investment. United Nations Economic and Social Commission for Asia and the Pacific (ESCAP). http://econpapers.repec.org/bookchap/untecchap/tipub2543_5fzhang.htm.

2 Morality, Markets, and the Gospel of Prosperity

Simon Coleman, University of Toronto

If you walk into any airport bookstore in Europe or North America and head for the section selling advice on how to succeed in business, in relationships, or simply in life there is a good chance that you will find books by Joel Osteen. His bestsellers include *Become a Better You: 7 Keys to Improving Your Life Every Day* (2009) and *Making Wise Choices: Your Decisions Determine Your Destiny* (2005). But Osteen is not just a successful author of self-help books; he is also a televangelist renowned in charismatic circles around the world for his prosperity message and for being the head pastor of Lakewood Church in Houston, Texas. His father, John, founded Lakewood Church in the late 1950s and in the process shifted theological positions away from southern Baptism toward a more charismatic, Pentecostal orientation. Arguably, though, Joel has made a still more significant transition in his career, and one that is rarely achieved even in the noisy, confident world of contemporary American televangelists and prosperity preachers. For he has reached a stage at which he not only holds the interest of self-confessed believers – and there are quite a few of those, as Osteen's services are beamed out from Houston to some 100 countries each week – but has also visibly penetrated a global, secular market such as that represented by airport bookstores, which must appeal to generic rather than specifically Christian tastes. Osteen now inhabits a similar niche to that which Norman Vincent Peale made his own in the middle of the twentieth century by offering variations on a theme of positive thinking. He was featured as one of ABC News's "Most Fascinating People of 2006," and he has had the dubious pleasure of being interviewed on CNN by Piers Morgan. Presidential candidate John McCain called him "inspiring." In sum, his appeal goes far beyond religion.

When I see Joel Osteen's books for sale at airports I often think back to the first interview my colleague Katrin Maier and I did with a member of the Redeemed Christian Church of God in London (RCCG). The RCCG is an immensely successful Nigerian charismatic denomination, also run on broadly prosperity lines, that has expanded globally over the last three decades, typically following the migration patterns of its aspirant members away from West

Africa into Europe and America. Katrin and I were talking to a young man to whom I gave the pseudonym Chris, and he was telling us about the glossy magazine that he had started to edit on behalf of the denomination. We were sitting in his office at Jesus House, the largest RCCG church in the United Kingdom, located in an industrial/commercial zone in north London. To the surprise of both Katrin and me, sitting on Chris's desk were not just a Bible but also some distinctly "secular" publications, such as *GQ* and *Esquire*. By way of explanation, Chris told us that his aspiration was to see his magazine for sale in high street stores like W. H. Smith, and so he needed to know how to produce the right format to hit that kind of market. He remarked that he was keen to "learn from the best" publications, even if his aim was not to offer advice on sex or clothes, as they did, but "something better." According to Chris, there were around two million Christian men in the United Kingdom, and "they need[ed] to be reached" with a prosperity message. But his ambitions did not stop there. By referring to W. H. Smith he was indicating his desire to be represented in a store well known to the entire British population, and one with no obvious religious associations; furthermore, he added that, some day, he hoped to expand his operation into Europe. In a subsequent conversation, I was to encounter Chris's ambitions in another direction as well, when he asked me for advice on how to pursue a master's degree in anthropology. He explained that he wanted to deploy the research tools of the social sciences to understand how most effectively to understand – and reach – his target readership.

Now imagine that you are going into an airport store or even W. H. Smith just one more time – actually, at a specific time, December 2009. As you search for a magazine your attention is caught by the front page of the *Atlantic Monthly*, a venerable American journal covering culture, politics, and literature. You notice the startling question on the cover: "Did Christianity Cause the Crash?" (Rosin 2009). Browsing through the piece, you see that it states:

> America's mainstream religious denominations used to teach the faithful that they would be rewarded in the afterlife. But over the past generation, a different strain of Christian faith has proliferated – one that promises to make believers rich in the here and now. Known as the prosperity gospel, and claiming tens of millions of adherents, it fosters risk-taking and intense material optimism. It pumped air into the housing bubble. And one year into the worst downturn since the Depression, it's still going strong.

We see here something of a "millennial capitalism" (Comaroff and Comaroff 2000) message gone mainstream. In other words, a form of pariah capitalism is being highlighted in the context of the diagnosis of an economic catastrophe, albeit one that – somewhat parochially, in this passage – is taken to concern primarily America rather than the entire globe. So a message that is presented as empowering in the Osteen version of the faith becomes, instead, matter deeply out of place in this piece: an unwanted and supposedly irrational meddling in economic activity, contrasting with the assumed Protestant asceticism of earlier times.

What are the issues raised by these intersections of prosperity ideas with ostensibly secular markets? They clearly interweave economic and religious imagery, but this observation is where analysis must begin, rather than end. I am intrigued by the ways in which ostensibly secular and religious spheres of material activity are sometimes represented as adjacent or overlapping, but also sometimes as inhabiting very different, epistemological and ontological worlds. Osteen's success as an author shows how an adapted message of prosperity may resonate well with the aspirations of people who belong, or wish to belong, to the mobile business classes in Euro-American circles and probably beyond. At the same time, the comments from Chris, our RCCG informant, tell us something else about the priorities and desires of Christians who actively promulgate a prosperity message: selling books or magazines with inspiring content is important, but the very act of reaching into, penetrating, a particular kind of market can bring its own reward. Simply gaining a *presence* within a global, demonstrably secular (in Christian eyes) sphere of commerce provides its own, self-validating evidence of "breakthrough" in Pentecostal terms. This attitude reveals an understanding of the secular market not only as an enabler of open commerce but also as a somewhat exclusive space to which access is restricted but desired. As an arena for action, it is desired not only because it reaches beyond already Christian territories, but also because it indicates a huge enlargement of the potential scale and scope of evangelical action.

In making these points, I am touching on older Weberian debates about the relationship between religion and capitalism. But notice also how the apparent proximity of prosperity ideology to assumptions of the secular market brings its own risks. One of the fascinating dimensions of the *Atlantic Monthly* is the sheer agency it grants to religion in the public sphere – an agency that most Christians can in reality only aspire to from a considerable distance. With agency, of course, comes accountability: the point of the article is to present Christianity as a powerful but fundamentally disruptive ghost in the market machine, with such an accusation potentially serving to protect the plausibility of "purely" secular economic assumptions by indicating how the latter were subverted by unreasonable – and irrational – optimism.[1]

Prosperity discourse[2] has attracted both attention and ire from fellow Christians, academics, and journalists since at least the 1970s. Osteen is often accused of promulgating a highly selective part of the Christian message – the bit that talks about money and success – while omitting to mention the consequences of sin and suffering, though he defends both his positive tone and, in line with the independent character of his calling, has denied that he should be seen as promulgating a prosperity gospel in a conventional sense.[3]

Nonetheless, from the perspective of some classic Pentecostalists, let alone liberal Protestants or Catholics, prosperity-oriented Christians such as Osteen have developed a "preying" rather than "praying" relationship to more traditional forms of the faith. His neo-Pentecostalism appears to resonate all too well with forms of neoliberalism, representing a commoditization of faith and a marketization of self.

This is not going to be a piece specifically about Joel Osteen. But I begin with him because he raises central questions about the phenomenon, and the study, of prosperity Christianity: How might we determine the relationship between this religious ideology and believers' valorization of the "free market," but also – and perhaps more interestingly – what is ideologically *at stake* for supporters or critics of prosperity ideas in defining this relationship? Why should either party consider the market, however conceived or evaluated, an important dimension of the spiritual life of such Christians?

Along with Chris and the *Atlantic* article, Joel Osteen helps us gain an initial overview of prosperity Christianity as a phenomenon that readily touches very different discursive worlds: those of believers, cultural commentators, theologians, and social scientists. I want to explore and juxtapose these discursive worlds in this chapter, with the ultimate purpose of indicating whether (and, if so, how) it is possible to construct a broad theoretical framework for understanding the resonances between ideologies of "prosperity" and shifting notions of the market and its associated moralities. My point will be that such resonances exist, but not necessarily in the ways we might at first expect. We shall see, for instance, how common understandings of prosperity theology as simply an expression of self-interested consumerism[4] do little justice to the subtle mediations of discipline and personhood that engagement in such practice can imply. I shall draw on Marcel Mauss as well as Max Weber to indicate how believers draw on transactional models of interaction and exchange in constituting notions of the entrepreneurial Christian subject – a subject whose orientation is toward not only the cultivation of interior conviction but also the outward, materialized, constitutions of religious engagement. Intriguingly, the same blend of authors is deployed by Arjun Appadurai (2013: 3–4, 233–235) in his reflections on the links between risk-taking and globalization at both individual and societal levels. Appadurai's interest is in "the capacity to aspire" (Chapter 9) as well as ways in which dispositions are cultivated that might exploit uncertainty in contexts of attempting to manage both risk and the future. We might seem a long way from prosperity Christianity here but we shall eventually see some intriguing resonances between aspiration and prosperity discourse, including the latter's occasional cultivation of risk-taking and "reaching out" into the world as part of its central constituting practices.

A focus on these themes raises questions of how prosperity practice relates to the evocation of risk and uncertainty in the creation of "modern" Christian subjects, even as I am also wary of reducing analysis of Christianity to a narrative of modernity itself (see also Cannell 2006; Marshall 2009). Here we might return again to the example of Chris and his magazine: this is, after all, a venture that involves the risk of monetary capital but also much more, an expression of the Christian as bold crosser of boundaries that he or she perceives to exist in the wider world. In this sense, Chris is both attempting to accumulate and is putting into play a form of "aspirational capital," making (and narrating) plans whose fulfillment will index not only his success as an editor, but also the performative power of his convictions.

All of this is not to say that the existence of prosperity discourse is somehow explained only as a means of mastering risk-taking, however. Nor should we ignore the "dark side" of the prosperity gospel: its regular appearance in contexts where uncertainty appears less a matter of celebration and more one of anguish and incomprehension, as we see in discussions of the occult economy, discussed further below (Comaroff and Comaroff 1999, 2000). In this chapter, then, I try to bring together two characterizations of prosperity attitudes to risk that are often kept apart in the literature. There is of course a long history to questions relating to the morality of the market. Ash Amin and Nigel Thrift (2004) point out that Adam Smith, acclaimed as father of modern economics, was the author not only of *Wealth of Nations* but also *Theory of Moral Sentiments*, and came to view the practice of economy also as a practice of moral judgment. In his view, modern society should be seen as "a moral order of sympathy, with participation in the feelings of others, existing alongside economic individualism "as the driving force of wealth creation" (Amin and Thrift 2004: xvi). It is notable that they redefine the neoclassical genealogy as part of an attempt to reframe the notion of the economy: thus they invoke Smith as part of their call for more attention to be paid to cultural economy and the ways in which "the production, distribution, and accumulation of resources – loosely the pursuit of prosperity – have always been a cultural performance" (Amin and Thrift 2004: xii). Anthropologists might easily agree with Amin and Thrift about "the utter constructedness of apparently pure entities like markets" (Amin and Thrift 2004: xix), and ethnographic interest is likely to be focused on the particular methods through which an ideology of purity is constructed in any given social or cultural circumstance. Of course, we are used to hearing neoclassical depictions of the autonomous market, implying the possibility of maximizing action both unfettered by the state and somehow perfectly indexical of the results of competition among putative equals. Such action can supposedly take place at very different scales, from the immediately proximate to the apparently global. But as Kalman Applbaum points out, the anthropological reflex is both to point out distinctions between physical marketplaces and more abstract market principles and to soften such distinctions in actual market ethnographies, thus exploring and perhaps challenging "a list of oppositions drawn between types of relations and even mentalities associated with economic exchange beyond markets per se: gift versus commodity, mutuality versus impersonal or self-interested calculation, local (place) versus global (placeless), and so on" (2012: 257).[5]

One of the things that is intriguing about such themes in relation to debates over prosperity Christianity is how anthropologists and other social scientists, normally "blurrers" and "softeners" par excellence, frequently become more purist (and sometimes downright intellectually puritanical) when it comes to reflecting on people such as Osteen or others who are considered more "extreme" prosperity preachers. Such Christians may or may not succeed in penetrating markets that they themselves perceive as "secular," in other words those such as an airport store where consumption patterns are not overtly related to religious identity. Nonetheless, as noted earlier, the aspirations of such Christians to reach these markets sometimes inflame social scientific sensibilities.[6] Here, I imply more than the issues involved in Susan Harding's (1991) well-known depiction of the difficulties of studying "the repugnant cultural other," where she discusses the mistrust felt by colleagues of her decision to study Christian fundamentalists. Of course, it is often hard to research frequently close-at-hand religion that appears to be in bad taste (and politically challenging) according to most middle-class Euro-American standards. But there are deeper issues at play relating to how we view and analyze Christianity as a whole, and they take us back to issues of how believers relate to markets and associated processes of commoditization and consumption. Fenella Cannell (2004: 7–8) refers to the ways in which a partially Weberian, ascetic stereotype of Christianity is still embedded in anthropology (let alone much of Euro-American culture at large), and how such a view may reinforce broader tendencies to define Christianity through theories prioritizing narratives of modernity that, in turn, identify the importance of interiority in relation to modern forms of morality and conscience (Cannell 2006: 20). My suggestion is that prosperity Christianity provides a particularly powerful way of unsettling not only such ascetic assumptions, but also the central place of interiority as a component of what we understand as defining the modern. In my development of these points, notions of market and morality are useful to focus on for a number of reasons: they often juxtapose conceptions of intentionality with those of materiality, as well as constructions of interiority and exteriority, and do so in ways that range in expression from physical practice to abstract metaphor, as well as across cultural and political fields.

Prosperity Christianity: What, Where, When?

Recall that Joel Osteen has *denied* that he is promulgating a prosperity gospel. His attitude hints at the largely thankless task of attempting to provide a satisfactory definition and characterization of what may be seen as a movement,[7] a network, an idiom, a theology, a heresy – or indeed not any single thing at all – and is surely the product of interactions not only among Christians themselves, but also among believers and their many detractors, as well as structural catalysts ranging from postwar religious revival to the global expansion of neoliberal forms of governance and economy.

In exploring the varied historical influences behind prosperity ideas in America, Kate Bowler (2013:13) cites Ralph Waldo Emerson's philosophical idealism, Emmanuel Swedenborg's Neoplatonic theory of correspondence, and Helena Blavatsky's theosophical quest for uniform spiritual laws, while noting the considerable influence of Phineas Parkhurst Quimby, a nineteenth-century touring mesmerist and physician who developed notable ideas about the human subconscious, including notions of a "talking cure" that preceded modern psychotherapy. Another key and equally maverick figure was E. W. Kenyon (1867–1948), a New England preacher deeply influenced by New Thought metaphysics (see also Yong 2012: 15). Bowler argues that Kenyon's tracing of the shift of the person from guilty sinner to empowered saint drew on New Thought ideas claiming that humans could harness God's power through deploying the spoken word (Bowler 2013: 19). Mind power and overcoming faith reinforced each other and overlapped with aspects of early Pentecostalism, producing what Bowler calls an "amplified anthropology" (Bowler 2013: 20).

Abstruse as these ideas might seem, they manifested in numerous popular forms in the self-help literature of the first part of the twentieth century. In due course, they would reinforce newly confident and increasingly well-resourced Pentecostal revivals of post–Second World War North America. The same decade that saw the publication of Norman Vincent Peale's blend of Methodist evangelism, Dutch Reformed Calvinism, and New Thought in *The Power of Positive Thinking* (1952; Bowler 2013: 57) also saw Oral Roberts produce *God's Formula for Success and Prosperity* (1956). Roberts's "Blessing Pact" combined imageries of speculation and calculation, contract and anonymous exchange, claiming that donors to his ministry would receive at least sevenfold returns on their investment (see Bowler 2013: 49). In subsequent decades, these and similar ideas would be picked up by other preachers both outside and within Pentecostal circles, and promulgated through such techniques as visualization and utterance of "positive confession" over all areas of life, from work to finances to family and health.

One particular image permeated the language and the practices of many believers while developing – in keeping with its own metaphorical as well as metaphysical implications – a life of its own. Roberts's "Seed Faith Principle" evoked agricultural language drawn from the Bible[8] (and, no doubt, the American Midwest) in describing the specific investments people made through prosperity practices. Thus, for Bowler, "Unlike tithes given after income, seed faith money added an element of risk by donating money on the hope of receiving more in return" (2013: 67). She points here to an element of disciplining the self that seems far from ascetic ideals and yet contains a notable dimension of self-governance: the cultivation of risk through a calculus that appears to act as an index – often a publicly expressed one – of ideological commitment. Thus the seed metaphor works through uniting basic elements of prosperity praxis: seeds, like empowered words or anointed money, can be passed between people, but also associated with a particular "broadcaster" who can expect to reap benefits from the work involved and risk taken; seeded actions grow through immutable laws; and finally, seeds may recall not only farming but also fertility, and at times preachers have indeed suggested the generative and always "overflowing" character of positively oriented religious practice. This imagery also opens up the possibility of imagining action occurring at numerous scales – "seeds" can be "planted" within one's immediate life circumstances or on the other side of the world.

If the metaphor of reaching out through "sowing" lends itself to multiple forms of appropriation, it has found expression in institutional forms that have helped the widespread diffusion of the message. Katherine Attanasi (2012: 2) notes how prosperity preaching came especially into its own within the last of three historical waves of evangelical "renewal" over the past century: the classical Pentecostalism that emerged in the early part of the twentieth century was followed by the charismatic movement of the 1960s and 1970s; but prosperity ideas have been "broadcast" most effectively through the recent expansion of neo-Pentecostalism, which is often to be found in newer, independent or semi-independent churches, and is associated with a relaxing of the strict holiness orientations of earlier, more sectarian forms of Pentecostalism. Over time, an identifiable religious network has begun to crystallize that comprises characteristic teachings, key preachers, conferences, and skillful use of mass media (Attanasi 2012: 53). A loosely knit organization called the International Convention of Faith Churches and Ministries (ICFCM) has provided some ideological unity in more recent years, alongside powerful educational establishments such as Oral Roberts University and Kenneth Hagin's Bible School, both based in Tulsa, Oklahoma. And yet, no single church form or organization has held definitive sway. For instance, the suburban, middle-class, post-denominational megachurch phenomenon of the late twentieth and early twenty-first centuries has provided an important venue for dimensions of prosperity teaching, and one that allows it to be diffused widely and subtly across congregations in the United States that may not even see themselves as explicitly "prosperity"-oriented (see also Yong 2012).

Of course, my focus on the American origins of prosperity ideas tells only part of the story. Amos Yong (2012: 15–16) points to the pervasiveness of prosperity themes around the world, including their location in the Yoido

Full Gospel Church in South Korea (the largest Christian congregation *anywhere*) as well as the Redeemed Christian Church of God in Nigeria, both of which also plant missionary congregations around the world, alongside independent churches such as the Brazilian-based but also globally missionizing Igreja Universal do Reino de Deus (Universal Church of the Kingdom of God [UCKG]). Attanasi (2012: 3) observes that nations displaying the most obvious propensity for prosperity beliefs in their neo-Pentecostal congregations are Brazil, Nigeria, and South Africa. In each of these contexts, local churches and Christians respond to particular genealogies and missions, even if prosperity orientations as we currently understand them have emerged most strongly within the last thirty years or so. A case in point is the RCCG: this denomination, now enormous and transnational in scope, has roots in an obscure, pious, "Aladura" foundation from the 1950s (e.g., Ukah 2008). Indeed, the RCCG remained in the shadows until the 1980s, when a combination of its shift to prosperity doctrines, the more general explosion of Pentecostal discourse in the country, and economic and political "push" factors leading to middle-class migration out of Nigeria, all contributed to a striking transformation of fortune (and expansion of scope) within a relatively short space of time.

So we are hardly dealing with a single, identifiable "movement." Some parts of the network(s) I am describing are in close touch with each other, and others are more independent. The complex relationships and expanding trajectories contained within the prosperity label do have intriguing parallels with the so-called southernization of Christianity (e.g., Jenkins 2007) and the considerable significance of Pentecostalism and neo-Pentecostalism in postcolonial landscapes. Some commentators, such as Gifford et al. (1996), have argued that the spread of prosperity ideas often represents an Americanization of non-Western religious contexts. To some degree, their argument is reinforced by the high profiles of key preachers, many of whom indeed come from North America, who travel around ministries and conferences around the world, in effect tracing a cartographic imaginary of prosperity-oriented organizations where some nations figure more prominently than others. Yet, it is clear not only that certain non-Western denominations such as the RCCG and UCKG are performing powerful feats of reverse mission in North American and European cities, but also that certain preachers from the global South, such as Pastor Adeboye, head of the RCCG, are becoming significant figures in themselves. The *Newsweek* "Top 50 Global Power Elite" List for 2008–2009 contained just two people of African descent: Barack Obama and Pastor Adeboye.

The "Why" Question

Yong rightly refers to "the pluralistic shades of prosperity embraced by Christians around the world" (2012: 16). The meanings of materiality, success, and "sowing" take on different resonances and associations in different contexts; they may involve exclusive adherence to a prosperity-oriented church or more of an occasional brush with prosperity thinking and activity; they may be allied with considerable self-discipline over personal consumption patterns, or not; their relationship to political discourse also varies; and so on. It is, however, the case that prosperity Christianity – like Pentecostalism as a whole – is highly prone to become tangled up in debates over the meanings of "modernity" wherever it is encountered. In some contexts such as the United States, as I have suggested, it may be seen as *both* irrational *and* too close to aspects of secular modernity; in others, for example, the fascinating case of Chinese entrepreneurs in Wenzhou, analyzed by Nanlai Cao (2012), it may signify aspirations toward establishing connections or at least parallels with Western, cosmopolitanism; in still others, as in the unusual case of Mensa Otabil of the International Central Gospel Church, Ghana, it may involve self-conscious resistance against both magical thinking and dependence on international structures, leading to attempts to create a more specifically African version of professionalism and economic engagement (Warikobo 2012: 50–51). However, we should not assume that prosperity's varied articulations with questions of the modern indicate that analytical frameworks oriented around the latter somehow provide us with a comprehensive *explanation* for the diffusion of prosperity ideas or their articulation with market imageries. Thus Ruth Marshall, in reflections prompted by work on Nigerian neo-Pentecostalism, notes the tendency for anthropologists to see in such new forms of religiosity the elaboration of a "vernacular language" that functions "to translate into a form of popular knowledge destabilizing processes, such as globalization, relations of domination, and socioeconomic crises – in short, to see them principally as forms of the domestication of modernity" (Marshall 2009: 22; see also Cannell 2006; Coleman 2011). Arguably, such an anthropological approach itself indicates a kind of social scientific domestication of prosperity, a reduction of it to a single, apparently secular, cause.

If we look at the ways in which scholars have drawn on economic tropes to explain the popularity of prosperity Christianity, two approaches have tended to dominate the field (see Coleman 2011). One is a neo-Weberian model. Numerous examples of this approach exist, though it is often associated in its most ideal-typical form with Peter Berger. R. Andrew Chesnut summarizes the approach by stating, "On the plane of macroeconomics it is clear that prosperity theology, in both practice and theory, reinforces and even promotes the existing global capitalist order," while it "was birthed in capitalism as a theology conceived and developed in the United States, the world's leading free market economy" (Chesnut 2012: 215). In these terms, prosperity advocates share with Liberation theologians a concern with the material effects of Christian activity, but seem to search for instant, individualized benefits rather than longer-term, collective and systemic ones. Prosperity aspirations and activities are assumed to appeal most strongly to poorer classes of people, though also to some extent to those who have already achieved wealth, according to their own reckoning, and indeed "the theology's emphasis on individual prosperity also jibes with the zeitgeist of the contemporary labor market" (Chesnut 2012: 218), where people are compelled to compete as individuals in capitalist labor markets, and cannot rely on the fallback of a functioning welfare state.[9] Stephen Hunt's interpretation of the links that are thus made between faith and perceived "need" is that they represent an example of a "hegemonic model" of explanation, with echoes of dependency theory and assumptions that Christianity is acting as an inherently modernizing, Westernizing force (2000: 333).

More could be said about this model but my main aim is to juxtapose it with an analytical alternative (see also Coleman 2011). Jean and John Comaroff's "Occult Economies and the Violence of Abstraction" (1999) describe what they see as the results of encounters between an optimistic faith in free enterprise and the challenges of neoliberal economics, including unpredictable shifts in demands for labor at global scales, an equivocal role for the state, and uncertainties surrounding the nature of civil society (Comaroff and Comaroff 1999: 294). For them, these are the kinds of contexts where "the magical allure of making money from nothing" indicates a "millennial moment" where "capitalism has an effervescent new spirit – a magical, neo-Protestant zeitgeist – welling up close to its core" (Comaroff and Comaroff 1999: 281). Importantly, this ideology invokes the ability to gain wealth without perceptible production, but it also implies – especially to those at the bottom of the economic pile – the working of insidious forces and even sorcery as means of accumulation (1999: 282). We see the key juxtaposition of these occult economies, as they point both to the pursuit of new, magical means for otherwise unattainable ends, and at the same time to worries that some people will enrich themselves through illegitimate means (1999: 284).

So how might these characterizations relate to specific prosperity discourses? Jean and John Comaroff provide an extended example from fieldwork in rural Tswana, a place where Pentecostalism meets neoliberal enterprise but also where "discourses of the diabolical" often focus on the UCKG, while "appealing frankly to mercenary motives, mostly among the young" (1999: 281). Their argument is extended a year later in reflections on how the occult economy is a significant dimension of "millennial capitalism" (Comaroff and Comaroff 2000). Again, the focus is on ways of generating value associated with concomitant increases in economic speculation (Comaroff and Comaroff 2000: 295). The "fee-for-service, consumer-cult, prosperity gospel denominations" appear to be especially close to the new neoliberal spirit of the age (Comaroff and Comaroff 2000: 314). Thus, millennial capitalism is said to contain a confusing and contradictory blend of hope and hopelessness, alongside a privatized sense of religious participation in relation to a market whose benefits remain ever more unattainable, constituted through rapid flows of value across space and time.

More recently still, Jean Comaroff has returned to these issues in an overview of her work. She sees faith-based organizations seeming to thrive in many contexts where "the architecture of modern social institutions" appears to be eroding, even as "the solid lines between the sacred and profane, the private and public – lines that seem synonymous with liberal modernity" are "under attack in many places" (Comaroff 2012: 13). Furthermore, she notes that "if ever there was a figure that typified the sudden rise of joblessness, the mysterious production of wealth without work, and the apparently occult grounding of neo-liberal capitalism in local experience, it was the zombie" (Comaroff 2012: 10). The zombie represents here the ultimate embodiment of flexible, nonstandard, asocial labor. We seem ideological worlds away here from the optimistic risk-taking chronicled by Bowler, but what Comaroff's material is doing is both providing a much wider structural, cultural, political, and economic landscape through which to assess these ideas, and presenting the important moral flip-side of a ritualized emphasis on the positive and the endlessly and effortlessly attainable. While the Bergerian perspective summarized by Chesnut raises the specter of a postsecular neo-Weberianism (if that is not a contradiction in terms), Jean and John Comaroff add a sophisticated dose of Marxism (and perhaps nostalgic Durkheimianism) to the mix.

If we are to see the prosperity gospel as in any sense a meaningful anthropological object, we need to bear in mind that in different contexts it produces the figure *both* of the thrusting entrepreneur and of the listless zombie. The prime economic and experiential alchemy that is presented as producing both is uncertainty itself, expressed variously through worries over the labor market, the sources of wealth, or the efficient cultivation of investment. So both analyses are powerful, but I worry about the sometimes one-dimensional qualities of their models, even as they operate on the interface between emic and etic understandings of the current efflorescence of prosperity Christianity (Coleman 2011). In both cases, we are encouraged to see religious action predominantly as a *response* to other events, in particular to a current conjoining of the global and the neoliberal (compare Rudnyckyj 2009). This kind of explanation focuses on structural positioning – in terms of class, generation, and sometimes ethnicity – and to aspirations for economic improvement or consolidation. We may wish to question the assumption that what appears to the secular observer as the irrational must be explained ultimately through an analytical rationale based on societal or emotional need.

Here I take account of Bill Maurer's (2010) recent piece discussing the religion in and of the current financial crisis – what he calls "credit crisis religion." Maurer produces his own reconsideration of Jean and John Comaroff's (2000) essay, and argues, "If the occult economies of millennial capitalism were seen as efforts to grasp the violence of capitalist abstraction, it is because the social scientific attempt to describe those occult economies also partakes of the same hierarchism in the construction of the object of that analytical effort" (Maurer 2010: 149). Here, he agrees with Marshall (2009) in critiquing the implicit privileging of the economic as primary source and site of explanation, but also suggesting that such analyses may be telling a story whose conclusions are already known from the very start.

Alternative Frames

What other analytical models might be deployed to characterize prosperity Christianities, understood very broadly as a globally diffused and internally heterogeneous set of ideologies and practices? We might, for instance, wish to move away from direct "why" questions to other analytical pathways. One approach might be a discussion of rhizomes influenced by Deleuze and Guattari (1987) and the endlessly generating semiotic chains that such religious discourses seem to generate, although I am not sure that this approach would do more than merely redescribe the dynamic and fractal landscape of expansion that currently exists. It lacks the sheer analytical and political force of talk of millennial capitalism and occult economies. Sharper analytical purchase might come from Anna Tsing's (2004) metaphor of "friction" and zones of awkward engagement as a way of thinking about the complex and convoluted production of forms of "universalism" in response to the diffusion of capital. I do not discount such a possibility, but my approach in this chapter moves me more toward the questions I posed at the beginning of this chapter, toward a closer examination of prosperity discourse as a site of practice where we can move toward a reexamination of some common assumptions about Christian, and particularly Protestant, interiority, asceticism, and moral conscience.

First, we need to acknowledge once more the ambiguity of our site of religious practice, to recognize the chronic "promiscuity" of prosperity ideas and practices as objects of study in their own right. In fact, this is an approach that is itself well grounded in social scientific studies of Pentecostalism as a whole, which have been intrigued by its striking ability to articulate with so-called local cultural forms while also giving them new moral and political valences, or even polarities (e.g., Coleman 2011). Prosperity, like Pentecostalism, is good at adding certain *dimensions* to ritual practices and economic aspirations (and here we might think back to Bowler's invocation of an "amplified anthropology").[10]

Thus prosperity orientations and trajectories tend to invoke issues of scale, distance, and projection, mediated and expressed through different forms of materiality. To put the point another way, it is striking how often a prosperity orientation is constituted by ritual activity that establishes links between forms of giving and the creation of value: as we have seen, certain manifestations of giving are perceived as productive in themselves (seed-like), while indexing the degree of conviction of the self as giver – or, as that person is often perceived, investor. Admittedly, "giving" in my sense can mean a number of things, and they are not necessarily exclusive to neo-Pentecostalists: it may involve tithing to a church; it may involve more spontaneous donations of money to individuals, charities, or other churches; but it may also involve investments of time, or even the kinds of "speaking out" of prayers and tongues that reach out into the world with performative intent. Such intent provides a complex mixture of human agency and divine compact, while combining risk and hope within the same action, and we might remember here the etymology behind "*pro spe*," indicating a sense of "supporting hope."[11]

Prosperity practices in these senses produce a strange hybrid of the shades of Mauss and Weber, with a bit of Hegelian externalization thrown in. But it is important to add a further dimension to such expressions of self-projection: they may invoke hope and intent, but they may also, in many ethnographic cases, imply a more subtle, subjunctive attitude toward prosperity discourse that might at first appear to be the case. Let me give an example of what I mean by going back to the context of the global financial crisis. Referring to his fieldwork at an American prosperity convention, Jonathan Walton quotes the well-known preacher Jerry Savelle (2012: 107–108):

> American households have lost 14 trillion dollars in wealth....But that will not affect me. Dow Jones is not my source. United States government is not my source. Social Security is not my source. God is my source of supply!...Stop worrying and start sowing.... If you don't have enough money to pay your bills sow a seed. When a worry about money pops into your mind, sow – this is the spiritual law.

On the face of it, there is no sign of holding back here. Hope and risk are pushed aside by law. God is an infinite source and resource, and one that can be accessed through externalization of resources from the self, even at a time of personal lack. We see here the indexing of personal conviction (or at least publicly expressed confidence) expressed in the process of reaching out, where sowing becomes not mere speculation but rather investment; both the secular state and the secular market are significant reference points but in this case they are not merely penetrated, but actually surpassed, as the crisis is depicted as not affecting the believer.

Such a message seems uncompromising, and we can see how it would prompt heavy critique from the kind of people who might read – or write for – publications like the *Atlantic*. There is no doubt that what might conventionally be seen as reckless behavior sometimes results from such rhetoric. But let me add two further dimensions to this interpretation. One is simply a contextual one. Rather than "reducing" our understanding of such giving/investment as depicted by Savelle to self-interested economic behavior, we need to bear in mind how "sowing" itself has an economic dimension but also much wider references in a prosperity context such as this: it parallels other forms of "reaching out" (externalization) such as prayer, the deployment of performative language, the conversion of others, the raising of one's perspective toward wider geographical horizons. Furthermore, as Walton himself notes, taking such preaching at face value could lead the observer to somewhat overdetermined accounts of "hailed" subjects who embrace such ideology wholesale. He prefers instead to see participants as improvisers: "There may be an operative chord structure or repetitive rhythmic refrain within the Word of Faith Movement to which persons adhere, but adherents strategically riff and creatively improvise within the system" (Walton 2012: 109). Arguably, such improvisation is aided precisely by the promiscuous character of prosperity teaching, with prosperity often acting as much as an adjectival practice describing or giving a certain flavor to other theologies and activities as forming a theology in itself. Walton refers to the ways in which adherents tend to reinterpret teachings to exercise their own forms of spiritual capital, adding "these are not closed ethical systems" (Walton 2012: 127). Thus the language of strict adherence to the Bible, or even to the laws of constant investment, becomes a catalyst for *reflection* on issues of scale and aspiration rather than a demand for strict adherence. And such a point begins to point us toward one of the problems of representation that I half hinted at in referring to Osteen's uneasiness with the term "prosperity." Believers themselves tend not to use the economistic, one-dimensional appellations of "prosperity" or "health and wealth" to describe themselves, preferring specific denominational terms or phrases such as "faith" adherence (as in the ICFCM, mentioned earlier). The purely economic metaphors used to describe believers are normally deployed by outsiders, and serve in effect to point to what they see as the most distinctive (and problematic) aspect of such religious ideology, while ignoring the numerous ways in which prosperity Christians may resemble others considered mainstream.

If the Walton example encourages us to nuance our views of how prosperity rhetoric is enacted in practice, I think we can add a warning note about the seeming hyperindividuality of much prosperity rhetoric as well. In thinking about prosperity as quality of action with implications for ideas of scale and the crossing of boundaries, I may be describing a tension between an adapted Maussian model of mediation and transactionality and a more Weberian model of the autonomous actor. This point takes us back to the ways in which anthropologists have recently been thinking about the construction of the Christian subject, including notions of interiority.

Jon Bialecki has recently provided an analysis of what he refers to as the "unstable subject of Protestant language ideology." He posits that "Christian language use can be understood by delineating two sharply contrasting, but both valued, forms of speech – "centripetal" and "centrifugal" – each of which has different implicit concerns about the importance of self-identity and the sorts of boundaries that comprise the ethical subject" (2011: 679). In Bialecki's account, these two models initially take concrete expression in two fieldwork contexts. Webb Keane's model of the Protestant semiotic ideology evident among the Sumbanese Calvinists generalizes toward a tendency of Christianity in general, and Protestantism in particular, to valorize both sincerity and an isomorphism between externally directed speech and internal subjectivity (Bialecki 2011: 682). The autonomous, bounded subject produced by this stance toward language "is one that is closely related...to the confessional, agentive, self-fashioned subject of contemporary modern secular language ideologies" (Bialecki 2011: 682).

In contrast, Bialecki uses my analysis of the Swedish Word of Life prosperity gospel ministry to illustrate a religious logic "where the borders of the self are much more porous, and where the concept of speech acts as being rooted in the specificities of the individuated person does not have the same importance" (2011: 683). Here, words take on value *because* of their exterior source, while the subject's own agency is carried forth beyond the limits of the person by a further circulation of both words and money. Expansive circulation and a kind of dividuality are valorized. The very prosperity of such Christians is about a mediation and reconstruction of the spiritually empowered self through interaction with others. Bialecki argues reasonably that any rigid opposition between the centrifugal and the centripetal can be collapsed, as what we are seeing here are religious modalities that can be found in widely diffuse locales, just as there may be a tendency for adherents of each of these language ideologies to take up the practices of the other. What interests me here, however, is the way in which a model of an unstable, transactional self provides a means through which to read prosperity Christianity as rather more than egocentrism spiritualized.

Such transactionalism clearly requires certain media through which to operate, and we might think of markets as one powerful site of exchange, of translation, and not only because they can exist on the boundaries between the secular and the sacred. This is part of what I meant, for instance, by referring to Chris's desire to penetrate the market represented by W. H. Smith, and the fact of this very penetration as having a self-validating quality for such Christians. However, again I think there is more here than meets the eye, and this time my point has to do with the location and character of some of the markets that prosperity Christians encounter – and create. The kind of global, secular market penetration achieved by a figure such as Joel Osteen is rare. However, it is possible to claim that, to some degree, prosperity-oriented congregations and denominations are good at constructing largely *internal* markets that nonetheless partake of some of the valorized qualities of secular counterparts: the clear crossing of lines between Christian and non-Christian spheres is lost, but the sense and experience of "reaching out," of externalization, of scaling up, of broadcasting "seeds" across certain boundaries, is still achieved. This strategy has the advantage of permitting investments and exchanges to take place, often over large distances, and may involve money but also wider forms of materiality and movement.

My point here refers to a dimension of Pentecostal life in general that seems relatively neglected by researchers: the contact between fellow believers who are separated by distance and/or nationality. Joel Robbins (2011) has referred recently to ways in which Pentecostal sociality is marked by a high degree of mutual ritual performance and the creation of an intersubjective sense of coordination of action. My suggestion is that apparently "economic" activities can, from a certain perspective, also be seen as forms of intersubjective, semi-ritualized coordination. For instance, the purchasing of a book by a famous preacher does not merely involve the paying of money for an item in a short-term interaction: it is also an investment of the resources of the self, indeed at a certain level also the self, in a good that is expected to yield returns for the self and others. At a much broader level, we can see groups such as the Redeemed Christian Church of God (Nigeria and beyond) and the Universal Church of the Kingdom of God (Brazil and beyond) as creating neo-Pentecostal franchises that may in practice have little direct, face-to-face contact with each other, but all involve the considerable intradenominational (and to a lesser extent interdenominational) movement of goods, people, and what I have earlier called aspirational capital within and across nation-states. If there are networked arenas of transaction being constructed here, the trajectories of vertical and horizontal integration and nonintegration are complex, fascinating, and both politically and historically loaded.

Conclusion

The prosperity gospel helps to constitute a "broad" and promiscuous church, but I have been following a thread that I argue can be discerned – sometimes strongly, sometimes faintly – in the congregations where it appears. If prosperity is an orientation, an ethic, then it is one that involves a certain discipline but not conventional asceticism; a valorization of the *idea* of the open market, but a more frequent engagement with more restricted forms; an idealization of self-governance but a set of practices that also involve forms of externalization and mutual engagement, even if exchange partners are sometimes distanced or only imagined. The language of laws and ineluctable processes is juxtaposed with attitudes that may be more experimental, subjunctive, even ironic in character. Intellectual context for such an orientation is to be found not only in Pentecostalism per se, but also in a longer history of metaphysical movements that themselves have challenged the notion of a bounded humanity – of the very idea of boundaries itself. But, as we have seen, the dark side to an ideology of endless expansion and entrepreneurship may be the construction of more occult realms of operation, where explanations for undeserved accumulation or dispiriting stagnation may be sought.

While exploring a number of analytical frames to comprehend the prosperity phenomenon, I have devoted most time to exploring its relationship to materiality and interiority, as mediated through discussions of relationship with various notions of the market. Such a focus inevitably brings me into dialogue with work that explores connections between Christianity and modernity, although as noted I am not assuming that Christianity, even Pentecostal Christianity, should be analyzed only through a modernist analytical lens. In a recent essay Eitan Wilf describes the ways in which Webb Keane (2007) has greatly contributed to anthropological understandings of modernity's ways of imagining itself and the modern subject through the argument that "the idea of the modern subject has been embedded within a specific semiotic ideology that requires the materiality of semiotic forms to be subordinate to immaterial meanings." This is a subject precisely defined "as an interiority that must be kept autonomous vis-à-vis any form of materiality, broadly defined, such as the body, ritual, received tradition, other people, and words, in order to maintain its freedom and moral integrity" (Wilf 2011: 462).

Wilf highlights the distinguishing features of a different semiotic ideology, and one that he sees as relatively unexplored yet also crucial to contemporary notions of modern subjectivity: the normative ideal of self-expression emergent from Sentimentalism and Romanticism (see also Campbell 1989) – movements that have their own affinities with New Thought through such common heroes as Emanuel Swedenborg and Ralph Waldo Emerson. The crucial point for me is the way in which such an ideal has ideological determinants and practical manifestations very different from that of the dematerialized modern subject. According to Wilf,

> The difference hinges on the ideological distinction between situations in which the subject conveys an already fully formed interiority (best epitomized in the notion of sincerity...) and situations in which the subject articulates an inchoate interiority in the process of becoming (best epitomized in the notion of self-expression). The materiality of semiotic forms in the first case is supposed to be reflective of the subject's interiority; in the second it is supposed to be constitutive of this interiority. (Wilf 2011: 463)

Intriguingly, we are also back to another dimension of uncertainty here – that of a negotiation of open-endedness – though not one that sees it as primary causal determinant of religious, or modern, consciousness. Rather, the point is that explicit interaction with the materiality of semiotic forms may help the subject to "find" him- or herself.

One of the places that Wilf finds to explore such themes takes us right back to the beginning of this chapter, for he presents American self-help literature as a prime context to discuss the explicit incorporation of the materiality of semiotic forms in the constitution of the modern subject. In a case study (of a man he calls Weinstein), Wilf notes how the subject is pitched as exercising his imagination and objectifying it by writing it down as a means to an end, thus revealing *to* himself his interiority. In effect, external stimuli (we might see them as "externalized") are seen as somehow preceding the articulation of interiority, and such constitution of the self may also be articulated by the exchange and consumption of goods (Wilf 2011: 469; see also Campbell 1987).

There is a world of difference between the desperate, noxious immobility of a South African township and the anxious ambition of an American business executive. The relationships between religion and materiality in two such contexts will have very different genealogies and trajectories. And yet in both cases, we see how themes of prosperity may involve the dynamic articulation of a Protestant subject made and remade in chronic, materialized performance, where the workings of the market may be seen as invoking the moral or the immoral, but never quite the *a*moral.

Notes

I would like to thank the editors for their stimulating suggestions on an earlier draft of this piece, as well as all the participants at the conference from which this volume is drawn. Julie Chu proved an insightful discussant for the first presentation of the ideas at the conference.

1 We might be reminded here, as the editors have suggested, of former Chairman of the Federal Reserve Alan Greenspan's reference to "irrational exuberance" in a speech to the American Enterprise Institute in 1996. The term was recalled in the context of stock market collapses from 2000 on. For a discussion see, e.g., Shiller (2006).

2 For a discussion of the organization and diffusion of Prosperity-oriented discourses, see Coleman (2016).

3 To gain a sense of the academic and popular critique of Osteen, and his response, see "Joel Osteen Answers His Critics," CBS News *60 Minutes*. 2007-10-14, at www.cbsnews.com/news/joel-osteen-answers-his-critics/ (Accessed September 15, 2014).

4 See note 3. Such an attitude has been displayed in academic circles in my experience as well as that of Bowler (2013). See also the character of the critique in, e.g., Brouwer et al. (1996).

5 Compare Applbaum's claim with Rudnyckyj's (2014) argument that anthropologists should also be more attuned to ways in which abstract market principles are inculcated into human practices, and that (ibid.: 122) "economy is not so much an objective reality within the world as an instrument dedicated towards its transformation."

6 Bowler (2013: 9) notes that the prosperity gospel is reviled by media and academics alike: "After a public lecture, I am frequently told that there is nothing to study in the prosperity gospel except naked greed" (2013: 9).
7 The idea that prosperity Christianity represents a "movement" is sometimes expressed by its critics; see, e.g., www.charismanews.com/opinion/41054-10-ways-the-word-of-faith-movement-went-wrong (Accessed September 15, 2014). Some academic commentators stress its distinctiveness, as, for example, Stephen Hunt's statement that the gospel "constitutes a distinctive wing of contemporary Pentecostal movement, with its own style and ethos and clearly overlain with a materialistic culture" (2002: 6).
8 See, e.g., Genesis 8:22, Matthew 17:20.
9 As Chesnut notes, there is a remarkable lack of major studies of the actual possible socioeconomic impact of the practice of prosperity theology, so "it is impossible to draw conclusions on the larger secular impact, if any, of the health and wealth gospel" (2012: 219).
10 We might also think here of Aihwa Ong's (2006) discussion of the sheer malleability of neoliberalism as a technology of governance.
11 Compare, for example, the Online Etymology Dictionary, at www.etymonline.com/index.php?term=prosper&allowed_in_frame=0.

References

Amin, Ash, and Nigel Thrift. 2004. "Introduction." In *The Blackwell Cultural Economy Reader*, edited by Ash Amin and Nigel Thrift, x–xxx. Oxford: Blackwell.

Applbaum, Kalman. 2012. "Markets, Places, Principles and Integrations." In *A Handbook of Economic Anthropology*, edited by James Carrier, 257–274. 2nd ed. Cheltenham: Edward Elgar.

Attanasi, Katherine. 2012. "Introduction: The Plurality of Prosperity Theologies and Pentecostalisms." In *Pentecostalism and Prosperity: The Socio-Economics of the Global Charismatic Movement*, edited by Katherine Attanasi and Amos Yong, 1–12. New York: Palgrave Macmillan.

Bialecki, Jon. 2011. "No Caller I.D. for the Soul–Demonization, Charisms, and the Unstable Subject of Protestant Language Ideology." *Anthropological Quarterly* 84(3): 679–703.

Bowler, Kate. 2013. *Blessed: A History of the American Prosperity Gospel.* Oxford: Oxford University Press.

Brouwer, Steve, Paul Gifford, and Susan Rose. 1996. *Exporting the American Gospel: Global Christian Fundamentalism.* London: Routledge.

Campbell, Colin. 1987. *The Romantic Ethic and the Spirit of Modern Consumerism.* Oxford: Blackwell.

Cannell, Fenella. 2006. "Introduction: The Anthropology of Christianity." In *The Anthropology of Christianity*, edited by Fenella Cannell, 1–50. Durham, NC and London: Duke University Press.

Cao, Nanlai. 2012. "Urban Prosperity as Spiritual Resource: The Prosperity Gospel Phenomenon in Coastal China." In *Pentecostalism and Prosperity: The Socio-Economics of the Global Charismatic Movement*, edited by Katherine Attanasi and Amos Yong, 151–170. New York: Palgrave Macmillan.

Chesnut, R. Andrew. 2012. "Prosperous Prosperity: Why the Health and Wealth Gospel Is Booming across the Globe." In *Pentecostalism and Prosperity: The Socio-Economics of the Global Charismatic Movement*, edited by Katherine Attanasi and Amos Yong, 215–223. New York: Palgrave Macmillan.

Coleman, Simon. 2011. "Prosperity Unbound? Debating the Sacrificial Economy." *Research in Economic Anthropology* 31: 23–45.

2016. "The Prosperity Gospel: Charisma, Controversy and Capitalism." In *The Brill Handbook of Contemporary Christianity: Movements, Institutions, and Allegiance*, ed. Stephen Hunt, 276–296. Leiden: Brill.

Comaroff, Jean. 2012. "Religion, Society, Theory." *Religion and Society* 3: 5–16.

Comaroff, Jean, and John Comaroff. 1999. "Occult Economies and the Violence of Abstraction: Notes from the South African Postcolony." *American Ethnologist* 26(2): 279–303.

2000. "Millennial Capitalism: First Thoughts on a Second Coming." *Public Culture* 12(2): 291–343.

Deleuze, Gilles, and Félix Guattari. 1987 (1980). *A Thousand Plateaus: Capitalism and Schizophrenia*. Minneapolis: University of Minnesota Press.

Gell, Alfred. 1992. "The Technology of Enchantment and the Enchantment of Technology." In *Anthropology, Art and Aesthetics*, edited by Jeremy Coote and Anthony Shelton, 40–63. Oxford: Clarendon Press.

Gifford, Paul, Steve Brouwer, and Susan Rose. 1996. *Exporting the American Gospel: Global Christian Fundamentalism*. New York: Routledge.

Harding, Susan. 1991. "Representing Fundamentalism: The Problem of the Repugnant Cultural Other." *Social Research* 58(3): 373–393.

Hunt, Stephen. 2002. "Deprivation and Western Pentecostalism Revisited: Neo-Pentecostalism." *PentecoStudies* 1(2): 1–29.

Jenkins, Philip. 2007. *The Next Christendom: The Coming of Global Christianity*. Oxford: Oxford University Press.

Keane, Webb. 2007. *Christian Moderns: Freedom and Fetish in the Mission Encounter*. Berkeley: University of California Press.

Marshall, Ruth. 2009. *Political Spiritualities: The Pentecostal Revolution in Nigeria*. Chicago: University of Chicago Press.

Maurer, Bill. 2010. "Credit Crisis Religion." *Religion and Society* 1: 146–155.

Ong, Aihwa. 2006. *Neoliberalism as Exception: Mutations in Citizenship and Sovereignty*. Durham, NC: Duke University Press.

Osteen, Joel. 2005. *Making Wise Choices – Your Decisions Determine Your Destiny*. Houston: Joel Osteen Ministries.

2009. *Become a Better You: 7 Keys to Improving Your Life Every Day*. New York: Howard Books.

Robbins, Joel. 2011. "The Obvious Aspects of Pentecostalism: Ritual and Pentecostal Globalization." In *Practicing the Faith: The Ritual Life of Pentecostal-Charismatic Christians*, edited by M. Lindhardt, 49–67. New York: Berghahn.

Rosin, Hanna. 2009. "Did Christianity Cause the Crash?" *The Atlantic*, December. www.theatlantic.com/magazine/archive/2009/12/did-christianity-cause-the-crash/307764/.

Rudnyckyj, Daromir. 2009. "Spiritual Economies: Islam and Neoliberalism in Contemporary Indonesia." *Cultural Anthropology* 24(1): 104–141.

2014. "Economy in Practice: Islamic Finance and the Problem of Market Reason." *American Ethnologist* 41(1): 110–127.

Shiller, Robert. 2006. "Irrational Exuberance Revisited." *CFA Institute Conference Proceedings Quarterly* 23(3): 16–25.

Tsing, Anna Lowenhaupt. 2004. *Friction: An Ethnography of Global Connection*. Princeton, NJ: Princeton University Press.

Ukah, Azonzeh. 2008. *A New Paradigm of Pentecostal Power: A Study of the Redeemed Christian Church of God in Nigeria*. Trenton, NJ: Africa World Press.

Walton, Jonathan. 2012. "Stop Worrying and Start Sowing! A Phenomenological Account of the Ethics of 'Divine Investment'." In *Pentecostalism and Prosperity: The Socio-Economics of the Global Charismatic Movement*, edited by Katherine Attanasi and Amos Yong, 107–129. New York: Palgrave Macmillan.

Warikobo, Nimi. 2012. "Pentecostal Paradigms of National Economic Prosperity in Africa." In *Pentecostalism and Prosperity: The Socio-Economics of the Global Charismatic Movement*, edited by Katherine Attanasi and Amos Yong, 35–59. New York: Palgrave Macmillan.

Wilf, Eitan. 2011. "Sincerity Versus Self-expression: Modern Creative Agency and the Materiality of Semiotic Forms." *Cultural Anthropology* 26(3): 462–484.

Yong, Amos. 2012. "A Typology of Prosperity Theology: A Religious Economy of Global Renewal or a Renewal Economics?" In *Pentecostalism and Prosperity: The Socio-Economics of the Global Charismatic Movement*, edited by Katherine Attanasi and Amos Yong, 15–33. New York: Palgrave Macmillan.

3 Religious Myths Retold: Masters and Servants in India's Corporate Culture

Nandini Gooptu, University of Oxford

"The god of strength, Hanuman, to whom people turn to alleviate their pain and sorrows, is now also gaining importance in this world of globalisation as a management guru. Vijay Agrawal has written a book called *Sada Safal Hanuman* that tells us that Hanuman possesses some of the great qualities needed for management."[1] With these comments, the newsreader on a popular Hindi-language television channel in India drew attention to the striking new interpretation of a familiar revered figure from India's greatest Hindu epic. "Mythology was written so that it could be interpreted and used in your daily life."[2] This is the rationale offered by, Kishore Biyani, chairman of Future Group, India's supermarket giant, to explain why in his business practice he relies on religious myths, as interpreted by Devdutta Pattanaik, Chief Belief Officer of his company and author of several highly popular books on mythology. Works by Agrawal and Pattanaik represent a growing trend of the interplay of religious belief, management ideas and business practice in contemporary India's market economy and corporate culture. This is in keeping with a well-documented "cultural turn" in global corporate practice in recent decades,[3] marked by a tendency to invoke religious traditions and cultural belief systems, with a view to defining moral norms and ethical standards that would shape individual conduct, institutional behaviour and organizational practice in business (Calas and Smircich 2003; Browne and Milgram 2009; Nandram and Borden 2010). The extant literature on this subject shows how existing religious and cultural ideas are pressed into the service of business and management. It is, however, insufficiently appreciated that this entanglement of cultural and market imaginaries offers radical new interpretations and seeks to create new corporate sensibilities and subjectivities, which is examined in this chapter.

It is now known that with the "cultural turn," lessons in effective human resource management and authoritative business leadership have been drawn from cultural traditions, including Greek heroic myths, medieval legends of kingship, folkloric sagas of just rule and Islamic religious principles (Koprowski 1983; Kessler and Wong-MingJi 2009; Rudnyckyj 2010). Both the state and private corporations, in many parts of the world, have asserted the superiority, authority and authenticity of indigenous religion and culture as the inspiration for capitalist development and managerial practice. In East and Southeast Asia, for instance, the concept of distinctive, spiritually informed "Asian values" and other cognate cultural ideas have been mobilized to enunciate forms of communitarian capitalism in Malaysia and Singapore, on the one hand, and management philosophies in China and Japan, on the other (Ong 1999: 74–77, 203).

In India too, since the 1990s, when a state-controlled and closed economy began to be liberalized, and the private corporate sector gained steady ascendance, religious ideas, especially Hindu thought, were increasingly harnessed to frame business ethics and management. Similarly, spiritual values animate individual action and behaviour in the corporate sector, sometimes with the aim of transcending mere material pursuit or competitive self-advancement (Chakraborty 1993; Srinivas 2000; Fuller and Harriss 2005; Sharma 2007; Birtchnell 2008; Narayanswamy 2008; Sinha 2008: 18, 29; Das 2009). Spirituality is also often disseminated to, and espoused by, corporate employees as a source of self-help practices (Upadhya 2013). In addition, cultural traditions have been invoked in recent celebrations of a distinctive and unique "Indian way" of innovation and enterprise, as the winning formula for the country's spectacular economic success in the early twenty-first century (Biyani 2007; Nath 2008; Nilekani 2008; Narayana Murthy 2009; Pitroda 2013). Discussions on the "Indian way," with a positive valence, have also developed to enlighten and entice overseas investors (Cappelli 2010). Verging on cultural essentialism, the assertion of a quintessentially Indian mode of conducting business is highly reminiscent of similar expressions of "Asian values." Popular authors and management experts are now engaged in distilling out the putative essence of the "Indian way" and in identifying its key characteristics through enquiry into religious and cultural traditions. In doing so, they offer novel readings of religious ideas to derive lessons for appropriate conduct and practice in a contemporary corporate setting.

Although this turn to religion and culture in business and enterprise is now widely acknowledged, it is scarcely appreciated that religious myths and mythology have come to play a central role. This is surprising, given the well-recognized importance of the mythic imagination in India. Devdutta Pattanaik, the most high-profile exponent of mythology in India in the corporate context, explains as follows:

> Myth is essentially a cultural construct, a common understanding of the world that binds individuals and communities together.... If myth is an idea, mythology is the vehicle of that idea. Mythology constitutes stories, symbols and rituals that make a myth tangible.... Myth conditions thoughts and feelings. Mythology influences behaviours and communications. (Pattanaik 2006: xiv–xvi)

In scholarly literature, it has been noted, from a psychoanalytical angle, that myths provide a framework for the everyday experience of interpersonal, familial and community relationships and hierarchies (Kakar 1978; Roland 1988: 297–289). This is argued to lend Indian culture its "mythic orientation." Similarly, anthropologists and scholars of literature and religion have argued that the symbolic narratives of religious epics and other myths, through tales of virtuous and evil characters, of gods and demons, of humans and animals, express complex perspectives on, and offer insights into, life's moral and practical dilemmas and choices (Doniger O'Flaherty 1980; Ramanujan 1989). Scholars such as Wendy Doniger hold that myths do "not record an actual event.... [They] reveal to us the history of sentiments rather than events, motivations rather than movements" (2009: 23). Yet in popular conception, some myths, notably those related to the Hindu religious epics *Mahabharata* and *Ramayana*, are considered to be renditions of historical fact. Hindu nationalists, for instance, claim that the *Ramayana* presents a factual account and they identify physical sites in the country as the actually existing location of events from the epic.

The complex, contested and polysemic nature of myths lends them to plural, contextual interpretations, suited to varying places, periods and communities. The *Ramayana*, for instance, has been shown to have multiple regional and social variations, while its meaning and significance have changed in the course of social and political transformation in various historical periods (Lutgendorf 1991; Richman 1991). A recognition of the multivalent nature of myths, as well as their power to inspire new thought and action, have stimulated contemporary authors in India to re-narrate various myths. They seek to promote and institutionalize new modes of thought and practice and to formulate a new set of canonical interpretations of myth, suited to contemporary India's corporate culture and business environment.

This chapter explores two recent reinterpretations of religious myths to analyse how sacred concepts are being creatively harnessed to construct India's corporate ethos. The two cases for analysis here have been chosen for their popularity and high visibility, both in print and electronic media. The chapter specifically focuses on conceptions of ideal masters and servants, managers and employees, as expressed in a religious idiom and with reference to myths. What do new renderings of myth reveal about the desired role of workers and their duty of service? What kind of a management ethic and leadership ideals are sought to be forged by deploying religious myths? It is not, however, implied here that these religious ideas determine the nature of India's corporate economy in the way that the Puritan ethic, for instance, shaped Western capitalism in Weber's analysis. Instead, new interpretations of religious myth are examined to gain insight into key emerging ideas in India's corporate culture and to shed light on the use of religious myths to mould the subjectivity of corporate personnel. This analysis also illuminates how religious notions are assuming public relevance in India in new ways through emerging ideas and practices in the corporate economy.

The Ideal Corporate Servant

Always ask this of God, "O God fill me with the sense of a servant and fortify it each day." (Agrawal 2011, KL 2147–2149[4])

Sada Safal Hanuman (literally, "always successful Hanuman"; hereafter abbreviated SSH) was presented by Dr. Vijay Agrawal as a television series of twenty-two episodes in Hindi on the popular *Zee Jagaran* channel (now widely available on YouTube), along with an eponymous book, first published in 2008, with a sixth impression in 2013 (Agrawal 2013). An English translation titled *Hanuman Who Never Failed* was published in 2011, including an electronic Kindle edition (Agrawal 2011). The book received much news coverage, and the author was interviewed on Aaj Tak, the popular Hindi television channel. Agrawal, a retired civil servant, now specializes in producing self-help and motivational literature and Hindi television shows. SSH is one such product. It is a manual aimed at individuals and is distinctive in drawing upon Hindu mythology to deliver lessons in self-help and success in the corporate milieu. Agrawal's mainly vernacular-speaking viewers and readers are largely based in non-metropolitan, provincial towns and cities, and they aspire to upward mobility through participation in India's emerging market economy.

SSH is based on a chapter or canto of the ancient epic *Ramayana*, as it was re-narrated in the sixteenth century by one of India's greatest Hindi poets, Tulsidas, in the *Ramcharitmanas*, which is the most popular and widely known version of the epic in India (Lutgendorf 1991). The canto, titled *Sundarkand* (The Beautiful Episode), recounts the exploits of Hanuman, the simian follower of Lord Rama, hero of the *Ramayana*. Hanuman performs a range of tasks assigned to him by Lord Rama, the most important of which was to rescue Rama's wife Sita, who had been abducted by the demon king Ravana and taken to Lanka, Ravana's kingdom, where most of the action in *Sundarkand* takes place. Agrawal wonders why the canto title should refer to "beauty" instead of the geographical location of the action, as do all the other canto titles of the epic. He arrives at the following conclusion about the beauty of work being the key theme of that canto: "Hanuman is the chief architect in this chapter. Hanuman is synonymous with 'workaholism'. Any work that is good or noble in nature would contain processes that are inherently beautiful" (SSH, KL 789–797).

SSH is a celebration of the work ethic and spirit of service of Hanuman as the perfect servant to Lord Rama, executing all tasks with unsurpassed efficiency, untrammelled dedication, unerring steadfastness, unwavering loyalty, unimpeachable work ethic and, of course, unfailing success. Agrawal explains, "The great thing about Indian culture is that it has not only accepted the importance of being a servant, but also given this a high place.... The reason that he [Hanuman] is so popular with Indians is that Indian culture values sacrifice, giving and service." Agrawal then asks, "Don't you think you can become very successful simply by being a servant?" (SSH, episode 8). Seeing that Agrawal served as a life-long civil servant, it is tempting to interpret SSH as a vindication and valorization of such service, with Rama embodying the Indian state. The subtitle of SSH, however, reveals a different orientation: "Lessons learnt from Hanumanji about success and management." Moreover, Agrawal salutes Tulsidas, the author of the *Ramcharitmanas*, as a super "management guru" (SSH, episode 1), who paints the character of Hanuman in such a way as to epitomize the virtues of a highly successful servant in the realm of business and management. Introducing his television show, Agrawal states,

> In this programme ... these are the things we will look at: what great qualities did Hanuman have, how did he think, what was his philosophy, what were his communication skills, what was his attitude to work, how did he discipline himself, ... how did he behave towards his boss, how did he manage stress? (SSH, episode 1)

Agrawal draws attention to the fact that despite being a mere monkey and a servant, in popular Hindu practice Hanuman has been deified and is worshipped as an independent god, with temples exclusively dedicated to him, while Lord Rama is the only other character from the epic to enjoy such stature. Hanuman has been enshrined in temples, Agrawal explains, precisely because of his unusual and exemplary character:

> It is extraordinary and an exemplary incident when a slave becomes a deity, and a unique deity at that.... we endorsed his personality, work-ethics [sic], and achievements and gave them our mandate for all times to come. (SSH, KL 104–107)

Agrawal acknowledges that this is a novel reading of the story of Hanuman. However, he justifies his thorough reinterpretation of Hanuman with reference to verses from the epic, which he cites throughout his books and in television presentations. He cites not only the *Ramcharitmanas*, but also the *Hanuman Chalisa*, a text dedicated to Hanuman based on the *Sundarkand* of the *Ramayana* and also written by the poet Tulsidas. The *Chalisa* is a highly popular text, extracts from which are daily recited by devotees, and audio-recordings of chants are widely available. Hanuman is normally depicted as possessing immense physical prowess, and is often referred to as "*Bajrang Bali*" or the powerful one, whose limbs are as strong as the celestial weapon thunderbolt. Based on this idea, the militant Hindu youth organization *Bajrang Dal* is named after Hanuman. Furthermore, he is considered "*sankatmochan*," or a trouble-shooter. Fears and insecurities are dispelled, and obstacles can be miraculously overcome or wishes granted by appealing to him (Lutgendorf 2007), especially if the *Hanuman Chalisa* is recited as an expression of reverence. Agrawal's understanding does not adopt any of these established ideas. Instead, he draws attention to the opening verse of the *Hanuman Chalisa*, which does not mention physical strength but rather mental and intellectual acumen, by hailing Hanuman as an "ocean of knowledge and exceptional qualities" (SSH, KL 348–353). Moreover, Agrawal does not urge passive devotion or prayer to Hanuman in facing obstacles, but advocates that Hanuman's actions and attitudes be imitated for success. The devotee then ceases to be a supplicant seeking blessings and miracles, but an active agent who seizes the initiative to work and succeed by emulating the example of Hanuman. As Agrawal states: "The idea then is not to recite the *Sunderkand*, but to learn from it, and put it into practice" (SSH, KL 789–797).

In Agrawal's widely watched television shows and the book, Hanuman, "who never failed," did not rely on muscle power or brute force but on a range of intellectual and attitudinal skills. Accordingly, the second chapter of SSH is entitled "It's all a mind game." Agrawal hails Tulsidas, the author of *Ramcharitmanas*, as a "psychologist" (SSH, episode 1) for his masterful depiction of Hanuman's mental faculties and psychological competencies as the source of his success. Hanuman's mindset is described as having three distinct aspects: "a happy mind, dedication to work, and emotional intelligence." Agrawal goes on to stress, "Once we get to understand and work upon developing these, we could make a positive change in our lives" (SSH, KL 194–197). Agrawal attaches utmost importance to emotional intelligence – an idea that is now globally widely prevalent (Rudnyckyj 2010: 146–147, 180), but he appears to glean it mostly from Western literature. Agrawal writes: "the uniqueness in Hanuman is not in his strength but in his knowledge and *other qualities* [emphasis added]. Knowledge wouldn't have sufficed.... But more importantly the intelligence of its optimal use is essential" (SSK, KL 353–361). Citing Daniel Goleman's *Emotional Intelligence: Why It Can Matter More Than IQ*, Agrawal states, "In this path breaking book, he has explained that success in life does not only depend on the sharpness of one's intellect. The success of a person is directly proportional to his emotional intelligence" (SSK, KL 369–372). Similarly, Agrawal refers to "Thomas Stewart of *Harvard Business Review*, [who] clearly believes that a good moral character and emotional intelligence are a must for people with talent to reach their goals" (SSK, KL 432–446).

"Emotional intelligence" is not the only concept that Agrawal has drawn from recent management literature. Some of his television programmes are dedicated to the issues of anger and stress management, and he starts one episode of SSH with this comment: "Friends, I would like to address those who feel stressed out by work" (SSH, episode 2). The question of overcoming stress and anger is addressed in the notion of the "happy mind" of Hanuman, and his "enthusiastic" countenance, that are said to be ubiquitous in Tulsidas's description of Hanuman (SSH, KL 273–274). Hanuman, Agrawal argues, was never angry or unhappy and never suffered from stress or tension, and he always remained calm and cheerful, even in the face of difficult or arduous tasks. Agrawal notes that "In the whole of *Ramcharitmanas* barring one or two instances we do not ever find Hanuman disheartened or unhappy" and he is the only character who "never loses his calm and poise throughout" (SSH, KL 198–205). If he does lose his temper, then his anger productively motivates him to achieve specific goals, such as the annihilation of evil. As such, his anger is " 'pure' or 'satvik' in the sense that something 'good' would result from it," as compared to the demon-ruler Ravana's "tamasik" or "impure" anger that does not lead "to any goodness for anybody except for his own perception [sic]" (SSH, KL 200–207). Hanuman's mental equipoise enables him to accept all jobs and assignments, whatever their nature, without the slightest hesitation, dismay, irritation or complaint, and to execute all orders and instructions without question.

> He does what needs to be done, and not that what he is fond of doing. He doesn't "choose" his assignments, or think negatively about the jobs delegated to him.... whatever is asked of him he does that diligently and with complete commitment. And because of this he succeeds in doing all that he sets off to do, and in a way that is exemplary. *Some of us who are less irritable, and are less complaining about their institutions and bosses would be much closer to Hanuman.* (SSH, KL 1833–1838; emphasis added)

Here Agrawal explicitly advocates a work ethic at the core of which lies a blind and unquestioning acceptance of corporate priorities, verging on unthinking submission to one's boss, without applying one's own judgement or discernment, and surmounting one's reticence or resentment.

The next set of virtuous qualities with which Hanuman is endowed relate to his own self-perception and capacity for self-management and self-discipline. Hanuman is held up for his unusual ability to make a realistic assessment of his own strengths and weaknesses, and to overcome the latter. As a result, he does not suffer from a sense of inadequacy; he invariably achieves success by virtue of his self-confident attitude.

> [Hanuman] teaches us that when we accept our weaknesses and work towards mending them, we are infused with boundless energy that becomes a source of our self-confidence and strength.... people who wallow in self-pity [find] their confidence is eroded and their aspirations become soggy.... But the moment we choose to get a grip on our weaknesses, we are on the path of becoming Hanuman ourselves. Therefore the essence of Hanuman is the acceptance of realities with courage, and an effort to overcome those with some undaunted resolve. (SSH, KL 132–135, 148–155)

Agrawal, thus, argues that both self-reflection or introspection and a steadfastly positive resolve to face up to and reverse one's inadequacies exert a transformative influence on one's own personality, and altogether pave the way to success.

By far the most important character trait of Hanuman is his attitude toward work – the work of his master Rama or *Ram-kaaj*, as evidenced in his motto: "How could I take rest before completing the Ram-Kaaj?" (SSH, KL 60–61). His essence is that of a servant to Rama, which gives him the focus and purpose to undertake his disparate tasks, and unifies and animates his actions with a singular goal – that of serving Ram: "one fine thread connects them all, … 'Ram-kaaj' or 'the task assigned by his Lord Ram'" (SSH, KL 274–276). In particular, Agrawal praises Hanuman's "joy of work" or the fact that he derives such satisfaction, pleasure and enjoyment from his work, and does not merely perform his duties mechanically. Agrawal quotes Tulsidas, who describes Hanuman's solitary journey into the dangerous land of Lanka in search of the abducted Sita, as "an unstoppable arrow of Ram." He is described by Tulsidas as "running" while carrying a mountain that contained a vital medicinal herb to save the life of Rama's brother Lakshmana. In all this, Agrawal points out, Hanuman's "momentum came through being joyful and self-assured, … even in grave situations and extreme tiredness." Further, Agrawal clarifies "the great poet describes him as, 'His joyful face reflected the sheen of his mind, having done the Ramkaaj somehow'" (SSH, KL 285–293).

Hanuman is also distinguished for his "reverence for work." Agrawal argues:

> Happiness and reverence are interlinked. Reverence is an emotion so refined that it is superior to respect.… With such a feeling towards our work, we render it a form in our subconscious that is akin to God, whom we worship. And in doing so our work becomes an act of worship and our life becomes a prayer that resounds in the "temple" that our bodies have now become. (SSH, KL 293–299, 304–306)

Agrawal, then, is not merely celebrating a work ethic but also according it a spiritual or religious status. Work, in this view, sanctifies mortal existence and elevates the corporeal act of labour to sacred or divine activity. The notion of work as worship here evokes Weber's analysis of the Puritan conception of work as a sacred duty, performed to fulfil God's purpose. More importantly, however, SSH reflects more closely the ideas of the Indian leader Mahatma Gandhi, who considered work to be akin to making sacrificial offerings to God, and espoused the idea that work is a moral imperative that must be undertaken without any desire to reap the fruits of one's labour, as laid out in the religious text *Bhagavat Gita* through the concept of "*karma yoga*" (Madan 2011: 104–108).

Hanuman is the embodiment of the dutiful servant whose being and existence are defined by the work he does for his master. Further,

> Hanuman had conquered his ego, and submitted himself to the all powerful Raghunaath (Ram). He drew upon Ram's energies and became invincible himself. It is because of this that before any difficult job Hanuman would seek Ram's blessings.… His uniqueness is his total commitment, bordering upon reverence, and his ever readiness to do his job. (SSH, KL 327–334)

It is but a small stretch to translate this dictum into the modern corporate context where such a conception of work implies submission of the self to the organization and to one's institutional superiors. At the same time, it suggests that the employee derives power and energy from the organization and so achieves individual success. Agrawal treads a fine line between portraying an image of abject servility and that of an empowered servant, whose sense of self, achievement and fulfilment derives from the workplace and corporate organization. Moreover, this is not a passive servant who merely executes orders, but one who is an active, self-motivated agent whose aims and goals are perfectly aligned with that of the corporation. While ideas of this nature about proactive, enterprising subjects are now in wide circulation and are typical of global human resource management principles, Agrawal's approach demonstrates how these seemingly universal conceptions are culturally inflected and socially embedded with reference to preexisting myth and religious ideas, albeit in radically reinterpreted forms. Such exhortations encourage those who already revere Hanuman, and now seek mobility through corporate employment, to develop the persona of an ideal servant, inspired by Agarwal's new perspective on Hanuman.

Richman has drawn attention to the multitude of "*Ramayana* tellings in light of their structure, diversity, and context" (1991: 8). SSH is one of its most recent iterations with a focus on Hanuman, directed towards upwardly mobile, Hindi-speaking, communities and individuals in non-metropolitan India, who seek to enter and succeed in the corporate world. Philip Lutgendorf (2007: 361–371), in his seminal study of the varied and changing nature of Hanuman worship, shows that while Hindu nationalist narratives project his muscular image as an expression of, or inspiration for, a physically powerful Hindu community identity, the high caste character of Hindu nationalist ideology also contributes to an emphasis on the servile role of Hanuman and his place as a god revered by intermediate castes or those seeking status accretion. Lutgendorf characterizes Hanuman as a "pan-Indian 'middle-class god' par excellence." Hanuman appeals to these classes as a figure who divinely intercedes on their behalf, in the same way that they routinely rely on intermediaries and brokers, "for access to required persons and resources", in their dealings with the Indian state and other institutions, which they find difficult to access directly due to a range of structural and hierarchical constraints. Lutgendorf, therefore, identifies Hanuman as a deity of upwardly mobile and often struggling middle classes, who see Hanuman as *sankat mochan* (problem solver, trouble-shooter) in tackling their daily tribulations and trials. Lutgendorf also notes that Hanuman has even been represented as an office worker or a secretarial character to an office boss, "whose intervention alone guarantees access to the Boss – as the *Cālīsā* declares: 'You are the guardian of Rama's door; none enters without your leave'" (Lutgendorf 2007: 375).

Agrawal's now extended interpretation of Hanuman as "*sada safal*" (always successful) would easily chime with these classes, especially the increasingly large numbers who are aspiring to get ahead in corporate jobs. He now offers them a range of self-help and self-empowering lessons from Hanuman's life and work, promising to enable them to seize the initiative of their own lives and succeed in corporate work.

Crucially, Agrawal glorifies and valorizes the quotidian experience of servility and pressures of corporate work, with reference to Hanuman's cheerful commitment to "Ram-kaaj." While Agrawal's aim appears to be to strengthen individuals and launch them on the path of success, he is simultaneously helping, wittingly or unwittingly, to create pliable and compliant corporate servants, who while being self-driven and motivated, are also willing to submit themselves unconditionally to the organization, and whose superhuman qualities of self-control and self-propulsion verge on that of robotic automatons working in the interest of the company. Agrawal liberally and unreservedly borrows from (and explicitly cites) Western and global management literature, as seen earlier, although some of his ideas are similar to notions of respect for authority and corporate loyalty as expressed, for instance, in Japanese management literature (which he does not mention). He recasts management notions in a familiar cultural idiom and re-expresses them as age-old truths, with reference to existing religious beliefs and practices, thus seeking to enhance their appeal and ensure their uptake.

Others, however, have invoked religious myths for the opposite purpose, to repudiate stridently what they see as management theories and practices of Western provenance, and formulate instead what they project as culturally grounded management principles that will be more effective in the Indian business context by virtue of their indigenous origin. The following section turns to this latter form of engagement with religious myth.

Benevolent Paternalism and Harmonious Business

Belief in multiple lives establishes a worldview that is comfortable with the absence of binary logic, where there are no fixed goals, continuously changing plans, dependence on relationships, celebration of trust and loyalty, uneasiness with rules, actions dependent on crisis, preference for short-term results over long-term vision, and a reliance on resourcefulness that gives rise to contextual, non-replicable improvizations: the jugaad. This is the Indian way. (Pattanaik 2013: 39)

Devdutta Pattanaik, formerly an executive in the healthcare and pharmaceutical industry and a business advisor at the international consultancy firm Ernst and Young, is now recognized in the popular press and electronic mass media as India's modern mythologist par excellence. He is the author of numerous books in English on myths and mythology as well as a regular columnist on newspapers and business magazines, and a presenter of several television programmes. Pattanaik has laid down his own conception of culturally embedded forms of leadership, business management and organizational behaviour in his numerous media appearances and his social media presence. His book *Business Sutra: A Very Indian Approach to Management* (Pattanaik 2013; hereafter abbreviated BS) draws on a television series broadcast on CNBC, one of the most influential business channels of India. He is also the Chief Belief Officer of one of India's most prominent business houses, the Future Group, where his brief is "to expand the mind [sic] of those involved in business so that they could see the misalignment between business practices (that they blindly followed) and beliefs of the people (that they remained oblivious to)" (BS: 1). As cited earlier, Pattanaik takes the view that beliefs shape behaviour, including business behaviour, and hence beliefs need to be engaged with and transformed to shape successful business. Like Agrawal in SSH, Pattanaik's exercise is aspirational, seeking to create a better, more effective corporate world, but in his case the target is senior managers rather than ordinary employees. He delivers his lessons by offering novel interpretations of mythic tales, characters and symbols in the form of "*sutras*" for business. Sutras refer to aphorisms, or short pithy principles or precepts, which were often collected in the form of a manual, sometimes of a religious nature. It is in this tradition that Pattanaik has presented his collection of management maxims in BS, and each aphorism or sutra is then explained with reference to mythic tales or characters. BS represents a normative exercise to develop a humane framework for business, and to connect it to familiar cultural ideas and symbols, with reference to religious myths. Pattanaik fashions a new universe of myths in the corporate context to offer nuggets of management wisdom, and to create a mythic sensibility as a resource for managers.

Pattanaik's point of departure in BS is the inadequacy of traditional management practices, apparently derived from the West. He finds them incompatible with Indian culture and beliefs. Pattanaik's key contention is that prevalent business practices that are standardized around the world, and adopted in India, are based on Western epistemology and belief systems grounded in Judeo-Christian and Greco-Roman myths. In his view, "the value placed on vision, mission, objectives, milestones, targets and tasks in modern business practice resonate with the Greek quest for Elysium, the heaven of heroes, and the biblical quest for the Promised Land, paradise of the faithful" (BS: 4). As he sees it, the focus of Western management science is on growth, measurement and tangible indicators, and it values accumulation, the single-minded pursuit of profit and institutional interest over individual well-being, and privileges the intellect over emotions. These impair business performance in the Indian setting, because they have a dehumanizing effect by privileging the institution over the individual. The knowledge imparted in business schools predisposes managers and executives to impose culturally alien "modern management systems" on their organizations, "focused on an objective institutional truth, or the owner's truth, rather than individual truths," or cultural and subjective truths as contained in myths (BS: 13). At the heart of Pattanaik's exposition is the utmost value he attaches to diverse subjectivities, imagination and beliefs, which focuses his attention on myths:

> Mythologies of Indian origin value the *nirguna* (intangible and immeasurable) over *saguna* (tangible and measurable), in other words, the subjective over the objective. Subjectivity tends to be more appreciative of the irrational. Subjectivity draws attention to other subjects and their subjectivity. Respect for other peoples' worldview allows diversity. (BS: 16)

Pattanaik here posits not only an alternative management model, but also a contested view of capitalism based on human subjectivity, instead of the calculative rationality with which capitalism is commonly associated.

Pattanaik's target audiences are leaders of business, executives and managers, whom he aims to expose to an "Indian way" of thinking through a mythic imagination. The expectation is that these leaders will then be able to "take better decisions, ones that ensure a viable, sustainable and happy business" (BS: 1, 15). A mythic idiom is used to reveal multiple frameworks of Indian thought and practice, because Pattanaik believes that the "most popular mode of expression, in India, was the mythic", to be found in a "grand jigsaw puzzle of stories, symbols and rituals" of Hindu, Jain, Buddhist and Sikh provenance (BS: 14). Pattanaik uses the appellation "*very* Indian" in the title of his book to denote his own approach to management. In this, unlike Agrawal mentioned earlier, Pattanaik signals that he does not aim to create merely a new Indian-language management vocabulary to be mapped onto cognate terms and models from existing business school orthodoxy. Instead, he aims to generate entirely new ideas and concepts attuned to what he sees as an Indian way of thinking (BS: 19–20).

Pattanaik's central metaphor and mythic imagery is that of the *yagna*, which refers to Vedic fire rituals from ancient India. In this ritual, various offerings or *svaha* are cast in the sacred fire, either to propitiate gods or in the expectation of accumulating religious merit and beneficial outcomes. Pattanaik sees the yagna ritual as a form of business or a "process of exchange" (BS: 69: 432). The yagna, or business transaction, is conducted by the *yajaman*, whose offerings into the fire are seen by Pattanaik as investment in business, and equivalent to "goods, services and ideas" (BS: 70). The aim of yagna is to satisfy or please various *devatas* or gods, who in the business context constitute multiple stakeholders and actors, ranging from the client and customer, to workers and employees, to creditors and suppliers, to colleagues and subordinates (BS: 168–169). In response to offerings or investment, the stakeholders or devatas grant the yajaman (businessman) his wishes – that is, the return on investment. A yagna is successful if it "ushers in wealth and prosperity" (BS: 69). The yajaman acts in a variety of ways to engage with all the numerous devatas, in the same way as one would make different sets of offering to multiple gods, each of whom has a different need (BS: 171–173). Thus, all yagnas cannot be reduced to one yagna; all devatas cannot be forcibly aligned to a single framework imposed by the yajaman; in other words, all stakeholders and actors cannot be brought in line with a unitary corporate strategy. Recognition of, and attention to, the diverse needs of devatas is the key to the best possible mode of doing yagna for the yajaman, who is required to develop plural approaches, catering to each specific devata in a different way. By analogy, the key to successful business is to appreciate this diversity and individuality and to shun the imposition of one uniform set of institutionally approved norms and rules on all concerned (BS: 168–173). As Pattanaik expounds, the emphasis here is on multiple visions and perspectives, or on the "gaze" (*drishti*). The "gaze" or vision is at the heart of Pattanaik's management model, highlighting the importance of sensitivity to diverse contexts and actors, as opposed to what he sees as a counterproductive singular fixation on goals and targets (BS: 105–108). This approach also enables the proper appreciation and recognition of individuals, their needs and their contributions, and thus generates a corporate environment that is inclusive, collaborative and harmonious.

To illustrate the ideal ethos of such a cohesive and balanced organization, Pattanaik invokes an image of churning that involves force and counter-force, give and take, in order to achieve a state of equilibrium and stability, which is in contrast to a fractious corporate culture of tug-of-war, consisting of competitive individuals pulling in opposite directions (BS: 185, 190–191). Pattanaik emphasizes that a business organization should not be a *rana-bhumi* or battleground of investors, managers, clients, customers, employees, creditors and others, but a *ranga-bhumi* or a playground, where everyone is happy. The key to this organizational culture of mutuality and trust are the leaders, senior manager and directors, whom he calls the "*karta*," as distinct from a "*karya-karta*" or worker who takes and executes orders, and has a limited gaze or vision. A karta is a pro-active "doer," a decision-maker, who gives orders. Those kartas who additionally bear the responsibility of enabling others to take action are the yajaman – a more powerful karta with greater authority and capacity to hire and fire, and with the ability to achieve a gaze scanning all directions and stakeholders. A yajaman has the mentality to take risks, irrespective of facts, figures and statistics, and he is decisive and ruthless in determining other people's lives, in order to enable them to become actors (BS: 110–116). He directs all towards change in such a way that their gaze is fixed on the market and not on the leader, thus collectively achieving the best business outcome (BS: 210–11). Describing the importance of the right "gaze" for such a leader,

Pattanaik compares them with a "*chakravarti*" or king from religious mythology, who is "the master of all he surveys" and whose "gaze is that of a leader determined to stabilise an established organisation and shape the destiny of his people" (BS: 216–217). In doing so, the leader's "sharpness of determination" has to be tempered with "sweetness of vision," especially in managing all those involved with the company (BS: 210). Pattanaik describes the leaders of a balanced organization as those who successfully manage numerous unique individuals and harness their diverse potentials and talents for a common purpose. He compares such leaders with an astrologer "*jogi*" (ascetic, wise person) who brings into alignment all *graha* and *taraka* (planets and stars) to achieve an auspicious outcome (BS: 186). The yajaman as the leader sees the bigger picture by virtue of his superior gaze or vision.

Managing and motivating staff is the key function of a leader emphasized in BS. This lies at the heart of a successful business in which the subjective human dimension is given not only due recognition but also the highest priority. Pattanaik's key contention, and an implicit critique of established economic theory, is the view that it is human imagination or vision, and hunger for knowledge and success, that drive business, and not the mere pursuit of profit or rational self-interest (BS: 83–87). Pattanaik recounts mythic tales to illustrate "subjective truths" about human nature and behaviour in India that would help to frame appropriate corporate policy and the conduct of managers. He draws attention to the unique form of ritual tribute and worship offered to every god through the ceremony of *aarti* (adoration), to elucidate that people are affected by how others view them and that everyone seeks recognition and wishes to be valued (BS: 219–228). He concludes: "praise empowers us" (BS: 228); "insult disempowers us" (BS: 230); "comparison grants us value" (BS: 232); "we seek hierarchies that favour us" (BS: 234); "we would rather be unique than equal" (BS: 236); "organisations grant us value" (BS: 238); and "everyone seeks a caring gaze" (BS: 322). These insights are then intended to aid the human resource manager to adopt practices that express appreciation of the value of staff. However, Pattanaik further points out that objects or material symbols of commendation or approval merely help to position individuals in a status or power hierarchy in an organization. These are not adequate to the task of motivating staff or eliciting corporate loyalty, for "transactions involve things, but relationships are about thought", feeling and emotional support, that make people feel secure within an organization (BS: 256, 258–261). Thus personalized human interactions and interpersonal relationships with an emotional content are emphasized, rather than a system of material rewards and incentives, in order to inspire enduring commitment of staff, and enhance their performance to the overall benefit of business. Growth and expansion are ensured if a leader is enlightened, humane, inclusive, cooperative, reciprocal, generous, compassionate, accommodating and reflective, even while he takes risks and tough decisions with adverse or detrimental consequences for some people (BS: 355–370). In Pattanaik's view, a model of such ideal leadership is the mythological character Vasudev, described in myths as "a worthy being, an action-driven hero" and "master of the earth and the elements". He clarifies:

> *A vasudev's gaze is that of the passionate entrepreneur*, who … takes decisions and makes things happen, taking full responsibility for consequences. He knows that without violence the wealth of the earth cannot be drawn out. He knows that things need not be done nastily; there is always nice ways to do things. *He knows how to churn, pull and push, adapt, transform the rigid organization into a nimble organism.* (BS: 107–108) (emphases added)

Pattanaik's method of using religious myths to develop management practices in a familiar cultural idiom has been applied in practice in a corporate setting. A much reported and highly publicized application is by the Future Group, led by Kishore Biyani, one of India's most reputed entrepreneurs, who owns the Big Bazar chain of retail outlets. Biyani is one of the key proponents of the "Indian way" (Biyani 2007), and has widely embraced Pattanaik's theories for application in the Future Group's business operations, particularly in human resource management (HR) and in customer relations. The idea of providing selfless service or "*seva*" as a means of accruing spiritual merit is invoked from Hindu thought to underpin customer care, and is marked by the award of "*sevak*" (service-giver) badges to employees. More importantly, in HR, the model of benevolent leadership is applied through the idea of the "karta" as the store manager. A ceremony to induct the karta has been initiated that entails the karta being enthroned on the manager's seat with a traditional turban that symbolizes authority; the karta is blindfolded before assuming office and being given the keys to the store. This signifies the importance of vision, the adoption of a new perspective befitting a leader, and a "mind-shift" that encourages "a wider, longer, deeper and more mature line-of-sight to accompany the increase in responsibility" (BS: 17–18).

The karta's performance as manager is evaluated not through conventional management metrics of profit and loss, but through a set of fifteen criteria, each indicated by a symbolic object with religious association and mythological connotation, and each signifying a different managerial attribute, derived from Pattanaik's theories. Thus the conch-shell trumpet refers to clear and effective communication skills; the *gada* (mace or club) represents the capacity to enforce discipline; the lotus flower complements the club and indicates the ability to appreciate and motivate staff; the *parashu* (axe) signifies incisive analysis of problems; the *ankush* (goad) depicts the push and pull of implementation; the *ikshu* (sugarcane) shows the juice of innovation; the *pasha* (string) suggests binding ability and capacity for synthesis in solving problems; while the revolving *chakra* (wheel) draws attention to repetition and the fulfilment of regular 360-degree reviews and monitoring exercises (BS: 190, 212). In assessing the performance and well-being of store staff, entitled the "Happiness Index Review", familiar religious deities are invoked, namely, Laxmi, Saraswati and Durga. Laxmi, as the god of wealth, refers to the performance of employees in enhancing the commercial aspects of a business, such as relating to sales; Saraswati, as the goddess of learning, refers to the acquisition of knowledge and training by workers and their skill enhancement; Durga, as the embodiment of *Shakti* (power), serves as the yardstick to assess the extent of sense of empowerment, motivation, initiative and self-reliance of employees. From the company's perspective, the use of these well-known religious symbols helps to enliven and communicate dry and abstract management concepts and practices to staff and enables more effective personnel management, while emphasizing the importance of Indian cultural values in the business milieu.

Although Pattanaik's dichotomous characterization of Indian and Western management methods is somewhat overdrawn, his ideas have gained much publicity. They are also clearly enjoying growing application by corporate leaders, as the Future Group example shows. This is because Pattanaik's emphasis on subjectivity offers a culturally grounded theory of trust and cooperation that promises to temper the harshness of corporate culture and render it more appealing. Pattanaik's assertion of a distinct and unique "Indian way" is reminiscent of similar claims associated with the idea of "Asian values" and with a variety of Japanese, Chinese, Singaporean and other Southeast Asian management cultures that emphasize collectivism (Ong 1999). Pattanaik's normative description of a benevolent corporation is analogous to Ong's analysis of collective humanitarianism and communitarianism articulated by the neoliberal capitalist state in East Asia as a corrective or antidote to harmful capitalism of the Western variety (Ong 1999: 77, 203). Pattanaik, however, does not refer to such literature, instead asserting the cultural uniqueness of his own theories. It appears that various Asian corporate cultures have shared characteristics, even when they have autonomous trajectories of development: they tend to take the West as their point of reference, to which they seek to measure up (as Agrawal does in the preceding text) or in relation to which they proclaim the superiority of their indigenous capitalist traditions (as Pattanaik does). Moreover, even though Pattanaik claims to have put forward novel management concepts, many of his ideas resonate with existing and increasingly popular notions about the "Indian way." Following the classic essay "Is There an Indian Way of Thinking?" by the poet and literary scholar Ramanujan (1989) and similar analyses, it is now commonplace to conceptualize the "Indian way of thinking" as being able to assimilate and synthesize diverse perspectives, accommodate and balance contradictory logics and cognitive inconsistencies, and capable of modification and adaptation with sensitivity to specific contexts. Scholarly accounts of this kind on the "composite Indian mind," the capacious, plural and context-sensitive nature of Indian thought as well as its collectivist, inclusive orientation, are now often invoked in Indian management literature, and even outlined in some textbooks (Sinha 2008: 19, 30, 37). Pattanaik emphasizes precisely such ideas in his interpretation of myths for deployment in corporate settings.

BS is a treatise on culturally attuned behaviour, based on myths, in an organization seen as a harmonious, people-centred organism. However, as the analytical literature shows, myths frequently reflect social stratification by articulating contested perspectives and interpretations, and often serve as the vehicle of self-assertion of subaltern groups against dominant classes (Richman 1991). Pattnaik (2006: xiv) instead emphasizes the socially cohesive nature of myths, fostering "a common understanding of the world that binds individuals and communities together", which he then deploys to craft a unified corporate ethos, led by able managers and executives, where hierarchical management structures and decisions with adverse human consequences are alleviated with a caring appreciation and inclusive embrace of all stakeholders and operatives. The key role in such an organization, as seen previously, is played by benevolent paternalistic leaders. The well-being of staff and personnel ultimately relies on the enlightened and noble subjectivity and vision of great leaders, rather than on external laws and regulations. Pattanaik notes from his perusal of myths that the state of nature is violent – as is the ungoverned world of business (BS: 137–139) – and hence Lord Brahma values *sanskriti* or rules and laws that govern society and protect the weak. However, rules are double edged; they become instruments of power, oppression and exploitation, or they prevent innovation, transformation and creativity (BS: 264–282). Pattanaik, therefore, argues that such laws and rules cannot adequately mitigate violence and exploitation, but a simultaneous process of regeneration is required. "Regeneration ensures sustainable wealth", and in turn, "restraint ensures regeneration." Such "restraint" is achieved through the intellectual and emotional growth of the leader (yajaman) (BS: 156–157). Self-restraint, individual self-regulation, prudence, knowledge and the vision of leaders ensure regeneration, as opposed to regulations or laws designed to control the illegitimacy, arbitrariness, destructiveness or exploitation in business and the violent nature of the market (BS: 158–159). The implication is that inner conscience, wisdom and the personal subjectivity of the leader are a better source of stability and balance than external rules (BS: 160).

Such an organization, as an organism, relies on a personalized mode of appreciative and compassionate interaction between leaders (kartas, yajamans) and the led, including employees (karya-kartas, who execute orders). Here corporate power is legitimized and rendered acceptable through the figure of the humane leader, akin to personalized forms of feudal paternalism rather than the impersonal organizational authority of a corporation. Although seemingly offering a moral compass or an ethical code, this emphasis on the contextual sensitivity of Indian thought and its apparent aversion to universal values encourages a moral relativism, and even an amoral perspective, setting aside any normative value judgement.

> All decisions are contextual....Laws by their very nature are arbitrary and depend on the context. What one community considers fair, another may not consider to be fair.... Rules always change in times of war and in times of peace, as they do in times of fortune and misfortune. Thus, no decision is right or wrong. Decisions can be beneficial or harmful, in the short-term or long-term, to oneself or to others. Essentially, every decision has a consequence no matter which rule is upheld and which one is ignored....It has consequences that a yajaman has to face. There is no escape. This is a heavy burden to bear.... If the decision is harmful, the yajaman alone is responsible.... If the decision is good, the yajaman is the beneficiary. (BS: 122–23, 126, 132, 134)

Pattanaik here outlines an ideology of a powerful, but benign, corporate elite at the helm of an enlightened corporation, accountable to no one other than themselves and unfettered by any external regulation. They are both prudent and decisive, able to bear the supreme responsibility of exercising control over peoples' lives. In this concept of corporate leadership, consistent with neoliberal approaches to unregulated capital, the leaders are restrained only by their own exalted vision and sense of responsibility, but are also able to elicit employees' compliance through the exercise of benevolent paternalism.

Conclusion

In tandem with India's transition to a market-based entrepreneurial economy and the rapid growth of the private corporate sector, Hindu myths have been retold and deployed to shape individual conduct and organizational behaviour in corporate business. The two cases explored in this chapter reveal two contrasting approaches to the deployment of religious myths in India's private corporate economy. While they share the common characteristic of entering in a dialogue with western management thought and practice, they do so in very different ways. Writing and broadcasting in Hindi, Agrawal addresses provincial vernacular middle classes, and aims to empower those seeking upward mobility through success in the private sector. Accordingly, he offers guidance to individual corporate servants to enable them to serve their organizations with steadfast commitment and a robust work ethic, in complete conformity with organizational goals and needs. In delivering this advice, Agrawal wholeheartedly embraces global management norms and derives inspiration from prevalent management texts to uphold such ideas as self-management, emotional intelligence, positive thinking and a service ethos. Agrawal, therefore, defines strategies for his target audience to integrate themselves successfully into the private sector through an unquestioning espousal of extant management ideals.

He dresses these up as a set of principles derived from an exemplary deified mythological character Hanuman, whom he projects as a living ideal from the past.

In contrast to Agrawal's small-town middle classes, Pattanaik addresses English-speaking senior management of large corporations. He offers them lessons in culturally sensitive modes of organizational behaviour that would help to win the compliance of their workforces, gain them legitimacy in the eyes of their employees and thus enable them to run successful and effective business operations as harmonious entities in the global marketplace. He explicitly rejects Western management orthodoxy and propounds an "Indian way" of organizing business and management systems that is culturally cohesive, with its own integrity and normative values, distinct from global corporate culture. He also implies an understanding of capitalism and the market that privileges not rational calculations but intuitive knowledge, subjective relations and beliefs. While all this is in many ways reminiscent of the wider global "cultural turn" in business and of ideas associated with "Asian values," he nevertheless asserts the autonomy of a self-contained Indian corporate culture, which is supposedly superior to the West in its cultural authenticity. In this exercise, Pattanaik draws on prevailing ideas about the "Indian way," reinforced, extended and repackaged in a familiar idiom of religious myths. In the process, these religious myths have been corporatized, and a market metaphor of exchange and transaction has been introduced to recast myths in tune with contemporary business culture. This reengineering of religious myths is expected to culturally anchor corporate capitalism, management practice and business ethos, and to render them more acceptable, benign, humane and paternalistic – not least because corporate power is otherwise recognized to be unregulated and unaccountable.

In turning to religion in this way, neither Agrawal nor Pattanaik explicitly seeks to associate his teachings with contemporary forms of politicized Hinduism. Pattanaik, in particular, suggests that he has no truck with religious politics, and implies that he does not engage in religious exegesis, but merely seeks to elicit cultural and ethical dispositions from myths. However, Pattanaik's sole reliance on Hindu and related mythology, to the exclusion of Islamic ideas, normalizes and essentializes corporate India as Hindu. Similarly, Agrawal's obvious devotion to and reverence for Hanuman, as well as his expression of a desirable corporate work ethic in a religious idiom, evidently enhance the public significance of Hinduism. A religious sensibility underpins the theories of both, which heightens and extends engagement with religious symbols and ideas, and contributes to a conscious sacralization of everyday life and corporate culture. All this constitutes and consolidates the cultural substratum in which to embed politics based on exclusionary Hindu identity.

The two contrasting cases explored here form two sides of the same coin. On the one hand, according to Pattanaik, benign and harmonious corporations are run by wise, powerful leaders who value a balanced organization and human contribution; on the other, in Agrawal's account, devoted and loyal employees give their unstinting service and undiluted commitment to the company. In this arguably neoliberal conception of unencumbered corporate power, there is no call for external controls to rein in the excesses of private corporations, nor is there any need or room for supposedly self-empowered workers to contest or challenge managerial control and corporate power. Agrawal's instrumental deployment of religious myths, coupled with Pattanaik's reference to plural perspectives and contextual adaptations as the hallmarks of the "Indian way" of thinking, together imagine this seemingly ideal corporate world and seek to give it a firm ideological foundation. Yet contradictory messages are also conveyed. The idea of the subjugation of the individual to a corporate monolith can be potentially undercut by the notion of the value of each individual within a corporation and by the possibility of individual success and empowerment in a market economy. If myths with their ambiguities, ambivalent meanings and multiple layers of interpretation seem to be a suitable vehicle to reconcile these contradictions, they can also allow subversive and contested appropriations in the interstices of the dominant narratives. Although the aim of retelling myths so far has been to advance the cause of corporate entities, the message of the value and power of people within business may also help to unleash new expectations and embolden contentions against corporate power.

Notes

1 News programme on *Aaj Tak* television: www.youtube.com/watch?v=hYIKib57h0Y. Accessed 8 October 2016].
2 "Why Kishore Biyani Is on a Creation, Preservation and Destruction Mission," *Economic Times*, 4 April, 2014.
3 For example, see *Organization* 10 (2003), Special Issue on Spirituality, Management and Organization.
4 SSH refers to Agrawal (2011). The references are cited from the Kindle edition, where SSH stands for *Sada Safal Hanuman* and KL for Kindle Locations.

References

Agrawal, Vijay. 2011. *Hanuman Who Never Failed.* Bhopal: Benten Books.
2013 [2008]. *Sada Safal Hanuman.* Bhopal: Manjul Publishing House.
Birtchnell, Thomas. 2009. "From 'Hindolence' to 'Spirinomics': Discourse, Practice and the Myth of Indian Enterprise." *South Asia: Journal of South Asian Studies* 32(2): 248–268.
Biyani, Kishore. 2007. *It Happened in India: The Story of Pantaloons, Big Bazaar, Central and the Great Indian Consumer.* Delhi: Rupa.

Browne, Katherine E., and B. Lynne Milgram (eds). 2009. *Economics and Morality: Anthropological Approaches*. Lanham, MD: Altamira Press.

Calas, Marta, and Linda Smircich. 2003. "Introduction: Spirituality, Management and Organization." *Organization* 10(2): 327–328.

Cappelli, Peter. 2010. *The India Way: How India's Top Business Leaders Are Revolutionizing Management*. Boston: Harvard Business Publishing.

Chakraborty, S. K. 1993. *Managerial Transformation by Values: A Corporate Pilgrimage*. New Delhi: SAGE.

Doniger O'Flaherty, Wendy. 1980. "Inside and Outside the Mouth of God: The Boundary between Myth and Reality." *Daedalus* 109(2): 93–125.

Doniger, Wendy. 2009. *The Hindus: An Alternative History*. Clarendon: Oxford University Press.

Fuller, Christopher J., and John Harriss. 2005. "Globalizing Hinduism: A 'Traditional' Guru and Modern Businessmen in Chennai." In *Globalizing India: Perspectives from Below*, edited by J. Assayag and C. J. Fuller, 211–236. London: Anthem Press.

Kakar, Sudhir. 1978. *The Inner World: A Psychoanalytic Study of Childhood and Society in India*. Delhi: Oxford University Press.

Kessler, Eric H., and Diana J. Wong-MingJi. 2009. *Cultural Mythology and Global Leadership*. Cheltanham: Edward Elgar.

Koprowski, Eugene J. 1983. "Cultural Myths: Clues to Effective Management." *Cultural Dynamics* 12(2): 39–51.

Lutgendorf, Philip A. 1991. *The Life of a Text: Performing the Ramcaritmanas of Tulsidas*. Berkeley and Los Angeles: University of California Press.

2007. *Hanuman's Tale: The Messages of a Divine Monkey*. New York: Oxford University Press.

Madan, T. N. 2011. *Sociological Traditions: Methods and Perspectives in the Sociology of India*. New Delhi: SAGE.

Nandram, Sharda, and Margot Esther Borden (eds.). 2010. *Spirituality and Business: Exploring Possibilities for a New Business Paradigm*. Heidelberg: Springer-Verlag.

Narayanswamy, Ramnath. 2008. "Why Is Spirituality Integral to Management Education? My Experience of Integrating Management and Spirituality." *Journal of Human Values* 14(2): 115–128.

Narayana Murthy, N. R. 2009. A Better India: A Better World. New Delhi: Penguin.

Nath, Kamal. 2008. *India's Century: The Age of Entrepreneurship in the World's Biggest Democracy*. New Delhi: Tata McGraw-Hill.

Nilekani, Nandan. 2008. *Imagining India: Ideas for the New Century*. New Delhi: Penguin.

Ong, Aihwa. 1999. *Flexible Citizenship: The Cultural Logics of Transnationality*. Durham, NC: Duke University Press.

Pattanaik, Devdutta. 2006. *Myth=Mithya: A Handbook of Hindu Mythology*. New Delhi: Penguin.

2013. *Business Sutra: A Very Indian Approach to Management*. New Delhi: Aleph Book Company.

Pitroda, Sam. 2013. "Focus on Innovation in 'Indian Way' Need of the Hour: Sam Pitroda." *Economic Times*, 22 March.

Ramanujan, A.K. 1989. "Is There an Indian Way of Thinking? An Informal Essay." *Contributions to Indian Sociology* 23(1): 41–58.

Richman, Paula (ed.). 1991. *Many Ramayanas: The Diversity of a Narrative Tradition in South Asia*. Berkeley: University of California Press.

Roland, Alan. 1988. *In Search of Self in India and Japan: Towards a Cross-cultural Psychology*. Princeton, NJ: Princeton University Press.

Rudnyckyj, Daromir. 2010. *Spiritual Economies: Islam, Globalization, and the Afterlife of Development*. Ithaca, NY: Cornell University Press.

Sharma, Subhash. 2007. *New Mantras in Corporate Corridors: From Ancient Roots to Global Routes*. New Delhi: New Age International.

Sinha, Jai B. P. 2008. *Culture and Organizational Behaviour*. New Delhi: SAGE.

Srinivas, K. M. 2000. *Pilgrimage to Indian Ethos Management: A Look at Indigenous Approaches to Organizational Development*. Calcutta: Management Centre for Human Values, Indian Institute of Management.

Upadhya, Carol. 2013. "Shrink-Wrapped Souls: Managing the Self in India's New Economy." In *Enterprise Culture in Neoliberal India*, edited by Nandini Gooptu, 93–108. London: Routledge.

4 Divine Markets: Ethnographic Notes on Postnationalism and Moral Consumption in India

Sanjay Srivastava, Institute of Economic Growth, Delhi University

This chapter explores the connections between contemporary practices of religiosity and one of the most sociologically significant processes of contemporary Indian life: consumerism. The chapter builds upon other discussions that explore this relationship in different parts of the world (Stambach 2000; Eickelman and Anderson 2003; Oosterbaan 2009), as well as those which address India specifically (e.g., T. Srinivas 2010; Srivastava 2011). The discussion will proceed through outlining two ethnographic vignettes that illustrate the particular ways in which consumerism and religiosity are intertwined, while not being reducible to each other. In this way, the chapter seeks to interrogate two approaches to the study of religion, custom, and social and cultural transformation in India. The first of these concerns the so-called "Hindutva" project of "restoration" and purity that have formed staple topics in analyses of religious fundamentalism in India (see, e.g., Blom Hansen 1999; Bacchetta 2004). In these works, the idea of a return to a pure and untainted past is frequently represented as a reaction to processes of intense social and economic change. Hence, as Blom Hansen puts it, "To human beings experiencing social mobility, or a loss of socioeconomic and cultural status produced by urbanization or 'minoritization' the issue of identity – the urge to eradicate the doubt that splits the subjects – becomes more acute than in situations of relative social stability" (1999: 212). Indeed, the idea that an "inner" Indian self is sought to be protected during times of change has become scholarly commonsense in a wide variety of studies. These include the contexts of "colonial modernity" (Chatterjee 1993), postcolonial life (Singer 1972) and emotional life (Desjarlais and Wilce 2003). The ethnographic examples of this chapter seek to outline broader trends within Indian society where consumerism itself is the grounds for religiosity, rather than the latter providing a "refuge" from the processes of social and cultural change. Further, the chapter suggests that that this produces a context that is not significantly about a search for a pure and singular self. Rather, it points in the direction of a split subject, where splitting is not an act of enfeeblement but, rather, a strategy of engaging with a wide range of economic and social processes.

The second, related, perspective I seek to problematize is that which suggests that the relationship between old and new can be captured through discourses of denunciation regarding the decline of bonds of community and family life in the wake of rampant consumerism (e.g., van Wessel 2004). I will suggest that consumerism and its antitheses (however these are imagined) are easily reconciled in everyday life *through* recourse to consumerist discourses themselves.

My argument that religious and consumerist activities are intertwined – and that this, in turn, produces a market morality, such that markets become spiritualized and spirituality cannot be disentangled from the market – can be usefully discussed through comparison with an African example. Addressing Christian evangelism in northern Tanzania, Amy Stambach reports that they "today openly comment on the global 'culture industry,' and on the interconnections of religion and the world economy, with greater consideration than colonial missionaries ever did" (Stambach 2000: 171). Thus, during the twentieth century and continuing through the present, goods introduced to Tanzania by missionaries "held an attraction as signs of the free market and liberalizing economy" (Stambach 2000: 173). Even while Tanzanian youth used goods associated with Christianity in their daily lives, missionary activity that targeted them as objects of "reform" articulated the message that "conversion could help revival participants manage consumerism and social strife" (175). However, the young believed that "by being called Born Again…they would become part of a global world of schooled and 'church-educated people' " (175) and were keen to demonstrate their Born Again status through the use of consumer goods: T-shirts with religious messages, running shoes distributed by the churches, and similar commodities. This, as Stambach suggests, was the context of an unbridgeable divide between leaders of the evangelical movements and their young congregation. Consumption by converts "defies universal consumerist logic of rejection and participation and instead reflects a qualified, cultural involvement in commodity consumption" (2000: 177). That is to say, converts do not assign completely opposed meanings to spirituality and consumerism. As I will later point out, there are both similarities as well as differences between the situations Stambach describes and those discussed in this chapter. What is significant in each case is the intertwined nature of the relationship between consumerism and religiosity.

I wish to broach the relationship between consumerism and religiosity through two specific ideas. These are "postnationalism" and "moral consumption." These concepts – explored in the next section – allow me to both make connections between the worlds of religiosity and consumerism, as well as position the relationship within wider contexts where the meanings of such terms as "state," "citizen," "tradition" and "modernity" are contested. The two concepts also seek to encapsulate certain perspectives that are present in a growing body of scholarship that tracks the relationship between relatively new engagements with the market among groups that have historically had limited access to the "world of goods" (Douglas and Isherwood 1979). Speaking of a segment of Kolkata's self-identified middle-class population, Donner (2011) points out that "amidst the excitement that the triumphant media coverage of the new 'markets' for the growing middle class suggested, the actual transformation of middle-class lifestyles was always evaluated in markedly ambiguous terms" (Donner 2011: 60). And, Geert De Neve suggests that newly affluent industrialists in the garment manufacturing town of Tiruppur in Tamil Nadu, even as they have plunged headlong into the processes of consumerism, "seek to locate themselves at the heart of what is locally constructed as an integrated and *moral* Tamil society" (de Neve 2011: 75; emphasis added).

This chapter focuses, then, on the relay between the desires and pleasures of consumerism, and those perspectives where it is positioned in an anxious relationship to its putative antitheses, religiosity and "tradition." The relationship between religiosity, "community life" and consumerism and "the construction of religious identity during a period of intense globalization" (T. Srinivas 2010: 329) concern multiple contexts such as changes in urban life and aspirations to engage with globalized identity projects (see also S. Srinivas 2001, 2008). I investigate some of these contexts through multi-sited ethnographic vignettes and connect these sites using the frameworks of "postnationalism" and "moral consumption." In this way, I wish to demonstrate the wider applicability of these terms in explaining contemporary religiosity in India as it rubs against traditional forms of sociality, such as the family, and newer aspirations to be part of a consumerist world in the making. The argument I present here is similar to the one made by Jacob Copeman and Aya Ikegame who, in their discussion of the relationship between religiosity and the media, write that "despite the prediction of modernization theory that as mediating technologies of reproduction developed religiosity would lose its intensity and diffuse into modern secular sensitivities, many scholars of religion recognize…that the opposite has been the case" (Copeman and Ikegame 2012: 312).

Postnationalism and Moral Consumption

In this section, I provide a discussion of the two concepts I wish to employ as connecting threads between the different ethnographic contexts of this chapter. To begin with, the term postnational does *not* mean to suggest that the nation-state is insignificant as a context of analysis, or that we now live in a "post-patriotic" age where the most significant units of analysis are certain "post-national social formations" (Appadurai 1993: 411) – such as nongovernmental organizations (NGOs) – that putatively problematize nationalist and statist perspectives. Further, my deployment is also different from another recent usage, which posits postnationalism as "a distinct ethico-political horizon and a position of critique" and a concept "that can be instantiated by suspending the idea of the nation as a prior theoretical-political horizon, and thinking through its impossibility, even while located uncomfortably within its bounds" (de Alwis et al. 2009: 35). I use postnationalism to refer to the articulation of nationalist emotion with the robust desires engendered through new practices of consumerism and their associated cultures of privatization and individuation. I refer to it as *post*-nationalism to index a phenomenon that is both different from classical descriptions of nationalism (e.g., Anderson 1983; Gellner 1997) but is, nevertheless, about sentiments that gather around the idea of the nation. It is a form of nationalism that comes *after* the period when the sentiment was elaborated through the vocabularies of personal and collective sacrifice, duty and valour. As I explain later, postnationalism grows out of a location within cultures of consumerism.

A fruitful way of approaching the topic – and providing concrete illustrative examples – is through an exploration of the contemporary politics of urban spaces in Delhi. I hope, through this brief digression, to not only establish the relevance of the idea of postnationalism to the discussion of this chapter, but also point to the wider contexts within which the theme "religion and the morality of markets" is embedded. The following discussion seeks, then, to illuminate a context in which newer relations with the nation-state are being formed through changes wrought by the market and its effects.

In 1999, soon after being elected to office, Delhi's erstwhile chief minister, Sheila Dikshit, "called for an active participation of Residents Welfare Associations [RWAs] in governance" (Ojha 1999: 1). The rationale for this was the "failure" of civic agencies to carry out their normal tasks. The chief minister's secretary noted that the call to actively involve RWAs in urban governance heralded a new era, marking "the first step towards a responsive management of the city" (Ojha 1999: 1). Positing a distinction between the state and the "community," the secretary further noted that the failure of civic agencies meant that "it's really time for the community to be given direct control of managing the affairs of the city" (Ojha 1999: 1). Subsequently, the government decided to "empower" RWAs to "take certain decisions on their own." It was proposed that RWAs be given control over the management of resources such as parks, community halls, parking places, sanitation facilities and local roads. A more direct relationship between the state and RWAs was also mooted through the idea of joint surveys of "encroached" land – that is, land that had been "illegally" occupied, usually by slum-dwellers – with the possibility that all illegal structures would "then be demolished in a non-discriminatory manner" (Ojha 1999: 1). Finally, it was proposed that RWAs be allowed to impose fines on government agencies that failed to carry out their assigned tasks.

In 2005, the Delhi state government announced that it would raise the electricity tariff by 10 percent. A body known as the Delhi Residents Welfare Association Joint Front (RWAJF) was formed in the same year to agitate against the measure. The Front consisted of 195 separate member RWAs from around the city. The increase in power rates for domestic consumers was the second one since the state-owned electricity body was "unbundled" in June 2002 as part of power sector "reforms." As a result, three privately owned companies secured contracts for electricity distribution (Sethi 2005).[1] There was vigorous protest over the price increase and, in addition to the RWAJF, NGOs such as People's Action and another group known as Campaign Against Power Tariff Hike (CAPTH) joined the campaign. Individual RWAs asked their members to refuse payment of the extra amount, while the RWAJF lobbied the government and organized city-wide protests. These gained wide coverage in both print and electronic media and, echoing Gandhian anticolonial strategies, the organizers were reported to have deployed "the ideas of 'civil disobedience' and 'people's power' " (Sethi 2005: 5). The parallels drawn between the Gandhian anticolonial moment and the present were even more explicit with the Convener of the RWAJF referring to the protests as "non-violent *Satyagraha* [resistance]" (Sirari 2006: 5). Eventually, the Delhi government backed down and the price rise was shelved. According to Sanjay Kaul, president of the People's Action NGO, the success of the protest heralded the making of a "middle-class revolution" (Sirari 2006: 5). Kaul is one of many who has rediscovered and deployed anticolonial vocabulary on behalf of the "people" at a time when the colonial era itself has become integrated into consumerist discourses through marketing strategies that invoke it as an era of genteel living and tastes. More recently, in the wake of the 2011 anticorruption movement led by the activist Anna Hazare, popular yoga guru Swami Ramdev invoked "Gandhi in calling for a '*satyagrah* against corruption' " (Copeman and Ikegame 2012: 318).

The circulation of the ideas of "civil disobedience" "Satayagrah" and "revolution," and the consolidation of the notion of a "people" contesting the state, index a situation of classical nationalism, but there are significant differences that lead me to characterize this context as postnationalism. By this, I mean a situation in which the original moral frisson of these terms – provided by anticolonial sentiment – no longer holds. Indeed, in an era of post-Nehruvian economic liberalization characterized by consumerist modernity (Mazzarella 2003; Fernandes 2006; Osella and Osella 2009), the moral universe of the anticolonial struggle is no longer part of popular public discourse. As noted earlier, a colonial ambience is now the stuff of popular marketing strategies. For instance, the Spencer's department store in the privately developed DLF City that borders Delhi (see Srivastava 2012) outlines its history through a series of billboard-size sepia photographs placed at the entrance. The photographs – of fashionable European ladies shopping for fine goods at Spencer's – are from the colonial period and represent an efflorescence of colonial chic in the Indian public sphere. Other contiguous sites include the five-star Imperial Hotel in central Delhi, its corridors liberally decorated with early twentieth century photographs from an imperial gathering to commemorate the coronation of King George V, and themed restaurants such as Days of the Raj and Sola Topee (the pith helmet that came to characterize Englishness), also in Delhi. The postnational context does not have a hostile relation to colonialism, and the earlier emphases on the ethics of saving and delayed gratification for the "national good" – indispensable ideological accompaniments to nationalist "civil disobedience" and "satyagrah" – do not find any resonance in popular discourses on the role of the state or the duties of citizens. Given this background, postnationalism also refers to the changing relationship between the state and the middle classes. Hence, with regard to the RWAs, postnationalism indicates an era of the "gentrification" and "re-spatialization" of the state (Ghertner 2011: 526) such that the consumer-citizen becomes the key focus of policy debates. This is a significant shift from the ideologies of the Nehruvian-era developmentalist state that succeeded the colonial one, with the poor as its key focus (Gupta 1998). It may not be adequate to summarize what I have described so far as neoliberalism, as this concept is unable to account for the specific *national* histories that transform into postnational ones. Further, as my examples will demonstrate, it is unclear that the "enterprising" subject of neoliberalism (Gooptu 2013) is the same everywhere and that the issue of agency can be transparently captured through speaking of a universal neoliberal moment.

The most significant manner in which the postnational moment resonates within the politics of urban space concerns the repositioning of the language of anticolonial nationalism from the national sphere to the suburban one. This, in turn, also indexes the move from the "national family" – an abstraction that sought to overwrite actually existing social and economic differences – to the nuclear and middle-class family as the object of state interest, and the translation of the notion of nationalist solidarity across classes to middle-class solidarity. Manifestations of a new consciousness of middle-classness can be found across a number of contexts including "urban beautification" and slum demolitions (Baviskar 2006; Ghertner 2011; Arabindoo 2011), forms of leisure (Brosius 2010; Donner 2011) and marriage (Uberoi 2008). It is in this context that new urban forms that are key to notions of middle-classness – such as gated residential communities – require attention. The rapid proliferation of gated communities across India (Brosius 2010; Srivastava 2014) signifies not only major topographical changes but also broader discursive transformations relating to family life, state, nation and citizenship. So, for example, gated communities in India have created a specific relationship between gender, consumerism and the morality of the markets. It is a relationship that – as I will discuss in the next section – speaks to the long history of anxiety about women in public through the question: How can the public woman belong both to the world as well as the home?

By moral consumption I refer to the context in which consumerist activity is glossed by explicit and implicit discourses on the possibility of exercising control over it. This is different from viewing it as a *threat* to established life-ways (van Wessel 2004). That is to suggest that contemporary contexts of consumerism indicate that long-standing cultural discourses of, say, the sacrificing and nurturing mother that *proscribe* "indulgent" consumption are encompassed *within* acts of consumerism by women (see Donner 2011). Hence, female visitors to the Disneyfied (and hyperconsumerist) Akshardham temple complex in Delhi can move seamlessly between roles as consumers *and* devoutly religious persons precisely because the same space provides opportunities for both (Srivastava 2011). Masculine anxieties over female consumption at the complex are assuaged through a process of moral consumption whereby women take part in hyperconsumerism *and are also* able to withdraw to the realms of its putative antithesis, namely religiosity. Though these domains interpenetrate, each is imagined as separate. At the Akshardham temple complex – built along the lines of Florida's Disney World and Hollywood's Universal Studios theme park – religiosity is located on the grounds of consumerism and makes possible the relay between the two, in turn naturalizing the relationship between them and consolidating the discourse of moral consumption.

I have explored this idea in relation to the contiguous publication of remarkably explicit articles on sex and sexuality with those on religious festivals and rituals in a variety of Hindi-language magazines geared toward women (Srivastava 2007). There I suggested that the magazines address a readership that views itself as taking part in moral consumption inasmuch as it can imagine itself as being able to move between modernity and tradition, rather than be determined by the former.

Postnationalism and moral consumption redefine the representation of the "people" in a time of consumerist modernity.[2] They are relevant for this discussion on the relationships between religiosity and the market inasmuch as they constitute the grounds on which these relationships are naturalized, through the figure of the consumer-citizen. Just as the latter is able to recast the relationship with the state through consumerist discourses, he or she also reconfigures engagements with religion. The concept "divine markets" seeks to capture the relationship with commodities "produced through an articulation between economic and religious practices" (Osella and Osella 2009: 215).

Gated Religiosity: Janmashtami Celebrations at Birmingham Garden in DLF City

The 3,000-acre, privately developed DLF City is located south of Delhi, immediately across the border in the Gurgaon district of the state of Haryana. DLF City was constructed by the Delhi Land and Finance (DLF) corporation, beginning in the mid-1980s. Its hypermalls, gated residential communities and corporate offices (occupied, among others, by call centres, business processes outsourcing companies and prominent multinational corporations) speak of an urban transformation that is also the making of a new, modern, middle-class, Indian self. DLF was established in 1946 by Chaudhury Raghvendra Singh, a civil servant and landowner. Until the mid-1950s, DLF had a significant presence in the private real estate market in Delhi. However, following the 1951 publication of a highly critical report of an inquiry into the functioning of the state-run Delhi Improvement Trust (established 1937), the government promulgated the Control of Building Operations Ordinance of 1955, leading to the establishment of the Delhi Development Provisional Authority. The Provisional Authority was, in turn, succeeded by the Delhi Development Authority (DDA) in 1957.[3] With the establishment of the DDA, opportunities for private real estate activity were severely restricted; even "while the DDA was in the process of preparing a Master Plan for the city, the government announced a freeze on all vacant undeveloped land within the urbanizable [sic] limits.... Establishing itself as the sole agency legally authorized to develop and dispose of land, the State [sic] left little, or no role for the private land developer" (Dasappa Kacker 2005: 72).

From the early 1980s, DLF began to acquire land in Gurgaon district in the bordering state of Haryana to re-invigorate its real estate business. After some initial hiccups (Gurgaon was considered too far away; there was much termite infestation; the local, largely rural populations were considered "threatening"),[4] DLF's townships, gated communities and office complexes proved an unprecedented success. Within a span of two decades, fuelled by changes in the economy since the 1980s, farming lands were turned into spaces of global commerce, malls and gated communities. The rapid expansion of the retail banking sector, which made it relatively easy to obtain home loans, was a significant component of the changes in the housing sector. Aggressive market forays by both state-owned and new private entrants (including foreign banks) sought to target "young and highly educated professionals who began their careers through the 1980s, [but] could not afford to own their own homes" (Khanna 2007: 107).

According to a recent report, the areas falling under the recently (2008) constituted Municipal Corporation of Gurgaon (that includes DLF City as well as several other privately developed residential enclaves) contained roughly

1.2 million inhabitants.[5] DLF City itself is divided into five "phases" that contain independent housing; corporate offices; shopping malls; leisure facilities such as theme parks, food plazas and a golf course and, of course, gated residential enclaves. It also has a privately built metro rail system owned by DLF. DLF City is regarded in both scholarly (King 2004; Dupont 2005) as well as popular works (Jain 2001) as a key site for the making of contemporary cultures of transnational urbanism in India. Birgit Meyer notes in her discussion of religion in a mediatized transnational world that "in order to [be] experienced as real, imaginations are required to become tangible outside the realm of the mind, by creating a social environment that materializes through the structuring of space, architecture, ritual performance, and by inducing bodily sensations… [and further that] in order to become experienced as real, imagined communities need to be materialized as in the concrete lived environment and be felt in the bones" (Meyer 2009: 5). This section explores the relationship between religiosity and new contexts of urban life through focusing on concrete practices of everyday life as it unfolds in one particular gated community in DLF City.

Birmingham Garden (name changed) is one of the most prominent gated residential enclaves in DLF City. It has an active Residents Welfare Association (RWA) that organizes a variety of social and cultural functions. These include events relating to Republic Day (January 26), Independence Day (August 15), popular religious festivals such as Diwali and Holi, dance competitions, sporting events, consumer-goods fairs and a variety of religious rituals focused on women (such as *karva-chauth*) that have been popularized by Bollywood cinema. Apart from Christmas, which has taken on the form of a secular festival, no non-Hindu festivals are celebrated. Different kinds of worlds – religious, national and transnational – lie within the gates, and women are visibly a part of it.

The Janmashtami festival that celebrates the birth of the god Krishna is a popular event at Birmingham Garden. Celebrated "on the eighth day of the waning half of the lunar month of *bhadrapad*" (Hawley and Goswami 1981: 62), which falls during August and September, the festival has elaborate local roots that draw on kinship networks, relationships in the neighbourhood and religious ties. In the north Indian city of Brindavan (famed as the place where Krishna spent a great deal of his childhood), Janmashtami celebrations involve a variety of priests, performing artists (who enact "nativity" plays) and lay worshippers, each group drawing on localized myths and resources. Janmashtami celebrations at Brindavan (similar to those in other parts of India) are also organized around acts of commensality – feasts and fasts – that further institutionalize community bonds through residents' participation in a nonmonetized ritual activity (Hawley and Goswami 1981).

Since 2008 the festival at Birmingham Garden has been organized by the International Society for Krishna Consciousness (ISKCON), founded in

New York in 1966 by Srila Prabhupada. Members of ISKCON who live within the complex took an active part in convincing the RWA to allow the organization to take over the festival from residents. In 2012, the celebrations began with a *bhajan* (prayer song) by a group of ISKCON devotees who sat on a large stage that faced several rows of chairs. A powerful sound system ensured that the singing reached all parts of the complex. To the right of the stage, there was a large screen. A laptop and video projector were used to project swirling colour images onto the screen. As the lead singer repeatedly requested that residents join the gathering, the crowd built to around a hundred, and a group of women, including one from a Birmingham Garden family that belongs to ISKCON, began to dance in an empty space in front of the stage. It was an improvised performance that followed the ISKCON "street dance" pattern seen in many western cities. The dancers exhorted others in the audience to join, and a few, all women, did so.

Soon after, two male ISKCON devotees joined the dancing. However, they danced to the right of the stage, away from the women. Then some other male residents from the complex also began a slow dance with this group. While the women danced in front of the *jharokha* (a tableau depicting Krishna as a child) in gestures of bliss and devotion – hands and faces raised to the sky – the men, perhaps appropriately, given the association between masculinity and technology, danced in front of the laptop and the video projector. Two specially attired girls came forward to dance to verses recited from the Gita, and an ISKCON devotee offered a discourse on the text. By then, the cinema screen was displaying graphics of flying machines, flaming arrows, a twirling globe and a variety of psychedelic animation. The ceremony was building to a crescendo. The women dancing improvised and also did Indian dances such as the *garba* and *gidda* popularized by Bollywood. The ceremony concluded with an *arti* (lamp) ceremony and the cutting of a "Krishna birthday cake," which was then offered as *prasad* (sanctified food). The screen now showed scenes from cities in the United States where white American *bhakts* (devotees) danced, sang and spoke about their lives as "Krishna bhakts." The ceremony lasted three hours, during which the laptop united the Birmingham Garden space with an American one. The "West" was in Birmingham Garden via a confident cosmopolitanism that could include within it a broader tableau of Indian culture. Especially notable was that this situation was unmarked by anxiety and angst regarding "cultural imperialism" or India's colonial legacy. We ate our cake and dispersed.

The suffusion of local space with cultures of transnationalism also happens in other, more obvious, circumstances. One of the most common ways in which group interaction takes place at Birmingham Garden is around promotional stalls for consumer goods manufacturers. Every other week, a mobile van or a portable tent promoting a variety of goods can be found at different places within the complex. In August 2011, Honda advertised its newly launched Jazz model by inviting residents to inspect the car, which had been parked next to a mobile information booth within the condominium complex. A young woman exhorted adults to "come down and see for yourself," while children took part in dancing competitions and were rewarded for composing songs about the vehicle. Some days before, an electronic goods company had displayed its wares at the same spot.

The relationship with the market is fundamental to – even though it does not exhaust – the senses of space and community at Birmingham Garden. It generates specific types of sociality: of a space where women may publicly dance with men at Bacardi-sponsored Holi (the festival of colours) celebrations without encountering the risks of the sexual economy that is common in Holi celebrations. It is imagined as a liberal space where women may drink alcohol provided by Bacardi in public, conjuring a new public that is ensconced within a private space that is liberated from the dangers and "uncivilized" nature of the old (Pow 2007). Expressions of the female body are a significant aspect of life within the gates: whether during Holi, Janmasthami, morning walks or other rituals, the female boy is allowed considerable visibility in the public spaces of the enclave. In these spaces, children and adults sing, dance and experience the physical sensuality of commodities that come to them, transporting the aura of the showroom to their doorstep and becoming one with their domestic lives.

The preceding text describes the related contexts of postnational modernity and moral consumption. Gated communities are exemplary sites of the making of suburban religiosities in tandem with the consolidation of the suburban (middle-class) family as the focus of postnational consumerist modernity. That is to say, if national spaces, such as the state-run educational system and factory towns (Roy 2007), were once the imagined space of personal and familial transformations from premodern to modern subjectivity, that role now appears to have passed to the more intimate localities of domestic residence. The postcolonial era in India witnessed earlier periods when residential spaces *were* part of the state's imagination of social life and change. Today, in contrast, the state loiters outside the home, and its relationships with domestic space are of a different nature. This has specific consequences in terms of new relationships between different kinds of spaces (domestic and public, for example), religiosity, gender and new notions of the self. Within gated communities, where the street is not the street, and, for precisely that reason, is the site of intense middle-class activity, public women both can be the guardians of tradition *and* take part in sexualized presentations of the self, rather than having to choose between the two (Phadke 2007). So, on the night of the Hindu festival of *karva-chauth*, traditionally attired women of Birmingham Garden pray for their husbands' well-being, and, the morning after, they pace the condominium grounds on their exercise rounds dressed in latex clothing. Consumerism, here, is the grounds for the making of a moral middle class that is able to combine "modernity" and "tradition" in appropriate measure. Women, in particular, are able to take part in consumerist modernity and return to tradition when required. Postnational consumerism provides the grounds for the making of moral consumption: for one must take vigorous part in consumerism in order to display one's ability to withdraw from it. One must display modernity to remain traditional.

Between the Temple, Reality Television and Time Management: Young Men in Haridwar

If non-religious spaces such as gated communities act as sites of moral consumption, there are other, more explicitly religious contexts in which religiosity is itself an entry point to the world of material goods. This occurs through "a continuous balancing act between reaching out and staying apart, between embracing the world and staying aloof, between addressing and appealing to the public and imposing some kind of boundary through which believers are set apart" (Meyer 2009: 21).

Dev Sanskriti Vishwavidyala (DSVV) is a private university located in the (Hindu) holy city of Haridwar in the state of Uttarakhand in northern India. It was founded in 2002 and is one of several educational institutions run by the All World Gayatri Pariwar, a Hindu religious organization founded by Pandit Ram Sharma Acharya (1911–1990) in 1958. Pandit Acharya was born in the village of Anwalkheda near Agra in the state of Uttar Pradesh. The headquarters of Gayatri Pariwar is Jyoti Kunj Ashram, also in Haridwar. The Ashram, like many others in Haridwar, is popular with pilgrims from around the country. Jyoti Kunj is a mini-city and contains temples and other religious spaces, accommodation for visitors, restaurants and dining halls, kitchens that prepare foods to be used during religious festivities, printing presses, administrative units that deal with domestic and international visitors and a variety of other offices. According to its website, "Spiritual refinement of the suksma vatavarana (subtle environment) has been the predominant focus of the mission and it has endeavoured a Yagya-based movement on the lines of the Vedic tradition to achieve this virtually impossible goal."[6] The current head of mission is the son-in-law of the founder of Gayatri Pariwar. He is also the chancellor of the Dev Sanskriti Vishwavidyala, which is located on an eighty-four-acre campus, approximately three kilometres from Jyoti Kunj Ashram. The university was established under a special act of the state government of Uttarakhand.

I was first introduced to DSVV in March 2011 by Ankur Patel, who, along with his wife Malti, is in charge of distance education for the university. On my initial visit, Ankur arranged for me to stay at the Ashram. When I arrived at Jyoti Kunj on a cold January morning, the air was thick with smoke from a number of *havans* (sacred fires) that form part of rituals of "yagya," originally a Vedic sacrifice ritual.[7] The havans were surrounded by devotees. Loudspeakers installed upon pillars blared chants that devotees were expected to repeat. Ankur told me that the yagya ritual at Jyoti Kunj has a very specific dress code: men are required to wear *dhotis* (an unstitched garment, tied at the waist and covering most of the legs) and the women must be in "Indian" attire. Among the crowd of devotees were a number of European and Japanese women wearing loose-fitting "harem" pants. I was met at the Ashram gates by Ashish Kumar Singh, who is a volunteer at the Ashram. He is in his mid-twenties and comes from the town of Jabalpur in Madhya Pradesh. He has an engineering degree. Like many other volunteers at the complex, Ashish was wearing saffron dhoti–kurta.[8] I checked into the Patanjali Bhavan ("Patanjali Mansion") guest house, named after the Sanskrit grammarian of ancient India. Ashish had become familiar with All World Gayatri Parivar (AWGP) at the age of thirteen when he became involved in some of their activities as a schoolboy. He is the only child in his family, so when he decided to join the organization as a full-time volunteer, his parents were unhappy with his decision. Now, he told me, they have reconciled with his membership.

Ankur Patel and his wife both have management degrees and earlier worked in corporate jobs in Bangalore. Malti's family had long been part of AWGP, but Ankur knew nothing about it. Before marriage, they visited Jyoti Kunj in 2008. Shortly thereafter, they decided to get married at the Ashram, but then returned to their respective jobs in Bangalore. However, Ankur said, he realized that he was increasingly "missing something" in his middle-class corporate life. He and his wife decided to meet with the head of AWGP. They told him that they wanted to "give their time to the mission." The head told them that, given their jobs, he thought that they might be able to spend only a short period with AWGP. Malti responded as follows: "If we decide, it will be forever." Shortly thereafter they moved to Haridwar. Their families, they said, "were completely shocked." Ankur tried to mollify his parents by telling them that he and Malti would get a salary of 20,000 rupees per month (approximately $330) each, whereas they actually received a stipend of 700 rupees per month (approximately $12). The stipend was recently increased to 1000 rupees per month. When his mother found out, she broke down and accused him of lying to her. His father supported him, saying, "He is not asking for any money from us and he is earning whatever he does with *izzat* [honor]." When Ankur and Ashish took me to meet the AWGP head, they touched their foreheads to his feet in a traditional sign of deference, and sat on the floor rather than occupy chairs. The same ritual is performed at the morning *darshan*, when the head and his wife (daughter of the founder of AWGP) "bless" the large crowd of devotees who queue up to see them.

Ankur was my chief guide to the DSVV campus. The university vice-chancellor told me that the institution caters "mainly to poor students," including many from rural areas from states such as Bihar, Madhya Pradesh, Rajasthan and Uttar Pradesh. The university has nine departments, including Sanskrit, English, Indian History and Culture and Scientific Spirituality.[9] The academic day consists of six hours of classroom teaching. DSVV offers certificate, diploma, graduate and post-graduate degrees in courses such as Holistic Health Management, Journalism and Mass Communication, Human Consciousness and Yogic Science and Applied Yoga and Human Excellence.

DSVV is located – along with many other such institutions – within a specific geography of the underfunding of provincial education. This sense of backwardness is keenly felt by the inhabitants of these spaces. They are marked not only by uneven development of educational facilities, but also by lack of confidence in them and a general sense that there is little of worth in an upbringing that is confined to the province. The following quote from an article by anthropologist Chaise LaDousa on schooling and the politics of language in Banaras (Varanasi) provides a succinct summary of this viewpoint:

> Although most people living in Banaras send their children to the city's schools, a small number find it necessary to send their children away for schooling. The case of my neighbour [during the period of fieldwork] demonstrates that not everyone in Banaras focuses on medium differences within the city. Indeed, the neighbour believes Banaras to be unable to offer the kind of English that he sees necessary for success. (LaDousa 2005: 468)

Within this context of social and economic disadvantage, a tertiary institution, such as DSVV, that provides relatively inexpensive education is likely to be popular. However, DSVV is, in the first instance, a religious institution and its key aim is the propagation of Hindu identity. Irrespective of how this is imagined, this activity has raised the now relatively familiar concern regarding the "Hinduization" of education in particular and the public sphere in general (Sundar 2004; Chopra 2008). At first glance, DSVV's moral and physical geography would certainly seem to confirm such concerns.

To begin with, DSVV bases itself on the "gurukul" model of education, the modern roots of which lie in the establishment of gurukul schools by the Arya Samaj movement in 1902 (Pandit 1974; Kumar 1993). Organized around ideas of gender segregation, strict hierarchy between students and teachers and the "timeless" relevance of "ancient Hindu knowledge," the schools were intended to return Indian education to its "ancient" past through purging it of "foreign" (i.e., Muslim and Western) influences. Within the (modern) gurukul movement, temple and religious life were central to the life of the student. The centrepiece of the DSVV campus is a temple to the god Shiva. Every evening, students gather at the temple to hear lectures on religion and morality delivered by teachers. This is followed by recitations by students of writings of Gurudev ("the Holy Guru"), as the founder of DSVV's parent body (the All

World Gayatri Pariwar) is referred to. Following the recitals, there is discussion between students and teachers, during which the latter seek "clarifications" on Gurudev's writings. As in almost all other contexts, boys and girls sit separately and at the feet of their teachers. These activities are followed by fifteen minutes of meditation during which religious music plays over the public announcement system. The meditation period is common to the campuses of Jyoti Kunj Ashram and DSVV, and gates to both institutions are locked for fifteen minutes, during which everyone present is expected to mediate. Thus, the university and the religious Ashram are united as a single space and the distinction between secular and religious education is dissolved.

Given certain analyses of Indian religious and social spheres (outlined in the introductory section of this chapter), one interpretation of DSVV's activities could be that they manifest the Hindutva project of "restoration" and purity and a condemnation of the decline of "authentic" Indian social and cultural beliefs. With respect to the concepts of postnationalism and moral consumption, however, I suggest that the case of DSVV provides another example of a different tendency in Indian society in which consumerism itself is the condition of possibility for increased religiosity. Furthermore, this context is not marked by a search for a pure and singular self. Rather, it signifies the *un-remarkable* consolidation of a divided subject that ranges across consumerist and religious subjectivities, encompassing both positions but determined by neither. It is also in this way that the Indian example, though apparently similar to the case described by Stambach (2007), differs from her Tanzanian case.

Stambach points to a tension at the heart of the relationship between consumerism and religiosity in the Tanzanian evangelical context. Discourses of gender and deference to authority and the strictly enforced austere routine of daily life at DSVV would also seem to position it in opposition to the pervasive practices of consumption, leisure and individuation outside its gates. A student's day begins at 4 A.M. and ends at 9:30 P.M., which is bedtime. In between there are multiple periods devoted to prayer, meditation, and activities such as "wandering through the levels of physical body, to sub-conscious and then super-conscious," "musicmantra" and "submission of your whole work to god." It is a rigorous daily routine, particularly marked by activities designed to produce "pure" Hindu subjects, "recovered" and corralled from the tumult of the outside world. "Time for entertainment" consists of sporting activities and "cultural evenings," which entail student performances based on exclusively religious themes.

One afternoon, as I wandered around the campus during the time set apart for "entertainment," I came across a group of young boys huddled around their music teacher. The boys were all part of the *bhajan* (prayer) singing group and performed regularly at various public events at the university. The group is rigorously trained in bhajan singing, as that is the key form of musical performance both at the DSVV campus as well Jyoti Kunj Ashram. This afternoon, however, they were attentively looking at the music teacher's phone as it replayed a recording of Bollywood singer Sonu Nigam's performance on a television musical reality show. Nigam displayed his virtuosity by alternating, in rapid order, between a 1950s songs, contemporary pop numbers, bhajans and Urdu ghazals. Santosh Singh, the music teacher, told me that that he wanted all his students to become as "versatile" as Sonu Nigam.

I asked Santosh about the implicit institutional policy where the only form of musical training students allowed is in bhajans and other forms of devotional music. Would aspirations to be Sonu Nigam-like not undermine the "socio-moral discourse" (Stambach 2000: 171) that DSVV sought to propagate? And, did the students not risk "losing their material-moral-grounding" (Stambach 2000: 173) that lay at the heart of DSVV pedagogy? Santosh Singh appeared not to address my question at all. Instead, he said:

> You know, I have studied music at BHU [Banaras Hindu University] and I can't even begin to tell you about the *sanskar* [ritually correct behaviour or a respectful manner] I learned there. We always touched the feet of our teachers and as we ascended the stage for a performance, we also respectfully touched our heads to the steps….

Try as I might, I was unable to draw him out any further, as he appeared to consider this an adequate response to my inquiry. After this, he and his students went back to watching the Sonu Nigam video. The reason for his apparent disinterest in engaging with my questions became clearer later on.

Soon after the aforementioned encounter, the registrar of the university sent word that he wanted to see me. When we met, the registrar asked if I might be able to do some casual teaching in DSVV's classes titled Essence of Lifestyle Management and Time Management. These, he said, were part of "PD" (Personality Development) courses that DSVV had recently initiated. Some other nearby universities, such as the Garhwal University, he continued, had also expressed an interest in initiating these courses on their campus. Other subjects within PD included Ideal [sic] of a Successful Personality, Building Confidence through Public Speaking, Ideal Leadership, Developing Leadership Skills, Preparing Self Evaluation Chart and How to Become a Goal Achieving Personality. The courses, the registrar went on to say, were based on "the latest management theories as well global psychology principles."

There is, of course, a long history to the coupling of Western knowledge with Hindu-nationalist projects. These include "proof" of the fit between "ancient" Hindu principles and modern science (Chatterjee 1993; Prakash 1999), and specific demonstrations of the imbrications of "Ancient Precepts and Modern Teachings" with respect to sexuality (Pillay ca. 1940), and caste as a biological fact (Srivastava 2007). It is possible to invoke this lineage as an explanation for the contemporary situation, where an institution such as DSVV (and its parent body, the Gayatri Parivar) combine the production of a Hindu subject with ostensibly global discourses of scientific management and personality development. I would like to suggest, however, that these identity projects differ from those characteristic of the era of "high" nationalism that characterized the decades following independence from colonial rule. The most significant aspect of this is the decline of what might be called the anti-consumerist and pro-industrialization nationalism of the Five Year Plan state (Chatterjee 1993; Gupta 1998) and the subsequent incorporation of consumption as a way of life. Within this context, "consumer-citizenship" forms the cornerstone of quotidian relationships between the state, citizens and private interests (Fernandes 2006; Roy 2007). Hence, in the case of agitation by RWAs against the electricity price hike cited earlier, the issue of how resources should be distributed among different sections of the population was most frequently articulated in terms of the difference between "good" consumers (the middle classes) who were forced to subsidize "bad" consumers (the slum-dwellers) who "stole" electricity (Srivastava 2014). It is this aspect that plays out with a further twist in the case of DSVV.

Conclusion

DSVV is, as I have suggested, located within the twin contexts of Hindutva identity politics and non-middle-class (and economically disadvantaged) education. Practices of moral consumption within the campus are located at the juncture of these two aspects. The seemingly contradictory positioning of discourses of Hindu identity alongside global ones of "personality development" that draw on management science and psychology and that many teachers and students saw as linking DSVV to the broader consumer culture was a frequent topic of discussion among teachers and students. And, just as frequently, it was the juxtaposition that was itself invoked as providing a coherent rationale, as well as a reason for why DSVV *differed* from other arenas of consumption. The juxtaposition, as the registrar once explained to me, "proved" that DSVV provided training to its students such that they are able to take part in "global ways" and yet "return to Indian traditions" when required. This, he suggested, was what differentiated members of the Gayatri Pariwar from "other kinds of Indians" who took part in consumerism, but were not in control of this activity. The latter were, I interpret him as suggesting, determined by their modernity, unable to withdraw from it at will and, hence, effect the seamless movement between globally sourced PD courses and locally developed Hindu perspectives. The latter aspect constitutes moral consumption. Further, as a final rung to my argument, moral consumption is also the making of a moral middle class that seeks to differentiate itself from other, historically prior, economically better off and "westernized" middle classes. Hence, moral consumption, in the context of DSVV's relationship to the world beyond its gates, relates simultaneously to religious and class identities. It is also the context of the rise of new class fractions involved in the process of establishing "distinction" (Bourdieu 1984) within contexts of postnational consumer modernity. Further, postnationalism and the production of consumer citizens is crucial to the process of class differentiation, as it is only through intensive participation in consumption that one proves one's ability to return to "Indian" culture. This is what music teacher Santosh Singh meant to suggest, without stating it explicitly, when he juxtaposed the "sanskar" (training in morally approved behaviour) gained at Banaras Hindu University with the world of reality television. Unlike the case of Tanzanian youth, who are warned off consumerism by Christian evangelists but take part in consumerism *despite* the proscription, in the Indian case, consumerism is both a source of anxiety as well as a solution to it. This, perhaps, is the most significant aspect of the postnational era.

While I mean to describe the ways in which consumer culture constitutes significant and indispensable grounds for the making of contemporary religious identities in India, I am not suggesting that religious life is completely determined by the latter. The key focus of my discussion is the manner in which the two should be seen as interwoven contexts. The divine life of markets and consumerist manifestations of religiosity provide us with a way of understanding aspects of social life "as a combination of piety and economic calculation" (Osella and Osella 2009: S204). This way of thinking about the relationships between market forms and religious lives is not, of course, unique to India. Fenggang Yang (2005) provides an account of young Chinese Christians who favour McDonald's restaurants as a meeting place for religious gatherings, interpreting the restaurant space as one of "modernity and cosmopolitanism" (Yang 2005: 425). And, Daromir Rudnyckyj (2010) discusses an Indonesian context where "The creation of a spiritual economy involved elucidating and implementing a number of compatibilities in the ethical practice constitutive of both Islam and neoliberalism" (Rudnyckyj 2010: 23). While building upon analyses such as these (and others cited throughout the chapter), I have suggested that, for the Indian case, it is crucial to keep in mind an additional context that relates to the interweaving of consumer culture and religious life. This, I have argued, concerns the making of new class identities, located in the crucible of consumerist and religious activities.

DSVV and the gated localities of DLF City are, this chapter has suggested, sites that signify the making of a new relationship between markets and religiosity. In particular, they are contexts of an *explicit* dialogue that seeks to posit a contemporary Hindu identity whose religiosity is in tune with the cadence of neoliberal capitalism and whose neoliberalism is informed by the requirements of religious belief. This is the context – and the process – I have referred to as moral consumption. A significant background to this is what I have referred to as postnationalism, an era that sees the consolidation of new class identities built around consumerism and a relationship with the nation-state that is, increasingly, mediated through private capital. This is in marked contrast to the situation that prevailed in the decades immediately following the end of colonial rule. Postnationalism and moral consumption, are, in turn, the overlapping contexts for the making of divine markets where consumers find solace through spiritualizing their relationships with commodities and commoditizing relationships with spirituality.

Notes

1 For a more benign view of privatization, see Kanbur (2007).

2 The articles in the recently (2013) published volume edited by Nandini Gooptu on *Enterprise Culture in Neoliberal India* traverse a territory contiguous to that in the present discussion.

3 The inquiry was constituted under the chairmanship of the leading industrialist G. D. Birla and the report came to be known as the Birla Report (BR). In blunt terms, it concluded that "the story of the Trust is the story of failure" (Birla Report 1951: 7); that its record of slum-clearance had been "meagre" (3); the Town Expansion Schemes had merely resulted in the "freezing" rather than "development" of considerable land areas (3); it had commissioned neither a "civic survey" nor a "Master Plan"; and its strategy of selling land to the highest bidder had only exacerbated the housing problem (4).

4 Interviews with residents of DLF City, November 2011–December 2012.

5 Sanjeev K. Ahuja, "11.53 lakh population: The Numbers Lie, Say Residents", *Hindustan Times*, 10 August, 2010, p. 4. The website of the Municipal Corporation of Gurgaon pegs this figure at 876,824. Citizens groups complain that the under-reporting allows the Corporation to escape its responsibility of proper provisioning of infrastructure.

6 www.awgp.org/MissionVision/Philosophy (Accessed 1 May 2014).

7 The Vedic period refers to the ancient era during which Hinduism's oldest scriptures were composed. At the current time, right wing Hindu movements use terms such as "Vedic Hinduism" to refer to a "pure" form of religious belief and practice.

8 Saffron is the colour identified with both Hindu religious identity as well as right-wing religious groups that propound "Hindutva" (Hinduness) as a political movement. See, for example, Basu et al. (1993).

9 The Scientific Spirituality course seeks to demonstrate the rational basis of ancient Hindu religious thought and its relevance in the current period. This builds upon a modern Indian preoccupation with establishing parity between western and Indian knowledge regimes and belief systems (see, e.g., Chatterjee 1993 and Prakash 1999).

References

Anderson, Benedict. 1983. *Imagined Communities. Reflections on the Origin and Spread of Nationalism*. London: Verso.

Appadurai, Arjun. 1993. "Patriotism and Its Futures." *Public Culture* 11: 411–429.

Arabindoo, Pushpa. 2011. "'City of Sand': Stately Re-Imagination of Marina Beach in Chennai." *International Journal of Urban and Regional Research* 35(2): 379–401.

Bacchetta, Paola. 2004. *Gender in the Hindu Nation: RSS Women as Ideologues*. New Delhi: Women Unlimited.

Basu, Tapan, P. Datta, T. Sarkar, and S. Sen. 1993. *Khakhi Shorts and Saffron Flags: A Critique of the Hindu Right*. New Delhi: Orient Blackswan.

Baviskar, Amita. 2006. "Demolishing Delhi: World Class City in the Making." http://www.metamute.org/en/Demolishing-Delhi. Accessed 27 July 2015.

Birla Report / DIT Enquiry Report (Report of the Delhi Improvement Trust Enquiry Committee). 1951. Vol. I. New Delhi: Manager, Government of India Press.

Bourdieu, Pierre. 1984. *Distinction: A Social Critique of the Judgment of Taste*. Translated by Richard Nice. London and New York: Routledge.

Brosius, Christiane. 2010. *India's Middle-Class: New Forms of Urban Leisure, Prosperity and Consumption*. Delhi: Routledge.

Chatterjee, Partha. 1993. *The Nation and Its Fragments: Colonial and Postcolonial Histories*. Princeton, NJ: Princeton University Press.

Chopra, Rohit. 2008. *Technology and Nationalism in India: Cultural Negotiations from Colonialism to Cyberspace*. New York: Cambria Press.

Copeman, Jacob, and Aya Ikegame. 2012. "Guru Logics." *HAU: Journal of Ethnographic Theory* 2(1): 289–336.

Dasappa Kacker, Suneetha. 2005. "The DDA and the Idea of Delhi." In *The Idea of Delhi*, edited by Romi Khosla, 68–77. Mumbai: Marg.

de Alwis, Malathi, Satish Deshpande, Pradeep Jeganathan, Mary E. John, Nivedita Menon, Aditya Nigam, and S. Akbar Zaidi. 2009. "The Postnational Condition." *Economic and Political Weekly* 44(10): 35.

de Neve, Geert (2011) "'Keeping it in the Family': Work, Education and Gender Hierarchies Among Tiruppur's Industrial Capitalists." In *Being Middle Class. A Way of Life*, edited by Henrike Donner, 73–99. London: Routledge.

Desjarlais, Robert, and James Wilce. 2003. "The Cultural Construction of Emotion." In *The Oxford India Companion to Sociology and Social Anthropology*, edited by Veena Das, 1179–1204. New Delhi: Oxford University Press.

Donner, Henrike. 2011. "Gendered Bodies, Domestic Work and Perfect Families: New Regimes of Gender and Food in Bengali Middle-class Lifestyles." In *Being Middle-Class in India: A Way of Life*, edited by Henrike Donner, 47–72. London: Routledge.

Douglas, Mary, and Baron Isherwood. 1979. *The World of Goods*. London: Routledge.

Dupont, Véronique. 2005. "The Idea of a New Chic Delhi through Publicity Hype." In *The Idea of Delhi*, edited by Romi Khosla, 78–93. Mumbai: Marg.

Eickelman, Dale F., and Jon W. Anderson (eds.) 2003. *New Media in the Muslim World: The Emerging Public Sphere*. Bloomington: Indiana University Press.

Fernandes, Leela. 2006. *India's New Middle Class: Democratic Politics in an Era of Economic Reform*. Minneapolis: University of Minnesota Press.

Gellner, Ernest. 1997. *Nationalism*. London: Weidenfeld and Nicolson.

Ghertner, Asher. 2011. "Gentrifying the State, Gentrifying Participation: Elite Governance Programs in Delhi." *International Journal of Urban and Regional Research* 35(3): 504–532.

Gooptu, Nandini. 2013. *Enterprise Culture in Neoliberal India: Studies in Youth, Class, Work and Media*. London: Routledge.

Gupta, Akhil. 1998. *Postcolonial Development: Agriculture in the Making of Modern India*. Durham, NC: Duke University Press.

Hansen, Thomas Blom. 1999. *The Saffron Wave: Democracy and Hindu Nationalism in Modern India*. Princeton, NJ: Princeton University Press.

Hawley, John Stratton, and Srivatsa Goswami. 1981. *At Play with Krishna: Pilgrimage Dramas from Brindavan*. Princeton, NJ: Princeton University Press.

Jain, Madhu. 2001. "Tyrannies at Work." *Seminar*, First City? A Symposium on Remembering Delhi, No. 515: 38–41.

Kanbur, Ravi. 2007. *Development Disagreements and Water Privatization: Bridging the Divide.* Available at www.arts.cornell.edu/poverty/kanbur/WaterPrivatization.pdf (Accessed 18 January 18, 2014).

Khanna, Tarun. 2007. *Billions of Entrepreneurs: How China and India are Reshaping their Futures*. Boston: Harvard Business Press.

King, Anthony D. 2004. *Spaces of Global Cultures: Architecture, Urbanism, Identity*. London: Routledge.

Kumar, Krishna. 1993. "Hindu Revivalism and Education in North-Central India." In *Fundamentalisms and Society: Reclaiming the Sciences, the Family, and Education*, edited by Martin E. Marty and R. Scott Appleby, 536–557. Chicago: University of Chicago Press.

LaDousa, Chaise. 2005. "Disparate Markets: Language, Nation and Education in North India." *American Ethnologist* 32(3): 460–478.

Lal, Vinay. 2009. *Political Hinduism: The Religious Imagination in Public Spheres*. New Delhi: Oxford University Press.

Mazzarella, William. 2003. *Shoveling Smoke: Advertising and Globalization in Contemporary India*. Durham, NC: Duke University Press.

Meyer, Birgit. 2009. "Introduction: From Imagined Communities to Aesthetic Formations: Religious Mediations, Sensational Forms, and Styles of Binding." In *Aesthetic Formations: Media, Religion, and the Senses*, edited by Birgit Meyer, 1–30. New York: Palgrave Macmillan.

Ojha, Abhilasha. 1999. "RWAs will soon have direct control over sanitation and community halls." *Indian Express*, January 12, www.indianexpress.com/res/ple/ie/daily/19991201 (Accessed 11 December 2014).

Oosterbaan, Martijn. 2009. "Purity and the Devil: Community, Media, and the Body. Pentecostal Adherents in a Favela in Rio de Janeiro." In *Aesthetic Formations: Media, Religion, and the Senses*, edited by Birgit Meyer, 53–70. New York: Palgrave Macmillan.

Osella, Filippo, and Caroline Osella. 2009. "Muslim Entrepreneurs in Public Life between India and the Gulf: Making Good and Doing Good." *Journal of the Royal Anthropological Institute* 15(s1): S202–221.

Pandit, S. S. 1974. *A Critical Study of the Contribution of the Arya Samaj to Indian Education*. New Delhi: Sarvadeshik Arya Pratinidhi Sabha.

Phadke, Shilpa. 2007. "Dangerous Liaisons: Women and Men, Risk and Reputation in Mumbai." *Economic and Political Weekly* 42(17): 1510–1518.

Pillay, A. P. ca. 1940. *The Art of Love and Sane Sex Living: Based on Ancient Precepts and Modern Teachings*. Bombay: D.B. Taraporevala and Sons.

Pow, Choon-Piew. 2007. "Securing the 'Civilised' Enclaves: Gated Communities and the Moral Geographies of Exclusion in (Post-) Socialist Shanghai." *Urban Studies* 44(8): 1539–1558.

Prakash, Gyan. 1999. *Another Reason: Science and the Imagination of Modern India*. Princeton, NJ: Princeton University Press.

Roy, Srirupa. 2007. *Beyond Belief: India and the Politics of Postcolonial Nationalism*. Durham, NC: Duke University Press.

Rudnyckyj, Daromir (2010) *Spiritual Economies. Islam, Globalization and the Afterlife of Development*. Ithaca, NY: Cornell University Press.

Sethi, Aman. 2005. "The Price of Reforms." *Frontline* 22(19): 5–6.

Singer, Milton. 1972. *When a Great Tradition Modernizes: An Anthropological Approach to Indian Civilization*. Chicago: University of Chicago Press.

Sirari, Tanvi. 2006. *Civil Uprisings in Contemporary India*. Centre for Civil Society Working Paper No. 161, p. 5. Delhi: Centre for Civil Society.

Srinivas, Smriti. 2001. *Landscapes of Urban Memory: The Sacred and the Civic in India's High-Tech City*. Minneapolis: University of Minnesota Press.

2008. *In the Presence of Sai Baba: Body, City and Memory in a Transnational Religious Movement*. London: Brill.

Srinivas, Tulasi. 2010. "Building Faith: Religious Pluralism, Pedagogical Urbanism, and Governance in the Sathya Sai Sacred City." *International Journal of Hindu Studies* 13(3): 301–336.

Srivastava, Sanjay. 2007. *Passionate Modernity. Sexuality, Class and Consumption in India*. New Delhi: Routledge.

2011. "Urban Spaces, Disney-divinity and the Moral Middle Classes in Delhi." In *Elite and Everyman: The Cultural Politics of the Indian Middle Classes*, edited by Amita Baviskar and Raka Ray, 364–90. New Delhi: Routledge.

2012. "National Identity, Kitchens and Bedrooms: Gated Communities and New Narratives of Space in India." In *The Global Middle Classes: Theorizing through Ethnography*, edited by Mark Liechty, Carla Freeman, and Rachel Heiman, 57–84. Santa Fe: School of Advanced Research Press.

2014. "Urban Spaces, Post-nationalism and the Making of the Consumer-Citizen in India." In *New Cultural Histories of India*, edited by Partha Chatterjee, Tapati Guha Thakurta, and Bodhisattava Kar, 409–436. New Delhi: Oxford University Press.

Stambach, Amy. 2000. "Evangelism and Consumer Culture in Northern Tanzania." *Anthropological Quarterly* 73(4): 171–179.

Sundar, Nandini. 2004. "Teaching to Hate: RSS' Pedagogical Programme." *Economic and Political Weekly* 39(16): 1605–1612.

Uberoi, Patricia. 2008. "Aspirational Weddings: The Bridal Magazine and the Canons of 'Decent Marriage'." In *Patterns of Middle Class Consumption in India and China*, edited by Christophe Jaffrelot and Peter van der Veer, 230–262. New Delhi: SAGE.

van Wessel, Margit. 2004. "Talking about Consumption: How an Indian Middle-Class Dissociates from Middle-class Life." *Cultural Dynamics* 16 (1): 93–116.

Yang, Fenggang. 2005. "Lost in the Market, Saved at McDonald's: Conversion to Christianity in Urban China." *Journal for the Scientific Study of Religions* 44(4): 423–441.

5 Merit Economies in Neoliberal Times: Halal Troubles in Contemporary Sri Lanka

Farzana Haniffa, University of Colombo

On the evening of 15 June 2014, violence erupted in southern Sri Lanka. During two days of violence, Sinhala mobs systematically attacked Muslim shops and homes in the towns of Aluthgama, Dharga town, Welipanna and Beruwela, causing three deaths and massive damage to property.[1] Anti-Muslim sentiment had been simmering in postwar Sri Lanka for some time, and was mobilized through the 2012 launch of the BoduBalaSena (BBS), a Sinhala Buddhist nationalist group led by monks.[2] Their massive public meetings – featuring saffron-robed monks and white-clad lay audiences, loudspeakers blaring rhetorical exhortations to violence – led to many incidents of harassment of Muslims throughout the island. The first issue that the BBS chose by which to mobilize Buddhists against Muslims was *halal* certification of consumer goods.

In late 2012, the BBS objected to halal labels appearing on products on retail shelves, arguing that it was an imposition of the practice of one religious group onto citizens of other religions. They stated that while halal labelling was permissible for export purposes, if practiced locally it should be restricted to Muslim-only shops, perhaps run by mosques, and not forced on those who were not Muslim. This chapter examines how Sri Lanka's halal economy was variously characterized by the BBS, Muslim organizations and press commentators, both in terms of the market logic that has been applied to the Sri Lankan economy since the 1977 liberalization and in terms of a particular postwar modality of nationalism. I will argue that the ethnic animosity targeting Muslims in contemporary Sri Lanka was precipitated by long-term policies of economic liberalization which, in recent years, have been framed by the logics of neoliberalism. Whilst the BBS and other nationalist groups wanted Muslims (and other minorities) to acknowledge their place as a secondary social group in a Sinhala-Buddhist nation, they were also committed to the government's development strategy directed towards making Sri Lanka more economically competitive. Committed to the state's project of neoliberal reforms, the Muslim entrepreneurial and professional classes, in turn, analysed the crisis in economic terms. They engaged in a resignification of halal purely as an economic activity. They anticipated that a "professional" management of the halal economy was what was required for Muslims to retain the right to certification and protect Islamic consumption practices, while continuing to provide a necessary service to the large business houses that provided Sri Lankan halal products to the global market. The Muslim business elite saw the All Ceylon Jamiathul Ulema (ACJU) theologians' administration of halal certification as the problem, owing to their overtly Muslim identification (long beards, Muslim caps and thawb). These vestments were seen as inappropriate to the work of running a business, and their lack of acceptance within the business community was finally considered the element requiring change. Within the Muslim business elite's self-assessment of the problem, a clean-shaven, tie-wearing "corporate" person with the accompanying language abilities was considered more appropriate to the process of resignifying halal as a purely *business* practice and a response to market demands (Ong 2006: 6). The establishment of the new Halal Accreditation Council (HAC) in January 2014 won halal both legitimacy among the business elite and some respite from the BBS. However, the continuation of attacks against Muslims revealed what many had known all along: the BBS and the regime needed a Muslim Other against which to project its criticisms. The regime would permit the mobilization of anti-Muslim sentiment so long as it was politically expedient.

Sri Lanka is home to four major ethno-religious communities. Although most of the population is Sinhala-Buddhist, there are substantial Hindu, Muslim and Christian (mainly Catholic) minorities.[3] Sri Lanka was engaged in a civil war from the late 1970s to 2009, in which the state engaged in a protracted struggle with the Liberation Tigers of Tamil Eelam (LTTE), a militant organization claiming to represent the Tamil minority fighting for a separate Tamil homeland in the north and east of the country. In 2009 the government armed forces defeated the LTTE in a brutal and controversial campaign resulting in thousands of Tamil civilian deaths. In the aftermath of the war, a state-endorsed Sinhala triumphal ethno-nationalism influenced all aspects of politics and society in the country. It is in the aftermath of state repression of the LTTE and, by extension, of Tamils that emergent Buddhist nationalist groups – especially the BoduBalaSena (BBS), RavanaBalaya and SinhalaRavaya – started to target the Muslims (Haniffa 2016 (a)).[4]

Muslims are demographically dispersed throughout the island, with significant concentrations in the western, southern central and eastern provinces. Since the 1980s Muslim communities have been influenced by reformist groups such as Tablighi Jama'at, Salafi/Tauheed groups and Jamaathi Islami (Zackariah and Shanmugaratnam 1997; Nuhman 2007; Haniffa 2013).[5] Reformist-inspired transformations in self-presentation and a greater emphasis on authenticated practices have accompanied the emergence of "Muslim" forms of consumption (Deeb 2006). A halal economy for food and other goods took root, together with Islamic banks and a "white list" of equities suitable for Muslim investors because they do not engage in "haram"[6] business practices. Sri Lanka's largest group of Muslim theologians, the All Ceylon Jamiatul Ulema (ACJU), provided certification designating food and other commodities as halal (permissible according to Islam). In operation since the 1990s, goods certified as halal by the ACJU – food products, bottled water, cosmetics and drugs, for instance – carried a label on the packaging and were widely available in local supermarkets and retail outlets.[7]

Methods and Fieldwork

As a citizen of Sri Lanka in 2012, I witnessed the emergence of the BBS as a formidable force in the Sri Lankan public sphere. I observed with unease their increasingly strident public stance regarding halal. I viewed it from the perspectives of both an academic studying Sri Lanka's postwar transition and as someone who might be confronted with the violence that such agitation appeared to inevitably precipitate. I participated in many community gatherings to discuss the phenomenon and how best to address it. I was in the margins of many of these meetings as one of just five or six women among seventy to eighty people. I was also part of an organization, the Secretariat for Muslims, that documented hate speech and discriminatory incidents reported in the press, and conducted briefings for local and international actors – nongovernmental organizations (NGOs), members of the diplomatic community, UN agency representatives – on the growing anti-Muslim sentiment. When the halal controversy was gaining momentum I tracked BBS press conferences and collected newspaper articles and YouTube footage of BBS rallies and television appearances. Owing to increasing tensions and incidents of anti-Muslim violence, I did not attend BBS meetings or attempt to interview BBS members. My analysis of the BBS, then, is based mostly on publicly available material. I also interviewed Muslim friends and colleagues who were closely involved with attempting to resolve the halal issue, including members of the Muslim Council and the CEO of the Halal Accreditation Council.

Of the many Muslim communities dispersed throughout the island, the southern Muslims are widely viewed as traders or businesspeople and often represent themselves as such (Ismail 1995). Muslim-owned businesses are a visible presence in the Sri Lankan. These range from the Brandix group (one of the largest apparel exporting companies) and Akbar brothers (which has large-scale plantation holdings), to retail clothing chains such as Fashion Bug, No Limit, and Hameedias. Moreover, almost all small towns in the Sinhala speaking areas of the country have Muslim shops and eateries engaging in small-scale food, textile, hardware, and other retail commerce. The Muslim community at large includes people from all classes and engages in all forms of employment;

Muslims constitute a substantial part of the urban poor of Colombo. The professional middle class that emerged in Sri Lanka in the aftermath of 1977 economic liberalization includes sections of the Muslim community as well. The adoption of Islamic styles of self-presentation and fashion makes the Muslim middle class's conspicuous consumption patterns extremely visible, especially in Colombo.

Since the 1990s, Sri Lanka supermarkets carried halal-labelled consumer goods, halal certified restaurants served special meals for *ifthar* (the breaking of the fast during Ramadan) and specialized businesses catered to the consumer needs of the Muslim middle class. In a country in which Muslims are a minority and where successive regimes have been less than sympathetic to ethno-religious minorities, the market had nonetheless been well equipped to enable Islamic piety by facilitating Islamic consumption through halal labelling and sophisticated choices of Muslim attire.[8] Moreover, a substantial quantity of the country's food exports have targeted Muslim markets in the Middle East and Southeast Asia, hence requiring halal certification.[9] However, by March 2013 the BBS's anti-halal campaign had escalated tensions. Ultimately a settlement was reached – mediated by the country's Chamber of Commerce – where the ACJU, producers and retailers agreed to remove halal-labelled goods from retail shops. The settlement had the effect of reinforcing Muslims' status as the quiescent minority.

The 2009 military victory over the LTTE legitimized nationalist monks' wartime ethno-religious ideology which defined Tamils as a minority politically inferior to the Sinhala Buddhist majority. The Tamil nationalist project had envisioned the creation of a separate state of Tamil Eelam, or, failing that, a substantial dismantling of the country's unitary state structure to give more powers to the regions on a federal model. Groups of nationalist monks, to which the BBS's antecedents can be traced, accommodated none of the Tamil claims, and called for decisive military intervention to defeat the rebels. In the postwar years, the BBS has sought to marginalize other minority groups, Muslims in particular, and to ensure that the abject status of all minorities is socially and institutionally recognized (Haniffa 2016(a)). It received clear institutional support from the state, for which we must understand the economic causes that underpin ethno-nationalism in Sri Lanka.

Economic Liberalization in Sri Lanka

In 1977, Sri Lanka embraced policies that were later to be named neoliberal and was thereby among the first countries of the global south to adopt "economic liberalization" policies (following Chile and Indonesia: Venugopal 2011b). After the United National Party's electoral victory that year, President J. R. Jayawardena promoted an "open economy". This was a response to the crisis faced by the country that decade caused by the failure of development policies of industrialization for import substitution. At various stages from 1956 to 1977 the country had been ruled by the Sri Lanka Freedom Party (SLFP), which instituted an economic policy of state accumulation through nationalization, regulation of private enterprise and import substitution (Lynch 1999). Although somewhat stymied by the war, the economic transformation initiated in 1977 by Jayawardena's radical economic policies entailed, in subsequent years, the introduction of trade liberalization and foreign investment, the curtailment of labour rights to allow for greater labour flexibility and various rounds of privatizations of state enterprises and services (Venugopal 2011b; Kadirgamar 2013).[10] The end of the war in 2009 inaugurated a new wave of economic liberalization sustained by an influx of foreign direct investment. Following the 2008 global financial crisis, global capital pursued a strategy of investments in the emerging market of countries such as Sri Lanka (Kadirgamar 2013). Today prosperity is palpable in Colombo, for some. European luxury cars, the beautification of Colombo, the construction of expensive hotels and apartment blocks, the expansion of the country's main road network and large investments in the tourism sector suggest a chimera of economic growth. For the middle and upper classes equipped with the skills necessary for success in a liberalized economy, imported luxury cars and shiny new apartment blocks indeed stand for the materialization of the country's postwar promises of fast economic development. This prosperity, though, has been accompanied by rising inequalities, consumption-driven indebtedness among the poor, a military occupation of the (Tamil-majority) north and militarization of everyday life in the south of the Island, increasing social unrest and the violent suppression of dissent. Five years after the end of the war, the Rajapaksa regime continuously reiterated that the country was well on its way to reaching the goals of becoming the economic "wonder of Asia". The island has already been declared a middle-income country, and it is anticipated that it will reach high-middle-income status in the next few years.[11]

Being the first country in South Asia to accompany state-led developmentalism with market-driven policies of economic liberalization, Sri Lanka has been quick to absorb neoliberal ideologies and practices underpinning and fostered by the globalization of capital. However, as many have pointed out, in the Sri Lankan case, liberalization was not accompanied by a shrinking of the state. In fact, the state has expanded considerably. As Ong notes, neoliberalism is also a "bio-political mode of governing that centres on the capacity and potential of individuals and the population as living resources that may be harnessed and managed by governing regimes" (2006: 6). In such regimes, there are two kinds of optimizing technologies in operation: technologies of subjectivity (by the self) and technologies of subjection by the state and other authorities.

Of particular concern for this chapter, technologies of subjectivity entail the production of "knowledge and expert systems to induce self-animation and self-government so that citizens can optimize choices, efficiency and competitiveness in turbulent market conditions" (Ong 2006: 6).

Given its long engagement with liberalized economic practices, the Sri Lankan private sector – where one finds some of the most obvious beneficiaries of liberalization – includes a middle class and an elite that subscribes to the ethics of conduct within a neoliberal system. Middle-class Muslims who participated in the liberalized economy, but who also pursued a spiritual life centred on the accumulation of religious merits, engaged in such self-animation and self-government towards an optimization of "choices, efficiency and competitiveness". They did so not only to deal with turbulent market conditions but also, as I have argued elsewhere, to manage the tensions of an increasingly ethnically polarized social context (Haniffa 2013), and to foster individual and collective religiosity under the demanding extractive ethical regimes of the liberalized economy (Povinelli 2006). The self-regulation characteristic of the urban upper-middle-class elite, however, is not reflected among the working classes and the regional middle classes that constitute the country's primary voter base. Among these populations, the large state with its multiple patronage networks persists.

Many analysts of post-liberalization Sri Lanka have attempted to theorize a connection between the escalation of the ethno-religious conflict and the shift in the country's economic policies. Different theories regarding the impact of reforms on different ethnic communities have been offered (Bastian 1990; Moor 1990; Gunasinghe 2004; Venugopal 2011b). However, timelines of economic change and increased state and insurgent violence seem to follow similar trajectories that predate liberalization; the youth insurrection of 1971 followed austerity measures by the United Front government. After liberalization in 1977, the country's most intense ethnic violence occurred in 1983. The 1983 riots are in fact documented as being instigated with state support. State violence often accompanied state ideology as borne out both in the post-election violence of 1977 directed mainly against Malaiyaha Tamils and the anti-Tamil pogrom of 1983. As I have discussed elsewhere, it is noteworthy that the state seems to collude with the working classes when attacking the lives and properties of minorities (Haniffa 2016(b)). The Rajapaksa regime had dynastic political interests but their strategies drew from a set of tried and tested practices. The government that came to power through the presidential elections of 2015 moved away, at least rhetorically, from ethnonationalist populism, but it needed to adopt measures such as decreasing fuel prices and approving wage hikes in its first budget to maintain its relevance among the poorer classes.

Halal in Sri Lanka: Moral Economies as Merit Economies

Prior to the emergence of the reformist piety movement and economic liberalization, halal was a loosely practiced non-formal institution with particular emphases in different regional settings. As I was growing up in a struggling middle-class household in Colombo in the early 1980s, halal meant not eating pork, and consuming only fish when in doubt about meat dishes in non-Muslim friends' houses. The 1977 open economy led to the emergence of a large consuming middle class of all ethnicities, and the capital itself was transformed with the establishment of supermarkets and restaurants, including global fast food brands and local franchises. The Islamic piety movement's success occurred in tandem with economic liberalization, and consuming goods in keeping with the new religiosity became one way of engaging in a Muslim merit economy as well.[12] Muslims organize their religious rituals and everyday bodily practices according to guidance regarding merit accumulation from the Qur'an and *hadith*. Instructions that exist for the minute actions of everyday existence that lead to greater merit accumulation – such as licking one's fingers after a meal before cleaning one's hands – pervade the *hadith*; learning different *dua* or supplications for different acts is also pursued as an act of additional merit accumulation by Muslims. Muslims then engage many such "technique(s) of optimization" to bolster their merit accumulation processes.[13] Practicing halal consumption and the decision of how strictly one adheres to halal requirements may involve calculations regarding merit accumulation.[14] Practicing Muslims anticipate that the merit accumulated will finally outweigh their sins on judgement day. The halal food industry soon became equipped to facilitate Muslims' accumulation of merit through consuming halal-certified products in supermarkets and patronizing halal restaurant chains.[15] Of course, these middle-class Muslims were, at the same time, conspicuously engaging in middle-class consumption practices – patronizing supermarkets and restaurants, purchasing fashionable clothing and so on.

In the Buddhist groups' rhetoric against halal, the All Ceylon Jamiathul Ulema (ACJU) – the council of theologians responsible for administering the halal certification process – stood accused of implementing a "Muslim extremist" plan. The ACJU involvement with the halal certification process began in 1999, and the first halal certification was granted in 2000 to two companies producing poultry products. The ACJU engaged professionals from the fields of food science, agriculture and chemistry prior to beginning to certify food-processing establishments in 2004. In a bid for greater professionalization, in 2005 they visited halal certification bodies in Malaysia, Indonesia, Singapore and South Africa and sought government authorization to be the sole certification provider for Sri Lanka in 2006. There had been an institution issuing certifications prior to the Jamiathul Ulema, but with the increasing influence of reformism and Muslims' preoccupation with authenticity and authentication (Deeb 2006), the ACJU, as a more clearly authoritative entity with "gatekeeper" aspirations, was considered by sections of the Muslim community (and endorsed by the political leadership) to be best suited to ensure halal compliance.[16] Many Muslims claimed that the systematization of halal had been driven by the expansion of halal-certified exports to Muslim majority countries. Providing acceptable certification was a way of placing the Sri Lankan economy within the flourishing circuits of halal for profit, and many Muslims believed that halal certification was systematized not for the benefit of individual consumers but rather to benefit big non-Muslim exporters. It seems to have achieved both. The ACJU website claimed that as of 2011 they had certified 4,000 products from 150 Sri Lankan companies as halal.[17]

Five years after its establishment as an accrediting body, the ACJU attempted to get government recognition as the sole legally entitled body to provide certification. The attempt failed in that, according to the government's commitment to market principles, the state could not endorse a monopoly even on the provision of religious authentication. Other groups that also offered certification protested against the ACJU. Therefore two gazette notifications, one giving the ACJU sole authority for halal certification and the second demanding an accrediting agency to provide authentication prior to the usage of the halal label, were rescinded.

When the halal controversy erupted in early 2013, there was no directive on halal by the Consumer Affairs Authority. Muslim representatives' claims that the ACJU's halal certification was similar to accreditations offered by institutions such as the Sri Lanka Standards Institute (SLS) were viewed with suspicion.[18] The ACJU was accused – by the then-leader of the opposition, among others – of having no legal basis to provide certification. The opposition leader echoed sentiments that were widely expressed in both traditional and social media: halal was said to be immoral, illegal and an unethical trade practice.[19] The ACJU's claim that it was issuing certification on the basis of its religious authority, and the endorsement received from international halal certification bodies, was considered inadequate. The lack of state authorization for halal certification meant that the halal accreditation done by the Jamiathul Ulema had no legitimacy within the world of commercial transactions.[20] Muslims who had long revered the ACJU's authority had to face the startling revelation that what they held to be authoritative had no relevance in the broader public sphere of the country.

State endorsement of halal certification was seen as a requirement for public, open market legitimacy. The Muslim community's response to the accusation of illegitimacy was to make the authority of the institution that succeeded the ACJU more recognizable in an idiom that was not confined to Muslims alone. The Halal Accreditation Council was registered according to the Companies Act and branded itself as a "market responsive" and a "market friendly institution."[21]

Halal Troubles

On 19 November 2012, we saw the secretary of the BoduBalaSena, the soon to be famous Venerable Galagodaththe Gnanasara, first introducing halal as a problem on primetime television news. I later watched the entire press conference on the BBS website. The Ven. Gnanasara stated that the BBS was looking to raise awareness about "this evil conspiracy called halal that was forcibly, unethically and in contravention of humanist principles, foisted on to the heads (*hisgedi*) of all Sri Lankan people, Buddhist, Catholic and Hindu alike, regardless of religious orientation."[22] He stated further that "in the aftermath of a decisive military victory to solve a troubling conflict, Muslim extremism [*Islam anthavadaya*] was spreading across the island in various guises and casting its dark shadow." The monk said the BoduBalaSena was struck by the presence of a "new" logo on many of the products they had received as alms that month. "What was this new logo?" he asked, "It was Halal!" he said, rhetorically answering his own question. "Goods that were brought as offerings to the temple were first dedicated to Allah." He further stated,

> Muslims are demanding halal by threatening businesses that they will not buy food that was not halal, and will not patronize establishments that were not halal.[23] This is a Mafia, this is highway robbery! (*Mankollakaamak*). If ten percent of the products are halal we don't have a problem, but why should the remaining ninety percent be halal? We have to inform the country about this. If this is so important let them have a shop in each mosque. All the mosques are in central urban locations, so let them have shops in there. We have no problem with that.

The Ven. Gnanasara then criticized the ACJU certification process, saying,

> "If we are taking halal certification we have to give them the recipe! These are trade secrets, they are asking for the secrets of our country! Of our race (jathiya)!"[24]

The monk was quick, however, to draw a distinction between halal certification available locally and that which is done to enable export, intoning, "We have no problems about halal for the sake of export to foreign countries."

Later in the press conference he revealed:

> The kind of freedoms that the Muslims are enjoying in this country, they don't have anywhere else in the world; *not even in their own country*! (emphasis mine) Even the Muslims who live in the Middle East don't have the freedoms that the Muslims here have. We won't let this freedom be the death of our race (Jathiya)!

The BBS critique of halal used both the logic of Sinhala majoritarianism and the language of free market competition. In asserting that halal was imposed on

Sinhalese businesses by Muslim threats to boycott non-halal establishments, the Ven. Gnanasara suggested that Muslims were unduly interfering with the laws of supply and demand. In referring to halal as a violation of trade secrets, the monk was invoking copyright and confidentiality. Halal certification, here, is represented as a conspiracy to undermine businesses' confidentiality and thereby to affect the economy of the Sinhalese. According to the monk, if halal was necessary, it should be executed in a localized and limited manner. In other words, these minority practices should be ghettoized. The BBS was calling for the isolation and distancing of Muslims and Muslim consumption from ethnic others. Yet the monk also accused the Muslims of using halal to introduce a *samajabedumvadaya* (social separatism).

The monk does not represent the expansion of halal labelling as a market-driven response to Muslims' consumption needs, but as an attempt by Muslims to impose consumption of halal goods on Sinhalese, to compel Sinhala businesses to sell halal goods, and to access trade secrets of Sinhala businesses. The monk rhetorically characterizes Muslims as aliens in Sri Lanka by referring to the Middle East as "their own country." The monk later drew selectively on popular media discourses about Al Qaeda and Hamas: "extremist" movements to which local Muslims supposedly had allegiances. Soon newspaper articles, Facebook pages, blogs and political discussions on television featured the issue of halal and questioned its legitimacy as both a social and an economic practice.

The response of the Muslim business elite and middle class, as I frequently encountered it at community meetings and in everyday conversation, was summed up by the lawyer Hejaz Hisbulla:

> When the big international fast food chains came to Sri Lanka they did not have halal certification. However, subsequently most of these chains went "halal". This had nothing to do with any "Islamist" conspiracy to take over Sri Lanka. It was a pure case of demand and supply and the pursuit of profit. The same applies to Islamic banking... So this whole brouhaha about "halal" really defies logic. The only reason why the All Ceylon Jamiyathul Ulema (ACJU) is a body of choice for it's the only body that the Muslim consumers accept and find legitimate and in marketing – [the] consumer is king.[25]

Thus, for Hisbulla, halal certification was driven by a search for profit that was well within the norms of market practice. It had nothing to do with a Muslim compulsion to subject non-Muslims to halal food, as was being argued by the BBS. Such recourses to the market spoke to the Muslim elite's interest in portraying halal not as a requirement of Islamic practice imposed on other communities, but as the instrumentalization of Muslim cultural practices for the benefit of the Sri Lankan export economy as a whole.

Sinhala Buddhist representatives frequently criticized halal practices for impeding food sharing between ethnic and religious groups in Sri Lanka and contributing to the social distance between Muslims and others. It rarely featured, however, in Muslims' analyses or in thinking about solutions. While I heard many Muslims articulate a critique of the social distance cultivated by the reformists, practicing halal was never understood as exacerbating this distance. Udaya Gamanpila, then a representative of the Sinhala nationalist political party the Jathika Hela Urumaya (JHU), wrote an article with reference to eating *kiribath* (milk rice), for the Sinhala and Tamil New Year.[26] He argued that if Muslims would throw away the *kiribath* because it was not halal, there was no point in sharing it with Muslims, as was traditional in the mixed neighbourhoods in which he grew up. Muslim commentator Hameed Abdul Kareem responded to Gamanpila's essay about sharing *kiribath* by accusing him of peddling a narrow political agenda.[27] Kareem addressed the issue by dismissing Gamanpila's inadequate understanding of the halal principle as a deliberate lie: vegetarian food such as *kiribath* was halal by definition and there was no question of throwing it away. I read Gamanpila's critique as reflecting Sinhala Buddhist anxieties regarding minority assertions of social superiority through rejecting food sharing. Kareem was not able to understand Gamanpila's position as anything other than disingenuousness.

The BoduBalaSena held a public meeting in Kandy in February 2013 where more references were made to food-sharing practices. One of the monks stated:

> Now the Sinhala New Year is approaching. And you know what they say about the Sinhala New Year. While we Sinhalese and Tamils celebrate the New Year the persons who really celebrate the New Year are the Mudalalis. And you know which Mudalalis. The ones that wear caps. Now you may have unknowingly gone and patronized their food shops. Do you know that there is a law in their Qur'an? The law is that anyone who is not a Muslim, anyone who belongs to another race, another religion, if they are giving either food or drink to such a person, they must spit three times in to it before they serve it to that person. The tea that you have had would have been spat on; the food that you have eaten at a Muslim hotel would have been spat on without your knowledge. That is the Sharia law, that is what their Al-Qur'an says, that is their belief and that is how they treat anyone who does not believe in their Allah.[28]

Most Muslims were outraged by this statement, which they saw as blasphemous and also as representative of the BBS monks' strategy of lying with impunity to mislead the Sinhala masses. Some read it as a strategy to discourage Sinhalese from patronizing the small Muslim retail food shops and tea houses ubiquitous in the country. At the Secretariat for Muslims, we used this example in our information sessions to illustrate the concerted attempt to affect Muslims' economies and livelihoods.

This depiction also invokes Muslims' halal culture and their perceived sense of superiority over others. This was not immediately appreciated by Muslims who suddenly found themselves under attack in all forms of media. The status of food exchange is an indication of a group's place in Sri Lankan caste/community hierarchy. As described by Marriott in relation to caste in Hindu culture, those who can refuse to accept food from others but are able to feed these same people are generally considered to be (or claim) higher status in the caste hierarchy.[29] Muslims, although a minority who according to prevailing Sinhala nationalist logics should consider themselves to be lesser than the Sinhalese, were accused of claiming social superiority by refusing to consume common food. We can read the logic of caste hierarchy not only in Sinhalese framings of the halal issue in terms of status claims, but also in the monk's reference to pollution via bodily fluids. By claiming that Muslims spit on food served to other communities, the monk mobilized caste sensibilities regarding pollution to persuade Sinhala Buddhists to avoid Muslim food and boycott Muslim restaurants. I am arguing here that halal invoked a variety of responses in the Sinhala populace of which their Muslim interlocutors were barely aware.[30]

The growing communal tension engendered by the anti-halal campaign took the shape of death threats to Muslim shop owners in a remote town in the Kurunegala district, attacks against mosques, harassment of Muslims dressed in identifiable Islamic clothing, vitriolic articles in the press and monks using all available platforms (including religious schools and almsgiving for the dead) to talk about the Muslim threat. There were also reports of small businesses being compelled to close down due to lack of patronage from non-Muslim customers. The tension reached such a fever pitch in March 2013 that most Muslims expected riots to be the inevitable outcome of the anti-halal protests. Those who were old enough recalled the tension and rumour-mongering that thirty years earlier led to the July 1983 anti-Tamil pogrom, seen by many as the beginning of Sri Lanka's protracted conflict. These fears were not misplaced. In June 2014, almost a year after the halal issue had been "resolved," the inevitable finally took place; organized anti-Muslim violence erupted in Aluthgama in southern Sri Lanka.

Muslim Reactions to the BBS

In January and February 2013 I was invited by the Muslim Council to attend two meetings: one at the Hotel Ranmuthu in Kollupitiya and the other at the Moors Islamic Cultural Home building in Wellawatta. Both gatherings were held in large meeting rooms with provisions for prayers, and were attended by the Jamiathul Ulema, minor politicians, the Young Men's Muslim Association, a large representation from the business community, academics, members of different reformist groups and more. The participants were largely English-speaking[31] middle- and upper-class people.

These meetings featured a brief introduction from the organizers and then an open floor for people to both voice their concerns and offer solutions. Most speakers stated that something needed to be done, even the withdrawal of halal, if it was going to "diffuse" the tension. However, there was a clear understanding among those gathered at both meetings that what was happening was not simply about halal. Many saw halal as a "non-issue" turned into something contentious for political purposes. Both meetings also included questions as to what Muslims should do if violence erupted. At the second meeting, the formation of an advisory council comprising a group of community leaders was suggested, and a plan to set up committees tasked with different activities was presented. A list of emergency phone numbers for a lawyers' group that was on standby as a rapid response team was handed out. Some participants stated with bravado, "If they hit us we will hit back!" During the meetings many repeatedly stated that the current regime, if not directly behind the attacks, was colluding with BBS. The local government representatives that attended the community meetings were especially vociferous. One person described how the BBS, after receiving a fifteen-minute appointment with the president of Sri Lanka, spoke with him for two hours. When the Muslim representatives met the president on the same issue, he had little sympathy, they said. President Rajapaksa allegedly accused the Muslims of building too many mosques and colonizing Sinhala neighbourhoods.

Tensions over the halal issue were seriously affecting Muslim businesses and many wanted a quick resolution. Others argued, "If we give in now, they will raise some other issue later on." While many agreed and were sympathetic to this stance, others stated that if the halal controversy was not addressed immediately, the entire April season's sales would be lost, and many would have to go out of business.[32] During this meeting an academic asked the ACJU in very strong terms to shut down the halal certification process. Members of the ACJU urged patience and wanted people to wait until the Parliamentary Select Committee on halal made a decision on its findings.

Halal and the Muslim Self-critique

At these meetings, there was a substantial element of self-critique in relation to the commercialization of halal and the minutiae of piety. Many claimed that Muslims ate halal food even before certification and that the entire certification process was little more than a business enterprise. Through raising this point, they were calling for a rejection of the commodification of halal. There was also criticism of Muslims' large investment in the symbolic accoutrements of piety and the effect that it was having on other ethnic communities' perception of Muslims. Many spoke critically about the new expressions or forms of Muslim piety; invoking the notion of *ahlaak*,[33] one person argued that the Muslims as a community had spent too much time on outward manifestations of faith. Many used the phrase, "We have to live here," targeting reformists who had for long years thought of community only in exclusively Muslim terms and of ethnic and religious others as a foil against whom Muslimness needed to be constantly reinforced (Haniffa 2013). There were critical comments about the manner in which Muslims sometimes called Sri Lanka "Dar Ul-Kufar" (the Land of the Kafir) and referred to the country as "the land of the Sinhalese."[34] The halal issue became a flash point for all the problems that Muslims were facing as a consequence of the intense engagement with reformist piety movements during the time of the war. Many who had long been uncomfortable with reformists took the opportunity to criticize their practices openly. They expressed anger at the manner in which southern Muslims' longstanding and cultivated goodwill with the majority community had faded during the time of the conflict, when the reformists were most successful (Haniffa 2013, 2012). Some who were well entrenched in a southern Muslim political sensibility (Haniffa 2012), which sought to avoid attention focussed on outward signs of Islamic piety, stated that it *was* in fact unfair to foist halal on others. The Muslim middle class, including representatives of reformist groups, seemed to realize that their engagement and economic exchanges with non-Muslims needed to be reconsidered. It was time to reframe their merit economy in a manner that included relations with the ethnic and religious others among whom they lived every day.

The Resolution of the Halal Question

The ACJU had a history of cooperating with the government in power. They had been helpful in garnering votes in favour of Sri Lanka from countries of the Organization of Islamic Conference represented in the UN Human Rights Council. [35] As a consequence, the representatives of the regime did not initially openly support either the BBS position on halal or their criticisms of the ACJU. However, they were also much less accommodating of the ACJU than Muslim leaders had expected.[36] In February 2013 the regime seemed to be waiting out the controversy, doing little to restrain the increasingly vehement and offensive tone of the BBS invectives. It was soon clear that the government would do little to defuse the situation in a manner that was critical of the BBS or could be seen as favouring Muslims over the monks.[37]

ACJU press statements on the principles of halal and the manner of certification were met with stony disinterest from the local press. At community meetings ACJU members stated that they could not even buy space in the newspapers. The ACJU also attempted to persuade producers to provide two sets of products: one with the halal logo and one without, but this was considered to be unfeasible.[38] On 15 February 2013, the press reported that the government had decided to take action to address the mounting tensions and that a Parliamentary Select Committee (PSC) would examine "whether locally- or internationally-funded religious extremism had infiltrated Sri Lankan society."[39] The government uncritically accepted the BBS's framing of the issue in setting up the PSC.[40] Given the manner in which the mandate was framed – it included no criticism of BBS discrimination and no acknowledgement of Muslim concerns – it was not clear that the PSC would deliver in any way. Throughout the period of heightened communal tensions, the ACJU advised the Muslim population – through Friday sermons by its nation-wide networks – to remain calm and not respond to violence. There was little interest among the fearful and tense Muslim population in initiating a violent response of any sort. The ACJU was also reluctant to follow the advice of those Muslims who advised the complete withdrawal of halal certification. The economic benefits that halal certification had for the export market were too great to be ignored, and the ACJU seemed reluctant to take a measure that would have an impact at the national level.

The eventual resolution of the halal controversy emerged through a powerful combination of interests that preserved both the economic status quo and existing ethnic hierarchies. The importance of halal certification for large business houses engaged in export meant that the Ceylon Chamber of Commerce had a role to play. The big conglomerates and garment industry magnates from the different Muslim communities (including Memons and Bohras[41]) took an interest in the issue, and together with the Muslim Council got the Ceylon Chamber of Commerce involved in a mediatory role. It was rumoured that both the Defence Secretary and the MP Milinda Moragoda, an elite Colombo businessman and later an SLFP politician, were involved in the process of mediation. After extensive discussions between large local export companies, the ACJU, sections of the Buddhist clergy not connected with the BBS, and the chamber of commerce, a deal was struck removing halal labeling from retail shelves. This diffused tensions, first by acknowledging that Muslim consumption needs should not impinge on the wider economy or the practices of other communities; second, it ensured the continuation of the certification for export purposes, thus facilitating national engagement with the global economy. Furthermore, the deal allowed provision of free certification for all those who wished to obtain it.[42] The ACJU also committed to handing over the certification process to a new, registered body by the end of 2013.

Indeed, by January 2014 newspapers reported that the ACJU had handed over the halal certification process to a private company, the Halal Accreditation Council of Sri Lanka. The latter differed from the ACJU in that it is a self-proclaimedly "professional" non-profit organization. Their publicity material reads, "HAC is primarily, a not for profit organization which is founded and managed by some of Sri Lanka's top professionals who assures [sic] the country's business community that international best practices will be maintained in Halal certification, whilst keeping within the guidelines."[43] They are affiliated with certification authorities in Malaysia, South Africa and Indonesia and ensure their own legal status by registration under the companies act. They charge a nominal fee for their services, their new logo does not have Arabic (religious) lettering and the use of their logo is not compulsory. The opening banner on the website reads: "The gateway to a two trillion (dollar) global market."[44] The HAC has branded itself as part of the Sri Lankan "professionalized" private sector that conforms to the shared and accepted ethical standards of a business community within a global market economy. By establishing the HAC, the business elite has attempted to resignify halal as a business practice rather than a religious practice; the HAC branded itself as supplying a service to both businesses and consumers. The fact that halal continues to be important for businesses accessing both local and foreign markets made such a resignification possible.

The Muslim middle class has internalized a notion of the constantly improved-upon entrepreneurial citizen, isomorphic with what the labouring individual is transformed into within the neoliberal economy. I have argued that reformist Muslims utilized this sensibility in relation to pious practices as well. However, in the Sri Lankan context, they must be seen to perform their "professionalism" in keeping with the requirements of a liberalized economy alongside or instead of their Islamic piety. I see the Muslim business elites' attempt to resignify the business end of halal as an economic activity alone as mobilizing a similar sensibility among Muslims and others alike. As the CEO of the new HAC stated, the new entity sought to ensure that halal certification could not be seen as "something by which to push a particular religious agenda." Instead it would "facilitate businesses having access to more markets and provide halal certified products for consumers who are looking for it." Today Muslims have access to a list of halal certified goods at all mosques, a mobile app and a website through which halal can be identified, and many larger manufacturing companies use the new HAC logo.

While the Muslim community may have overcome its problems at the level of the market, it was unclear if inroads were made in relation to any of the underlying issues that remained at the heart of the halal crisis. The threat of halal was perceived and articulated by the BBS not just as a problematic economic practice. It was a threat because a minority group was seen to be getting ahead of itself in a Sinhala majority country. While the HAC was successfully established in January 2014, Muslims remained fearful. Those professing anti-Muslim sentiment found ways to draw strength from the resolution of the halal question and the status quo remained largely unchanged. In June 2014 Aluthgama happened.

Many Sri Lankan citizens did not benefit from the liberalized economy; they were distracted from their progressive dispossession through the spectacle of the civil war, and were managed partly through being absorbed into the military (Venugopal 2011a).[45] Under the Rajapaksha regime sections of the urban poor were mobilized to act as perpetrators of violence within the new ethnic conflict. The episodes of anti-Muslim violence in Aluthgama are telling and similar to many other such incidents in Sri Lankan history. The businesses and homes that were attacked belonged to middle- and upper-middle-class Muslims, and those who did the damage were Sinhala Buddhists from a poorer economic strata. The security forces are documented as having looked away without attempting to stop the violence. In Rajapaksha Sri Lanka, the regime mobilized the poor for a "riot" against Muslims in Aluthgama to ensure its own existence and longevity.

It is therefore unclear what purpose was ultimately served by the professionalization of halal and its resignification as a market practice alone. The anxiety that the Sinhala populace feels at what are perceived as assertions of Muslim superiority is grounded in a sense of Sinhala ascendency being under threat. And what was primarily at stake institutionally was Sri Lanka's age-old problem of how the state that politically cultivates such majority anxieties relates to its minorities. In Sri Lanka's postwar, post-Rajapaksha era if these two questions are not addressed by both constitutional and institutional means, such problems of violence against minorities through sections of a majority under threat will continue.

Notes

1 Previous violence targeting Muslims took place in 1915 (Sri Lanka's first "modern" ethnic violence), 1977, the 1980s and in the early 2000s. However, violence of the scale of June 2015 had not been seen for decades.

2 The BoduBalaSena is an organization of monks established in May 2012 that has as its stated intention the preservation of a Buddhist way of life in Sri Lanka. So far this has included a highly successful campaign of discrimination against Muslims and several violent attacks against Christian prayer centres.

3 2011 census of population and housing: 70% Buddhist, 12.6% Hindu, 9.66% Muslim, 6.194% Catholic, 0.015% Other Christian. See www.statistics.gov.lk/PopHouSat/CPH2011/index.php?fileName=FinalPopulation&gp=Activities&tpl=3.

4 Muslims are not their only target. Both Evangelical Christians and "recalcitrant" Buddhists have also been chosen as targets of interventions.

5 The Jamaat-i-Islami in Sri Lanka, unlike in most other parts of South Asia, are not yet registered as a political party or seen to be directly participating in electoral politics.

6 The white list, maintained by stockbrokers, is a list of companies that have no investments in alcohol or pork products and whose primary businesses are not interest based.

7 After the agitation by the BBS the ACJU no longer offers halal certification and the process has been handed over to an entity registered under the Companies Act.

8 The coming together of reformist or Islamist ethics and market-driven consumer practices has been explored by Yael Navaro-Yashin in the case of Turkey, where reformist politics were also influenced by the opposition between the Islamists and the Kemalist republicans. However, the similarities with Sri Lanka remain noteworthy, especially regarding how the Muslims of the country became most pious during the time of conflict and economic liberalization (Navaro-Yashin 2002).

9 According to economist Saman Kelegama, 9 percent of all exports are to the Middle East and 7 percent to the ASEAN region of Southeast Asia. PowerPoint presentation at www.ips.lk/staff/ed/news/2013/10_01_2013.../xeport_nce.pdf (Accessed 19 March 2014). Further, Sri Lankan tea exports mainly focus on the Middle East, targeting countries such as United Arab Emirates, Iran, Jordan, Syria and Saudi Arabia. The Netherlands and Russia are also significant markets for tea. See also Jayaranjani and Dharmadasa (2011).

10 There is a substantial body of literature addressing the impact of neoliberalism on the Sri Lankan psyche as well. Nimanthi Perera-Rajasingham has recently written on the manner in which the state domesticated the contradictions of economic liberalization and the ethic of self-sufficiency upon which the ancient Sri Lankan kingdoms were valorized in local critiques of colonialism. Perera-Rajasingham describes the manner in which this was done in the celebratory festivals organized around the Gam Udawa (village reawakening) programs of the UNP government of the 1980s that were paid for by foreign loans (Perera-Rajasingham 2012).

11 www.worldbank.org/en/country/srilanka/overview.

12 The term "merit economy" has been used with slight variations by Joll (2013) and Jansen (2004).

13 See Sahih Muslim, Book 23: The Book of Drinks (Kitab Al Ashriba), found at www.iium.edu.my/deed/hadith/muslim/023_smt.html.

14 See, for instance, Schielke's (2009) discussion of merit accumulation during Ramadan.

15 Such Muslim eateries include Queen's Café, Dine More, as well as Marry Brown, KFC, McDonalds, Pizza Hut and, most recently, Burger King.

16 Information obtained from the Halal Accreditation Council (HAC). The ACJU also has a large representation of the Tablighi Jamaath, and it would be important to engage in greater research to ascertain what influence the Tablighi movement has had in the ACJU takeover of the certification process. Even today, there are many who oppose the certification process from a Muslim religious perspective. A person who identifies as a Salafi stated in an interview that ACJU certification was done with no authorization, that halal should be based on trust and that the certification process was nothing but a "money making operation."

17 The ACJU website has now been changed and no longer carries any information related to halal. It provides contact information for the new institute that has been set up instead.

18 This was brought up as an issue by the Ven. Gnanasara in an interview with the Sunday Leader newspaper on 17 March 2013. www.thesundayleader.lk/2013/03/17/the-cessation-of-halal-is-a-violation-of-rights/.

19 www.thecolombotimes.com/political-news/14079–govt-and-ulamas-reiterate-halal-certificate-voluntary. For instance, the leader of the opposition made a statement in parliament on 6 February 2013 in which he stated that halal certification

is provided by a religious organization that lacks authorization to do so. In his response to the opposition leader, the leader of the House, Nimal Siripala de Silva, stated that the ACJU was providing a purely voluntary religious service and therefore did not require government approval.

20 The BBS too kept reiterating that the ACJU had no legal authority to charge fees for its services, or even to provide such certification services.

21 Interview with CEO of the Halal Accreditation Council (HAC).

22 Paraphrasing of the Ven. Gnanasara's statement at the Press conference. Available on YouTube at www.youtube.com/watch?v=CeJY0WkDVXU.

23 He also stated that the ACJU charged 175,000 rupees (roughly US$1,350) for certification every year, and that they charged this amount for 4,000 goods that have certification. He stated that 175,000 rupees multiplied by 4,000 meant that the ACJU was making 700,000,000 rupees (US$5.4 million) per year on halal certification. The ACJU website responded to the monk's claim by stating that the certification charge per item was nominal and cost the consumer "less than a rupee."

24 The hyperbole was a feature of the monk's rhetoric. He later stated that the ACJU uses the money for various Muslim religious purposes – translating and printing books for madrasas, having Islamic collective meetings, and so forth. And he asked, why should we be contributing to funding such activities? It was not until several weeks later that the BBS claimed that halal certification funded Hamas and Al Qaeda.

25 Hejaaz Hisbulla, "Who Needs Halal?" *Groundviews*, 16 February 2013, http://groundviews.org/2013/02/16/who-needs-halaal/.

26 Udaya Gamanpila, "Halalization and End of Sri Lanka Food Culture," *Ceylon Today*, 24 February 2013. Gamanpila went on to say that the "social segregation" that was being carried out through halal by the ACJU was worse than the "territorial segregation" attempted by the LTTE leader Pirapaharan.

27 See www.colombotelegraph.com/index.php/keep-your-kiribath-mr-gammanpila/.

28 Bodubala Sena meeting in Kandy, February 2013. Also see Haniffa 2016a.

29 See, for instance, McKim Marriott's discussion of transactional rules and terms in the case of a South Indian village that he studied. Marriott (1968: 142) states, "A cardinal assumption of ranking in such statements about food could be formulated very simply: givers are higher, receivers are lower. If a member of caste A gives food to a member of caste B, then the whole of caste A must be regarded as higher than caste B. If the member of receiving caste B also gives food to a member of caste A, then caste A and B are of the same rank once more. Concern for transitivity is evident wherever three or more units are involved: if A gives to B and B gives to C, then A is higher than C even if there is no direct transfer of food from A to C. Arithmetic computations are also implied. If A gives to C while B does not, A is higher than B; if A gives to C and D while B gives to D but not C, then A is higher than B."

30 While the monk was arguably reflecting and mobilizing resentment based on caste sentiment, another way of understanding such resentment regarding the refusal of food is Mauss' (1990) ideas regarding the gift. Accepting a gift is as important to Mauss' schema as the other two components of gift giving and reciprocating.

31 There were a few Tamil speakers, but they were a minority.

32 13 and 14 April are the Sinhala and Tamil New Year and the time when the most frenzied consumption takes place in Sri Lanka. Muslim business owners make

their profits for the whole year on April sales. The BBS targeted their hate rhetoric towards undermining these April profits.

33 This refers to good conduct and is here stated in opposition to merely the symbolic manifestations of piety.

34 The language also reflects long-standing Sinhala nationalist claims.

35 In March 2012 the United States sponsored a resolution promoting reconciliation and accountability in Sri Lanka. The resolution passed with Qatar, Saudi Arabia, Kuwait, Indonesia and Maldives voting no, and Jordan and Malaysia abstaining. www.ohchr.org/Documents/HRBodies/HRCouncil/RegularSession/Session19/resolutions/votingprocess/L2.pdf.

36 Stated at the Muslim Community meeting in March 2013.

37 The Muslim Council and members of the YMMA met repeatedly with the defence secretary, the president's brother, Gotabhaya Rajapaksha, to ask for some state intervention against the BBS and the rising tide of anti-Muslim sentiment. The defence secretary, however, repeatedly stressed that the BBS were a fringe group and taking action against them would only exacerbate the situation.

38 ACJU press release of 21 February 2013.

39 "Muslim Sinhalese Neighbours Defend Communal Harmony; the Government Moves to Stop Rogue Elements from Inciting Tensions Against Muslims in Sri Lanka," *Khabar South Asia*, http://khabarsouthasia.com/en_GB/articles/apwi/articles/features/2013/02/15/feature-01.

40 "Jamiyyathul Ulama Scoffs halal Certification Solution," www.hirunews.lk/53850/jamiyyathul-ulama-scoffs-halal-certification-solution.

41 Small communities of Muslims who have considerable business interests in Sri Lanka.

42 The funding for the certification was to be taken up by the Muslim business community until a new "professional" entity was to be set up to provide halal certification.

43 http://hac.lk/media.php.

44 www.hac.lk/.

45 See Tisaranee Gunesekere, "A Garrison State?" *Himal Southasian*, 13 October 2014, http://himalmag.com/garrison-state/. Gamburd (2004) has documented the place of the military in the employment choices of rural youth.

References

Bastian, S. 1990. "Political Economy of Ethnic Violence in Sri Lanka: The July 1983 Riots." In *Mirrors of Violence: Communities Riots and Survivors*, edited by Veena Das, 206–304. New Delhi: Oxford University Press.

Bergeaud-Blackler, Florence, Johan Fischer, and John Lever. (2015) *Halal Matters: Islam, Politics and Markets in Global Perspective*. London: Routledge.

Deeb, L. 2006. *An Enchanted Modern: Gender and Public Piety in Shi'i Lebanon*. Princeton, NJ: Princeton University Press.

Fischer, J. 2009. *Proper Islamic Consumption: Shopping among the Malays in Modern Malaysia*. Copenhagen: Nordic Institute of Asian Studies Press.

Fischer, J.. 2016. *Islam, Standards and Technoscience in Global Halal Zones* London: Routledge.

Gamburd, M. R. 2004. "The Economics of Enlisting: A Village View of Armed Service." In *Economy, Culture and Civil War in Sri Lanka*, edited by D. Winslow and M. D. Woost, 99–114. Bloomington: Indiana University Press.

Gunasinghe, N. 2004. "The Open Economy and Its Impact on Ethnic Relations in Sri Lanka." In *Economy, Culture and Civil War in Sri Lanka*, edited by D. Winslow and M. D. Woost, 99–114. Bloomington: Indiana University Press.

Haniffa, F. 2012. "Conflicted Solidarities? Muslims and the Constitution-Making Process of 1970–1972." In *The Sri Lankan Republic at Forty: Reflections on Constitutional History, Theory and Practice*, edited by A.Welikala, 219–252. Colombo: Center for Policy Alternatives.

2013. "Piety and Power amongst Muslim Women in Contemporary Sri Lanka." In *Islamic Reformism in South Asia*, edited by F. Osella and C. Osella, 171–201. New Delhi: Cambridge University Press.

2016 (a). "Minorities in the Post-War Context: The Case of the Muslims of Sri Lanka." In *The Struggle for Peace in the Aftermath of War*, edited by A. Amarasingham and D. Bass, 109–128 London: Hurst.

2016 (b). "Stories in the Aftermath of Aluthgama." In *Militant Monks and Muslim Minorities: Buddhist/Muslim Conflicts In Modern Sri Lanka*, edited by John Holt, 164–193. Oxford: Oxford University Press.

Ismail, Q. M. (1995). "Unmooring Identity: The Antinomies of Elite Muslim Self-Representation in Modern Sri Lanka." In *UnMaking the Nation*, edited by P. Jeganathan and Q Ismail, 55–105. Colombo: SSA.

Jansen, W. 2004. "The Economy of Religious Merit: Women and *ajr* in Algeria." *The Journal of North African Studies* 9(4): 1–17.

Jayaranjani, S. R., and R. A. P. I. S. Dharmadasa. 2011. "A Study of Tea Export Marketing in Sri Lanka: Application of Boston Consulting Group Matrix." *Proceedings of International Conference on Business Management* 8. http://journals.sjp.ac.lk/index.php/icbm/article/view/291.

Joll, C. 2013. *Muslim Merit-making in Thailand's Far South*. Dordrecht: Springer.

Kadirgamar, A. 2013. *Second Wave of Neoliberalism: Financialisation and Crisis in Post-war Sri Lanka*. www.colombotelegraph.com/index.php/second-wave-of-neoliberalism-financialisation-and-crisis-in-post-war-sri-lanka/.

Lynch, K. 1999. "Good Girls or Juki Girls? Learning and Identity in Garment Factories." *Anthropology of Work Review* 19(3): 18–22.

Maranci, G. 2012. "Defensive or Offensive Dining? Halal Dining Practices among Malay Muslims Singaporeans and heir Effects on Integration." *The Australian Journal of Anthropology* 23: 84–100.

Marriott, M. 1968. "Caste Ranking and Food Transactions: A Matrix Analysis." In *Structure and Change in Indian Society*, edited by M. Singer and B. S. Cohen, 133–171. New Brunswick, NJ: Transaction Publishers.

Moore, M. 1990. "Economic Liberalization versus Political Pluralism in Sri Lanka." *Modern Asian Studies* 24: 341–383.

Mauss, M. 1990. *The Gift: Forms and Functions of Exchange in Archaic Societies*. London: W. W. Norton.

Navaro-Yashin, Y. 2002. "The Market for Identities: Secularism, Islamism, Commodities." In *Fragments of Culture: The Everyday of Modern Turkey*, edited by D. Kandiyoti and A. Saktanber, 78–113. London: I. B. Tauris.

Nuhman, M. A. 2007. *Sri Lankan Muslims: Ethnic Identity Amidst Cultural Diversity*. Colombo: International Centre for Ethnic Studies.

Ong, A. 2006. *Neoliberalism as Exception: Mutations in Citizenship and Sovereignty*. Durham, NC: Duke University Press.

Perera-Rajasighnam, N. 2012. "The Factory Is like the Paddy-field: Gam Udawa Performances, Ethnicity and Neoliberalism in Sri Lanka." *South Asian Review* 33(3): 275–292.

Povinelli, E. 2006. *The Empire of Love: Towards a Theory of Intimacy, Genealogy, and Carnality*. Durham, NC: Duke University Press.

Rudnyckyj, D. 2010. *Spiritual Economies: Islam, Globalization and the Afterlife of Development*. Ithaca, NY: Cornell University Press.

Schielke, S. 2009. "Being Good in Ramadan: Ambivalence, Fragmentation and the Moral Self in the Lives of Young Egyptians." *Journal of the Royal Anthropological Institute* 15 (special issue): S24–S40.

Van Nieuwkerk, K. (ed.). 2011. *Muslim Rap, Halal Soaps and Revolutionary Theatre: Artistic Developments in the Muslim World*. Austin: University of Texas Press.

Venugopal, R. 2011a. "The Politics of Market Reform at a Time of Civil War: Military Fiscalism in Sri Lanka." *Economic and Political Weekly* 46(49): 67–75.

Venugopal, R.. 2011b. "The Politics of Market Reform at a Time of Ethnic Conflict: Sri Lanka in the Jayawardena Years." In *Liberal Peace in Question: Politics of State and Market Reform in Sri Lanka*, edited by C. Stokke and J. Uyangoda, 77–102. New Delhi: Anthem Press.

Vora, N. 2013. *Impossible Citizens: Dubai's Indian Diaspora*. Durham, NC: Duke University Press.

Zackariah, F., and A. Shanmugaratnam. 1997. "Communalisation of Muslims in Sri Lanka: A Historical Perspective." In *Alternative Perspectives: A Collection of Essays on Contemporary Muslim Society*, 75–104. Colombo: Muslim Women's Research and Action Forum/WLUML.

6 "Structural Adjustment Islam" and the Religious Economy in Neoliberal Mali

Benjamin Soares, University of Amsterdam and University of Florida, Gainesville

This chapter analyzes some of the dramatic and much-discussed changes in modalities of religious expression, including ways of being Muslim and modes of belonging in contemporary Mali, a secular state (*laïc* on the French model) whose population is overwhelmingly Muslim. I do not directly address the 2012 Islamist takeover of northern Mali that received considerable international media attention, particularly when Islamists destroyed Muslim saints' tombs in places like Timbuktu, but rather broader transformations in relation to which those developments must be understood.[1] This is part of a larger ongoing effort inspired by the work of Max Weber in such works as *Economy and Society* (1978) as well as some of Weber's interpreters to grapple with how "religion" and "economy" intersect and influence each other over time. Religion and economy – abstractions for understanding religious and economic practices – have long been deeply intertwined in this part of West Africa, perhaps most notably in the direct involvement of Muslim scholars and religious leaders in such economic activities as the precolonial trans-Saharan trade in gold, salt, and slaves that spanned centuries (see Lydon 2009). What I want to do here is build upon some of my earlier analysis of religion and economy in Mali to understand religion in the current era.

However, I would like to emphasize the need to proceed cautiously in any such discussion of religion and economy.[2] Rather than treating religion, as in some older models, as a mere function of political economy, a form of adaptation or resistance, or culture, for example, in reified, static notions of "African Islam" or African "traditional" religion, as I argue, one must analyze religion – understood as discourses and practices encompassing modalities of religious expression – as a heterogeneous field in which there is considerable debate, contestation, and transformation. Arguing against equally simplistic and teleological models of Islamization, reform, and totalizing notions of ethical self-fashioning, I draw on research on transformations in religious practice to propose new ways of thinking about religion that foreground how religious practice has changed in the context of Mali's neoliberal reforms.

In addition, I do not want simply to apply or impose my own analytical language. I work from my respondents' understanding of changes in modalities of religious expression and their participation in debates about them to develop my own analytical optics about some of the momentous changes in Mali. In fact, I pay particular attention to some of the economic and market metaphors about religion that Malians frequently deploy to make sense of recent changing modalities of religious expression. As I will suggest, certain Malians' modalities of religious expression have come to resemble the neoliberal market economy but without being necessarily reduced to its logic.

"Religion" and "Economy"

In recent years, anthropologists and sociologists have devoted considerably more attention to the intersections of religious and economic action in a variety of settings (e.g., Comaroff and Comaroff 1999; Haenni 2005; Soares 2005; Osella and Osella 2009; Rudnyckyj 2010; Obadia and Wood 2011), and others have usefully explored religion and the commodity form and processes of religious commodification in the contemporary period (e.g., Jones 2010; Kitiarsa 2010; Turner 2012). Some economic theories of religion have drawn directly on rational choice theory – for example, Nile Green's model of a competitive market of religions in his book, *Bombay Islam* (2011). But the use of such economic theories has not been uncontroversial (see Lehmann 2010; van der Veer 2012). In fact, many analysts resist thinking about religion in economic or market terms, as Nile Green does when he employs such analytical notions as entrepreneurs to discuss religious figures or "firms" to talk about religious organizations such as Sufi groups. Some criticism of such models can be easily faulted for idealism or the patent refusal to consider religion and economy together. Certain critics (e.g., Ahmad 2013; cf. Green 2014) even seem to think the use of such models makes one an apologist for free market capitalism or neoliberalism, which is to confuse a theoretical apparatus with normative positions about religion and the market. My own reservations about the facilely reductive nature of rational choice theory certainly inform how I approach the intersection of religion and economy. Be that as it may, I find the analytical framework of a religious economy or plural religious economies with markets, consumers, and supply and demand, as in Green's work, useful for understanding how religion and economy are mutually imbricated in contemporary Mali.[3] Indeed, I use the notion of religious economy to get at what is effectively a changing economy of religious practice in Mali. Moreover, as I will show, such a framework is actually evocative of how some Malians themselves talk about contemporary religion in Mali and critique religion and religious practices within the context of neoliberal reforms.

Although I certainly recognize the difficulties in clearly defining neoliberalism (see Mirowski and Plehwe 2009; Mirowski 2009) and some of the challenges in its application in contemporary social science (Ganti 2014), in my way of thinking it is useful to talk in shorthand about a neoliberal era in a place like Mali. In this era, a number of key economic reforms and policy prescriptions, which include deregulation, liberalization, and privatization, along with currency devaluation, have been implemented over the past few decades. In Mali, one of the effects of such policies has been the erosion, if not the complete end of the developmental state. Indeed, there have been significant cutbacks to state services and the hollowing out of state capacity to meet the demand for services that has increased, not least through demographic expansion. In this neoliberal era, there has been massive un- and underemployment and economic decline for many alongside fantastic wealth for a select few. Another particularly important feature of this era has been the proliferation of post-Fordist forms of economic organization in the wake of the privatization of state-owned enterprises or their dissolution, the closing of factories unable to compete in the face of cheap imports, the increased casualization of labor with more fixed-term and flexible contracts, and the informalization of labor with the proliferation of the so-called informal sector. Entrepreneurialism and a range of "practices of survival" or *débrouillardise* (Masquelier 2016) have become increasingly privileged modes of action – even in religion – for Malians of all sectors of the society. A central premise of this chapter is that the particular context of neoliberal reforms is key to understanding transformations within the realm of religion. However, before discussing the recent context and transformations in the practice of Islam in Mali, I would like to revisit some of my earlier ideas about the intersection of religious and economic practice.

Mali's Religious Economy

In earlier work I traced transformations in religious practice over the course of the twentieth century in a celebrated Islamic religious center in Mali (Soares 2005) and broadened the discussion to include another Islamic religious center in the country (Soares 2004a). One of my main arguments was that over time religious authority had come to be personalized in certain Muslim religious leaders – leaders of Sufi orders from lineages of Muslim religious specialists – who had reputations as saints. These charismatic figures are thought to be closer to God, have greater access to God's favor, and are known for "miracles." That is, they have reputations for association with wondrous things (*karamat* in Arabic) and for the ability to make desired things happen. For this reason, ordinary Muslims treat such persons with great respect, awe, and even fear. From the perspective of many reformist Muslims and Islamists in particular, all of this is objectionable, indeed, a form of idolatry or *shirk*

(Arabic, associationism), that is, associating things other than God with Him. This helps partly to explain why certain Islamists wanted to destroy Muslim saints' tombs in northern Mali where people ask for intercession with God. In their way of thinking, all are equal in their proximity to God, and no person or his tomb should be an object of veneration. Such critiques of Muslim religious leaders and their practices relate to more general critiques of Sufism in Mali and beyond that are longstanding and shared among such strange bedfellows as many Islamists, ardent secularists, leftists, and modernists of various sorts.

Following Murray Last, I analyzed what I called the prayer economy, an economy of religious practice with more privatized saints around whom the exchange of gifts for blessings, prayers, and intercession with God had flourished (Soares 2005, chapter 6). As I argued, the commodity form – personal and impersonal Islamic religious commodities in the form of blessings, prayers, amulets, and saints' images – was key to the development of such a religious economy around a group of saints with veritable superstar status (Soares 2004b). In Mali, a number of these Muslim saints had become "free-floating sanctifiers" in a religious economy that had come to be much more like a market with fee-for-service religion in ascendance (Soares 2005: 246). One of the consequences of this economy of religious practice was that the organizational form of the Sufi order had become much less important than had been the case at earlier historical moments in some places in the region. In any case, I also reported how many Malians claimed that there were actually no living saints – like the saintly superstars – present (other than in passing or in transit) in Bamako, the Malian capital, the largest city and most important center for economic activity in the country. Rather, such saintly superstars were ordinarily ensconced in some of the main Islamic religious centers at considerable distance from the capital where lineages of Muslim religious specialists have historically resided. As I show later, in the era of neoliberal reforms religious entrepreneurs began to flourish outside such Islamic religious centers that dot the landscape and more specifically in the previously largely secular space of Bamako, the colonial city that become the postcolonial capital and center of government, politics, business, and commerce.

In addition to such saintly superstars, I identified two broad categories of notable Muslim religious figures in Mali's religious economy, who, I argued, were considerably less important than the privatized Muslims saints (Soares 2005: 251–253; see also Soares 2004b; cf. Dumestre and Touré 2007). First, there are the numerous minor figures whom many Malians have characterized as *marabouts d'affaires*, a term that is a play on words between the French term for businessman (*homme d'affaires*) and the notion of *marabout* from the French colonial lexicon, which indexes a broad range of Muslim religious specialists, including imams, teachers, scholars, preachers, saints, Sufis, diviners, and healers. Marabouts d'affaires refers more specifically to Muslim religious specialists known for their use of the Islamic esoteric sciences, so-called *maraboutage* in French colonial parlance or "magic" by most anthropological definitions. The emblematic figure of the marabout d'affaires is a religious entrepreneur in Mali's burgeoning fee-for-service religious market who offers "services" via the esoteric sciences for obtaining wealth, success, and well-being, particularly in exchange for money or commodities.[4] It is important to note how the actions of marabouts d'affaires are often referred to as "work" in the region's vernaculars, with work here having a broad semantic range in meaning from the sense of physical or wage labor but also encompassing the various practices and techniques – such as divination, geomancy, the confection of amulets, spiritual "exercises," and so forth – that might be employed in exchange for remuneration.

Although some of the marabouts d'affaires exhibit signs of considerable wealth, the overwhelming majority merely seems to eke out a living or supplement their income from their "work" in the esoteric sciences in the fee-for-service religious market. I know one rather successful figure considered a marabout d'affaires, a descendant of a nineteenth-century Muslim scholar, who lives in a sumptuous villa in a neighborhood favored by Bamako's elites and owns a luxury sports-utility vehicle with tinted windows; this person apparently flies regularly to neighboring countries where he has a clientele that pays handsomely for his services. Someone seeking a job promotion in the civil service or private sector, a businessman, politician, or university student's parents might ask such a marabout d'affaires "to work" for him or her. The marabout d'affaires would most likely engage in one or more diagnostic techniques such as forms of divination to identify which solution was required to solve the person's particular problem, and this would almost invariably require the payment of a considerable sum of money once the desired results had been achieved and possibly even before the marabout d'affaires' "work" begins.

In striking contrast with most Muslim religious leaders and Sufi leaders in Mali and elsewhere in West Africa, those deemed marabouts d'affaires have no real followers constituting anything like a corporate group. If the saintly superstars have followers, as well as clients for their services, the marabout d'affaires, as their moniker suggests, are more likely to have a business-like or more market-oriented relationship with their interlocutors. As many Malians note, the marabout d'affaires has a clientele that is more akin to customers who solicit and pay them for the various services they are able to provide. However, there are many more minor Muslim religious specialists who provide various services to a largely local clientele in exchange for limited remuneration or payment in kind.

The second, more disparate group comprises some of the many new religious figures – preachers, writers of books and pamphlets, activists, media personalities, and others such as the young, new-style Sufis (see Soares 2007,

2010, 2016a) – almost all of whom are men of a younger generation, if not youths, with a public presence in large urban centers, particularly Bamako. Some of these figures, most of whom employ various media forms, do have followers (actual and/or virtual) and "fans." Most notably, there is the case of Mali's most celebrated Muslim preacher, Chérif Ousmane Madani Haïdara, whose sermons have circulated on cassette since the 1980s (and later on video, DVD, and private radio stations). In the 1990s, he founded a modern-style Islamic organization with formal membership and structure, which has many members in large parts of the country and among the Malian diaspora elsewhere in Africa, Europe, and beyond.[5] Although Haïdara is himself not a Sufi, he has been on quite good terms with Sufi leaders and even comports himself like a charismatic Sufi leader, dispensing blessings to followers and supplicants. A recurrent theme in Haïdara's sermons has been a sustained critique of Islamists and those he usually calls "Wahhabis" (a term used loosely to refer to all Muslim reformists, particularly those who are anti-Sufi) whom he regularly accuses of dishonesty, hypocrisy, and intolerance.

However, it is important to note how until somewhat recently such figures with very few exceptions – like the preacher Haïdara – have tended to lack the charisma of the celebrated Muslim saints and have not been able to command much authority. Although some have been able to gain a measure of popularity, celebrity, and even at times notoriety, they have been qualitatively different from some of the other figures who have emerged more recently.

Transformations in the Religious Economy

In recent years, the religious economy in Mali has experienced a series of important changes. In fact, over the past decade, several important developments have prompted me to revisit and update some of my earlier analysis of the country's changing religious economy. One much-discussed, significant development is that some of the minor religious figures living in Bamako, including several I had been following since the 1990s, have since gone on to become major religious figures in their own right. Previously, the country's most influential Muslim religious leaders and the saintly superstars in particular did not have much of a physical presence in the capital. In addition, the broader context has also changed considerably. The death of several celebrated saints in the late 1990s and 2000s was much discussed and commented on. However, in most cases, no charismatic figures (sons, brothers, nephews, or followers) have been able to succeed the deceased saintly superstars or, when someone has done so, he has usually failed to command much authority. On several occasions I have listened to close followers of some of the saintly superstars talk about their deaths and the void left in their wake. Some with an allegiance to a particular recently deceased saint specifically told me that they were looking for a new Muslim religious leader, presumably a saint, to whom they might turn given the deficit in charisma among the saint's kin and close followers. In the words of the Mauritanian sociologist Abdel Wedoud Ould Cheikh, there is the possibility that "the charisma" of the saintly lineage might be "exhausted" (*épuisé*) and the saintly lineage unable to reproduce itself (quoted in Soares 2005: 158). Although the new religious figures have not necessarily supplanted the celebrated Muslim saints, who are diminished in number, I am not advancing a structural functionalist argument, as in the work of social anthropologists such as Ernest Gellner (1981), that these new figures can simply replace the saintly superstars and all will eventually continue as before. Rather I want to show how the broader changes are such that the larger religious economy is coming to be more like the neoliberal market economy. One can see this in the rise of new religious entrepreneurs who seem to be able to meet the strong demand for persons with charismatic authority and their services in the religious economy in the current era, which is characterized by incredible uncertainty and débrouillardise. Such new figures cultivate an ethics of entrepreneurship and flexibility in tune with the market, rather than relying primarily on inherited charisma (like the saintly superstars) or preexisting patron–client ties to try to deliver the various kinds of paid services in the esoteric sciences many Malians increasingly seek out.

It is important to note that Malians do not necessarily use the analytical language of religious economy, which I employ here, or even refer directly or specifically to neoliberalism for that matter. But over the years I have heard many Malians use economic and market metaphors to talk about contemporary religious practice and changes to that practice. During visits to Mali – usually at least once each year over the past decade – I have also regularly heard friends and acquaintances reflect on some of the dramatic changes as far as religion is concerned. Some of this language I find particularly productive for thinking with and building upon for my analysis, as does Green (2011), who also uses the market as metaphor in his analysis of the history of religious practice in nineteenth-century Bombay. For example, I have heard committed Malian secularists regularly condemn what they call the new religious marketing in the country, whereby various religious figures use mass marketing techniques to proselytize and market their images, activities, and services. In fact, I recall a newspaper headline in the 1990s calling for an end to such "religious marketing" because of its potentially deleterious effects on relations between different religious groups in the country.[6] Pejorative views about religion and religious marketing techniques aside, many Malians have been commenting on a larger trend of the commodification of religion, the marketing of religion and religious commodities through a range of media, and the consumption of such religion and new religious commodities, which have become much more widespread over the past twenty years (see later).

During fieldwork I frequently heard Malians talk about religion in ways that I have found helpful for my own analysis. I think the following vignette also helps to illustrate some of those changes, as well as the ways in which some Malians themselves have been trying to make sense of those changes and the limits to their comprehension. In late 2004, I was talking with two Malian men in their 40s whom I had known for quite some time, both journalists. I had known the older man, whom I will call Almamy, for more than a decade; he had followed a "traditional" Islamic education in Arabic that included memorization of the Qur'an and advanced studies in Islamic jurisprudence as well as supplementary training in journalism in Cairo. The other man, whom I will call Babou, earned a university degree in journalism before becoming a radio journalist. They were both committed Muslims with close and longstanding ties to some of the country's eminent Muslim saints, which was the reason I had first come to know them. Both would speak often about Islam and being Muslim. While we were sitting and chatting in Almamy's home, the two men emphasized how much "disorder" there was in Mali since the fall of General Moussa Traoré's authoritarian regime in 1991, which had ushered in major changes, including political liberalization, multiparty elections, and stepped up economic reforms and restructuring according to neoliberal prescriptions.

When the conversation turned to the subject of Islam, Babou stated there was now a "cacophony" of dissonant Muslim religious voices in Mali, and this was precisely what globalization (*mondialisation*, the French loan word he used) meant. Almamy questioned whether this was, indeed, globalization – a term that had been increasingly invoked and bandied about in Mali at the time. They agreed that many Malians do not know any more what is true or correct as far as Islam is concerned or even whom to trust. For example, Babou noted that one Muslim preacher such as Chérif Ousmane Madani Haïdara might say one thing about Islam, and another something entirely different. Moreover, Almamy interjected, almost anything now seemed permitted, particularly among the young, who might even dabble in things that are deemed un-Islamic. Here he was alluding to "traditional" ritual practices (often related to blood sacrifice), which most Malian Muslims consider un-Islamic. This was a rather illuminating exchange for me, as it illustrated how the two men seemed to yearn for greater certainty without exhibiting any obvious nostalgia for the authoritarian past of the Traoré regime that had lasted more than two decades and had been characterized by economic stagnation and decline.

Almamy and Babou were well aware of the possibilities of the new era of political liberalization – greater freedom of expression and freedom of assembly – and associated media liberalization. But they were rather apprehensive about the multiplicity of available options, which such greater freedoms seemed to allow, and rather uncertain about what the future might possibly bring. The two men (like many of their peers and other members of their generation I encountered) often disparage much of what they see among their fellow Muslims in a country where many people had embraced Islam only over the past few decades. But they are particularly dismissive of many Muslim youths who are no less concerned with uncertainty in the present and the future. Almamy also regularly voiced his concerns that Islamists might get a foothold in the country (as they eventually did in northern Mali in 2012) or that sectarian violence as witnessed in Iraq and elsewhere might eventually come to Mali (which it has largely not). He said those were things he could well understand even if he abhorred them. However, he also said he was truly at a loss when faced with some of the recent and dramatic changes in the practice of Islam in Mali he had been witnessing, particularly among the country's Muslim youth, and the rise of a range of new religious figures whose success would have been unimaginable a short time ago. Indeed, Almamy seemed quite exasperated, saying he could not understand how things had been developing and where they might eventually lead.

Over dinner one evening in the autumn of 2004, another friend whom I will call Kalidou – a self-styled former Marxist, who was, at the time, the local representative of a major international corporation, an erstwhile militant atheist who had become a committed Muslim and a Tablighi (a member of Tablighi Jama'at, the world's largest Muslim missionary organization, founded in colonial India) – told me that the key to understanding Islam in Mali today was good old-fashioned materialist analysis. Kalidou said that many of the changes witnessed among Muslims in Mali and especially among youths – new religious figures, styles, and organizations – are concrete examples of what he and some other Malians call, not without irony and certainly with a sense of regret, "structural adjustment Islam." Indeed, in subsequent conversations the former atheist and leftist Kalidou talked about the quest to lead a proper Muslim way of life, which seemed to be in tension with the postcolonial "secular" society in which he lived, with its various distractions and temptations that might lead him away from "correct" practice and morally upstanding behavior. He readily conceded that his own organization's presence in Mali with its many young members was one of the effects of globalization and greater transnational interconnections in the world today. In other words, Tablighi Jama'at, spreading, if not arriving, as it did in the recent period of more openness to the outside world and presenting a novel way of being Muslim that differed from preexisting options, was just another instantiation of so-called "structural adjustment Islam."

This term "structural adjustment Islam" is arguably quite compelling, getting as it does at the possible links between religion and economy and the particular historical moment of the structural adjustment program, which the Malian state started to implement beginning in the late 1980s. Given Mali's diligence in meeting International Monetary Fund and World Bank targets for such reforms, including privatization schemes and reductions in state budget deficits in part through cutbacks in state services, some policymakers in Washington have sometimes even heralded Mali (without apparent irony) as a "poster child" for such reforms (Soares 2006). Although I prefer to retain the use of the language of religious economy and the market, notions that I do think still need to be refined further, the term structural adjustment Islam, evoking as it does structural adjustment and its attendant processes, is nevertheless useful for making sense of some of the broader recent changes in religious practice in Mali, which are not necessarily shifting toward a uniform global or globalized Islam (cf. Roy 2004; Green 2014).

As I have suggested, the religious economy is an analytical device, which helps to get at the mutual imbrications of religion and economy in the *longue durée* in a place like Mali. But this religious economy is also an economy of religious practice that has changed considerably within the context of the implementation of structural adjustment programs and more generally in the era of ongoing neoliberal reforms. If the prayer economy with its more privatized saints who were descendants of key nineteenth- and twentieth-century Muslim religious figures has been centrally important to Mali's religious economy, there has been a shift in the religious economy. When some Malians talk about structural adjustment Islam they are gesturing toward the "cacophony" of voices Almamy and Babou invoked, as well as how some religious practices in the fee-for-service religious market, have come to quite closely resemble market-oriented behavior with entrepreneurialism as a key mode of action. But this is not to suggest that all Islamic religious practices are being reduced to the logic of the market or a singular globalized Islam has emerged.

Since the 1990s, as the country's political system and economy were liberalized and with cutbacks in state services in accordance with neoliberal prescriptions, the religious economy has in a sense also been liberalized. Prior to the end of authoritarian rule there had been the country's sole officially authorized national Islamic organization – the Association Malienne pour l'Unité et le Progrès de l'Islam (AMUPI, Malian Association for the Unity and Progress of Islam) – ostensibly for all Muslims, regardless of their differences, that operated alongside the prayer economy. Modeled after the one-party state, AMUPI was supposed to manage intra-Muslim tensions and conflicts as well as coordinate aid inflows from such Muslim donor countries as Saudi Arabia, Libya, and Iran. With economic and political liberalization, there was a concomitant opening up of the religious economy, which has become much more diversified and competitive. There has been a proliferation of literally dozens of new Islamic associations for youths, students, preachers, and women with diverse memberships, goals, and orientations, advocating "development," "reform," human rights, and so forth (see Soares 2005: 228–229; Soares 2006). Some of these new associations have come to rival AMUPI, the national Islamic organization, whose influence has been much diminished, even if it is not completely defunct.

Faced with the sharp decline in the quality of public education and massive un- and underemployment, many youths have undertaken initiatives to enter the religious economy and have become major actors therein, particularly in Bamako. Many Malian Muslim youths got involved in new forms of Islamic associational life, including some – perhaps a small minority – in groups we might characterize as Islamist. An array of new religious entrepreneurs, both Muslim and non-Muslim, have entered the religious economy, especially in urban Mali and its fee-for-service religious market. In the era of neoliberal reforms, Bamako became an active arena for experimentation in the religious economy and has gone on to become the country's most important center of fee-for-service religion. An important feature of the changing religious economy is the greater use of media, including new media technologies, and techniques for publicity and the marketing of religion in general and religious services in particular.

The religious economy in Mali, no longer composed simply of saintly superstars and an array of relatively less influential minor figures, has changed markedly and in some ways now seems to parallel the neoliberal economy. The religious market is a much more crowded and diverse market with a "cacophony" of different entrepreneurs offering their services to consumers, who also might be followers. Although there has been (and continues to be) marketing around the saintly superstars, it tends to be relatively sober and restrained as, for example, in photographs that are like studio portraits showing them in poses looking pious, wise, and beneficent that are sold individually or printed on calendars alongside stock images of the Ka'ba and the hajj in Mecca. Such sobriety contrasts with some of the marketing around the new religious entrepreneurs, which seems designed to generate comment, debate, and even buzz. In practice, media use in the religious marketing among the new young religious entrepreneurs and their entourages has ranged quite widely in its sophistication, from the relatively simple use of photos on badges to the increasingly slick use of the Internet and social media, and such media use has changed a great deal over the past decade. But such marketing has reached unprecedented levels and scope around certain new religious figures.

In recent years, various entrepreneurs have employed increasingly sophisticated media strategies and an array of marketing techniques aimed at different and changing audiences. They produce (or have others produce) and market various religious commodities (t-shirts, printed fabric, badges, lapel buttons, photos, posters, calendars, and so forth); they are also adept at using the print and audiovisual media (newspapers, radio, video, DVD, loudspeakers, signs, and billboards) for publicity in Mali's liberalized media landscape and increasingly on the Internet (websites, Facebook, YouTube, and so forth). While all of these media are used for proselytizing, they are perhaps used even more so for the marketing of the charismatic figures and their services, including during various religious gatherings. In some cases, the use of media and the array of Islamic religious commodities have contributed to certain religious leaders being marketed almost like brands, which people embrace if they find them alluring or appealing (cf. Kitiarsa 2010). Some religious figures even seem to market themselves actively. For example, there is the young Sufi leader Bilal Diallo, a.k.a. Soufi Bilal (see later), one of the new-style Sufi leaders who have been nicknamed Rasta Sufis because they sport dreadlocks or braids (see Soares 2007, 2010, 2016a). Bilal seems to market himself openly when he appears in public actually wearing clothing made of printed fabric bearing his own image, alongside followers who might also sport images of him. This development has generated much discussion about whether it is immodest or unseemly.

Most of the new religious entrepreneurs leave much of the marketing and branding work to their associates, employees, followers, or even "the market" – those with the entrepreneurial wherewithal interested in entering and possibly capitalizing on such a market. There is another so-called Rasta Sufi, Adama Yalcouyé, a.k.a. Soufi Adama (see later),[7] around whom there has been considerable marketing since the early 2000s organized by various entrepreneurial individuals close to him who have sought to earn income and sometimes give a portion of the sales proceeds to him. In Bamako one can readily purchase laminated badges with photos of Adama side by side with photos of Chérif Ousmane Madani Haïdara, as well as a celebrated deceased Malian saintly superstar, which for some people clearly adds to Adama's allure.

In recent years, a number of such new religious entrepreneurs have been particularly adept at taking advantage of spaces the neoliberal era has opened up. Some of these "new young preachers and millionaires," as they have been described in the Malian press,[8] have risen to great fame, particularly for their reputations for making desired things happen quickly – in short, the "miracles" they perform and the wealth they have accumulated. One such figure is the relatively young preacher cum marabout d'affaires Moussa Traoré (no relation to the former president), a.k.a. Moussa Bagadadji, Moussa from Bagadadji (Baghdad in local parlance), the name of the crowded neighborhood in central Bamako where he lives in a compound outside of which there is a large painted sign stating, "Moussa Traoré Marabout." Since at least 2001 Moussa Bagadadji has run advertisements in local newspapers and subsequently on private radio stations, which have often billed him, in the words of one 2001 newspaper ad, as a "grand marabout" able to provide "solutions" to "all your problems."[9] The kinds of problems listed in that particular ad include health (headaches, stomach ailments, back troubles, and even leprosy), reproductive health, love and marriage, "management" (*gestion*), the quest for popularity, and “problems with spirits.” A decade ago, Moussa Bagadadji was one of the most talked-about young Muslim religious specialists who stood out from his peers. He was perhaps the first young Malian Muslim to use mass media actively not just to proselytize or to spread his ideas in sermons on cassette or video but also to advertise and market his services. In Bamako’s crowded media market he became somewhat of a minor celebrity after his exuberant radio appearances, during which he alluded to his seemingly great powers. In radio addresses he would regularly conclude a sermon, for example, about how to comport oneself as a proper Muslim, with tantalizing references to the requisite esoteric knowledge he knew to employ to obtain desired results in health, wealth, and success. Owing to his media presence Moussa Bagadadji relatively quickly gained a great deal of attention, attracted a clientele, and was able to exhibit some of the signs of wealth such as a nice car and other imported consumer items such as fine clothing and expensive wristwatches. However, he has remained a relatively minor figure in the fee-for-service religious market without any real followers or constituents (other than his not insubstantial client base).

In contrast, some of the new religious entrepreneurs, like the one with his sumptuous Bamako home and luxury SUV mentioned earlier, have seemingly amassed great wealth, exhibiting the most prominent and desirable signs of wealth for most people in this setting. The latter include massive villas in large residential compounds, expensive imported vehicles according to the fashion (the Hummer was *de rigueur* a few years ago), and many dependents with whom they are reputed to share some of their wealth. Another religious entrepreneur I know – a non-Muslim ritual specialist – receives a steady stream of clients, including former ministers, military officials, and large-scale traders, in his huge modern compound with special facilities for receiving guests in a tiny village outside the capital, where he has all the modern conveniences powered through generators and a fleet of vehicles at his disposal. Although most of the young entrepreneurs seem to eschew politics, some have in fact become public figures who make public statements about politics and government policy. However, it is striking that those religious entrepreneurs who have attained the most fame and success are also those who seem to be the most media savvy. Or, they surround themselves with media savvy handlers who are adept at interacting with graphic designers, television and radio producers, technicians, website designers, and so forth. In fact, being media savvy and knowing how to engage with the media to communicate with potential followers and customers seems to be an increasingly important element to charisma and ultimate success, which eludes most who might want to invest in such a career and undertake the risk to enter such a competitive religious economy.

As I noted earlier, such entrepreneurs have developed reputations for making desired things come to pass, and some are known for their expertise in certain areas or for resolving particular sorts of problems – financial, social, marital, sexual, and so forth. The reputations and fame of such entrepreneurs often seem to spread through word of mouth, and this helps to attract even more inquiring clients who might have also heard about them through the various marketing techniques in use.

At first glance, there appear to be fewer obstacles to entry into Mali's much more liberalized religious economy. On the demand side there is an avid interest in religion among all sectors of society, including by many who are disillusioned with multiparty elections that only seem to reproduce the country's elites. But perhaps even more important, there is the hope and quest for success and wealth in a country with staggering levels of poverty and lack of opportunity, especially for youths, alongside spectacular wealth for a few. The diminished number of saintly superstars has certainly been an important factor but the remaining ones continue to be relatively aloof from the burgeoning religious economy in Bamako. It would seem that any ambitious young man (they are almost all young men) might be able to try his luck in the religious economy, for example, by offering services in the fee-for-service religious market.

Clearly, aesthetic and affective elements have been important, helping to shape the demand for such figures and their services. To succeed, new religious figures must be able to meet such demand. They must be alluring, not least by having an aura of being able to make things happen, preferably also with the caché of being able to deliver clients quick results. Around some of them there is what might even be considered excitement, a certain *frisson*, or a sense of cool and fun, which are particularly prevalent among the Rasta Sufis with their unconventional albeit trendy sartorial style. In many cases, it helps to be able to gesture toward hereditary credentials, perhaps invoke a famous ancestor (as, for example, Soufi Bilal does) or origins from a place known in the social imagination for its mystique (as, for example, Soufi Adama does), or assert closeness to other usually deceased saintly figures (as most of the figures do). There is considerable buzz around many of these new religious figures about their abilities to make such-and-such a thing happen and their relative success in this era of insecurity and uncertainty. There is also considerable effort by such figures, those around them, and their clients to generate such buzz and make it proliferate. However, it is difficult to generalize about the processes that turn people into the clients and customers of such figures. What is clear is that competition has indeed been stiff. To use additional market metaphors, there are market pressures, which prevent just anyone from entering the market and succeeding in what has become crowded and competitive, and quite a number of entrants to the religious economy ultimately do not succeed or their success is of limited duration.

Within this religious economy, rival religious entrepreneurs sometimes impugn each other's integrity or denounce other figures, saying they are interested only in material gain rather than in religion. This relates to a broader discourse about morality, the sincerity of devotion in religion, and the intention (*niya* from the Arabic) of actors, especially religious actors who are frequently looked to as moral exemplars. But it also connects to a widespread discourse about the importance of mutual aid or reciprocity, which is frequently discussed in terms of how individuals should share what they have with others in a society characterized by great uncertainty, huge disparities in wealth, and widespread accusations of corruption.

Most Muslim reformists and Islamists in Mali see all such practices in the religious economy as no less than idolatry (or shirk) and fee-for-service religion in particular as charlatanism. The critiques of reformist Muslims and Islamists aside, many in the older generation, particularly members of the country's ‘ulama and those associated with some of the lineages of saintly superstars, malign many of the new religious entrepreneurs. They regularly cast aspersions on them, questioning their legitimacy and authenticity. They frequently claim they are ignorant about Islam and the Islamic esoteric sciences and interested only in making money rather than in promoting religion and its virtues. Interestingly, the latter perspective is widely shared by those Malians who are ardent secularists, many of whom think that religion should be confined to its proper place and not be mixed with economics or politics, as well as by leftists, who remain important especially among Mali's educated classes and elites.

In addition to such critiques from Islamists, secularists, and leftists, one can also see some of the tensions within the religious economy. Indeed, within a context of considerable competition in the religious economy, a select few seem to have the ability to accumulate great wealth and attain great fame. This also points to the considerable ambivalence about the market in which some persons' wealth might possibly be acquired through illicit means or through forms of corruption. In the current era, there is constant speculation about graft and corruption, and the major campaigns regularly launched ostensibly to stamp it out in the broader society seem to flow into discussions of religion. There is also great concern and frequently even heightened anxiety about the possibly nefarious means – via the Islamic esoteric sciences or forms of sorcery – some actors might be willing to employ to defeat a rival in the religious economy or on the fee-for-service religious market. In fact, there is regular discussion about the ends to which some religious entrepreneurs might go to prevent a rival from succeeding or what some might do to attract clients or even steal them away from another figure in the religious market.

Within this context of competition, rivalry, inevitable failure for some, and success for a few, many Malians try to act like discerning customers, indeed, consumers in the religious economy where the ultimate allegiance of the customer always seems elusive. They often seem ready to disparage, if not denounce, different entrepreneurs as hucksters or frauds and vote with their feet if they do not get the results they seek. In the event the religious figure to whom someone is linked disappoints, perhaps by not making desired things happen, not redistributing enough of his wealth, or through financial ruin, that person can shift his or her attention to one of the other figures, including new entrants to the market who might offer similar services, seem more alluring and appealing, or about whom there might be considerable buzz.

Some of those who have entered the market have been able to establish regional reputations for their services, and their fortunes might also wax and wane. For example, Soufi Lassana, another of the so-called Rasta Sufis, is based in Mali's third largest city, Ségou, which is known as an important Islamic religious center. In the 1990s Lassana developed a reputation as a Sufi master who was able to make desired things happen, and he attracted many followers and clients, particularly women, and accumulated considerable wealth and influence. He occasionally travels to Bamako at the invitation of wealthy and well-placed patrons who solicit him for his services. During such visits to the capital he might be able to attract new followers who might have heard about his reputation or be impressed by the high status and wealth of his hosts.

Other young religious leaders have been able to attain much wider fame and success. This is particularly the case for a number of the young, new-style Sufi leaders who are based in and around Bamako. Although they frequently invoke the names and memories of Mali's esteemed Muslim saints and Sufi leaders from the past, they usually claim to be independent of the country's existing Sufi orders (primarily the Qadiriyya, Tijaniyya, and their various branches), Sufi leaders, and their hierarchies, which have long been important in the country. Indeed, they often act as though they are completely *sui generis*, even if many Malians can point to those who might have been their teachers or those who might have initiated them into Sufism. Soufi Bilal, one of these young, new-style Sufis and allegedly a former protégé of Soufi Lassana, who claims to have reached the highest stage of Sufism, has actually founded a new formal Islamic association, Communauté Musulmane des Soufis du Mali (CMS-Mali, the Muslim Community of Sufis of Mali), which now has branches in large parts of the country (see Soares 2007, 2010; Bourdarias 2009). One of the first Malian religious leaders to have had his own website, he also has a considerable video presence on the Internet, and he has become increasingly active on social media, where he promotes his organization and his ideas about Sufism. Although initially Bilal seemed to appeal primarily to young Muslims of modest means and backgrounds, as his reputation has developed upwardly mobile educated urbanites and some members of the country's political and economic elites have been attracted to him for his pious reputation, as well as his services in the esoteric sciences (see Soares 2010). At the same time, some Malians see him as a possible alternative to reformist Muslims and Islamists. Be that as it may, much of the media around Bilal remains focused on him as the central charismatic figure to whom followers and clients – actual and potential – should turn if they would like to get ahead.

In fact, most of the new-style Sufis do seem to be operating in a postinstitutional context, that is, in line with the postinstitutional features of contemporary religion that many sociologists have identified (see Turner 2010). Here much attention is focused on such individual, charismatic figures like Bilal, even if he has founded a formal organization. This is also the case for someone like Soufi Lassana, as well as Adama, another of the so-called Rasta Sufis, who is based in Bamako. Although Adama calls himself a Sufi and considers himself a Muslim, unlike many of his peers, he also talks about wanting to unify all people – Muslims, Christians, and "pagans" or "animists." On some of the laminated badges marketed around Adama, he appears alongside Pope John Paul II, thereby suggesting the two are equals or interchangeable and generating quite a bit of buzz about an ostensible Muslim and self-styled Sufi who associates openly with Christianity. In addition to combining Christian symbols such as the cross and headdresses of high-ranking Roman Catholic clergy and such un-Islamic symbols and elements as the iconography of the country's best-known "pagan" (or "animist") masks in his and his entourage's dress and material culture, Adama is closely associated with Daouda Yattara, a.k.a. Satan, one of Mali's most prominent and even notorious non-Muslim ritual specialists. The charismatic Adama seems much more focused on the unity, which he calls for and seems to embody in his dress and comportment, rather than any institution building.

As I suggested earlier, these new entrepreneurs in the changed religious economy are not, however, only Muslims. In fact, they include non-Muslim ("pagan" or "animist") ritual specialists, often called *féticheurs* in French, some of whom have also gone on to great fame and social success like the village-based figure mentioned earlier. One of the most prominent of these in Bamako is the young former Muslim nicknamed Satan who offers good health, wealth, and success to clients. Satan attracted so much attention for his services and the bravado with which he, his entourage, followers, and clients talked about his abilities and services that he quickly gained notoriety as well as many detractors (see Soares 2016a, 2016b). For nearly all such entrepreneurs – Muslim or non-Muslim – critics, the machinations of possible rivals, and the risk of failure are almost always present factors.

Conclusion

In this discussion of the religious economy in Mali and what some Malians refer to as "structural adjustment Islam," I have shown how some religious practices in contemporary Mali, most notably, fee-for-service religion, have come to resemble market-oriented behavior quite closely. In the era of reforms and the liberalization of the economy, the religious economy, which is an economy of religious practice, also seems to have been liberalized. In recent years, this liberalized religious economy has become an important arena of experimentation as various religious entrepreneurs try their luck in the fee-for-service-religious market. When one considers the various new religious figures I have described and their involvement in fee-for-service religion, one can see how much entrepreneurialism has become a key mode of action even in the realm of religion in the era of neoliberal reforms. Many ordinary Malians' modalities of religious expression have also come to resemble the market economy, hence the term "structural adjustment Islam." As processes of becoming clients or customers in the religious market are open ended and can change over time, it is clear that modalities of religious expression have not been entirely reduced to the logic of the market. Indeed, the changing religious economy in which there has been considerable experimentation and innovation by entrepreneurial individuals remains rather unstable even if it does seem to mirror the market economy. Such instability might relate to the fact, as Max Weber noted, that charisma is always unstable. Although over time charisma can be tamed and routinized, it seems unlikely that charisma will necessarily be exhausted in a place like Mali any time soon. The demand for persons with charismatic abilities, miracles, and worldly success remains very strong in this region. Indeed, many Malians comport themselves like discerning customers, regularly on the lookout for new and presumably charismatic figures and sometimes even authentic saints who might help them get what they want in exchange for money. Given that such people's allegiances and their resources cannot be taken for granted, the supply of such new figures, some of whom seem able to embody some of the elements of the market and its success while simultaneously defying its logic, is unlikely to diminish any time soon.

In closing, I emphasize that I have tried to show in this chapter how such analytical devices as religious economy, fee-for-service religion, and religious marketing – although certainly in need of further theoretical refinement – can help us to make sense of some of the momentous changes in a place like Mali. Indeed, they help us understand some of the changing modalities of religious expression and new entrepreneurial figures that have accompanied processes of economic and political liberalization, the stepped-up implementation of neoliberal reforms, and the rise of entrepreneurialism in religion. As I have tried to show, such analytical tools and economic metaphors are not merely the language of the outside analyst such as myself. I have drawn from the perspective of Malians who have talked about and analyzed these much-discussed changes in the realm of religion. Islamist critiques of Sufism and fee-for-service religion in Mali and the broader region are longstanding. As I have shown, some have also lamented what they call "structural adjustment Islam," and others have decried the new religious marketing in the contemporary religious economy. Still yet others seem in awe of Mali's young religious leaders, some of whom have been able to become "millionaires," or they are condescending toward them. Distancing myself from such normative views, though mindful of the heavily laden normative perspective of many who talk about religion and neoliberalism, I have preferred to talk here about the religious economy in the neoliberal era. Such young religious entrepreneurs help us to see how religion in Mali is a heterogeneous field of competition, debate, and contestation. Clearly, such an insight about how religion and economy in the neoliberal era are deeply intertwined should not be mistaken as a form of apologetics.

Notes

This chapter draws on different periods of field research in Mali beginning in 1992 but particularly in the period since 2003, when I first met some of the key figures discussed here. The Malians who assisted me with this research and its analysis are too numerous to mention. However, I would like to single out the late Daouda Dia, Mohamed Aliou Sow, and Moussa Djiré for special thanks. I would also like to thank Filippo Osella and Daromir Rudnyckyj for their constructive comments on earlier drafts of the chapter.

1 Some of these saints' tombs had been designated UNESCO World Heritage sites. See De Jorio (2016). On the 2012 coup and its aftermath, see Soares (2012, 2013).
2 As I have written earlier, we know from Max Weber that, "the relationship of religious practices and [the 'economy' or] the market is very complex indeed. [Moreover,] ... it would be tendentious to claim that religion has been reduced entirely to the logic of the market" (Soares 2005: 252).
3 In his more recent book *Terrains of Exchange* (2014), Green addresses some of his critics, presenting even richer and more far-ranging materials to illustrate the applicability of his market model.
4 Gifts might also be involved but would seem to be not as important as money and commodities.
5 I have written about Haïdara elsewhere; see Soares (2004b, 2005, 2006, 2016c). See also Davis (2002), Holder (2009, 2012), and Schulz (2006a, 2006b).
6 "Halte au marketing religieux!" *Le Démocrate*, September 23, 1993, p. 2.
7 On Adama, see Soares (2007, 2016a, 2016b), as well as the study of Adama from the perspective of the poor Bamako neighborhood where Françoise Bourdarias has conducted long-term fieldwork in Bourdarias (2008, 2009).
8 M. H., "Ces nouveaux prêcheurs jeunes et millionaires," *Bamako Hebdo* (January 24, 2015), www.maliweb.net/societe/ces-nouveaux-precheurs-jeunes-et-millionnaires-761402.html.
9 "Moussa Traoré, le Grand Marabout," *Aurore* (704), February 6, 2001, p. 6.

References

Ahmad, Irfan. 2013. "Anthropology of Islam: History, Culture and Power." *Indian Economic and Social History Review* 50(4): 495–509.

Bourdarias, Françoise. 2008. "L'imam, le soufi et Satan: religion et politique à Bamako (Mali)." In *Les constructions locales du politique*, edited by F. Bourdarias and H. Bertheleu, 115–139. Tours: Presses Universitaires de France.

2009. "Constructions religieuses du politique aux confins de Bamako (Mali)." *Civilisations* 58(2): 21–40.

Comaroff, Jean, and John L. Comaroff. 1999. "Occult Economies and the Violence of Abstraction: Notes from the South African Postcolony." *American Ethnologist* 26: 279–303.

Davis, Kimberley. 2002. "Preaching to the Converted: Charismatic Leaders, Performances and Electronic Media in Contemporary Islamic Communities." MA thesis, Sociology and Anthropology, Concordia University, Montreal.

De Jorio, Rosa. 2016. *Cultural Heritage in Mali in the Neoliberal Era*. Urbana-Champaign: University of Illinois Press.

Dumestre, Gérard, and Seydou Touré. 2007. *Maléfices et manigances: chroniques maliennes*. Paris: Karthala.

Ganti, Tejaswini. 2014. "Neoliberalism." *Annual Review of Anthropology* 43: 89–104.

Gellner, Ernest. 1981. *Muslim Society*. Cambridge: Cambridge University Press.

Green, Nile. 2011. *Bombay Islam*. Cambridge: Cambridge University Press.

2014. *Terrains of Exchange*. London: Hurst.

Haenni, Patrick. 2005. *L'islam de marché: L'autre révolution conservatrice*. Paris: Seuil.

Holder, Gilles. 2009. "'Maouloud 2006', de Bamako à Tombouctou: Entre réislamisation de la nation et laïcité de l'État: la construction d'un espace public religieux au Mali." In *L'islam, nouvel espace public en Afrique*, edited by Gilles Holder, 237–289. Paris: Karthala.

2012. "Chérif Ousmane Madani Haïdara et l'association islamique Ançar Dine: un réformisme malien populaire en quête d'autonomie." *Cahiers d'études africaines* 206–207(2): 389–425.

Jones, Carla. 2010. "Materializing Piety: Gendered Anxieties about Faithful Consumption in Contemporary Urban Indonesia." *American Ethnologist* 37(4): 617–637.

Kitiarsa, Pattiana. 2010. "Toward a Sociology of Religious Commodification." In *The New Blackwell Companion to the Sociology of Religion*, edited by Bryan S. Turner, 563–583. Oxford: Blackwell.

Lehmann, David. 2010. "An Idea, a Tribe, and Their Critics: Rational Choice and the Sociology of Religion." In *The New Blackwell Companion to the Sociology of Religion*, edited by Bryan S. Turner, 181–200. Oxford: Blackwell.

Lydon, Ghislaine. 2009. *On Trans-Saharan Trails: Islamic Law, Trade Networks, and Cross-Cultural Exchange in Nineteenth-Century Western Africa*. Cambridge: Cambridge University Press.

Masquelier, Adeline. 2016. "'The Mouthpiece of an Entire Generation': Hip-Hop, Truth, and Islam in Niger." *Muslim Youth and the 9/11 Generation*, edited by Adeline Masquelier and Benjamin Soares, 213–238. Albuquerque: University of New Mexico Press.

Mirowski, Philip. 2009. "Postface: Defining Neoliberalism." In *The Road from Mount Pelerin: The Making of the Neoliberal Thought Collective*, edited by Philip Mirowski and Dieter Plehwe, 417–455. Cambridge, MA: Harvard University Press.

Mirowski, Philip, and Dieter Plehwe (eds.). 2009. *The Road from Mount Pelerin: The Making of the Neoliberal Thought Collective*. Cambridge, MA: Harvard University Press.

Obadia, Lionel, and Donald C. Wood (eds.). 2011. *The Economics of Religion: Anthropological Approaches*. Bingley, UK: Emerald Books.

Osella, Filippo, and Caroline Osella. 2009. "Muslim Entrepreneurs in Public Life between India and the Gulf: Making Good and Doing Good." *Journal of the Royal Anthropological Institute* 15(S1): 202–221.

Roy, Olivier. 2004. *Globalized Islam: The Search for a New Ummah*. New York: Columbia University Press.

Rudnyckyj, Daromir. 2010. *Spiritual Economies: Islam, Globalization, and the Afterlife of Development*. Ithaca, NY: Cornell University Press.

Schulz, Dorothea E. 2006a. "Morality, Community, Publicness: Shifting Terms of Public Debate in Mali." In *Religion, Media, and the Public Sphere*, edited by Birgit Meyer and Annelies Moors, 132–151. Bloomington: Indiana University Press.

2006b. "Promises of (Im)mediate Salvation: Islam, Broadcast Media, and the Remaking of Religious Experience in Mali." *American Ethnologist* 33(2): 210–229.

Soares, Benjamin. 2004a. "Muslim Saints in the Age of Neoliberalism." In *Producing African Futures: Ritual and Reproduction in a Neoliberal Age*, edited by Brad Weiss, 79–105. Leiden: Brill.

2004b. "Islam and Public Piety in Mali." In *Public Islam and the Common Good*, edited by Armando Salvatore and Dale F. Eickelman, 205–226. Leiden: Brill.

2005. *Islam and the Prayer Economy: History and Authority in a Malian Town*. Edinburgh/Ann Arbor: Edinburgh University Press/the University of Michigan Press.

2006. "Islam in Mali in the Neoliberal Era." *African Affairs* 104(418): 77–95.

2007. "Saint and Sufi in Neoliberal Mali." In *Sufism and the "Modern" in Islam*, edited by Martin van Bruinessen and Julia Howell, 77–91. London: I. B. Tauris.

2010. "'Rasta' Sufis and Muslim Youth Culture in Mali." In *Being Young and Muslim: New Cultural Politics in the Global South and North*, edited by Linda Herrera and Asef Bayat, 495–509. New York: Oxford University Press.

2012. "On the Recent Mess in Mali." *Anthropology Today* 28(5): 1–2.

2013. "Islam in Mali since the 2012 Coup." *Fieldsights – Hot Spots, Cultural Anthropology Online*, June 10. www.culanth.org/fieldsights/321-islam-in-mali-since-the-2012-coup.

2016a. "Malian Youth between Sufism and Satan." In *Muslim Youth and the 9/11 Generation*, edited by Adeline Masquelier and Benjamin Soares, 169–188. Albuquerque: University of New Mexico Press.

2016b. "Reflections on Muslim-Christian Encounters in West Africa." *Africa* 86(4): 673–697.

2016c. "New Muslim Public Figures in West Africa." In *Writing Boards and Blackboards: Islamic Education in Africa*, edited by Robert Launay, 268–284. Bloomington: Indiana University Press.

Turner, Bryan S. 2010. "Religion in Post-Secular Society." In *The New Blackwell Companion to the Sociology of Religion*, edited by Bryan S. Turner, 649–667. Oxford: Blackwell.

2012. "Post-Secular Society: Consumerism and the Democratization of Religion." In *The Post-Secular in Question: Religion in Contemporary Society*, edited by Philip S. Gorski, David Kyuman Kim, John Torpey, and Jonathan VanAntwerpen, 135–158. New York: New York University Press.

van der Veer, Peter. 2012. "Market and Money: A Critique of Rational Choice Theory." *Social Compass* 59(2): 183–192.

Weber, Max. 1978. *Economy and Society*. 2 vols. Berkeley: University of California Press.

7 Assembling Islam and Liberalism: Market Freedom and the Moral Project of Islamic Financc

Daromir Rudnyckyj, University of Victoria

On March 1, 2010, the *Wall Street Journal* published an article titled "Doing God's Work," which highlighted the impressive growth of Islamic banking and finance and some of the challenges that faced the industry as it expanded at unprecedented rates. Before presenting data on the proliferation of Islamic bonds and an array of statistical indicators for the achievements of Islamic finance at large, the article opened with a suggestive vignette that highlighted some of the moral questions raised by Islamic finance:

> At a party in Karachi a young man cradles a glass of whiskey and laughs when asked why he is in the Islamic banking industry. "It is the fastest-growing sector in Pakistan," he says. "I want to make money, so this is where I need to be. Who cares about religion?" A corporate-finance lawyer, who is a devout Muslim, gives a very different answer: "If you do not believe that Islam and its teachings can bring about positive change to the world, then you should not be in the business." (Phillips 2010)

The contrasting vignettes presented starkly different moral orientations toward managing Islamic money. On one hand, an Islamic banker is violating one of Islam's central prohibitions and attributing his motivation to market forces; on the other is an industry player who saw Islamic finance as a moral project capable of social change.[1] The central question that these contrasting vignettes raised was, How Islamic is Islamic finance? In other words, to what extent can Islamic finance, as a project simultaneously dedicated toward enacting Islamic values *and* facilitating capitalist economic action, successfully fulfill both mandates?

Indeed this is a central question that animates many of those engaged in Islamic finance today and is a recurring problem for most practitioners. This problem was evident several weeks later when I attended a public forum at the ultramodern headquarters of Malaysia's Securities Commission in the Bukit Kiara section of Kuala Lumpur. The meeting, jointly organized with the Oxford Centre for Islamic Studies, was titled "The Contribution of Islamic Finance, Post-Global Financial Crisis" and was headlined by a number of famous scholars and practitioners with international reputations in Islamic finance. The *Wall Street Journal* article, with its allusions to moral impropriety among those engaged in Islamic finance, was a hot topic of conversation among participants at the forum. In one afternoon session, before an audience of roughly 400 practitioners, a Gulf-based Islamic finance professional with more than two decades of experience in the field explicitly referred to the piece in the context of staffing Islamic financial institutions. Addressing the audience in the second person and in tones of moral reproach, he said:

> You might have seen the lovely *Wall Street Journal* article a few weeks ago – the opening paragraph about the Islamic banker in Pakistan enjoying his whiskey and explaining why he was in the business. So, even if you put on your best face at work and everything is fantastic, you're docile and humble in your sales approach. You say your prayers in front of the colleagues. Maybe you go home and have your whiskey? Who knows?

Perhaps intended to stir introspection, he referred to a moral problem that animates Islamic finance. Were Islamic finance practitioners living according to the moral code prescribed by Islam? Or was their Islamic practice simply a smokescreen, covering up their participation in distinctly un-Islamic activities? This reflection on the empirical practices of Islamic finance practitioners alluded to a broader question often broached in Islamic finance regarding the relationship between outward form and interior substance. To what extent does Islamic finance offer a real moral alternative to liberal freedom and the kind of market action that it presupposes? Or is Islamic finance simply a thinly veiled version of conventional finance? This question became more pressing in the wake of the global financial crisis that started in 2008, as many Islamic finance practitioners attribute the crisis to a lack of moral responsibility among those on Wall Street and elsewhere who created the exotic securities that precipitated financial quagmire and global recession. Indeed, a central problem in Islamic finance today is to what extent it can offer a moral alternative to market capitalism or whether it essentially replicates the basic moral structures of the market.

The question of the difference that Islam makes has been a widespread topic of discussion among scholars as well. Saba Mahmood has shown how women seeking to enhance their Islamic piety through participation in the mosque movement in Egypt question the universality of liberal freedom (Mahmood 2005). In so doing, she argues that liberalism is premised on the exclusion of religious practice as a legitimate form of political practice. Drawing on Foucault's genealogy of market freedom (Foucault 2008), I seek to build on this account of the relationship between Islam and liberalism. Whereas Mahmood showed how Muslim women in contemporary Egypt challenge the assumptions of liberal freedom, I seek instead to show how liberalism is an explicit object of reflection among proponents and practitioners of Islamic finance.

This chapter documents the debates over moral questions that pervade Islamic finance today. The techniques of self-cultivation in which Mahmood's

Egyptian interlocutors engaged indicate a form of self-discipline that challenges liberal notions of agency. She develops the concept of docile agency to characterize the practices of Egyptian women, suggesting an alternative to the configuration of freedom characteristic of liberalism (Mahmood 2001). In supplementing Mahmood's account, I seek to show how a different legacy of liberalism inflects the practices of Islamic finance experts today. The morality of market action is a recurrent problem for proponents and practitioners of Islamic finance. While Mahmood underscores the radical alterity of Islamic ethics and the failure of liberalism to meaningfully comprehend those ethics, I argue that such a focus may obscure the diverse assemblages of Islam and liberalism emergent today. Thus, this chapter seeks to demonstrate how moral questions about correct Islamic practice are common objects of reflection among Islamic finance experts. Empirically, I focus on the efforts of actors who both seek to reform Islamic finance and to preserve it in its current form. I conclude that Islamic finance illuminates one assemblage of Islam and liberalism and reveals how questions of personal propriety are profoundly linked to market action.

At the outset, it is critical to note that the tension between worldly and otherworldly concerns has been long debated in Islamic history. Hamid Hosseini has noted that early Muslim scholars created two distinct perspectives on trade, for "the first theory praised wealth for its own sake" while "the second theory...stemmed from the Islamic assumption that for Muslims this world is a preparation for the next" (Hosseini 2003: 92). Thus, he describes how scholars such as Dimishqi, writing in the twelfth century, developed something that looks like "what modern economics calls price theory" (94) insofar as Dimishqi documented the effect of supply and demand on market prices, which a trader must comprehend to be successful. Hosseini attributes the second theory of trade to the eleventh-century writings of Ghazali, who argued that economic participation could constitute part of a morally upstanding life, but only insofar as such a life was directed toward otherworldly salvation (Hosseini 2003: 95–96). Hossieni concludes that both authors "had a thorough understanding of the market mechanism" (106). In this sense, the arguments made by Islamic finance professionals today about the compatibility of Islam and liberalism can be understood as fitting well within the broad contours of reflection on economic phenomena in Islamic history.

Sovereignty and Market Freedom

To comprehend the moral project of Islamic finance and efforts to remake market practices according to Islamic norms it is useful to understand how liberal capitalism displaced moral concerns from the market. In the *Birth of Biopolitics*, a set of lectures that were delivered at the Collège de France in

1979, Michel Foucault sketches out a preliminary genealogy of liberalism as a way of explaining the principles and practices of neoliberalism. Foucault shows how the relationship of the state and the market was reconfigured from being a problem of moral intervention to one of producing truth. In Foucault's account, prior to the eighteenth century, the state's main objective in the market was to ensure that market prices were just (Foucault 2008: 30). The state monitored the market to ensure that prices were fair and to protect consumers from immoral merchants who might try to deceive their customers. Foucault further notes that fraud was a chronic problem in late-medieval and early modern marketplaces, as unscrupulous vendors recurrently deceived their clients by selling them flour riddled with weevils and milk that had already spoiled. Thus, an exercise of sovereign power ensured that values were negotiated justly, and the market became a site of state regulation.

Foucault argues that this relationship was altered in the eighteenth century, when the market was reconceived as "that which reveals something like a truth" (32), as what alone is deemed the site in which "natural" prices are realized (31). Natural prices here must be determined without state efforts to ensure justice by, for example, setting artificial prices indexed to concerns deemed external to the market, such as protection of the poor from unjust prices and protection of consumers from fraud. The transformation in market interventions is precipitated by the realization that the state can never know the multitude of economic actions that occur over the extent of its territory. Thus, authorities become aware of the limitations of sovereign knowledge and the market is transformed from a site of moral intervention to one for the determination of truth, or what Foucault terms "a site of veridiction" (32–33). Market freedom is defined as the state's noninterference, which enables prices to emerge naturally from the free association of buyers and sellers. This may appear familiar to contemporary readers, as it is a formulation that undergirds the predominant economic thought of today. The conviction that action within the market was capable of revealing the truth of price explains, in part, the ongoing attachment that liberals (and neoliberals) have to the market.

Foucault's genealogy of the market as a means to produce truth is key to understanding contemporary capitalism and the way in which capitalism separates moral questions from questions of livelihood. In reconfiguring the market from a site for the administration of justice to a site of veridiction, the problem of the market is reconfigured from a moral one to a technical one. That is to say, the market, rather than being a site in which sovereign power was required to ensure moral practice, is redeployed as a space that is devoid of moral problematization and free of state intervention. Thus, in creating the principle of market freedom, liberalism separated moral questions from action that was defined as amoral. Morality could then be divorced from economic action.

Defining Islamic Finance

In seeking to reconfigure economic action and financial forms according to religious principles, experts in Islamic finance question the separation between market freedom and moral questions that Foucault argued was constitutive of liberalism. In the eyes of reformers who have become disenchanted with the manner in which it has developed, Islamic finance should ground economic action not in the universal principles of market liberalism (such as self-interest, rational choice, and individual freedom), but rather in moral prescriptions drawn from the Qur'an. Experts most often refer to the Qur'anic prohibition against the payment of interest (or what is called *riba* in Arabic) as the central difference between Islamic and conventional finance.[2] Although historically there have been attempts to parse the meaning of *riba* by defining it as usury or excessive interest,[3] today there is broad consensus in the Islamic finance industry that any money that is created out of money, without a sale or improvement through labor, is contrary to the revealed word of Allah contained in the Qur'an (Warde 2010: 45–47).

In fact, according to most Islamic finance experts, charging interest is among the most immoral acts mentioned in the Qur'an. As one former conventional banker in Malaysia (who had by his own account "converted" to Islamic banking) noted, there is clear direction in the *hadiths*[4] regarding the immorality of collecting interest. With a wry smile he said, "The prophet Muhammad stated that collecting interest is a sin worse than committing adultery thirty-six times." This calculation was mentioned to me several times by other Islamic finance experts in defining the existential predicament confronting those who sought to engage in commerce and simultaneously live according to the moral principles inherent in key Islamic texts. Thus, irrespective of whether interest is the most efficient or productive manner of providing capital, the Islamic finance industry has increasingly sought to avoid it.

As Thomas Pepinsky has observed, the Qur'anic proscription of *riba* has led to two basic techniques that Islamic financial institutions use to avoid charging interest: trade-based transactions and profit-sharing agreements (Pepinsky 2013). Trade-based transactions involve a purchase followed by a deferred sale. The most commonly used such transaction is known as a *murabaha*, which is what practitioners call a "cost-plus contract" in which a financial institution purchases an asset and then sells it to a customer at a mark-up on a deferred payment basis. The transaction is deemed permissible (*halal*) because it involves a formal sale in which a financial institution takes possession of an asset and therefore the risk associated with that asset, even if only for as brief as a second. As Pepinsky notes, the charge that the financial institution levies "functions nearly identically to interest in conventional financial systems" (Pepinsky 2013: 159). Although there is scant precedent for murabaha either in *fiqh* or Islamic history, these are the most widespread instruments used in Islamic finance today, consisting of roughly 80 percent of total contracts, leading to what has been called the "murabaha syndrome" (Yousef 2004). Their ease of use has been seen largely as enabling the rapid growth of Islamic banking.

While some Islamic scholars have questioned trade-based contracts, such as murabaha, profit-sharing agreements are viewed far more favorably by virtually all Islamic jurists. These contracts appear more frequently in classical juristic texts and have a much longer historical precedent (Udovitch 1970; Çizakça 2011: 249–274). Profit-sharing contracts, such as *musharaka* and *mudaraba*, are considered "equity-based" rather than debt-based because they are premised on mutual investments in real assets and resemble the venture capital contracts commonly celebrated for spurring entrepreneurship in places such as Silicon Valley. A mudaraba, for example, is a profit-sharing contract in which a mudarib (entrepreneur) and a capital provider enter into a partnership. The mudarib typically possesses expertise and entrepreneurial acumen, but no capital of his or her own. Profits generated by the joint venture are split between the parties according to a predetermined ratio. However, the party providing the capital bears all financial losses, while the mudarib or investment manager bears the opportunity costs associated with managing the venture.

Questions regarding the Islamicity of murabaha and efforts to refocus Islamic finance on profit-sharing contracts such as mudaraba reveal how Islamic finance experts are debating the extent to which the moral values of Islam can be integrated with capitalism. Critics of debt-based financing and proponents of profit sharing base their arguments on features that do not conform to the economism that undergirds liberalism. In so doing, they may suggest a type of economic rationality not premised on the sovereign subject that is assumed in the liberal economic models that constitute the dominant economic paradigm of our times (Barry et al. 1996; Rose 1999). For example, risk-sharing in mudaraba contracts distributes economic hazards between a creditor and a debtor rather than expecting a borrower to assume the entire burden of risk (McKay 2009). Thus, Islamic finance may offer the possibility to create stronger collective relationships than conventional finance and ultimately a more stable system, as there is an acceptance of financial risk rather than a ceaseless attempt to find a counterparty to shoulder the burden.

Indeed, many Islamic finance experts have criticized trade-based contracts and seek to reform Islamic finance to make it conform more faithfully to the "goals of *sharia*" (*maqasid*), by more frequently using profit-sharing agreements. However, other experts have expressed caution. For example, at Harvard University's biannual forum on Islamic finance in 2012, one leading Islamic finance expert suggested that banks and venture capitalists make different types of risk calculations. He said that there is a "fundamental difference between traditional lending and partnership contracts...Bankers want to be repaid. Venture capitalists want to grow businesses. Most bankers are bad venture capitalists and most venture capitalists are bad bankers. Venture capitalists accept the fact that most businesses fail." Thus, some experts realize that the moral project that many proponents associate with Islamic finance is in need of substantial work.

Remaking Market Morality

The moral project of Islamic finance was further evident in an address delivered in a plenary session on the second day of the eighth International Conference on Islamic Economics and Finance, held in December 2011 in Doha, Qatar. During the session Dr. Asad Zaman, a professor of economics at the International Islamic University in Islamabad, delivered a blistering critique of financial economics. In front of an immense conference hall, with close to a thousand people in attendance, he pronounced "the methodology of modern economics is fundamentally flawed...all the basic theories are wrong!" Dr. Zaman, who holds degrees from Stanford and MIT, spoke eloquently amidst the opulence of Doha's brand new National Conference Center, large portions of which remained unfinished at the time of the meeting. The light from dozens of five foot tall teardrop-shaped lamps, each adorned with 12,700 Swarovski crystals, slowly rotated through a rainbow spectrum – scarlet...orange...gold...emerald...sapphire...indigo...violet – painting the room in an ever-changing glow that ranged from soothing blue to anxiety-inducing orange. Dr. Zaman's passionate oration stirred the audience from a mild mid-morning torpor that had set in among many of the jet-lagged attendees, as the infusion of attention-enabling caffeine from the last coffee break was rapidly dissolving in our bloodstreams.

Dressed in an elegant beige *shalwar kameez*, chocolate-colored turban, and olive vest, he cut an impressive figure with his long white beard and spectacles lending him an air of practiced dignity and moral authority. In escalating tones Dr. Zaman began to list what he saw as the fundamental fallacies of finance and economics, his voice rising as he leveled each indictment: "Consumer theory is WRONG! Consumers do not maximize utilities!...If you try to use consumer theory to make predictions, you will be incorrect...Firm theory is WRONG! Firms do not maximize profits!...Price theory is WRONG! Prices are not determined by supply-demand equilibrium." Amidst the extravagance of the outsized hall, Dr. Zaman invoked the recent financial crises that had shaken countries from Britain to Botswana as evidence for the shortcomings of economics. "Since World War II there have been more than ninety monetary crises. We have no understanding of how to prevent these monetary crises!" He argued that financial theory had demonstrated itself to be wholly inadequate to the task of stable economic growth. With no shortage of hyperbole, he then connected the failure of the discipline of economics to development. "There have been sixty years of World Bank efforts at implementing different types of development policies, and there is not one example of success!"

Shortly thereafter Dr. Zaman shifted away from the crescendo of prosecutorial invective and began to speak in more measured tones, arguing that the failure of conventional economics could be attributed to its faulty assumptions regarding human beings. As a solution, he urged conference participants to purge Western knowledge from efforts to reconcile Islam with conventional economics and finance, because "ignorance cannot be combined with wisdom – all attempts to do so have failed!" He urged participants to avoid combining Western knowledge and Islam and instead to start over "from the bottom up." He said this was necessary because "the Qur'an continues to provide complete guidance to solve our current economic problems...the key to Islamic approach is the transformation of human beings. Muhammad made Muslims moral people and the Qur'an teaches generosity and kindness and compassion." With that, Dr. Zaman exuberantly segued into his final argument, "These values, not the accumulation of wealth, will change the world!" His exasperation was palpable, and by the time he reached this climactic pronouncement he had moved many of the attendees, who had just minutes earlier been on the brink of slumber, to the edges of their seats.

After several more plenary panel speakers, the moderator solicited questions from the audience. The third response came from a man with a precisely clipped British accent wearing a finely tailored suit. He rose near the front of the room, which felt as if it could easily accommodate at least three-quarters of a football pitch, and in pointed terms delivered a polite but incisive rejoinder to Dr. Zaman. In calm and confident tones he offered a measured defense of some of the central tenets of economics. "For every example of non-maximizing you come up with, I can bring for you 100 examples of maximization!... Even Amartya Sen, when he went back to Harvard, said 'the offer was so big, I could not resist'...You simply cannot eliminate maximization from human life...The ideas in economics are so logical we cannot refuse them!"

The standoff between Dr. Zaman and the Islamic banker expressed an underlying problem in Islamic finance and the way in which moral problems are a recurrent object of reflection among practitioners. Dr. Zaman is representative of those who seek to reform Islamic finance by creating a system that is clearly demarcated from conventional finance, which would be wholly divorced from it and reformulated "from the bottom up." Such viewpoints are common among those who challenge the notion of the market as a discrete sphere of human activity, by asserting that there are other logics that might guide production, consumption, and exchange. These experts are often engaged in policing the boundaries of Islamic finance – it is quite common, for instance, to hear of practitioners speaking of "firewalls" between conventional and Islamic accounts within institutions that conduct both Islamic and conventional operations.

In contrast, those like the man who rose to challenge Dr. Zaman's vision conceptualize a different relationship between conventional finance and Islamic finance. Whereas Dr. Zaman envisioned the possibility of a new market morality grounded in Islam, the banker saw Islamic finance as an offshoot or subdiscipline within universal economic principles. For those like him, market reason was driven by what he took to be universal laws of supply and demand and the rational pursuit of profit.

Milton Friedman: Islamic Banker

In contrast to those like Dr. Zaman, Islamic finance practitioners operate with a tighter set of constraints and offer a more nuanced view of the encounter between Islam and liberalism. These actors see market principles as universal values that cannot be refused, but also embrace a moral vision that they recognize as endemic to Islam. Their conviction in the universality of market morality is evident in the way in which they argue that Islamic finance must "compete" with conventional finance. In addition, executives of Islamic financial institutions invert the moral arguments of reformers. Rather than seeing Islam and liberalism as necessarily opposed, they seek to find different ways of resolving the two. What I find most interesting about these practitioners is that they come to different conclusions about the terms of the resolution.

State officials in Malaysia assumed that the nascent Islamic finance must prove its competitiveness with conventional finance when they initially established the national Islamic banking system in the early 1980s (El-Din and Abdullah 2007). Whereas countries such as Iran, Sudan, and Pakistan attempted the wholesale transformation of their national banking systems from conventional to Islamic in one fell swoop, Malaysia adopted a more measured "dual banking system" model, in which the newly established Islamic system would operate alongside the conventional banking system that the country inherited from the British. The presumption that the Islamic system is in competition with the conventional system persists among many proponents. For example, as Dato' Razif, the former deputy governor of Malaysia's Central Bank who held the Bank's Islamic finance portfolio until 2011, proclaimed in a speech marking collaboration on Islamic Finance between the Malaysian and Bahraini stock exchanges, "Efforts, time and resources must be pooled among the Islamic finance community to expand the industry and compete healthily with the larger conventional finance markets" (Razif Abdul Kadir 2010).

The imperative to competition is further evident in recent policies pursued by Malaysia's Central Bank. For example, it has sought to spur growth and innovation by opening its borders to competition from Islamic financial institutions based outside Malaysia. These include the Gulf-based companies Kuwait Finance House, Asian Finance Bank, and the Saudi-based Al-Rajhi bank (which proclaims itself as the world's largest Islamic bank). The governor of the Central Bank, Zeti Akhtar Aziz, couched the opening of the domestic Islamic banking industry in the same idioms of competition that characterize liberal economics. She expressed optimism that "the new entrants...will have the opportunity to bridge the two regions [Southeast Asia and the Middle East], participate in the growing Islamic banking industry as well as tap new markets in Malaysia and in the region, and promote *healthy competition* thereby contributing to elevate the industry to new levels of dynamism" (Aziz 2005, emphasis added). The focus on competition demonstrates how the principles of market liberalism frame the policy decisions of those seeking to cultivate Islamic finance. The governor's exhortation that competition is "healthy" shows the positive moral valence accorded to market principles and the biopolitical value that is associated with competition. The governor's comments also show that while Islamic finance in its more ideal forms attempts to reconfigure economic rationality, in practice it is always already positioned in relation to the logic of conventional finance.

Whereas scholars such as Dr. Zaman had the privilege of criticizing Islamic finance without having to be accountable to the demands of customers and shareholders, those working in Islamic finance find themselves facing a more challenging set of moral and market constraints. Hamza,[5] an executive at an Islamic financial services firm with twenty years of experience in Islamic finance, resolved this complicated position by avowing to reconcile the moral disconnect between Islamic finance and market liberalism. I met Hamza in a room on the lavish fortieth floor of the Petronas Towers, the tallest twin office buildings in the world, as a huge storm cell built up over the mountains northeast of Kuala Lumpur. As we chatted, the storm moved in through the city, turning the landscape momentarily opaque, and then dissipated almost as quickly as it arrived.

My conversation with Hamza was illuminating because rather than seeing Islamic finance as opposed to conventional capitalism, he saw it as more faithful to liberal economic principles than the capitalism practiced in the North Atlantic. Gradually, he walked me through the steps in this argument. Hamza told me that instruments like deposit insurance create irresponsible behavior because they discourages customers from "doing their due diligence."[6] In the conventional banking system, deposit insurance guarantees deposits and therefore customers do not "read the financial statements" of banks and "don't ensure that the bank is acting responsibly with their money." Consumers simply depend on the government to ensure the credibility of the banks. Hamza argued that in an Islamic financial system there would be no deposit insurance, because "making profit requires taking risks." Thus, consumers would have to spend more time monitoring the activities in which their banks were engaged. As I pondered the unpleasant prospect of actually having to read my bank's financial statements, Hamza said:

> At a conventional bank you just put your money in and you get a guaranteed return. With deposit insurance you don't need to worry about the possibility of a bank's failure. But interest and deposit insurance don't exist in the Islamic system – you may profit off the investment the bank makes with your deposit. But you might lose your money as well! So consumers are going to have to go into it with their eyes open. They are going to have to read the financial statements and do a lot more research on where their money goes and what it is doing than they did before.

He continued along this line of analysis, explaining that deposit insurance enables banks to pay out low interest rates on deposits and then subsequently enables them to charge low interest rates on loans, because the actual rate is not important to them: their profit comes from the margin between rates. The deposit insurance subsidy created a "moral hazard" in which consumers "did not monitor" the actions of their banks because they had "faith" that the government was insuring the system.

To my astonishment, Hamza then claimed that "the mudaraba model of banking is actually the free market model." Rather than seeing Islamic finance as opposed to liberalism, he saw it as more authentically liberal than conventional finance. He argued that mudaraba more accurately "prices and distributes" risk. If people were dependent on profit sharing, he reasoned, rather than guaranteed interest from their banks, they would be more diligent and would demand a higher return from the banks, due to the higher risk entailed in profit sharing as opposed to interest-based banking. To bolster this contention, Hamza quoted Muhammad Yunus, the founder of the Grameen Bank, who held that scholars and analysts had assumed that theory reflected reality – but what was needed was to better ground theory in actual reality. Yunus had argued that the success of the Grameen bank proved that poor people knew a lot more about money than most theoretically minded analysts had believed. Hamza implied that it was the same with Islamic banking assuming a much greater knowledge on the part of ordinary consumers. The deposit insurance system infantilizes them and treats them as irresponsible and ignorant.

In contrast, Hamza advocated changing the conventional system along the lines of the Chicago school of economics, which he said was "in fact Islamic in principle." He sketched out a radical rethinking of conventional banking according to what he argued were the fundamental tenets of Islamic economic action. Banks would have two kinds of accounts: demand deposit accounts and investment accounts. Customers would choose which kind of account better suited them. Those with no appetite for risk would use the demand deposit accounts, which would have "100 percent risk weightage," meaning that funds on deposits would be held in full by the bank. This would mean an end to the fractional reserve system in which banks can create fiat money. Currently, under Basel II banking regulations, banks are required to hold only 8 percent of their funds on deposit in liquid form.

In contrast, the investment accounts would be profit generating. A customer would choose what kind of risk he or she wanted and then select a corresponding account. Low-risk accounts would be based on real estate financing and high-risk accounts would be based on credit card financing. The returns from each investment would match the risk profile, unlike the current system in which risk and returns are out of alignment because of the subsidy granted through deposit insurance and "the lender of last resort" dictum, in which the state bails out firms that are designated "too big to fail." Thus, depositing money in the bank would be much more akin to investing in the stock market. When depositing money in the bank an investor would have to do the same kind of research that he or she now does when investing in stocks. Because it forced individuals to bear more risk without the security of deposit insurance, Hamza argued that Islamic finance was in fact more liberal than conventional finance, at one point exclaiming, "Milton Friedman was actually a proponent of Islamic finance!"

Hamza inverted Dr. Zaman's formulation. Rather than seeing Islamic finance as an alternative to liberal economic principles, he viewed it as the manifestation of true liberalism. Hamza invoked examples such as federal deposit insurance and government policies that see some financial institutions are "too big to fail" as evidence that countries, especially the United States, which espoused liberal economic principles were in fact insufficiently attentive to those principles. In contrast, Islamic finance emphasized a kind of individualism that Western states abandoned in favor of state support when difficulty hit. In his eyes, an Islamic system made individuals more tightly accountable for the risks they took and required them to exercise due diligence in their fiscal action.

Reframing the moral project of Islamic finance was common among executives of Islamic banks and financial institutions. For example, Makruf Abdul Hadi,[7] the CEO of one of Malaysia's largest Islamic banks, echoed Hamza's ascription to liberal principles. He also had attended the forum at the Securities Commission in which the *Wall Street Journal* article had been a hot topic of conversation and expressed open disdain for most of the speakers. Indeed, he reversed the moral arguments of many of the reformers who had articulated a moral project for Islamic finance. He suggested that Islamic banking was guided by the same logic as liberal economics. Even though Islam seeks to strike a balance between "profit and social responsibility…at the end of the day" Islamic banking is a "pure business…that is driven by maximum profit." In a refusal of those such as Dr. Zaman espousing Islamic finance as a moral alternative, he instead reconfigured the maximization of profit as a shariah value. He told me that the paramount obligation for Islamic banks is to "protect the interests of their shareholders." Indeed, he argued, to ignore such interests and not seek to maximize profits for shareholders "would be contrary to Islam." Continuing this rebuttal against those seeking to develop profit-sharing agreements as opposed to trade-based transactions in Islamic finance, Hadi said that such experiments were anti-Islamic because it was "irresponsible to gamble with money under shariah."

Hadi is representative of those who offer a contrasting moral vision for Islamic finance. Indeed he reframes the moral project of Islamic finance by recasting the obligations of Islamic financial institutions. Thus, he defines ensuring maximal returns as an Islamic moral value, in contrast to those such as Dr. Zaman, who saw such values as inimical to Islam. Whereas Dr. Zaman saw Islamic values as characterized by "generosity and kindness and compassion," Hadi held that the moral responsibility of Islamic finance is to concrete shareholders, not to abstract principles of just action.

Among Islamic finance experts today, liberalism is the inescapable other to which both reformists and those seeking to preserve the status quo compare Islamic economic principles and values. On one hand, those seeking to reform Islamic finance see the moral values of Islam and liberalism as incommensurable opposites. In their eyes, Islam entails such values as compassion, mutuality, and partnership that are incompatible with liberal morality. On the other hand, regulators and practitioners of Islamic finance, who face a more stringent set of constraints, represent the moral values of Islam as complicit with those of liberalism. Thus, officials in the Central Bank and state officials take as a point of departure the liberal notion that efficiency is best achieved through competition. They argue that Islamic finance must demonstrate that it can compete against its conventional counterpart.

Practitioners such as Hamza and Hadi see the moral problem in slightly different terms. They take principles of liberalism (due diligence, self-interest, individual responsibility) as universal moral values that are endorsed by Islam. For example, Hadi observes that firms should seek to maximize profits because to neglect to do so would be detrimental to the interests of their shareholders, which he views as contrary to religious injunctions. He sought to observe obligations to honesty and partnership, but in so doing interpreted the liberal value of profit maximization as a frame within which these injunctions must be observed.

However, even practitioners who endorse liberal principles diverge in the ways in which they construct the assemblage of Islam and liberalism. Hamza and Hadi were divided over whether to emphasize profit-sharing instruments in contrast to trade-based instruments. Hamza viewed profit-sharing instruments as compliant with liberal principles, because they limited the intervention of the state in the market through state-guaranteed deposit insurance and the state as the lender of last resort. He viewed the endorsement of profit sharing by Muslim scholars and in key Islamic texts as an implicit endorsement of liberal morality, arguing that profit-sharing contracts would make people more individually responsible (and accountable). Thus, whereas most of those seeking to reform Islamic favored profit-sharing instruments because they saw them as creating stronger mutual bonds and partnership relationships (in contrast to the individualizing tendencies of liberalism), Hamza favored them for increasing individual accountability and mobilizing the knowledge of individuals, rather than relying on external experts or bureaucrats.

Hadi took an opposing view. Rather than viewing profit-sharing instruments as conducive to liberal values, he argued that they were in fact contrary to Islamic prescriptions on economic action. Whereas the proceeds in a trade-based murabaha transaction are known in advance and are thus certain, the proceeds from profit-sharing instruments are variable because profits from investment in a business are unknown in advance. An important tenet of Islamic economic action, in addition to the prohibition on the payment of interest, is that all terms in contracts are to be clearly defined and thus free of *gharar*, which is defined as uncertainty, risk, or excessive speculation. As Ibrahim Warde notes, the prohibition of gambling in the Qur'an is closely associated with the prohibition of speculation (Warde 2010, 56–58). Along these lines, Hadi argues that the variable yields from profit-sharing contracts are uncertain and akin to gambling and speculation. Both Hadi and Hamza sought to align Muslim moral principles regarding economic action with liberal values. However, whereas Hamza endorsed profit-sharing contracts as superior because they replicated the moral principles of liberalism, Hadi saw them as contrary to the Qur'anic prohibition against gambling, and thus impermissible. He instead favored preserving the trade-based contracts that his financial firm had developed.

Conclusion

Most accounts of the articulation of Islam and liberalism have focused on political liberalism. In contrast to these approaches, I have sought to draw on Foucault's observation that liberalism was premised on the exclusion of moral questions from economic action, to show how economic liberalism is a recurrent object of reflection and comparison among proponents and practitioners of Islamic finance. In designating the market as a space not subject to state intervention, liberalism produced a new morality premised on freedom, individual responsibility, and self-interest. Today, experts in Islamic finance are grappling with the universality of liberal economism and the extent to which Islamic economic action might offer an alternative to this logic.

Experts define Islamic finance (and Islamic economic action more broadly) through explicit or implicit comparison with liberalism. In Mahmood's account of the women's mosque movement in Egypt, liberalism and Islam stand opposed across a yawning gulf of different ontological assumptions. She draws on the forms of piety and self-subjectification characteristic of the Islamic revival to show that liberal models of political agency are not universal. However, her focus on the radical alterity of Islam may obscure the diverse assemblages of Islam and liberalism that exist in the world today. Indeed, this chapter has shown that in Islamic finance, a diverse array of experts seek to reconcile Islam and liberalism in sometimes surprising ways, often mirroring arguments about the compatibility of Islam and the "market mechanism" in the history of the religion. Although some practitioners, such as Dr. Zaman, see Islam and liberalism as incommensurable opposites, this view is not ubiquitous within Islamic finance. Experts such as Hamza and Hadi envision different combinations of (and commensurabilities between) Islam and liberalism. The question, "How Islamic is Islamic finance?" is often answered in relation to liberalism, and differently positioned actors draw on different definitions of Islam to answer it.

Notes

I thank all the participants in the "Religion and the Morality of the Market" workshop, held at King's College, London in June 2013, for which this chapter was originally prepared. The chapter especially benefitted from the insights and provocations of Matthew Engelke and Filippo Osella. I would also like to extend my gratitude to all my interlocutors in the world of Islamic finance who have generously shared their time and expertise with me. Research for this project was supported by a Standard Research Grant and an Insight Development Grant from the Social Sciences and Humanities Research Council of Canada. I am grateful for the Council's support.

1 In using the phrase "moral project," I draw on Tania Li's analysis of the word "project." She argues that "project" captures both the act of envisioning the future and the "purposive activity to bring about definite results" (Li 2008: 124). Thus, a project is both a representation and discursive practices deployed to bring that representation into being. I argue that experts who view Islamic finance as a moral project envision an alternative form of capitalism and see Islamic finance as a means to bring that alternative representation into being.

2 Bill Maurer notes that the Qur'an refers to *riba* twenty times (Maurer 2005b: 27). The most often invoked injunction against interest is Qur'an 2:275.

3 John Bowen provides an excellent overview of debates over whether Muslims living as minorities in Europe are permitted to participate in contracts that require the payment of interest (Bowen 2010: 137–143). As he notes, the situation in Europe is somewhat distinct in that these debates are often framed by the absence of any alternatives to interest-based financing.

4 The *hadiths* refer to the recorded words and deeds of the prophet Muhammad.
5 This is a pseudonym.
6 Bill Maurer has identified "due diligence" as critical to liberal economic organization (Maurer 2005a).
7 This is a pseudonym.

References

Aziz, Zeti A. 2005. "Building a Progressive Islamic Banking Sector: Charting the Way Forward." Bank Negara Malaysia. www.bnm.gov.my/index.php?ch=9&pg=15&ac=173&print=1 (Accessed August 19, 2012).

Barry, Andrew, Thomas Osborne, and Nikolas Rose. 1996. *Foucault and Political Reason: Liberalism, Neo-Liberalism and Rationalities of Government*. Chicago: University of Chicago Press.

Bowen, John R. 2010. *Can Islam Be French? Pluralism and Pragmatism in a Secularist State*. Princeton, NJ: Princeton University Press.

Çizakça, Murat. 2011. *Islamic Capitalism and Finance: Origins, Evolution and the Future*. Cheltenham, UK: Edward Elgar.

El-Din, Seif, and N. Irwani Abdullah. 2007. "Issues of Implementing Islamic Hire Purchase in Dual Banking Systems: Malaysia's Experience." *Thunderbird International Business Review* 49(2): 225–249.

Foucault, Michel. 2008. *The Birth of Biopolitics: Lectures at the College De France, 1978–1979*. Houndmills, UK: Palgrave Macmillan.

Hosseini, Hamid. 2003. "Understanding the Market Mechanism before Adam Smith: Economic Thought in Medieval Islam." In *Medieval Islamic Economic Thought: Filling the "Great Gap" in European Economics*, edited by S. M. Ghazanfar, 88–107. London: RoutledgeCurzon.

Li, Tania. 2008. "Contested Commodifications: Struggles over Nature in a National Park." In *Taking Southeast Asia to Market: Commodities, Nature, and People in the Neoliberal Age*, edited by Joseph Nevins and Nancy L. Peluso, 124–139. Ithaca, NY: Cornell University Press.

Mahmood, Saba. 2001. "Feminist Theory, Embodiment, and the Docile Agent: Some Reflections on the Egyptian Islamic Revival." *Cultural Anthropology* 16(2): 202–236.

2005. *Politics of Piety: The Islamic Revival and the Feminist Subject*. Princeton, NJ: Princeton University Press.

Maurer, Bill. 2005a. "Due Diligence and 'Reasonable Man,' Offshore." *Cultural Anthropology* 20(4): 474–505.

2005b. *Mutual Life, Limited: Islamic Banking, Alternative Currencies, Lateral Reason*. Princeton, NJ: Princeton University Press.

McKay, Deirdre. 2009. "Performing Economy Differently: Exploring Economic Personhood and Local Economic Diversity." *The Australian Journal of Anthropology* 20(3): 330–346.

Pepinsky, Thomas. 2013. "Development, Social Change, and Islamic Finance in Contemporary Indonesia." *World Development* 41: 157–167.

Phillips, Khan. 2010. "Doing God's Work." *Wall Street Journal*. March 1. http://online.wsj.com/article/SB10001424052748703315004575073483994358308.html.

Razif Abdul Kadir, Mohamad. 2010. "Deputy Governor's Special Remarks." Bank Negara Malaysia. www.bnm.gov.my/index/%3C/files/new_currency_declaration/files/publication/msb/2009/11/pdf/2.20.pdf?ch=9&pg=15&ac=340&lang=bm&print=1 (Accessed May 23, 2013).

Rose, Nikolas. 1999. *Powers of Freedom: Reframing Political Thought*. Cambridge: Cambridge University Press.

Udovitch, Abraham. L. 1970. *Partnership and Profit in Medieval Islam*. Princeton, NJ: Princeton University Press.

Warde, Ibrahim. 2010. *Islamic Finance in the Global Economy*. Edinburgh: Edinburgh University Press.

Yousef, Tarik. 2004. "The Murabaha Syndrome in Islamic Finance: Laws, Institutions, and Politics." In *The Politics of Islamic Finance*, edited by Clement Henry and Rodney Wilson, 63–80. Edinburgh: Edinburgh University Press.

8 Persistent Forms: Catholic Charity Homes and the Limits of Neoliberal Morality

China Scherz, University of Virginia

"Cleaning brushes. I'd say we need ten cleaning brushes and we need to replace them about once a month. So that's 120 brushes a year. At 700 shillings a brush we need 84,000 shillings a year for brushes." It was nearly midnight and we were still up working. The six Ugandan, Kenyan, and Tanzanian nuns who had been placed in charge of a home for orphans and children with disabilities were responding to my requests for an accounting of their current annual budget, not with a document but with a late night meeting in which they attempted to align their former mother general's sparse report with their own remembered accountings. Given this home's mission of providing care, accommodation, and access to education for around 100 children and adults who have found themselves outside of the networks of care usually made of kin, much of this budgetary conversation took the form of a micro accounting of household items. And on it went into the night. These calculations were accompanied by a good bit of laughter as we were all enjoying the chance to be together and energized by the arrival of Ruth Petersen, a sixty-one-year old Peace Corps volunteer with five years of prior experience working with children with disabilities.

The laughter was also the result of the novelty of the task at hand. The sisters were not in the habit of engaging in such prospective budgeting. Instead, they took the help that came their way and used it to meet the most pressing needs. This trust in divine providence was both a lived tenet of their theology (Scherz 2013) and a matter of necessity, as the few large donors they still had were not interested in providing funds for such quotidian expenses as brushes and soap. Most of the foundations that had once supported their work had moved on to more "sustainable" projects, preferring community-based projects, advocacy, and awareness raising campaigns to the forms of material charity provided by institutions such as Mercy House. In the end, their anticipated income fell short of their anticipated operating expenses (which totaled some 50 million Ugandan shillings, or approximately US$25,000), by nearly half.

This anticipated shortfall, which was ultimately carried up into a cell marked "other donors" to make the budget balance on faith that God would provide through sources yet unnamed, speaks to the financial difficulties many charitable institutions face even while private charity is lauded as the solution to the problems created by neoliberal privatization. The clinics, orphanages, and homes for the elderly and disabled that were integral to the architecture of Catholic mission stations in colonial Uganda still shape the built environment of many of Uganda's trading centers, but their varying states of repair and use reflect the divergent trajectories of elements of that earlier charitable assemblage as it has come to interact with new forms of intervention over time. In this chapter I argue that we might think of places like Mercy House as remainders, as places continuing to work within prior assemblages of care, even while elements of those assemblages have been taken up by other actors to do new kinds of work that is often so different that these remainders become impossible to include. The persistence of such places speaks to the incomplete nature of the transformations of charitable aid that have occurred in recent years. The concept of the remainder provides a way to think about these partial transformations that highlight the past's continuance in and relationship to the present.

The Moral Neoliberal

Andrea Muehlebach has recently articulated the increasing importance of private charity and volunteerism as essential elements in an assemblage of concepts, principles, techniques, and practices that she terms "the moral neoliberal," and that she posits operates alongside the market neoliberal so frequently described as central to the contemporary political and economic order (Muehlebach 2012:12). In her writings, she convincingly describes how an "opulence of virtue" has expanded alongside the ravages of austerity (Muehlebach 2013: 455). Muehlebach argues that under this moral neoliberal form the same states that designed the policies that produced so much suffering and dislocation have also called on people to respond to these private sufferings and humiliations through unremunerated acts of voluntarism. Through her research in Northern Italy, she demonstrates the affinities and concrete relationships between Catholic Social Teaching and post–Washington Consensus neoliberalism.[1] Muehlebach shows how elements of each have been recombined to create a form of social assistance premised on the sacralized and unremunerated work of thousands of ethical citizens whose voluntary efforts are motivated by structures of feeling carefully promoted by government trainings, programs, and media campaigns that merge elements of Catholic, socialist, and neoliberal imaginaries (Muehlebach 2012, 2013).

Muehlebach's reflections on the ways political actors bring together a heterogeneous and often unexpected array of elements to generate a response to a problem reflects other recent anthropological writing on assemblages. Building on Foucault's concept of apparatus (*dispositif*), the term assemblage has been used in reference to unstable collections of norms, practices, technologies, and forms of reasoning that come together in response to a particular problem, but that have not yet stabilized as apparatuses (Rabinow 2003: 56). Despite their differences with regard to questions of stability, as conceptual tools, both the apparatus and the assemblage have the advantage of avoiding an overreliance on the influence of a single coherent logic (Ong and Collier 2005: 12). Rather than focusing on purely cognitive or ideological elements, assemblages and apparatuses allow us to think about the influence of both discursive and material elements, and how these elements are rearticulated and rearticulate themselves in relation to one another over time.

Although Muehlebach does not claim that the moral neoliberal is universal or all encompassing, it may be alluring to see the recombination of elements of Catholic Social Teaching and neoliberal critiques of state-led welfare provisioning into this novel assemblage as showing the compatibility between neoliberalism and all forms of Catholic charity. Yet, as I noted earlier, there remain many strands of Catholic thought and practice that not only oppose neoliberal reforms, but that also prove unrecognizable or even repugnant to neoliberal policy and grant makers, a phenomenon that is also briefly noted in Muehlebach's work. I term these spaces, ideas, and practices "remainders." In using this term I aim to speak of that which is left behind even as other elements of a prior assemblage are taken up to fashion something new. While people who remain connected to these spaces, ideals, and practices may be aware of their separation from more dominant assemblages, their participation in these remainders is not necessarily motivated by an opposition to such assemblages, as in a situation in which a particular religious order's commitments to practices that prove repugnant to neoliberal grant makers are motivated by their own spiritual beliefs and commitments.

In my effort to articulate the relationship between assemblages and their remainders and to explore the boundaries of the moral neoliberal, I draw on a description of one site connected to this order, Mercy House.[2] Mercy House is a home for orphans, people with disabilities, and the frail elderly run by the Franciscan Sisters of Africa, about which I have written elsewhere (Scherz 2013, 2014). This home is situated in central Uganda, where I conducted ethnographic research over twelve months in 2007, 2008, and 2010. Although Mercy House is an exemplary model of Catholic charity, it has largely been excluded from the influx of development and orphan support monies that have come into Uganda since the end of the 1980s. In this chapter I argue that Mercy House's persistent commitment to programs centered on long-term, materially substantial forms of institutional care, its commitment to an ethic of virtue over an ethic of audit, and its attachment to forms of connection and outreach that fail to correspond to a market logic have made it unattractive to many donors. These elements can be thought of as remainders, as elements of a prior assemblage that have been left behind even as other elements of its practice have been taken up to fashion both Catholic Social Teaching and neoliberalism. So while I agree with Muehlebach that Catholic Social Teaching helped to shape neoliberal social policy, my goal in this chapter is to explain the perhaps unexpected exclusion of many Catholic charities from the moral neoliberal assemblage. How ought we make sense of the fact that organizations that might be viewed as paradigmatic exemplars of neoliberal social discourse often do not conform to the practices characteristic of neoliberalism and are thus excluded by donors? While some of Catholic charities have undertaken projects of internal transformation, so as to better align themselves with the moral neoliberal, others, such as Mercy House, have failed or refused to do so.

I want to be clear that sites such as Mercy House do not diminish the value of Muehlebach's arguments. Rather, thinking about the reasons why these spaces fall beyond the gaze of neoliberal policy and grant makers may help to provide greater specificity to the precise configuration of the moral neoliberal by exploring its boundaries and exclusions. In turn, this will allow for a more complex understanding of the relationship of neoliberalism to contemporary practices of charity. Such an analysis also warns against quick binary judgments that classify all nonstate activity as compatible with neoliberal prescriptions for a vibrant civil society. In addition, by demonstrating the plurality of perspectives and practices that exist within the Catholic Church, we come to a more complex understanding of the variation that exists even in such a seemingly monolithic institution. Finally, these problems of remainders and recognition not only highlight the simultaneous existence of the same element within multiple assemblages, but also challenge us to find a way to speak about these remainders that avoids what Johannes Fabian has called the "denial of coevalness," a phrase he uses to refer to "anthropology's persistent and systematic tendency to place the referents of anthropology in a time other than the present of the producer of anthropological discourse" and to instead see them as contemporaries (Fabian 1983: 31).

Catholicism and Neoliberalism

Andrea Muehlebach's writings are among several recent efforts to describe the increasing importance of civil society, voluntarism, and philanthropy under forms of neoliberal governmentality (Foucault 1979; see also Rose 1999; Elyachar 2005; Englund 2006; West 2006; Li 2007; Adams 2013). Muehlebach describes what she terms a "Catholicization of neoliberalism" in Italy and beyond, in which concepts drawn from Catholic Social Teaching have been taken up by neoliberal policy makers to create a sacralized society in which wealth and care can be privately redistributed (Muehlebach 2012: 70). This moral neoliberal regime is distinguished by acts of affectively motivated charity that replace state-sponsored welfare. The Italian volunteers Muehlebach describes are largely opposed to austerity measures and the retreat of the Italian state, which have endangered the long fought for entitlements at the center of the Italian social contract. Yet, the Italian state has also created a narrative that frames its would-be-opponents' status as good citizens as being contingent on their willingness to volunteer their time and labor to charity, thus replacing the leisure of their retirement with productivity and their opposition with collaboration. This move has also enabled the state to divest itself of some responsibility to the frail elderly and other vulnerable populations.

As with other elements of neoliberal policymaking, these private initiatives do not so much involve a total replacement of the state by the market and private voluntarism, as the state acting as an orchestrator, ensuring that conditions are in place for the existence and optimal functioning of markets and other forms of private initiative (Foucault 1979; Mirowski 2009). In the Northern Italian case, *gratuità*, a conception of free giving inspired by divine grace drawn from Catholic theology, is actively promoted by the Italian state through its inclusion in a 1991 law regulating voluntary activity, through its direct contracting of organizations to provide services to be performed by volunteers instead of by paid state employees, and through its promotion of voluntarism through media campaigns and classes directed at fostering a culture of giving (Muehlebach 2012: 57–58).

The themes of sustainability and community participation so central to neoliberal philanthropy are also well aligned with the value the Catholic Church places on subsidiarity, or the idea that actors and organizations closest to a given problem should be supported in their independent efforts to resolve it (Bevans and Schroeder 2004). This concept has become central to contemporary Catholic thought since it was formally introduced by Pope Leo XIII in *Rerum Novarum*, an 1891 encyclical that became the starting point for the body of writing often referred to as Catholic Social Teaching (Catholic Church 1939). It was further developed by Pope Pius XI's 1931 encyclical *Quadragesimo Anno*, which stated, "It [is] an injustice and at the same time a grave evil and disturbance of right order to assign to a greater and higher association what lesser and subordinate organizations can do" (Catholic Church 1931: 79). In recent years, numerous neoliberal thinkers have used this element of Catholic Social Teaching to speak about the importance of civil society and the problems of excessive state intervention. Yet, despite the ease with which subsidiarity joins Catholic Social Teaching and post–Washington Consensus neoliberalism, there are other elements of Catholic social practice, including commitments to a kind of quotidian materiality and a certain resistance to visibility and formalization of certain forms of charity, that require Catholic charitable organizations to change before they can be recognized as possible participants in the moral neoliberal.

The coupling of accumulation and charitable redistribution is further sustained by a Catholic "moral style" in which the moral subject vacillates between states of sin and repentance, accumulation and free gifting. Following Karl Marx, Muehlebach argues that through acts of charitable service the "material opulence" of capitalist wealth is coupled with "an opulence of clean conscience and good feeling" that follows these apparently selfless gifts (Muehlebach 2013: 455). Muehlebach contrasts this with a more Puritan form of moral personhood described by Max Weber in which the subject is judged as a uniform whole who must be constantly on guard against impious actions as he or she is a subject who is incapable of making up for periodic occasions of sin through good works (Muehlebach 2013: 461–462).

In Muehlebach's writings, religious practice does not so much offer a supernatural escape from the uncertainties of the neoliberal market as it does in the occult economies described by Jean and John Comaroff (Comaroff and Comaroff 1999). Nor is it mobilized for enhanced participation in the market, as it is in the spiritual economy described by Daromir Rudnyckyj (Rudnyckyj 2009). Rather, for Muehlebach religion provides the raw material necessary to craft a moral salve that some see as capable of healing the wounds precipitated by neoliberal markets.

As Muehlebach argues, the conjoining of market principles and moral sentiments is nothing new. Adam Smith and Karl Marx made similar arguments, albeit with opposing moral valences, but Muehlebach extends these classic analyses by demonstrating the concrete linkages between Catholic Social Teaching and neoliberal social assistance programs in post-Fordist Italy. Like neoliberalism, Catholic Social Teaching provides a critique of laissez-faire economics and proposes privately organized initiatives as alternatives to state-sponsored welfare. She describes the involvement of economist Joseph Stiglitz in the Vatican's Pontifical Academy of Social Sciences and the centrality of concepts drawn from Catholic Social Teaching in his social prescriptions. Catholic proponents of the benefits of the market have also proffered readings of church documents that point toward the compatibility of church teaching and neoliberal economics (Novak 1993), although other Catholic theologians have critiqued these interpretations of the church's teaching on economic issues (Whitmore 2001). The Catholic Church's opposition to embryonic stem cell research has even taken a market-based turn through the Church's recent investment in the nonprofit arm of a for-profit adult stem cell biotechnology company (Scherz 2013), suggesting that the connection between neoliberalism and Catholicism may also run in the other direction.

NGOs and Neoliberalism in Uganda

Muehlebach's work can be connected to a larger body of scholarship on the rise of nongovernmental organizations (NGOs) and civil society. Following the implementation of austerity measures imposed by the World Bank and International Monetary Fund in the global South during the 1980s, highly indebted states found themselves forced to cut public spending, thus endangering the welfare of many of their citizens. As the ravages of the austerity measures became clear, international development institutions began to search for possible ways to fill the gaps left by the retreating state. By the turn of the millennium, civil society came to be seen as a promising replacement for the programs formerly administered by national governments and a diverse range of nongovernmental, nonprofit, and for-profit organizations proliferated.

Uganda is arguably the African nation that most wholeheartedly embraced neoliberal economic and social reforms (Wiegratz 2010). It thus comes as little surprise that in Uganda NGOs took an even more pronounced role. Following the end of the civil war in 1986, President Yoweri Museveni's government promoted national and international civil society organizations as central for the development and reconstruction of the country (Dicklitch 1998; Bornstein, Wallace, and Chapman 2006). The importance of civil society organizations was also confirmed in their role in responding to Uganda's AIDS epidemic, where civil society organizations actively facilitated the open discussion and engagement critical to Uganda's successes in slowing the spread of HIV (Hunter 2003; Epstein 2007; Boyd 2015).

As years went on, NGOs "mushroomed" in response to the large numbers of orphans left behind after their parents passed away. By 2009, there were nearly 8,000 registered NGOs in Uganda (Uganda National NGO Forum 2009), many of which are faith based. As I have written about in detail elsewhere (Scherz 2014), the majority of interventions being implemented by both faith-based and secular NGOs in Uganda are at least formally committed to principles of sustainability, accountability, and community participation in and ownership of the development process. The focus on these principles has led NGOs to eschew programs that involve direct service provision and the distribution of material goods. Instead, they have focused on nonmaterial interventions such as trainings, workshops, and the creation of small self-supporting community institutions. Many in the development community think of these less materially intensive interventions as being less likely to create dependence where recipient communities rely on donor organizations for continual support. Members of local and international aid communities also view trainings and community institutions as capable of providing benefits into the future far beyond the initial, funded implementation period. These are trends that find resonance in many places in the world, but they are especially important in Uganda, given that the World Bank selected the country as a target for the implementation of participatory development exercises in the late 1990s (Mallaby 2004).

Persistent Forms

"We were doing this work before the donors came, and we will continue doing it even if they leave." – Sister Amelia Namukasa

Despite the shifts many charitable institutions have made to align themselves with neoliberal practices, some institutions have remained committed to older redistributive forms of charity, different styles of management, and other modes of interacting with potential donors. These institutions are awkward matches for foundations seeking to promote the sort of sustainable, participatory development that is constitutive of the neoliberal development assemblage. The difficulty such organizations face in seeking funding demonstrates a striking counterpoint to the organizations described by Muehlebach, and an acknowledgment of their persistence allows for a more specific and complex definition of the moral neoliberal.

Mercy House, a Catholic charity home for more than 150 orphans, children and young adults with disabilities, and the elderly, is one such organization.[3] Mother Mary Patrick, an Irish Franciscan nun, established Mercy House in 1923 to rehabilitate people who had been discharged from a small hospital, also operated by her Catholic missionary order, but who were still in need of nursing. In 1928 Mercy House was moved from its original site near the hospital to its present location in Namayumba so that the newly professed Ugandan nuns who were the first Franciscan Sisters of Africa might be able to better learn their Franciscan charism of service.[4] Today, it is one of the sites where the Ugandan, Kenyan, and Tanzanian women seeking to join the order receive their most intensive training as part of a nine-year process of religious formation. As I describe elsewhere (Scherz 2013, 2014), the Franciscan Sisters of Africa envision Mercy House as a "school of charity," a place where the virtue of charity can be learned and practiced. Through the daily work of tending to wounds, escorting children to the national capital for medical consultations, managing the gardens that provide food for the home, and seeking the resources necessary to send the children to school, the sisters understand themselves to be engaged in acts that simultaneously confirm their love of God and neighbor and allow for opportunities for self-transformation. The role that this particular form of charity plays in their religious training and in their daily lives highlights the fact that it is not only about serving the poor, but is in many ways also an end in itself.

Recognition

Given the disjuncture between the sisters' commitments and trends in international aid that have rejected these forms of direct charity and service, and the fact that they received no regular support from the order or from the Catholic

Church, the sisters who ran Mercy House were constantly struggling to meet the costs of running the home. In 2008, the total operating budget came to just 35.7 million Ugandan shillings.[5] The sisters raised nearly half of this sum through small income-generating activities including a poultry project, a piggery, and a bakery; the other half came in bits at a time in the form of sponsorships from a Dutch foundation for a small number of children with disabilities and from a range of individual donors. Many of these individual donors were less interested in contributing to ongoing operating expenses such as food, medical debts, and school fees, preferring instead to support large one-off projects such as a new dormitory. In 2008, the sisters received a new double-cabin truck and a beautifully designed, universally accessible playground, but were unable to find a donor willing to provide the soap and washbasins necessary to prevent a scabies outbreak.

The distinctions donors made between NGOs that embraced sustainability, community participation, and accountability and charity homes like Mercy House, between donations that would ideally create sustainable change and donations that would be consumed as operating expenses, and often with little formal record of their impact, illuminates the ways in which the moral neoliberal assemblage privileges charity over justice (Muehlebach 2013: 462) while simultaneously excluding some of the most basic forms of charity. The ways in which Mercy House's efforts were seen by potential donors as incommensurable with neoliberalism centered on the home's commitment to materially substantial forms of assistance, the awkward position of nuns who are neither employees nor volunteers, the sisters' resistance to practices of audit, and their insistence on a model of personal relationship rather than marketing as a method to attract potential donors.

Through their persistent commitments to other elements of the earlier charitable assemblage described in the text that follows, the sisters found themselves inhabiting a somewhat paradoxical situation. On one hand, the form of charity practiced at Mercy House was a prototype for the forms of private voluntary giving central to the moral neoliberal assemblage; on the other, the sisters' resistance to certain forms of neoliberal organizational transformation ultimately excluded Mercy House from the flows of money animated by the ascendance of that same assemblage.

Materiality

Given the ways that particular forms of materially mediated charity figured into the sisters' understanding of their charism and their own ethico-religious formation, they were unable and unwilling to abandon these forms of care to make their work more appealing to a neoliberal philanthropic field that sought to combine the private nature of charity with a commitment to promoting a vision of sustainable development and autonomous individuals and communities (Rahnema 1992; Stirrat and Henkel 1997; Green 2000; Cooke and Kothari 2001; Paley 2001; Kremer and Miguel 2007; Li 2007; Swidler and Watkins 2009).

Sister Reginald Gonza, a leading member of the Franciscan Sisters of Africa, explained the importance of embodied forms of charity and service by pointing me to a passage for a lesson plan for the novices on Franciscan spirituality where she wrote[6]:

> The nature of Francis and Clare's religious experiences can be said to be embodied. Whatever belongs to our human condition (joys, sorrows, weaknesses/failures, limitations, sickness and rejection) can lead us into an experience of the divine because of Jesus...Francis's compassion for the marginalized (the lepers and the poor) led him to have compassion for the crucified Christ...Thus the human experience with the lepers led him [Francis] to experience the divine.

In this passage, she speaks to the relationship between embodied forms of direct service and the sisters' aims of experiencing and understanding the divine. With this in mind, we can start to see that the sisters see their service work as an extension of the more contemplative work of worship they undertook each day in the chapel.

Sister Elizabeth Nagayi, a young sister who was working at Mercy House while still under temporary vows, explained how these embodied acts of service had been central to her own formation process, explicitly relating the story of St. Francis's personal transformation to her experience. She said,

> [Early in his life] St. Francis could not meet a man with leprosy and greet him...But [later] he was a friend of the lepers and could embrace them...When you have just come to this home and you have been somewhere else, you may even get scared of eating food in this place...When I had just come here, this boy Charles was sick and had sores all over the mouth and he was having a certain smell. I was giving him food and [the sisters] told me that his disease is contagious, [but] he couldn't take the food in the hands, you [had to] put it in the mouth. So I washed my hand and fed him and the boy ate and got satisfied... Before I joined, I had a lot of mercy, [but] would not [have] come back [to] eat with my same hand. But that [day] I ate and did not use a fork. I just thanked God because it is not easy.

Sister Elizabeth saw this moment of affective transformation as a gift of Divine grace a central turning point in her efforts to model her life on that of St. Francis (Scherz 2015). Feeding Charles was thus not only a good in itself or something that needed to be done on account of its necessity, but was also central to Sister Elizabeth's understanding of her own spiritual transformation.

These acts of charity also figured into the sisters' understanding of a Catholic economy of salvation that relies on both God's grace and one's good works. Referencing an oft-told passage from the Gospel of Matthew (Matt. 25:31–40),

Sister Roberta Namuyiga referred to the testimony of the poor before the throne of God as a "visa into eternity" in her contribution to a self-published magazine celebrating Mercy House's platinum jubilee.

> The residents of Mercy House are the true riches of the church in Uganda... [T]hey will pass on into eternity with us when we come before the throne of God for judgment. He will point to them, saying to us '[W]hen I was hungry, sick, naked, lonely ... you did it to me.' The poor will be our visa into eternity. They are a treasure we must care for very well.

In light of these understandings of embodied prayer and the role of direct service in this particular economy of salvation, concretely ministering to the bodies of the poor was not something that could be left behind, as doing so would mean abandoning their Franciscan charism.

This commitment to embodied, materially substantial forms of charity made Mercy House an awkward match for donors looking to support programs where a time-limited intervention might yield sustainable benefits. Recent attempts to avoid dependency and material gifts are exemplified in Vincanne Adams's ethnography of the role of for-profit corporations involved in the recovery of New Orleans following Hurricane Katrina. Adams describes how even the formaldehyde-ridden FEMA trailers that people had been living in for years could not be given as gifts, but were instead offered as commodities that consumer citizens could purchase for $25,000 on the assumption that to give the trailers out freely might turn people into passive and careless subjects of aid (Adams 2012: 195). In a different register, Britt Halvorson has written of the difficulties an American Lutheran mission faced as it attempted to incorporate the handmade bandages characteristic of a previous ethic of charitable caregiving into a more professionalized bureaucratic form (Halvorson 2012). Thus while Christian charity may serve as a motivating force for volunteers drawn into the moral neoliberal, classic forms of redistributive charity are excluded on the grounds that they will produce dependent subjects at odds with the empowered consumer citizens and resourceful self-provisioning communities that are also part of the neoliberal philanthropic imaginary. The sisters' insistence on continuing to provide materially intensive forms of care to the children and adults in the form of housing, food, clothing, medical care, and school fees thus positions them outside of this ethic of care, which denigrates material charity as productive of dangerous forms of dependency.

Volunteerism

Mercy House is further separated from the moral neoliberal by the position of its workers, who are for the most part not volunteers but nuns.[7] A large cadre of volunteers who give their time to the frail elderly populates Muehlebach's ethnography. These volunteers, formerly at risk of being denigrated as the unproductive unemployed (Muehlebach 2012: 151–159), are now interpellated by this new form of ethical citizenship. The nuns of Mercy House, in contrast, are neither employees working under a specific contract in exchange for a wage, nor are they volunteers providing uncompensated labor with carefully defined limits, temporal or otherwise; rather, they are professed religious women who have taken solemn vows. Whereas many of the volunteers within the regime of the moral neoliberal work on a temporary basis, contributing a few hours a week or a few weeks a year, the sisters have committed to this form of life on a permanent basis. Although the order may grant them some time away from their work for further schooling or a period of retreat, under the vow of obedience they have permanently consigned control over their lives to the order. Although they each joined the order after a long process of discernment and deliberation, their participation in any given post cannot be said to be voluntary. Further, given the lifelong nature of these commitments, we cannot speak of them as rendering the unproductive productive, of turning retirements, vacations, and periods of unemployment into opportunities for productive work, as was the case of the retired workers in Muehlebach's account. In many cases, a woman's decision to join an order actually removes a productive person from the workforce. Although some of her time will be spent in active service, much of it will be spent in prayer. Finally, the subjectivity achieved through this labor is not that of the ethical citizen participating in a sacralized and affectively saturated public sphere, but is rather oriented toward the sacred itself. Through their extensive training process and ongoing participation in works of charity and mercy, the sisters do not confirm their place within the public sphere through publicized acts of voluntarism. Rather, their acts of charity are the means through which they foster an ever-more intimate bond with God.

Audit

The difficulties Mercy House faced in attracting funders were also shaped by the sisters' resistance to developing auditing and reporting systems. During my fieldwork I watched as donors and volunteers accustomed to working with more conventionally managed organizations struggled to make sense of the sisters' lack of formal reports, budgets, plans, and resident files. Volunteers often initiated events such as the one described at the opening of this chapter to solicit budgets, resident lists, and long-term plans under the assumption that these absences had been created by problems of technical competence. These "capacity building" attempts were generally met with enthusiasm and good cheer, but the resulting documents were rarely used again. The sisters' lack of interest in maintaining these systems after these volunteers left Mercy House stems from their participation within an alternate system for ensuring ethical accountability that placed a premium on the achievement of moral subjectivity through an elaborate and ongoing process of ethical work. In a situation in which time was always in short supply, the sisters generally prioritized their obligations to attend a series of daily services in the chapel, including daily mass, adoration of the Eucharist, and the morning and evening offices of the liturgy of the hours. Although these services required a great deal of time, the sisters considered them to be important obligations and essential to their spiritual nurturance and development, as evidenced by the efforts they made to get up before dawn to attend them. Given the demands of their religious practice and the work required to keep Mercy House running, there was little time or energy left for maintaining paperwork. This did not worry the sisters, as their efforts were oriented primarily toward pleasing a Divine auditor who did not depend on technical accounting and saw their own religious training as a better method for ensuring moral accountability. Given this training, formal auditing and other "rituals of verification" (Power 1997) seemed superfluous. It is not so much that the sisters were opposed to these forms, but rather that these efforts seemed redundant given their existing practices. Their faith in the workings of Divine providence made them similarly ambivalent about long-term planning exercises and made them question donors who attempted to move them away from what they experienced as a providentially determined mission.

The sisters' lack of interest in practices of audit has also been central to their ability to maintain their commitment to more intensive interventions. As foundations have become increasingly focused on developing strong monitoring and evaluation practices, they have pushed organizations toward interventions that will yield large numbers of quantifiable beneficiaries. Within this framework, material interventions are not only conceived of as counterproductive because they are thought to produce dependency, but are also unattractive because they do not yield high beneficiary numbers (Adams 2012; Scherz 2014). The sisters' lack of interest in producing public accountings and reports has left them unable to participate effectively in a funding market that has become increasingly reliant on such reports as indicators of future organizational effectiveness.

Brand

While branding has long been a tool for marketing products to consumers, under neoliberalism an increasing array of things, including charitable organizations and the stories of those assisted by them (James 2010, 2012), have become marketable commodities. Organizations marketing these charitable experiences seek consumer loyalty by "invoke[ing] a particular imaginary of fidelity, standardization, quality control, and trustworthy distribution" in much the same way that Costas Nakasssis has written about nineteenth century trademarks (Nakassis 2013: 114). In this way, these organizations have increasingly sought to use the idea of the brand to attract and maintain consumer-donors. These practices are highly recognizable to these consumer-donors as they resemble their experiences of other branded commodities. Consumers of poverty, who are asked to click "add to cart" to purchase training for a microfinance group member or a community pit latrine, have already learned to attach themselves to, trust in, and define themselves through their relationships to commercial brands and are thus primed to respond to these sorts of overtures.

Documents produced by Catholic Relief Services, one of the largest charities in the United States, provide a helpful contrast to Mercy House in their articulation of this aim of achieving better "global brand management" (Catholic Relief Services 2014: 15, 18, 21) in their 2014 "From Hope to Harvest: Agency Strategy 2014–2018" publication. They define this process as "an initiative to strengthen our ability to communicate a coherent and consistent picture of who we are, what we do, how we do it and the results we achieve" (Catholic Relief Services 2014: 21). This agency-wide exercise is aimed at maintaining consistency in terms of values, quality, integrity, and staff commitment and better distinguishing the organization in the marketplace for global philanthropy. Analogous to the establishment of commercial brands, Catholic Relief Services hopes to cultivate this image to foster positive connections with Catholics in the United States and thus "encourage them to become more deeply involved" (Catholic Relief Services 2014: 21).

Catholic Relief Services' awareness of the need to fashion itself into a coherent and easily recognizable brand reflects the transformation of an increasingly wide array of things, including charities and the recipients of charity (James 2010, 2012; Adams 2013) into goods to be advertised on the market under contemporary neoliberalism. With potential donors conceptualized as consumers, Catholic Relief Services seeks to project its unique constellation of values and "signature program areas" as a brand with which these consumers can form a stable affective bond.

By contrast, most of the donations that Mercy House receives are motivated by personal relationships of trust with the sisters or with other individuals who have personally volunteered at Mercy House in the past. While Catholic Relief Services is conscious of the need to transform itself into an effective player in the highly competitive market for philanthropic donations and contracts, the sisters have yet to conceive of Mercy House as a participant in a market, let alone as a commodity capable of being stably branded. While they remain highly attuned to possibilities for seeking out patrons, their outreach is oriented primarily toward people and organizations they might be connected to by those who already trust them.

What Remains

The differences that set Mercy House apart are not only differences in scale and form, but rather represent more fundamental distinctions in terms of their perspectives on what can be accomplished through human agency and planning, how right action can be ensured, and what the goals of charitable action should be. In this chapter, I have argued that despite the very real Catholicization of neoliberalism that promotes certain kinds of charity as an alternative to state-sponsored welfare, longstanding sites of Catholic charity like Mercy House do not conform to these new configurations of care. This is partially due to the ways in which these sites continue to support forms of materially substantial charitable giving and ongoing relations of dependence, both of which are foreign to the practices of charitable giving intrinsic to the moral neoliberal. The difficulty these charitable sites face also stems from their refusal to engage with neoliberal managerial practices and their failure to market their activities successfully to potential donors.

Sites such as Mercy House constitute remainders in the sense that they represent both the continuation and differential evolution of prior forms of practice. Despite the ways in which elements have been drawn from older forms of charity to create new assemblages of governance and care, these older forms persist in sites like Mercy House. Acknowledging the existence of these remainders is important not only for its own sake, but also for what it can teach us about how to theorize assemblages. We can think of an assemblage as an emergent collection of heterogeneous elements, both discursive and nondiscursive, that are in the process of being rearticulated in relation to one another, many of these elements are borrowed from elsewhere and deployed to solve new problems (Rabinow 2003; Ong and Collier 2005). However, although elements may be borrowed, it is a duplicate that is borrowed, allowing a copy to stay in place. This does not mean that the original assemblage or apparatus remains static and unchanging, for it too may shift and transform along its own trajectory. A concept like free giving or subsidiarity may be operationalized in different ways, and in ways that may prove incommensurable to the people using them. Thinking about the coexistence of these multiple assemblages pushes us to think about their simultaneity. Mercy House is not "in the past," nor is it a foregone conclusion that more neoliberal forms of aid will supplant it in the future, as a progressive model of history might have us believe. Rather they exist alongside one another, sometimes interacting, sometimes not, in ways contingent on particular circumstances. In central Uganda, where indigenous ethics of interdependence align easily with personal, material forms of charity, the form of charity practiced at Mercy House remains a robust (if underfunded) presence across the region, often located just down the road from the field offices of other local NGOs that have refashioned their programs and funding solicitation strategies to better align themselves with the expectations of neoliberal development institutions.

Attention to the persistence of apparatuses from which certain elements have been copied and incorporated into emergent assemblages such as the moral neoliberal allows us to see how some charitable institutions might both fail to conform to the logic of neoliberalism to the point of being unrecognizable as legitimate partners while at the same time serving as points of origin for some of the most important features of neoliberal morality. Other authors have made us aware of the existence of charities and NGOs that have been created in response neoliberal preferences for decentralized service provision (Pfeiffer 2013; Whyte et al. 2013), governance through the responsibilization of individuals (Rose 1999; Zigon 2011; O'Neill 2013), and the possibilities for profit that exist in newly created markets of sorrow (Adams 2012). Other organizations, such as Catholic Relief Services, are engaged in an ongoing process of re-creating themselves in an attempt to court individual and institutional funders. Still other organizations are sought out by larger organizations in an attempt to co-opt their labor and credibility (Adams 2012). Coming to an understanding of the multiple ways in which organizations interact with emergent moral assemblages such as the moral neoliberal not only allows us to see the contingent futures of any given assemblage, but also warns us against the tendency to see any global form, no matter how powerful, as all determining.

Notes

1 Post–Washington Consensus neoliberalism refers to a modified form of neoliberalism that took root at the end of the twenty-first century. As the World Bank came to realize the human costs of the austerity measures promoted in previous decades, it sought to mitigate the effects of dismantling of state-managed social programs through the promotion of private charity, voluntarism, and community involvement (World Bank 1998; Li 2007; Muehlebach 2012: 93–94).

2 Mercy House, and all of the names given to the people and places associated with it, are pseudonyms.

3 I conducted fieldwork at Mercy House from November 2007 through April 2008 and in May 2010 as part of a larger study on orphans support NGOs in Uganda (Scherz 2014). During this period, I traveled to Mercy House on a regular basis, generally staying for a week at a time in the sisters' guesthouse or in a room attached to the boys' dormitory. At Mercy House, I spent my days observing activities and talking with the sisters, the residents, and the steady stream of volunteers who came to donate their time through an array of self-defined projects. I have stayed in regular contact with the sisters and residents of the home since that time and have also conducted interviews with many of Mercy House's donors.

4 The term charism in this context refers to the beliefs, commitments, and mission of a particular order.

5 This is approximately $21,000.

6 Francis of Assisi (1181–1226) founded the Franciscan order – the Friars Minor – in the early thirteenth century after giving up the lifestyle he had enjoyed as the son of a wealthy Umbrian cloth merchant. Saint Clare's request to follow a similar life in 1211 prompted him to found the order of Poor Ladies, a contemplative order now called the Poor Clares. Francis was also involved in founding a third order of lay confraternities and religious institutes that follow similar rules based on poverty, obedience, and chastity while taking up a more active role in the world.

7 With the exception of occasional foreign volunteers, who are arguably participating within the moral neoliberal, the other workers at Mercy House are employees. These employees are often underpaid, but cannot be conceptualized as volunteers.

References

Adams, V. 2012. "The Other Road to Serfdom: Recovery by the Market and the Affect Economy in New Orleans." *Public Culture* 24(1): 185–216.

2013. *Markets of Sorrow, Labors of Faith: New Orleans in the Wake of Katrina.* Durham, NC: Duke University Press.

Bevans, S., and R. Schroeder. 2004. *Constants in Context: A Theology of Mission for Today*. Maryknoll, NY: Orbis Books.

Bornstein, L., T. Wallace, and J. Chapman. 2006. *The Aid Chain: Coercion and Commitment in Development NGOs, Intermediate Technology*. Warwickshire, UK: Intermediate Technology.

Boyd, L. 2015. *Preaching Prevention: Born-Again Christianity and the Moral Politics of AIDS in Uganda*. Athens, OH: Ohio University Press.

Catholic Church. 1931. *Quadragesimo Anno. Encyclical on the Reconstruction of Social Order*. New York: The Paulist Press.

1939. *Rerum Novarum*. New York: The Paulist Press.

Catholic Relief Services. 2014. *From Hope to Harvest: Agency Strategy 2014–2018, Catholic Relief Services*. Baltimore: Catholic Relief Services.

Collier, S., and A. Ong. 2005. "Global Assemblages, Anthropological Problems." In *Global Assemblages: Technology, Politics, and Ethics as Anthropological Problems*, edited by S. Collier and A. Ong, 3–21. Malden, MA: Blackwell.

Comaroff, J., and J. Comaroff. 1999. "Occult Economies and the Violence of Abstraction: Notes from the South African Postcolony." *American Ethnologist* 26(2): 279–303.

Cooke, B., and U. Kothari. 2001. *Participation: The New Tyranny?* London: Zed Books.

Dicklitch, S. 1998. *The Elusive Promise of NGOs in Africa: Lessons from Uganda.* New York: St. Martin's Press.

Elyachar, J. 2005. *Markets of Dispossession: NGOs, Economic Development, and the State in Cairo*. Durham, NC: Duke University Press.

Englund, H. 2006. *Prisoners of Freedom: Human Rights and the African Poor.* Berkeley: University of California Press.

Epstein, H. 2007. *The Invisible Cure: Africa, the West, and the Fight Against AIDS.* New York: Farrar, Straus and Giroux.

Fabian, J. 1983. *Time and The Other: How Anthropology Makes its Object*. New York: Columbia University Press.

Foucault, M. 1979. "On Governmentality." *Ideology and Consciousness* 6: 5–21.

Green, M. 2000. "Participatory Development and the Appropriation of Agency in Southern Tanzania." *Critique of Anthropology* 20(1): 67–89.

Halvorson, B. 2012. "Woven Worlds: Material Things, Bureaucratization, and Dilemmas of Caregiving in Lutheran Humanitarianism." *American Ethnologist* 39(1): 122–137.

Hunter, S. 2003. *Black Death: AIDS in Africa*. New York: Palgrave Macmillan.

James, E. 2010. *Democratic Insecurities: Violence, Trauma, and Intervention in Haiti*. Berkeley: University of California Press.

2012. "Witchcraft, Bureaucraft, and the Social Life of (US)AID in Haiti." *Cultural Anthropology* 27(1): 50–75.

Kremer, M., and E. Miguel. 2007. "The Illusion of Sustainability." *Quarterly Journal of Economics* 122(3): 1007–1065.

Li, T. 2007. *The Will to Improve: Governmentality, Development, and the Practice of Politics*. Durham, NC: Duke University Press.

Mallaby, S. 2004. *The World's Banker: A Story of Failed States, Financial Crisis, and the Wealth and Poverty of Nations*. New York: Penguin Press.

Mirowski, P. 2009. "Defining Neoliberalism." In *The Road From Mont Pelerin: The Making of the Neoliberal Thought Collective*, edited by P. Mirowski and D. Plehwe, 417–456. Cambridge, MA: Harvard University Press.

Muehlebach, A. 2012. *The Moral Neoliberal: Welfare and Citizenship in Italy*. Chicago: University of Chicago Press.

2013. "The Catholicization of Neoliberalism: On Love and Welfare in Lombardy, Italy." *American Anthropologist* 115(3): 452–465.

Nakassis, C. 2013. "Brands and their Surfeits." *Cultural Anthropology* 28(1): 111–126.

Novak, M. 1993. *The Catholic Ethic and the Sprit of Capitalism*. New York: Free Press.

O'Neill, K. 2013. "Left Behind: Security, Salvation, and the Subject of Prevention." *Cultural Anthropology* 28(2): 204–226.

Ong, A. and S. Collier, eds. 2005. *Global Assemblages: Technology, Politics, and Ethics as Anthropological Problems*. Malden, MA: Blackwell.

Paley, J. 2001. "The Paradox of Participation: Civil Society and Democracy in Chile." *PoLAR: Political and Legal Anthropology Review* 24(1): 1–12.

Pfeiffer, J. 2013. "The Struggle for a Public Sector: PEPFAR in Mozambique." In *When People Come First: Critical Studies in Global Health*, edited by Joao Biehl and Adriana Petryna, 166–181. Princeton, NJ: Princeton University Press.

Power, M. 1997. *The Audit Society: Rituals of Verification*. Oxford: Oxford University Press.

Rabinow, P. 2003. *Anthropos Today: Reflections on Modern Equipment*. Princeton, NJ: Princeton University Press.

Rahnema, M. 1992. "Participation." In *The Development Dictionary: A Guide to Knowledge as Power*, edited by W. Sachs, 116–131. London: Zed Books.

Rose, N. 1999. *Powers of Freedom: Reframing Political Thought*. Cambridge: Cambridge University Press.

Rudnyckyj, D. 2009. "Spiritual Economies: Islam and Neoliberalism in Contemporary Indonesia." *Cultural Anthropology* 24(1): 104–141.

Scherz, C. 2013. " 'Let Us Make God Our Banker': Ethics, Temporality, and Agency in a Ugandan Charity Home." *American Ethnologist* 40(4): 624–636.

2014. *Having People, Having Heart: Charity, Sustainable Development, and Problems of Dependence in Central Uganda.* Chicago: University of Chicago Press.

2015. "Enduring the Awkward Embrace." Presentation at the Society for the Anthropology of Religion (SAR) 2015 meeting. San Diego, CA, 18 April.

Scherz, P. 2013. "Conflicting Models of Technology in Catholic Social Teaching." Presentation at New Wine, New Wineskins: Catholic Moral Theology Conference. Moreau Seminary, Notre Dame, IN, July 25.

Stirrat, R. L., and Henkel, H. 1997. "The Development Gift: The Problem of Reciprocity in the NGO World." *Annals of the American Academy of Political and Social Studies* 554: 66–81.

Swidler, A., and S. Watkins. 2009. "'Teach a Man to Fish': The Sustainability Doctrine and Its Social Consequences." *World Development* 37(7): 1182–1196.

Uganda National NGO Forum. 2009. "The NGO Sector in Uganda, Its Operating Environment and Relationship with Government: A Brief Meeting between Representatives from the NGO Sector and the 3rd Deputy Prime Minister and Minister of Internal Affirs-Hon. Kirunda Kivejinja." Kampala: Uganda National NGO Forum.

West, P. 2006. *Conservation Is Our Government Now: The Politics of Ecology in Papua New Guinea.* Durham, NC: Duke University Press.

Whitmore, T. 2001. "John Paul II, Michael Novak, and the Difference between Them." *The Annual of the Society for Christian Ethics* 21: 215–232.

Whyte, S., M. Whyte, L. Meinert, and J. Twebaze. 2013. "Therapeutic Clientship: Belonging in Uganda's Projectified Landscape of AIDS Care." In *When People Come First: Critical Studies in Global Health*, edited by J. Biehl and A. Petryna, 140–165. Princeton, NJ: Princeton University Press.

Wiegratz, J. 2010. "Fake Capitalism? The Dynamics of Neoliberal Moral Restructuring and Pseudo-development: The Case of Uganda." *Review of African Political Economy* 37: 123–137.

World Bank. 1998. *Beyond the Washington Consensus: Institutions Matter.* New York: Oxford University Press.

Zigon, J. 2011. *"HIV Is God's Blessing": Rehabilitating Morality in Neoliberal Russia.* Berkeley: University of California Press.

9 Marketizing Piety through Charitable Work: Islamic Charities and the Islamization of Middle-Class Families in Indonesia

Hilman Latief, Muhammadiyah University of Yogyakarta

This chapter underscores how the marketization of spirituality is evident in Islamic charitable practices in Indonesia. In particular, it analyses the philanthropic activities of Daarut Tauhid (DT) and their incorporation into the country's social-economic enterprises. DT is an Islamic organization that offers educational activities and training in both leadership and entrepreneurship. It represents in part a manifestation of what pious Muslims in Indonesia refer to as modern Islam: a mode of religious practice and spirituality characteristic of the urban middle classes in Indonesia. DT was founded by Abdullah Gymnastiar, a popular preacher who is widely known as "Aa Gym" (*Aa* means elder brother in the local Sundanese language). Aa Gym has received extensive coverage in the media, and his sermons have often been broadcast live by several national television stations.[1] Owing in large part to Aa Gym's visibility, his charitable foundation has become a popular medium through which middle-class Indonesian Muslims fulfil the third pillar of Islam, the payment of *zakat* or almsgiving.

Since its inception in 1990, DT has been active in collecting charity funds by maintaining a relationship with the middle class, whose members have in fact profoundly contributed to its social, religious and economic development projects. A reciprocal relationship between DT and the Muslim middle class has materialized in DT's response to the growing middle-class demand for Islamic childcare and Islamic education more generally. Through its zakat and charity organization, called Dompet Peduli Umat-Daarut Tauhid (DPU-DT), founded in 1999, DT provides middle-class families with morally and professionally reliable childcare workers, who are a labour force in high demand. As a matter of fact, young women trained in both childcare and the basic tenets of Islamic practice contribute to the Islamization of their employers.

This chapter proposes two central claims. First, Islamic charity (in the form of DPU-DT) draws on religious principles to create a spiritual economy whereby the religiously motivated contributions of pious middle-class Muslims funds the training of young women from rural parts of Java. Second, this spiritual economy is premised on equipping these women not only with the technical skills required of childcare workers, but also with a considerable amount of Islamic expertise. That is to say, the value of the young women's labour is enhanced through the acquisition of Islamic knowledge that they can then pass on to the children in their care. Thus, the chapter shows how the enhanced display of Islamic piety by middle-class Muslims in Indonesia today is instrumental to the emerging Islamic spiritual economy.

Charities, Market and Islamic Spiritual Economies

The significant growth of the Indonesian economy in the 1980s and 1990s resulted in the concomitant growth of the middle class, many of whose members were employed either in government bureaucracies or private companies and enjoyed wider leeway for religious practice in their daily lives following reduced constraints on Islamic piety during the later years of the Suharto regime. At the same time, an intensified process of Islamization occurred not only in the social sector, but also in the economic and political spheres (Hefner 1998; Salim 2008). The emergence of a wide range of Islamic-inspired economic activities and of market-motivated religious movements is one of the most visible examples of enhanced piety among the Muslim middle class in Indonesia.

The overlap between the market and religion in Indonesia today is evident in the emergence of a new pattern of Muslim popular culture and economic behaviour. The daily presence of popular Muslim preachers on national television (Howell 2008; Sunarwoto 2013), the expansion of an Islamic music industry (Barendregt 2011) and the popularization of Muslim fashions and cosmetics among the youths (Jones 2010; Afriani 2013) are all indications of an Islamization of popular culture (Fealy 2008; Hoesterey 2012). Moreover, the development of Islamic financial institutions – from Islamic banks to Baitul Mal wa al-Tamwil (BMT)[2] – and the growth of Islamic businesses and enterprises suggest that Islamic norms have been combined with economic action (Ariff 1991, 1991b; Sakai 2008). Different forms of Islamic entrepreneurship have had a significant impact on the production and consumption practices of Indonesian Muslims. These can be seen in the expansion in the provision and popularity of products such as Islamic tourism, Islamic media, Shari'a hotels, halal foods and more (Fealy 2008).

The interaction between religion and the economy has been of sociological interest for more than a century. Max Weber is one of the most influential scholars who have contributed to debates concerning relationships between religious and economic behaviours and practices. Max Weber's *Protestant Ethic*, which discusses the impact of Protestantism on economic action and the eventual development of capitalism, has been widely debated by scholars. Weber argues that Protestant asceticism has had a profound impact on the way Protestants acted in the world and on the formation of the ethical dispositions characteristic of capitalism in the North Atlantic. While Weber's thesis remains popular, especially among sociologists and religious studies scholars, his argument about the Protestant ethic remains a subject of debate. Questions about how Protestant ethics function among marginalized groups in the United Sates is one example of the complex relationship between religion and economic behaviour (Bruce 1990).

Asking whether or not other religions, including Buddhism, Catholicism and Islam, are conducive to a rational and economically motivated way of life can be another avenue to examine Weber's approach (Weller 2008). Likewise, Finke and Stark's exchange theory approach, which underscores notions of rewards and costs underpinning religious life, has been taken up in recent discussion of the commodification of religiosity (Hamilton 1995; Finke and Stark 1988; Van der Veer 2012), lending support to the formulation of what Bryan S. Turner calls "the religious markets approach" or "the economic interpretation of religion" (2008: 32–33). The religious markets approach goes beyond the secularization theory. It particularly addresses "the resilience of religion" and how religious communities attempt to compromise between the modern world and religious beliefs and practices. The approach also pays attention to the function of the "spiritual market" and how religious values and spirituality are marketized (2008: 34).

The marketization of spirituality is a fruit of a dynamic and intensified encounter between the logic of capitalism and the ethics of religion. It signifies the intervention of "market mechanisms" in conceptualising and expressing religious values and in turn in resolving the hardship faced by communities, especially among the poor. As a form of modification and convergence between religion and the market ethic, religiously motivated social and economic activities within society have been characterised by and attached to such terms as entrepreneurship, economic development, productivity, wealth and wage. Anke Schwittay speaks of "the marketization of poverty", by which she refers to the way that poverty is made the object of market mechanisms (Schwittay 2011: S72). I build on Schwittay's approach by documenting the marketisation of piety in contemporary Indonesia. Whereas Schwittay focuses on how poverty is remediated through market mechanisms, I have shown how a certain marketized spirituality is seen as the antidote to poverty in contemporary Indonesia. In the attempts to overcome poverty problems, religious denominations and charitable organizations such as DT persuade and urge poor families to be part of the market and to adopt the market ethics.

Despite modernist presumptions that secularization is an inherent feature of modernization, the use of religion and religious symbols for both social and economic purposes is a pervasive feature of the contemporary world. This challenges scholars to sharpen their analysis of the role of religion in shaping market logics and the power of economic action to elicit new forms of religious expression. The prevailing debates on the interaction between religion and the market are stimulated partly by the fact that religion and the economy are treated as incompatible. Religion is often associated with the holy and sacred, spirituality, piety and morality, while the economy is related to the profane, self-interest, capital accumulation and market (see Livingstone 1989; Hefner 1998). However, the distinction between a spiritual domain and the economic sphere is not always applicable to all religious traditions. Secular approaches may have developed in western Europe, but they are not a universal feature of globalization, and indeed, if Weber is correct, may not even accurately characterize the West. In many Muslim countries, religious symbols and Islamic spirituality often are mobilized toward social and economic objectives.

In recent scholarship, the increasing role of religiosity in public life and the consequent convergence between economic and religious practice has been discussed in terms of "the business of spirituality" (Carrette and King 2005), "the economics of religion" (Obadia and Wood 2011) or the emergence of "spiritual economies" (Rudnyckyj 2010). The notion of spiritual economy indicates a particular response or engagement with neoliberalism and globalization, whereby, to borrow Rudnyckyj's expression, "religious practices are conjoined to broader project of economic transformation as workers are enjoined to compete in an increasingly global economy" (2009: 105).

To narrow the analysis of the interaction between religion and the market, this chapter focuses on Muslim charities, and the way charitable action simultaneously shapes and is shaped by market ethics. Charity in the form of paying *zakat* (alms) is an important Islamic obligation and, in fact, is one of the five pillars of Islam: ritual activities required of all Muslims. Thus Muslims whose wealth exceeds a set amount are obliged to pay zakat annually to a trustworthy collector so that it can be dispensed for public benefit, particularly to assist the poor (Benthall 1999; Singer 2008). Beyond the rise of zakat organizations, most Muslims provide zakat independently to poor relatives or neighbours.

In Indonesia, the popularity of zakat has increased considerably in the past two decades, indicated, for instance, by the growth in numbers of zakat collector organizations established by the government, private companies and civil society. During the Suharto regime, which is also known as the New Order era (1967–1998), Muslim civil servants were required to pay zakat, or alms, to the government-sponsored foundations or agencies. The imposition of zakat on Muslim civil servants by the local government is still occurring in some regions of Indonesia (Fauzia 2013; Latief 2013a). This growing engagement with organized forms of charitable giving goes alongside, and is related to the proliferation of, various types of Islamic voluntary organizations, including those that I define as hybrid voluntary organizations. These are Islamic voluntary organizations whose objectives are inspired or even driven both by economic and socio-religious interests. Thus, hybrid Islamic voluntary organizations might run businesses and charitable activities in parallel with each other (Ibrahim & Sherif 2008; Latief 2013b).

After the fall of Indonesia's long-time authoritarian president, Suharto, in the late 1990s, Indonesia witnessed a significant growth of philanthropic organizations. During the early years of the *reformasi* era,[3] Islamic charitable organizations became increasingly active in public life, not only in *dakwah* (religious proselytizing) and social activities, but also in the operation of economic enterprises. Whereas in the past charities were managed by mosque-based voluntary committees, they increasingly became staffed by skilled volunteers. These charitable organizations have gained extensive support from the public, especially the middle class, which increasingly channels most of its *zakat* (alms), *sedekah* (charity) and *waqf* (endowment) donations through them (Latief 2013b, 2014).[4] At the same time, in the past ten years large firms and multinational companies have increasingly contributed to Islamic charities. Islamic charities, in fact, have received not only donations from individual Muslims through zakat and sedekah, but also support from corporations and business organizations as part of corporate social responsibility programmes.

Urban Muslims and the Marketization of Piety

Since the early 1990s, DT has been a magnet for university students and the Muslim middle class seeking Islamic knowledge and spiritual guidance, emerging as one of the most popular Islamic spiritual training centres in urban areas of Indonesia. DT stands out for its innovative ways of interpreting Indonesian Islam through a mixture of piety, entrepreneurial skills, human resources development, leadership training and education, as well as by promoting Islam as an easy, simple, and practical faith.[5]

Different groups of people, including high school students, the elderly, academics, senior managers and executives from national as well as multinational firms, regularly attend DT's training centre in Bandung, West Java. Here they participate in Islamic leadership and human resource training, called *Manajemen Qalbu* (MQ, Management of the Heart). This training is intended for human resources development and is a capacity building programme that draws on Aa Gym's interpretation of Islamic doctrine. MQ training includes motivation and mental and physical (outbound) training. Aa Gym uses a distinctive approach by emphasizing the necessity to "manage" the heart and cultivate Islamic dispositions. Some groups seek to cultivate their religiosity by spending a weekend at DT's guest house, where they perform prayers together (*tahajud berjama'ah*) and attend Aa Gym's lively Sunday morning religious sermons.

Aa Gym's popularity can be attributed to his focus on morality given the diversity of Islamic orientations in Indonesia and, in particular, the split between so-called modernist and traditionalist schools. The modernist is partly represented by Muhammadiyah and the traditionalist by Nahdlatul Ulama (Noer 1973; Feener 2007). Indonesian Muslims adhere to different strands of Islam and many Muslims are still sensitive to the discussion of differences in ritual practice, but themes of ethics and morality are less controversial.

An example of Aa Gym's message about cultivating religious faith for economic success was evident in an address he delivered in October 2008. At the time, Indonesians were anxious about the impact of the financial crisis that had affected major European, American and Asian countries. Following Friday prayers in DT's mosque in Bandung West Java, Aa Gym stood up in front of the audience and delivered a brief speech, saying

> With regards to the news about the world's economic crisis that we have recently heard, we have to remain undaunted because Allah is extraordinarily merciful. When we were in our mother's wombs, our livelihood and fortune had already been scripted. What we need to do is fulfil God's orders...Our fortune and livelihood cannot be blocked by anyone except by our own violation of God's law. Therefore, we have to be more confident about this crisis. Truthfully, this crisis encourages us to work wholeheartedly and to show our forbearance and attitude of resignation.[6]

This speech was delivered in response to anxiety about the impact of the crisis on Indonesian society. Aa Gym sought to remind worshippers in the DT mosque to draw on religious lessons to confront social and economic crises. In his eyes, Muslims should strive to improve their faith and self-confidence to face adversity. Thus, Aa Gym attempted to foster the engagement of Indonesian Muslims in strengthening their Islamic faith, self-assurance, mentality and ability to confront problems. As I demonstrate in the next section, DT has created a wide range of programmes dedicated toward the marketization of spirituality to redress the problems of poverty and economic underdevelopment.

Two decades since its inception, Aa Gym's *pesantren* (Islamic educational institution akin to a *madrassah*) has expanded considerably and now includes a wide range of facilities, including a mini-market, student dormitories, daycare centre and kindergarten, guesthouses and a convention centre. Aa Gym strives to cultivate professionalism and discipline among the employees of DT. At the same time, he has built up the Manajemen Qolbu Corporation (MQC), a holding company that manages a number of subsidiary companies that he and his organization established in fields including media, tourism and consumer goods. His umbrella organization, DT, is not only an Islamic educational institution, but also a successful business conglomerate, attesting to his business acumen. Alongside those activities, DT has expanded its core activities by running a charitable organization that collects and distributes zakat to support the provision of social services for the poor, as well as for the organization of emergency relief activities.

When he first started out as a religious leader, Aa Gym's main supporters were mostly women. His first wife was highly visible and was referred to by the familiar "Téh" (elder sister). However, when in 2006 it became known that he had taken a second wife – a DT staff member – his popularity amongst women declined sharply. Although Islamic law permits a man to marry up to four wives, polygamy is frowned upon by most Indonesian Muslims. Aa Gym's decision to take a second wife led to a drop in enthusiasm for his educational and social activities, as well as a dwindling base for DT business enterprises. The volume of visitors to his pesantren dropped and only a few travel agencies continued to organize trips to Aa Gym's spiritual training programmes. The staff who managed DT's charitable organization admitted that during the period following Aa Gym's second marriage zakat collections almost dried up completely. When I did my initial fieldwork at DT in 2008, the childcare training had just recently been revived after having been suspended in 2007 for lack of funds and prospective trainees. Reflecting on the consequences of the polygamy scandal, Hoesterey (2008: 96) notes

> Everything changed. Feeling heartbroken and betrayed, his female followers abandoned him and his polygamous marriage became the subject of national scandal. Infotainment shows and gossip magazines circulated stories of former admirers shredding his pictures, boycotting his television shows and cancelling weekend pilgrimage to his pesantren and a 'spiritual tourism' complex, Daarut Tauhid.

The situation deteriorated further when Téh Ninih, Aa Gym's first wife, announced in June 2011 that she wanted a divorce. However, a year later Aa Gym and his first wife reconciled. Since then, Téh Ninih has become a very active woman preacher and leads some of DT's programmes in Bandung. Although Aa Gym is not as popular as he was at the zenith of his stardom prior to 2006, he still has broad appeal among many middle-class Muslims in Indonesia.

The Formation of DPU-DT

In 1999, Aa Gym established a charity division called Dompet Peduli Ummat (DPU-DT) whose main task is to collect and manage zakat. Like other community-based zakat organizations operating in Indonesia, DPU-DT channels charity to a variety of social enterprises, ranging from poverty relief to community-based entrepreneurship training. A few years after its inception DPU-DT became a national zakat organization following formal recognition and authorization by the Ministry of Religious Affairs.

DPU-DT consists of three divisions: the Centre for Community Self-Governance (*Pusat Kemandirian Ummat*), the Centre for Education and Community Training (*Pusat Pendidikan dan Pelatihan Ummat*) and the Centre for Social and Humanitarian Affairs (*Pusat Sosial Kemanusiaan*). DPU-DT was recognized as a Regional Zakat Organisation (LAZDA) by the governor of West Java Province and as a National Zakat Organisation (LAZNAS) by the Ministry of Religious Affairs in 2002 and 2004 respectively. Since 2006, DPU-DT has worked with the Muslimah Centre, the women's wing of DT that was also founded by Aa Gym, to run a joint programme called "Baby Sitter Mitra Ibu" (BSMI – childcare workers and mothers' partnership), whose participants are mostly teenage women.[7]

The Muslimah Centre seeks to train women to become "good Muslims" by teaching them how to be Islamic role models in their families and communities. In this respect, one of the major planks of the Muslimah Centre's education system is the notion of a woman's "golden age" (*masa keemasan*). Training specifically directed to women older than fifty years of age is called "Muslimah's Golden Age Schooling" (*Bimbingan MuslimahMasa Keemasan*). "Golden age" here refers to the period in life when women are to begin withdrawing from "worldly affairs" and focus instead on cultivating pious dispositions by studying Islam and performing religious duties.[8] Normally training is conducted in DT's complex and caters to groups of women from different social and ethnic backgrounds, although private classes are also offered for individual women or single families.

Another meaning of the term "golden age" by the Muslimah Centre, though, refers to the early years of life, when a basic knowledge of Islam should be imparted, providing children with both religious and moral guidance that will shape their adult lives. The training of childcare workers by the DPU-DT in cooperation with the Muslimah Centre (to which I return later) works towards supporting children's religious learning during the "golden age" period. Their cooperation, I argue, underscores a novel intersection between Islamic religiosity and market action. The fulfilment of middle-class demands for childcare workers with skill in teaching religion signifies how Islamization ensues as a result of the inclusion of spirituality into the market. DT has attempted to marketize not only childcare the usual domestic skills of childcare workers, but also their talent in teaching Islamic basic tenets. Therefore, it can be said that organizations such as Aa Gym's DPU-DT epitomize a substantial shift in the orientation and practices of Indonesian Islamic philanthropic institutions.

Alongside "traditional" charitable activities, such as distributing groceries to those in need, providing wheelchairs or prostheses for people with disabilities and delivering basic healthcare for the poor, DPU-DT has engaged the Muslimah Centre to create development-oriented projects directed towards providing training and employment for rural young women. The lack of live-in domestic workers to provide child care and perform household chores is a persistent complaint among middle-class Indonesians; thus the training of childcare workers not only addresses problems of rural female unemployment, but also provides a much-sought service to Aa Gym's legions of middle-class followers. DT appeals for charitable donations in Islamic terms to support the childcare workers' scheme and to provide employment to these young women once they have completed training that is both vocational and religious in orientation.

Childcare Training

The history of the childcare training scheme begins with the needs of the DT's female staff who, in the early days of the pesantren, had to juggle their professional duties with family responsibilities. As their numbers increased, DT set up a daycare centre in the Muslimah Centre so that, as one of my research participants explained, "babies could receive the best nourishment from their own mothers' milk, and at the same time the mothers could dedicate themselves to their careers and religious proselytising." The childcare workers were appointed at both the daycare centre and kindergarten to look after the children of the DT's staff. While the main objective of the daycare centre and kindergarten was to support staff members and clients, after 2006 DT began recruiting childcare trainees from low-income households, which allowed DPU-DT to collect and utilize charitable donations to finance the training.

However, other factors contributed to DT's decision to establish the childcare worker training programme, in particular the economic crisis in the late 1990s and the increase in unemployment, especially among young women whose limited formal education and skills was deemed to make them vulnerable to human trafficking. The DPU-DT aimed to provide training that might lead uneducated rural women to jobs that would allow them to earn enough money to eke out a living. At the same time, there was a growing demand from the middle and upper middle classes for childcare workers with both vocational and religious training. It can be said that the training functions as DT's way to materialize its vision of an Islamic community (*ummah*) by helping poor teenagers, and to disseminate Islamic principles into society at large through the Islamization of middle-class families. In this respect, not only does the training programme seek to address the economic needs of unemployed women and the religious sensibilities of the middle classes while allowing DT to expand its business activities, but it also moulds childcare workers into agents of religious change.

According to DPU-DT's promotional materials, the objective of childcare training is the "empowerment" of Muslim women who are eligible as zakat beneficiaries. DPU-DT advertised childcare training as a way to communicate with the public and in turn to welcome people's zakat payments and charitable obligations through DPU-DT. A volunteer working for DPU-DT repeatedly emphasized that a zakat organization should address specific problems that people really face. According to him, childcare training can provide a means of earning a living wage to those from low-income families who have left school early and have few career prospects. Prospective trainees originate mostly from West Java, where both early marriage among teenagers and the recruitment of female migrant workers for placement abroad are widespread. Thus, it offers a means to prevent poorly educated teenagers who lack marketable skills from leaving to work as housemaids overseas and protects them from the threat of human trafficking.

While I was conducting the research, the participants in the training programme were predominantly teenagers younger than eighteen years of age, although a few of the trainees were in their twenties and had experience working in factories or in the informal sector. Two of the trainees explained:

> First trainee: "I was working as a salesgirl in a big supermarket in my hometown when I found brochures about this babysitter training. This coincided with my intention to find a new job that did not require me to use a lot of cosmetics like what I have done as a salesgirl. I decided to come to the address mentioned in the brochure and meet some other girls in the DPU-DT office to sign up for the training. Some of my friends admitted that they knew about this training from radio advertising, while others were informed by their relatives who found out about the programme from the Internet."
>
> Second trainee: "There was a gentleman from DPU-DT, who came to my village to look for prospective participants for the baby sitter training programme. At that time, I had been unemployed for one year after I finished high school. I needed a job and asked my friends and relatives who were in the same situation like me in my village to apply to join the programme. Twelve girls from my village are joining this programme."

These quotations indicate how DPU-DT programmes were advertised and marketed not only in urban centres but also in smaller villages. In addition to advertising the programme in the media and press, the recruitment process was conducted through direct visits to villages. The participants were teenagers who had just graduated from junior or senior high school and did not have access to jobs in their hometowns.

Despite Aa Gym's popularity and association with Islam, the DPU-DT found it difficult to recruit prospective childcare workers, a problem confirmed by a DPU-DT staff member responsible for the recruitment of trainees in rural areas:

> It is not always easy to convince parents to let their daughters join the childcare worker programme because of fears about human trafficking.... The parents were afraid that their daughters might be sent to work abroad or outside Java. I know that some participants attempted to convince their parents that they would not have trouble with this training because they often see Aa Gym, the leader of DT, on television.

Although the parents of the prospective trainees worry about human trafficking, and therefore sometimes hesitate to let their daughters enter the DPU-DT programme, Aa Gym's reputation as a popular preacher and religious leader in many cases has assuaged these concerns.

Spiritualization of Childcare Training

The childcare training programme was implemented in 2006. When I conducted fieldwork in 2008 and 2010, DPU-DT had already completed eight cycles of training, each one involving thirty young women, mostly from West Java. Once they passed an initial screening, the participants were invited to come to DPU-DT's headquarters in Bandung. Some came alone or with a friend while others were escorted by their parents. After arriving in Bandung all participants were required to take a number of tests, including a psychological assessment and a medical examination to ensure that they were free from tuberculosis and were not pregnant. As DPU-DT expects the childcare workers to become agents of Islamic renewal amongst urban middle-class families, trainees were tested on their ability to read the Qur'an properly or at least show a commitment to learning to do so if their reading skill did not meet the DPU-DT's standards. If they passed these tests, they would begin a three-month training programme.[9]

The training conducted by DPU-DT resembles similar schemes provided for prospective female migrant workers, in that in both instances participants are taught specific practical skills and correct dispositions towards domestic work (Rudnyckyj 2004; for comparative studies, see Huang and Yeoh 2007; and Mahdavi 2011). The training of childcare workers resembles what Rudnyckyj calls "technologies of servitude" through which trainees are habituated to performing domestic duties with the skills and poise required by middle-class employers (Rudnyckyj 2004: 431–434). The DPU-DT and the Muslimah Centre do not run the training scheme alone, but rely on partnerships with other institutions such as the nursing school associated with the Indonesian Air Force Nursing Academy, which provides teaching material on health and childcare, and the Indonesian Education University, which supplies didactic support on family life, domesticity, psychology and other relevant practical matters.

The childcare worker training is conducted in two locations: the Muslimah Center Building of Daarut Tauhid Complex and the nursing school associated with the Indonesian Air Force. The Muslimah Centre is located in front of Aa Gym's house in the Daarut Tauhid complex and was constructed in 2004 with financial support from former participants of DT Hajj and Umrah Travel. It functions as both a dormitory and training centre, with some rooms used as classrooms. Meanwhile, the nursing school of the Indonesian Air Force is located in another area quite far from the DT complex. During the course of healthcare training in this nursing school, every morning the participants are picked up by car from the Muslimah Centre to depart for the nursing school. The nursing school provides one classroom and laboratory for the childcare training.

The training is divided into three stages (*marhalah*): orientation, formal teaching and apprenticeship. In the first and second stages, the training covers three sets of subjects. The first stage deals with topics related to Islam and is directed towards cultivating the religious skills and moral dispositions of childcare workers, with the goal of producing not only devout Muslim women, but also competent religious teachers. Islamic *dawah* (proselytizing), after all, is the main driving force behind DPU-DT's social mission and charitable services. Specific subjects – such as Islamic ethics (*akhlaq*), theology (*'aqidah*) and jurisprudence (*fiqh*) – are taught intensively every night. Trainees are coached in Qur'anic recitation and are encouraged to memorize both short Qur'anic verses and daily prayers.

Trainees are encouraged to perform a voluntary fast every Monday and Thursday. In a Muslim community, performing these voluntary fasts is recommended by Islamic tradition and signifies a higher degree of individual piety, partly because this is more challenging than fasting only during the month of Ramadan. Every Monday and Thursday, all trainees are roused in the early morning for breakfast (*sahur*) before sunrise, and they may break their fast after sunset. Even women who are menstruating (and are therefore exempted from fasting) are encouraged to take part in the early breakfasts to demonstrate "solidarity." As there are differences among Indonesian Muslims in the performance of rituals such as daily prayers, childcare workers are taught different versions of ritual practices so that they adjust to their employers' religious traditions.

The second section of the training focuses on subjects and skills related to family and domesticity (*kerumahtanggaan*) that are taught by a group of lecturers from a state-run university in Bandung. Domesticity refers to the lifestyles of middle-class Indonesians. Thus the trainees learn how to operate modern domestic appliances, such as washing machines, dishwashers and vacuum cleaners. They are also taught how to purchase groceries at the supermarket, to prepare food and cook in an appropriate manner, how to act in a restaurant and, more generally, how to behave in middle-class contexts.

The third section comprises subjects pertaining to infant healthcare. Here, trainees receive both theoretical and practical teaching on health and childcare and for this reason the training takes place at the nursing school associated with the Indonesian Air Force in Bandung. In the babysitting classes, for instance, trainees learn basic theories about infant health and care, coupled with practical experience under the supervision of lecturers from the nursing school. Using mannequins of various sizes, from newborn to about three years old,

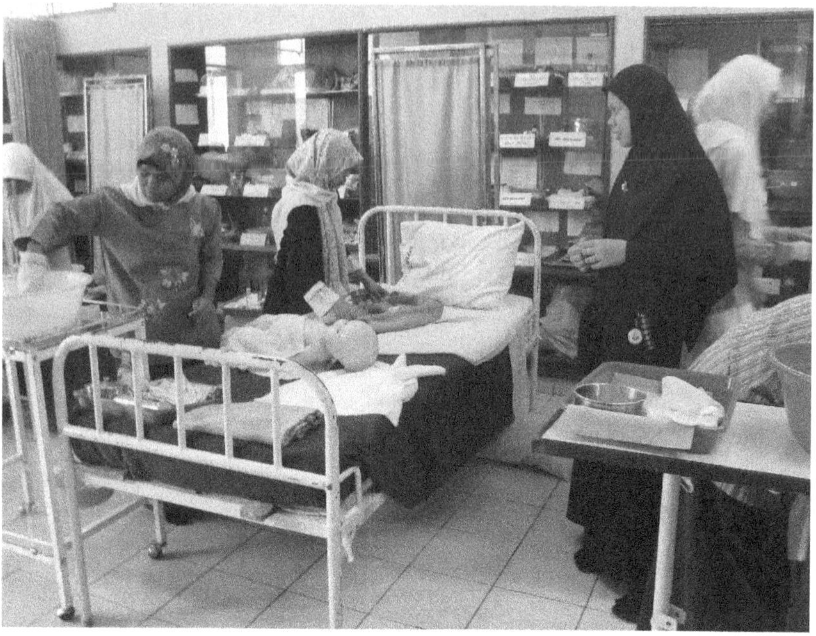

Figure 9.1. DPU-DT childcare trainees practice how to care for infant mannequins.
(Photo Credit: Hilman Latief)

they practice bathing and dressing, providing food and measuring nutrients and detecting illness and offering first aid (see Figures 9.1 and 9.2).

During my second visit to DT in 2010, the practical training was supervised by three young women, all staff from the Muslimah Centre. Unlike the trainees who wore a more casual Muslim dress, the staff wore long black or blue *abaya* as their uniform. One of the staff members led prayers and described the objective of the training, which she said was to develop not only trainees' skills, but also their mentality. When the training began in the workshop class, the staff walked around the class to make sure that the trainees understood the instructions and followed procedures. These women also kept an eye on the trainees' attitudes in giving first aid to the (baby) dummy and reminded the trainees not to forget to recite prayers before and after they accomplish their tasks. Yet, practically, the staff members' body language and hesitations eventually betrayed their lack of experience. Despite their authoritative positions, none of them had any formal training in childcare or any direct personal experience of raising babies.

On completion of the training, the trainees are required to practice what they had learned during the apprenticeship period. During the apprenticeship,

Figure 9.2. Staff at the Muslimah Centre/DPU-DT (wearing black and blue abaya) monitor childcare trainees practicing with infant mannequins. (Photo Credit: Hilman Latief)

DPU-DT or the Muslimah Centre staff observe and evaluate how the trainees implement their skills in childcare, their social attitudes, and their discipline in practising religious duties. The trainees spend four to six weeks as childcare workers in the homes of DT staff members. After passing this stage and attending the graduation ceremony, they are deemed ready to work for middle-class Indonesian families outside the immediate DPU-DT network.

Marketizing Childcare Workers

PT Global Solutions Provider (GSP), DT's commercial division, acts as a broker linking prospective employers and childcare workers, as the latter are not allowed to seek employment by themselves. Families wishing to employ a DT-trained worker pay a fee to GSP to be put on their waiting list, and they are required to take in Management of the Heart training programme and orientation, during which time they are introduced to the childcare workers.[10] The training programme, DT argues, ensures that care workers will not be subject to any mistreatment by their prospective employers.

The placement of childcare workers is a highly standardised and regulated process. The GSP determines a minimum monthly wage and the childcare workers' rights that should be honoured by employers, all of which are stated in the one-year contract signed by the three parties: the childcare worker, the provider (GSP) and the employers. Should GSP receive any complaints about the way the employing families treat childcare workers, GSP has the right to cancel the contract. Likewise, if a family complains about an childcare worker's performance, GSP will offer a replacement. Every three months, DT, through GSP, organizes meetings with the childcare workers so that they can share their experiences and support each other. The meeting functions not only to evaluate their performance, but also as a forum through which DPU-DT staff can give *tausiyah* (Islamic messages) and to make sure that the childcare workers do not face a great deal of difficulties while working with their employers. It is because of these arrangements that DPU-DT claims that the objective of childcare worker training is to help and protect unskilled and vulnerable young women from possible exploitation and trafficking.

The role of GSP as an intermediary between childcare workers and their employers leads to ambiguities with respect to the determination of wages. The minimum wage for Indonesian workers, especially for labourers in factories, has been a topic of conflict among trade unions, nongovernmental organization (NGO) activists, employer associations and the government in the post-Suharto years. There have been government efforts and NGO advocacy directed towards supervising the implementation of a regional minimum wage for labourers, but an overall agreement has not been reached. DPU-DT's childcare providers have been excluded from wage agreements. Furthermore, workers in informal sectors such as childcare or housework have not been included either in government policies concerning the minimum wage or in NGO advocacy. As a result, the DPU-DT, through the GSP, in 2009 determined unilaterally the childcare workers' minimum wage, ranging from IDR 650,000 to IDR 750,000 (US $65–75) per month, which according to the DPU-DT is higher than that received by ordinary childcare workers and housemaids. However, some trainees said that the employers should pay GSP IDR 1, 300,000 (US$120–130). In Indonesia, childcare workers, especially those not employed through agencies, are paid according to the individual agreement between employer and worker without any standardisation.

In response to this phenomenon, Yunianti Chudzaifah, chairperson of the National Commission for Women, has argued that the multitalented childcare workers trained by the DPU-DT actually deserve a much higher wage by virtue of the professional skills they have acquired (interview, February 2010). She asserts that training these employees to teach religious rituals, such as praying (*salat*), daily and short prayer recitation and Qur'anic reading for infants and children, are skills to their merit, different from those required for childcare or housework, thus requiring appropriate recognition and compensation. Chudzaifah also said, "this is unfair to pay the workers who have different skills such as teaching Qur'an, prayer, and childcare with such amount of money. They should be paid more than that." The statement implies that religious knowledge and domestic knowledge are equally important and both deserve appropriate compensation. Thus, the skill inherent in the ability to teach religious principles and practices is part of a market for religious knowledge that adds value to the labour of childcare workers.

Even though *childcare worker's duties* differ from those of a housemaid, in practice for Indonesian families who employ them this is seldom the case, and childcare workers are often assigned general domestic duties as well. Ordinarily childcare workers, who are quite common in middle-class Indonesian families, are not responsible for teaching religion or religious practices to the children in their care. In addition, newly trained care workers have little or no knowledge of working hours and salary, as neither is included in the contract signed by care workers, GSP and the employers, a contract that, according to DPU-DT, should ensure fairness and reduce abuse or exploitation.

Nevertheless, to ensure that care workers receive the agreed on wage, in 2009 GSP introduced a new policy requiring employing families to pay salaries directly to the GSP, which it then transfers to the workers themselves. The workers are encouraged by GSP to open a savings account with the *baitul mal wa al-tamwil* (BMT, an Islamic financial cooperative) owned by DT. According to DPU-DT, childcare workers may withdraw their money whenever they wish. Childcare workers are also encouraged to practise voluntary giving (*sedekah*) for dakwah. DPU-DT's effort to train pious Muslims who are economically productive is not simply a marketization of spirituality, but could also be seen as part of a broader spiritual economy, in which religious and economic ethics are promoted through distinctive forms of training (Rudnyckyj 2010).

The aggregate of religious charity and market practices can be seen in the relationship between the families who draw on GSP's services and DPU-DT. The families are, for the most part, followers or admirers of Aa Gym. They frequently attend religious gatherings or *pengajian* (Islamic study groups) at DT mosques to listen to Aa Gym's sermons. Over the years, they have contributed heavily to DPU-DT's charity funds. Not surprisingly, DPU-DT seeks to maintain good relationships with these benefactors, whose individual contributions are regularly announced during the pengajian.

On one hand, DPU-DT provides middle-class families with morally and professionally reliable childcare workers, who are a labour force in high demand. On the other hand, DT, in general, and its charitable organisation, DPU-DT in particular, rely on middle-class financial contributions for sustaining and developing its religious and social activities, as well as its business initiatives. Furthermore, DT's religious proselytization responds to the growing middle-class demand for Islamic childcare and Islamic education more generally. Young women trained in both childcare and the basic tenets of Islamic practice will contribute to the Islamization of their employers. Hence, the marketization of spirituality has become part of – and cannot be detached from – the process of Islamization engineered by DT to fulfil the demands of the growing Muslim middle class. By addressing specific needs of the middle class, DT accomplishes three objectives: it provides assistance to those who have not completed their primary or secondary education and to unemployed young women; it sustains dakwah; and it draws support from potential funders. In the meantime, charitable organizations such as DT, supported and funded by the middle class, eventually work towards reinforcing existing middle-class networks by providing services to the latter (see Clark 2004).

Conclusion

This chapter has addressed the interaction between religion and labour markets in contemporary Indonesia and illustrated the complex social and economic dimensions of Islamic charity. I have shown how DT through DPU-DT and Muslimah Center ascribes market value to religious knowledge and piety in the childcare training programmes that it has developed. These programmes are intended to help the poor by amplifying the religious piety of those they seek to assist. Thus, the enhancement of religious practice is a critical means through which poor women from rural parts of Java are able to participate more intensively in Indonesia's growing economy. Increasing the value of the labour of female teenagers from rural villages by cultivating religious skills, such as reading the Qur'an, and domestic skills, such as childcare, illustrates the marketization of piety.

Economic growth in Indonesia in recent years has fostered the growth of Muslim middle classes and stimulated the proliferation of charitable organizations whose activities focus on overcoming the hardships faced by the huge number of poor Indonesians. To this end, especially in the aftermath of economic crises in the late 1990s that caused tremendous upheaval in a country already characterized by social and economic disparities, a number of charitable organizations have attempted to provide various schemes to aid the poor. DPU-DT is one of many Indonesian Islamic charities whose duties are, among others, collecting *zakat* (almsgiving) and *sedekah* (charitable giving) and supporting disadvantaged segments of society, including orphans and the needy. Thus, charities such as DPU-DT illustrate the convergence of religious and economic objectives.

Daarut Tauhid (DT) has developed a reputation for its dakwah-based commercial enterprises and managing a wide array of businesses, ranging from spiritual training to Islamic media. DT's founder, Aa Gym, has effectively translated Islamic ethics and values into business practices. However, DT marketizes spirituality not only for commercial purposes, but also for social goals. Charitable activities run by DT and by its autonomous zakat agency, DPU-DT, are deeply influenced by market forces and economic interests. On the one hand, the training of skilled childcare givers stands for DPU-DT's efforts to address rural poverty and to protect vulnerable young women from exploitation and human trafficking. By doing so, DT responds to the demand among middle-class Muslim families for childcare givers who are simultaneously skilled in childcare and Islam. On the other hand, DT seeks to fulfil its dakwah mission through a re-Islamization of middle-class Muslim families. This is enabled, among other means, by training pious caregivers who enable raising children in an Islamic manner and environment. DPU-DT thus combines market principles, spirituality and charity activism in its childcare worker training programme. It should also be noted that DPU-DT has acted as an "intermediary" between the employees from poor families and middle-class employers in promoting mutual benefit between the two, in eradicating poverty and in marketizing piety among middle-class families at the same time. In this respect, DPU-DT has adopted and followed the market ethics in its charitable enterprises and poverty alleviation projects.

With reference to the roles played by DT's charitable organization, we may argue that the religiously motivated tradition of giving cannot be separated from economic and political interests. The process of marketizing Islam in Indonesia is still prevalent and even increasing. In this respect, religion is a means through which ethics conducive to market action are configured. Religiously inspired charity activism among Indonesian Muslims illustrates the reciprocal relationships between religious and market action, the ways in which religion is valued in the context of economic development and the extent to which religious ideas are translated to be in line with the increasing demand for specific types of labour. It is under these circumstances that Islamic charity activism and the efforts of Muslims to materialize notions of benevolent action should simultaneously be negotiated with the recent dynamic development of economic enterprises in their daily lives.

Notes

1 The emerging roles of preachers, including Aa Gym, on national television in Indonesia has been regarded as the rise of what Julia Howell calls "on-screen evangelism" or "televangelism" (Howell 2008: 51).

2 These are extremely popular cooperative lending institutions that offer small-scale loans based on Islamic economic restrictions.

3 Reformasi refers to the period of Indonesia's political reform, marked by the fall of the Suharto regime in 1998. Suharto had ruled Indonesia for thirty-two years after he usurped power from Sukarno, Indonesia's first president.

4 Both zakat and sedekah are practiced to assist the poor. *Waqf* are endowments by the deceased to benefit society. These are the three main forms that Muslims use to finance charitable activities.
5 There are other Islamic training programs in Indonesia that resemble Aa Gym's DT, such as Ary Ginanjar's ESQ (Emotional and Spiritual Quotient) and Yusuf Mansur's Wisata Hati ("the Journey of the Heart").
6 I observed and recorded this speech on 10 October 2008 at DT.
7 *Muslimah* is an Arabic term for Muslim women. The Muslimah Center was originally named *Daarul Akhwat* ("the House of Sisters") and founded by female students who lived in the dormitory near Aa Gym's house in 1995. Daarul Akhwat then formally became a division of DT in 2005, specifically to facilitate women's activities.
8 Interview with coordinator of childcare worker training and the staff of the Muslimah Centre, 10 and 11 November 2008, in Bandung.
9 I had the opportunity to attend the seventh childcare worker training in 2008, when the prospective trainees were tutored on healthcare and Islamic tenets, and the eighth training in 2010.
10 A similar type of training can also be seen in the ESQ (Emotional and Spiritual Quotient) project founded by Ari Ginanjar Agustian, a prominent and popular motivator who also attempted to incorporate spiritual approach into work and business (Rudnyckyj 2010).

References

Afriani, S. H. 2013. "Islamic Beauty: Socio-Semiotic Analysis of Facial Form and Body Lotion Advertisement." *Journal of Indonesian Islam* 6(2), 265–278.
Ariff, M. (ed.). 1991. *The Muslim Private Sector in Southeast Asia*. Singapore: Institute of Southeast Asian Studies.
Barendregt, B. 2011. "Pop, Politics, and Piety: Nasyid Boy Band Music in Southeast Asia." In *Islam and Popular Culture in Indonesia and Malaysia*, edited by A. N. Weintraub, 235–256. London: Routledge.
Benthall, J. 1999. "Financial Worship: The Qur'anic Injunction to Almsgiving." *Journal of the Royal Anthropological Institute* 5(1): 27–42.
Blackburn, S. 2004. *Women and the State in Modern Indonesia*. Cambridge: Cambridge University Press.
Bruce, S. 1990. *Pray TV: Televangelism in America*. New York: Routledge.
Carrette, J., and R. King. 2005. *Selling Spirituality: The Silent Takeover of Religion*. Oxfordshire and New York: Routledge.
Clark, J. A. 2004. *Islam, Charity and Activism: Middle Class Network and Social Welfare in Egypt, Yemen, and Jordan*. Bloomington: Indiana University Press.
Fauzia, A. 2013. *Faith and the State: A History of Islamic Philanthropy in Indonesia*. Leiden, the Netherlands: Brill.
Fealy, G. 2008. "Consuming Islam: Commodified Religion and Aspirational Pietism in Contemporary Indonesia." In *Expressing Islam: Religious Life and Politics in Indonesia*, edited by Greg Fealy and S. White, 15–39. Canberra Institute of Southeast Asian Studies and Research School of Pacific and Asian Studies, Australian National University.

Feener, R. M. 2007. *Muslim Legal Thought in Modern Indonesia*. Cambridge: Cambridge University Press.

Finke, R., and Stark, R. 1988. "Religious Economies and Sacred Canopies: Religious Mobilisation in American Cities–1906." *American Sociological Review* 53: 41–49.

Geertz, C. 1956. "Religious Belief and Economic Behavior in a Central Javanese Town: Some Preliminary Considerations." *Economic Development and Cultural Change* 4(2): 134–158.

1963. *Peddlers and Princes: Social Change and Economic Modernisation in Two Indonesian Towns*. Chicago: University of Chicago Press.

Hamilton, M. 1995. *Sociology of Religion*. London & New York: Routledge.

Harmsen, E. 2008. *Islam, Civil Society and Social Work: Muslim Voluntary Welfare Associations in Jordan between Patronage and Empowerment*. Amsterdam: Amsterdam University Press.

Hefner R. W (ed.). 1998. *Market Cultures: Society and Morality in the New Asian Capitalisms*. Boulder, CO: Westview Press.

Hoesterey, J. B. 2008. "Marketing Morality: The Rise, Fall and Rebranding of AA Gym." In *Expressing Islam: Religious Life and Politics in Indonesia*, edited by Greg Fealy and Shally White, 90–107. Canberra: Research School of Pacific and Asian Studies, Australian National University.

2012. "Prophetic Cosmopolitanism: Islam, Pop Psychology, and Civic Virtue in Indonesia." *City and Society* 24: 38–61.

2008. "Marketing Morality: the Rise, Fall and Rebranding of Aa Gym." In *Expressing Islam: Religious Life and Politics in Indonesia*, edited by Greg Fealy and Shally White, 95–112. Canberra: Research School of Pacific and Asian Studies, Australian National University.

Howell, J. D. 2008. "Modulation of Active Piety: Professors and Televangelists as Promoters of Indonesian 'Sufism'." In *Expressing Islam: Religious Life and Politics in Indonesia*, edited by Greg Fealy and Shally White, 40–62. Canberra: Research School of Pacific and Asian Studies, Australian National University.

Huang, S. and B. S. A. Yeoh. 2007. "Emotional Labour and Transnational Domestic Work: The Moving Geographies of "Maid Abuse" in Singapore." *Mobilities* 2(2): 195–217.

Ibrahim, B. L., and D. H. Sherif (eds.). 2008. *From Charity to Social Change: Trends in Arab Philanthropy*. Cairo and New York: American University in Cairo Press.

Jones, C. 2010. "Materializing Piety: Gendered Anxieties about Faithful Consumption in Contemporary Urban Indonesia." *American Ethnologist* 37, 617–637.

Kuran, T. 2004. *Islam and Mamon: The Economic Predicaments of Islamism*. Princeton, NJ and Oxford: Princeton University Press.

Latief, H. 2013a. "Islamic Philanthropy and the Private Sector in Indonesia." *Indonesian Journal of Islam and Muslim Societies* 3(2): 175–201.

2013b. "Islam and Humanitarian Affairs: The Middle Class and New Patterns of Social Activism." In *Islam in Indonesia: Contrasting Images and Interpretations*, edited by Kees van Dijk and Jajat Burhanuddin, 173–194. Amsterdam: Amsterdam University Press.

2014. "Contesting Almsgiving in Post New Order Indonesia." *American Journal of Islamic Social Sciences* 31(1): 16–50.

Livingstone, J. C. 1989. *Anatomy of the Sacred: An Introduction to Religion*. New York: Macmillan.
Mahdavi, P. 2011. "Questioning the Discursive Construction of Trafficking and Forced Labor in the United Arab Emirates." *Journal of Middle East Women's Studies* 6: 6–35.
Muzakki,A. 2008. "Islam as a Symbolic Commodity: Transmitting and Consuming Islam through Public Sermon in Indonesia." In *Religious Commodification in Asia: Marketing Gods*, edited by Pattana Kitiarsa, 205–219. London: Routledge.
Noer, D. 1973. *The Modernist Muslim Movement in Indonesia, 1900–1942*. Singapore: Oxford University Press.
Nuraeni, Z. 2005. "DT: Modernizing a Pesantren Tradition." *Studia Islamika*, 12(3): 477–509.
Obadia, L., and Wood D. C. (eds.). 2011. *The Economics of Religion: Anthropological Approaches*. Bingley, UK: Emerald.
Rudnyckyj, D. 2004. "Technologies of Servitude: Governmentality and Indonesian Transnational Labor Migration." *Anthropological Quarterly* 77(3): 407–434.
2009. "Spiritual Economies: Islam and Neoliberalism in Contemporary Indonesia." *Cultural Anthropology* 24(1): 104–141.
2010. *Spiritual Economies: Islam, Globalisation and the After Life of Development*. Ithaca, NY: Cornell University Press.
Sakai, M. "Community Development through Islamic Microfinance: Serving the Financial Needs of the Poor in a Viable Way." In *Expressing Islam: Religious Life and Politics in Indonesia*, edited by G. Fealy and S. White, 267–286. Canberra: Institute of Southeast Asian Studies and Research School of Pacific and Asian Studies, Australian National University.
Salim, Arskal. 2008. *Challenging the Secular State: The Islamization of Law in Modern Indonesia*. Honolulu: University of Hawai'i Press.
Singer, A. 2008. *Charity in Islamic Societies*. Cambridge: Cambridge University Press.
Sunarwoto. 2013. "Dakwah Radio in Surakarta: A Contest for Islamic Identity." In *Islam in Indonesia: Contrasting Images and Interpretations*, edited by Jajat Burhanuddin and Kees van Dijk, 195–214. Amsterdam: The International Convention of Asia Scholars and Amsterdam University Press.
Schwittay, A. 2011. "The Marketization of Poverty." *Current Anthropology* 52(3): S71–S82.
Turner, B. S. 2008. "New Spiritualities, the Media and Global Religion." In *Religious Commodification in Asia: Marketing Gods*, edited by Pattana Kitiarsa, 32–33. London: Routledge.
Van der Veer, P. 2012. "Market and Money: A Critique of Rational Choice Theory." *Social Compass* 59(2): 183–192.
Watson, C. W. 2005. "A Popular Indonesian Preachers: The Significance of Aa Gymnastiar." *Journal of Royal Anthropological Institute* 11(4): 773–792.
Weber. M. 1958. *The Protestant Ethic and the Spirit of Capitalism*. New York: Scribner's.
Weller, R. P. 2008. "Asia and the Global Economies of Charisma." In *Religious Commodification in Asia: Marketing Gods*, edited by Pattana Kitiarsa, 15–30. London: Routledge.

10 "A Poor Muslim Cannot Be a Good Muslim": Islam, Charitable Giving, and Market Logic in Sri Lanka

Filippo Osella, University of Sussex

In an article published in the *1970 Silver Jubilee Souvenir* of the Moors' Islamic Home, H. S. Ismail (1901–1973), a prominent Sri Lankan politician who became the first Muslim Speaker of Parliament, rebuked the Muslim middle class in Colombo for its apparent lack of concern for "social welfare work amongst the Muslims." Citing a recent newspaper article, he wrote, "Although the big commercial element of the Muslim population is about three per cent of the total…the popular impression of the Muslims is that they are a rich trading community." The wealthy Muslim elite lives "in luxury and comfort", wasting vast amounts of money on lavish marriage ceremonies so that "millions of rupees are literally thrown in the drain every year…with absolutely no benefit for the community at large." While those who live in "luxury and comfort" spend lavishly to keep up their prestige, "the near relatives, the orphans, the needy and the wayfarers get pittances which drag them into the mire of beggary." The shame of "beggary" is made worse by the way *zakat* is distributed during Ramadan, "when thousands of Muslims – men, women and children – roam the streets for the collection of their doles. The well-to-do must bear the blame for this sorry exhibition of poverty of our masses and our utter failure to maintain our so-called Islamic brotherhood" (Ismail 1970: 67–69).

That H. S. Ismail encouraged "the well-to-do" to pool resources to provide assistance "for those genuinely in need" should not come as a surprise. An early Tablighi Jama'at follower,[1] in 1956 he founded the Ceylon Baithulmal Fund,[2] an organization devoted to the collection and distribution of *zakat* (obligatory almsgiving) and *sadaqa* (voluntary charity) "to deserving Muslims in Sri Lanka." After more than fifty years and moments of instability, today the Fund has a pool of regular donors from whom it collects millions of rupees every year. Donors' zakat and sadaqa sustain a number of programs for poor Muslims: scholarships and vocational training, contributions to the expenses of marriage ceremonies, assistance to rural communities, acquisition of sewing machines for widows, and financial help for unforeseen life emergencies. In recent years, alongside these programs, Baithulmal has introduced more modern initiatives, such as interest-free loans collateralized with gold or a sponsorship system through which donors are asked to subsidize a specific person or project that is advertised on the Baithulmal's website.[3]

Baithulmal is just one of the many formal and informal organizations that have blossomed in Sri Lanka to collect and distribute zakat and sadaqa donations. This is part of a worldwide movement of hundreds of local and global nongovernmental organizations (NGOs) that mobilize religious donations to finance development projects across the Muslim world (see, e.g., the activities of the World Congress of Muslim Philanthropists; cf. Benthall 1999; Singer 2008; Atia 2013; Fauzia 2013). This corresponds with an increased emphasis on the redistributive nature of Islamic obligations to give (Singer 2008; for a critique, see Mandaville 1979; Kuran 2001, 2003), sometimes represented as an expression of an inherent Islamic humanitarianism (Dean and Khan 1997). These interventions often contrast capital accumulation with Islam's ethical imperatives, leading to calls for the revival of an Islamic moral economy opposed to the presumed immorality and excesses of Western capitalism (Rodinson 1978; Kuran 1986, 2001; Tripp 2006), and in which zakat is envisaged as a "total economic and social solution" (Fauzia 2013: 63).

To explore the local contours of the emerging Islamic moral economy centered on normative practices of almsgiving, this chapter documents how Muslims participating in various forms of religiously inspired giving in Colombo attribute both ethical and economic value to their actions. I show that material exchanges enabled by charitable acts allow for the objectification of pious dispositions and conversely that these dispositions are implicated in the production and reproduction of economic value. The apparent convergence of religious piety, humanitarian altruism and (spiritual and material) self-interest in zakat and sadaqa underpins the emergence of modalities of organized giving that are embedded in (apparently near-hegemonic) socio-religious pedagogies directed towards transforming the spiritual and material lives of middle-class givers and poor recipients alike. The former are enjoined to turn an individual obligation to God into a means for the spiritual and economic renewal of the Muslim community as a whole; the latter are encouraged, in turn, to utilize charity they receive to transform themselves into economically active and pious Muslims. Charting out understandings and practices of Muslim charity in Colombo from colonial times to the present, I will argue that the cultivation of specific ethico-economic dispositions through acts of religious giving have a complex history that cannot be too easily reduced to the long march of contemporary global capitalism and the neoliberal cultures that sustain it (cf. Muehlebach 2012; Atia 2013). At the same time, I will suggest that processes of subjectivation directed towards the habituation of givers and recipients of charity to an ethic of piety, social responsibility and economic virtuosity are necessarily incomplete and mediated by a number of concomitant or contradictory concerns. For many Colombo Muslims who give alms to the poor almost daily, zakat and sadaqa remain concerned primarily with the transformation of the (donor) self – a means to discharge a religious obligation, accumulate religious merits and ensure success in one's economic endeavors – rather than with the long-term material and spiritual welfare of "those genuinely in need." Finally, I will argue that the long-term purchase of connections between accumulation of religious merits and capital enabled by practices of almsgiving suggests caution in attributing to neoliberalism alone the power to co-opt religiosity as a means to foster or shore up economic practice (cf. Muehlebach 2012; Atia 2013).

The empirical material on which this chapter is based was collected in Sri Lanka's capital, Colombo, in 2012. Whilst in this Sinhala-Buddhist–dominated island Muslims make up roughly 10 percent of the total population, according to the 2012 census they account for 40.7 percent of Colombo Divisional Secretariat area. The vast majority of Sri Lankan Muslims are Sunni and follow the Shafi'i school of jurisprudence, but there are also two other Muslim communities with origins in northern India, Memons and Bohras. Although their population is small, these two groups have been highly successful in commerce, in concerns ranging from tea plantations and international trade to retail. There is no space here to summarize the rich history of Sri Lankan Muslims (see McGilvray 2008), but suffice it to say that they are a Tamil-speaking community whose middle-class elite rose to commercial prominence during the British colonial period. The debates over charity that I discuss in this chapter are taking place in a context in which Sinhala-Buddhist xenophobia has led recently to virulent, and oft violent, anti-Muslim campaigns (see Chapter 5 by Haniffa), making the Muslim minority increasingly anxious about its vulnerability and sensitive to criticism of their economic success and of their alleged exclusive and inward orientation (Ali 2014). Muslims have been accused of gaining unfair advantage over the Buddhist majority by circulating economic resources within the community; Muslims are chided for, for instance, patronizing only Muslim shops and restaurants, for investing in Muslim-owned business, and so forth (see Chapter 5 by Haniffa).

Islam and Charity

The relation between religious piety and economic practice has been a historical concern of Islamic scholars and thinkers, for instance through debates seeking to establish whether trade and commerce are morally neutral activities (and hence beyond the scope of religious intervention) or require a degree of ethical scrutiny (see, e.g., Hosseini 2003; see also Reda 2014). By and large, though, whilst Islamic traditions encourage various forms of almsgiving, they do not censure capital accumulation as inherently immoral. Researchers have argued that Islam is not hostile to the production and enjoyment of wealth per se, but sets prescriptions on its accumulation and use (Kuran 2004; Maurer 2005; Tripp 2006; Singer 2008), representing both piety and the objectification of worship through material donations to worthy recipients as a duty to God. Acts of giving result in the accumulation of spiritual merits in the afterlife and material returns in this world (Benthall 1999; Werbner 2003; Singer 2008). Muslim charitable practices, then, are neither necessarily opposed to the logic of market exchange, nor straightforwardly reflective of it (cf. Rajak 2011; Muehlebach 2012; Schwittay 2014).

Central to Islamic orthopraxis, zakat has been linked to prayer (Singer 2008), with Benthall defining it as "financial worship" (1999): a religious duty performed by giving a percentage of one's wealth to specific categories of deserving recipients (see Atia 2013: 14ff). It is distinguished from voluntary almsgiving, sadaqa, albeit the two words are often used interchangeably (Bashear 1993).[4] Whilst it can be considered as a tax, and indeed historically it has often been collected alongside other taxes (Scott 1987; Lev 2007; Singer 2008), zakat suggests notions of purification and increase. By giving a percentage of one's wealth, the remainder is purified. Although the ultimate reward for one's generosity is experienced only in the afterlife, the act of giving entails the promise of increased material prosperity and accumulation of religious merits. Zakat is also thought to purify recipients – the poor and needy – by reducing feelings of resentment towards the wealthy (Bashear 1993; Benthall 1999).

Scholars have underscored the complex history of zakat, tracing debates over who should be entrusted with its collection and distribution, who is entitled to receive it and for what purposes it should be utilized (for a review, see Kuran 2003). Others have explored the incorporation of Islamic almsgiving into pre-/non-Islamic gift-giving practices (van Hoven 1996; Soares 2005), and have considered instances of resistance against state-led reforms of zakat (Scott 1987; Fauzia 2013; May 2013). Although much attention has been paid in recent years to the development of Islamic banking (for a review, see Maurer 2005) and the emergence of novel forms of civic and social activism in the Muslim world associated with the rise of so-called "political Islam" (see, e.g., Sullivan 1994; Wiktorowicz 2001; Clark 2004; Deeb 2006; Bayat 2007),[5] social relations ensuing from the distribution of zakat and sadaqa have remained somewhat unexplored (for exceptions, see Singer 2008; Kochuyt 2009; Latief 2010).[6] Recent studies by Mona Atia (2013) and Amelia Fauzia (2013) on charitable practices in Egypt and Indonesia respectively have partially redressed this lack. They locate the emergence of contemporary forms of organized charity in these key Muslim-majority countries at the intersection of historically specific relations among state, market and public religiosity.

Whilst in contemporary Indonesia critiques of state corruption and mismanagement shifted the collection and distribution of zakat from the state to competing religious organization such as Muhammadiyah and Nahdlatul Ulama (Fauzia 2013: 157ff), post-economic liberalization Egypt has witnessed the emergence of a pious neoliberalism (see also Rudnyckyj 2010; Karaman 2013). Atia argues that state-led neoliberal reforms and the Islamization of public and private life – the outcome of attempts to rein in or repress Islamist organizations whilst co-opting Islam to lend legitimacy to the state – have led to the marketization of Islam and the Islamization of the social. Islamic charitable organizations in Cairo deliver services formerly provided by the state and have redefined the goals and ethics of Islamic charity. The latter is no longer solely a means for achieving a degree of social justice through redistribution of wealth through cash transfers, but it has become a tool for socioeconomic development in which religious proselytization and the ethics of market entrepreneurship go hand in hand (Atia 2013). Whilst the ethnography I discuss in the coming pages certainly resonates with the transformations of charitable giving outlined in Fauzia's and Atia's studies, it also underscores discontinuities and slippages in contemporary practices of charitable giving in Sri Lanka.

The Making of Modern Charity in Colombo

Across South Asia, the shift from traditional religious giving to modern forms of charity has been linked to the development of new middle-class aesthetics and to the politics of the colonial economy.[7] Describing the emergence of an indigenous bourgeoisie in colonial Ceylon, social historian Kumari Jayawardena (2002) has argued that from the mid-nineteenth century charitable giving became a means to establish individual status, to build political careers, to gain the goodwill of the colonial administration and to participate in the politics of community building and assertion. Jayawardena explains how traditional forms of religious giving – sustaining religious institutions or building temples and mosques, for instance – went alongside donations to support education or health projects and philanthropic initiatives promoted by colonial administration and British businesses, endeavors often rewarded with British titles and honors.

Echoes of these transformations can be found in the records of the Sri Lankan Wakf (*waqf;* endowment/trust, pl. *awqaf*) Board. Following the introduction of the Trust Ordinance in 1917 and the Succession and Wakfs Ordinance in 1931,[8] whilst some Muslim trusts remain primarily religious in orientation, others are designated a much wider remit. Take, for example, Noordeen Hajiar Abdul Caffoor (d. 1948), who was part of a family from Beruwala on the south-west coast of the island. He was one of the wealthiest Colombo gem traders of his time who, over the years, multiplied his riches by investing profits in the acquisition of large tracts of land in the centre of the city. Reputed to be a generous philanthropist, Abdul Caffoor made substantial donations to the Muslim-run Zahira College – paying for a science block, sixteen new classrooms and a hostel – as well as to other modern educational institutions and mosques – the Deaf and Blind School at Ratmalana, the Boy's Industrial School at Maharagama, and the Masjid Muhiyadeen in Colombo. In 1932 he established the Abdul Caffoor Trust, a religious and family waqf. In the deeds of the trust, he divided all his immovable properties among his four sons (who also become co-owners of the gem business and trustees of the waqf) and allocated 100,000 rupees to each of his two daughters as a premortem inheritance. The annual income from the rent of a multistoried building in central Colombo was devolved to the maintenance of the Gem Museum (founded by Caffoor himself), support for poor relatives, distribution of charity to the poor on the first day of Ramadan and the education of the children of "poor relatives and Muslim friends." Money left after these allocations was set for the education in Europe of "deserving Muslim boys." Finally, the profits from thirty-five acres of cultivable land were allocated to Maharagama Arabic College to provide fifty annual scholarships for "boys studying Arabic and Islam."

Private and public giving undergirded the economic and political ambitions of the Colombo-based Muslim trading elite, but, just as in recent years, economic success and public visibility (building of mosques, madrasas, schools and so on) became a liability that partially facilitated the sentiments that spawned the emerging Sinhala Buddhist nationalism. By the time of the 1915 anti-Muslim riots, Sinhala Buddhist anxieties about the dominance of Indian traders and commercial enterprises – amongst whom, though, Indian Muslims were a minority – were reframed as accusations of usury and exploitation against the Muslim community as whole (Ramanathan 1916; Jayawardena 1970; Ali 1981; Rowell 2009). In the meantime, philanthropic activities, and the recognition and honors that the British rewarded prolific donors, became the ground for confrontations between different sections of the Muslim community. Donations to and the management of prestigious institutions such as the Grand Mosque in Pettah, Maradana Mosque and Zahira College objectified the aspirations and orientations of diverse projects of community building, represented, at the time, by the rivalry between the All Ceylon Moors' Association and the All Ceylon Muslim League (Nuhman 2007: 38ff).[9] This was an antagonism that also reflected competition between the economic interests and status ambitions of different merchant dynasties, in particular those associated with Sir Mohamed Macan Markar[10] and N. D. H. Abdul Caffoor.[11] Finally, if donations toward and participation in the development of modern education for the Muslim community were an expression of the modernist orientation of the trading elite, colonial modernity and Anglophilia were shot through with the growing influence of different expressions of Islamic reformism circulating at the time (Nuhman 2007; cf. Osella and Osella 2008).[12]

In the aftermath of independence, and with the eventual nationalization of education, donations to schools and colleges dried up,[13] and the institution of waqf, amidst accusations of widespread corruption and increased state regulation (Mahroof 1985), lost its appeal. The few awqaf set up in the 1950s gave greater emphasis to the reproduction of relations of kinship and patronage. In 1959, for instance, Ebrahim Lebbe Marrikkar Hajiar Mohammed Salim (d. 1987) established the EL Ebrahim Trust. Born into a family of plantation owners, who by 1927 owned more than 1,700 acres of rubber and tea estates, he was one of Ceylon's rubber kings. A pious Muslim, he is known for funding through his *zakat* donations children's Qur'anic learning across the island, and for every Ramadan sending 100 kilogrammes of dates to each mosque in Sri Lanka, together with new clothes for old people.[14] Ebrahim allocated to the waqf five of his rubber estates whose income was devoted to sustaining the livelihood of more than 1,100 families living and working in his plantations, together with similar provision for an unspecified number of families in Colombo, and support for Qur'an teaching to 120 madrasas.

The fading away of religious-cum-family trusts took place in a post-independence environment in which the Colombo elite fraction of the middle class had, on the one hand, lost the colonial audience and rewards for its acts of largesse and, on the other hand, abandoned ambitions of rallying an ethno-religious constituency to forward its political objectives (McGilvray 1998; Nuhman 2007; Haniffa 2009). Whilst trusts and endowments continue to support religious institutions and mosques (Mahroof 1985), for the wealthy and socially mobile zakat and sadaqa became the main channels of religious and philanthropic giving.

From the late colonial period until the early independence years, religious giving morphed from individual acts of piety to a means for the public assertion of the Muslim elite's political and economic aspirations. In the mid-1950s, coinciding with parliamentary elections bringing to power a Sinhala nationalist party,[15] H. S. Ismail's Ceylon Baithulmal Fund marked the beginning of a novel orientation towards charity that articulated urban middle-class concerns about the socioeconomic circumstances of the Muslim community as a whole and its public image vis-à-vis other ethno-religious groups, with the reformist discourse of Islamic organizations such as Tablighi Jama'at and, later, Jama'at-e-Islami, and the Sri Lanka Thawheed Jama'ath. Contemporary debates about how, what and to whom to give, couched in discourses about middle-class responsibility to foster the spiritual and material development of the Muslim poor, are the outcome of this convergence.

Debating Contemporary Religious Giving in Colombo

Every year the Ceylon Baithulmal Fund, described at the outset of this chapter, launches a Ramadan Appeal targeting the professional or business acquaintances of its trustees. The Fund's secretary – a successful IT entrepreneur and Tablighi Jama`at follower – attributes Baithulmal's achievements to professional management and accountability, both ensuring that donations are entirely used to support "deserving Muslims," hence eliciting donors' trust. "Baithulmal has a very strict system for allocating money," he explained. "Everyone is interviewed. We have two hundred scholarships that are advertised, but for the rest of the schemes we get recommendations, especially from mosques. The mosques will check the background of the applicants, to make sure that they are entitled to receive, that will use the money properly, that they are Muslims and so on."

Questions as to whether the distribution of zakat and sadaqa to rightful or deserving recipients are done in person by the giver or delegated to an organization are often answered in terms of degrees of efficiency and efficacy. For many (formal and informal) Muslim charities, as well as Islamic reformist organizations, individual acts of giving – often stereotyped as donation of cash to beggars during the month of Ramadan – might discharge the obligation to give zakat, but do not address the root causes of poverty. The latter are routinely identified as the outcome of lack of (religious and secular) education and skills, which, in turn, lead to unemployment, family instability, an inability to plan life and defer gratification, promiscuity, criminality and plain laziness. For the CEO of a community television station and active member of the Sri Lanka Muslim Council,[16] the potential of organized religious giving is obvious:

> Millions and millions are available every year through zakat, as Muslims have to give [and] don't have a choice. With enough coordination, every year we could choose one of two areas and develop them, providing sustainable livelihoods to the poor. For example, if all the zakat from Gulf countries could be directed every year to a poor Muslims country, that country would be taken out of poverty. In Sri Lanka, if every year we could take two hundred people out of poverty for good, to make them self-sufficient, it would be a big success. But coordination is needed.

This rhetoric of planning, managerial efficiency, transparency and accountability that have become part and parcel of the language of contemporary Muslim charity chimes with the life-world of a new generation of professionals, businessmen and entrepreneurs who advocate and are involved in novel forms of organized giving (cf. Atia 2013). Practices, aesthetics and fashions of the market are here mobilized as a means to rationalize the giving of zakat and sadaqa, and as diagnostics to identify deserving recipients, as well as to monitor the use of charity.

Take, for example, Al Kafala, an organization consisting of a group of friends and business acquaintances (including lawyers, architects, accountants, and businessmen), which hoped to give zakat in a more "planned way." Al Kafala's executive director, an MBA graduate in his early forties who works as a management consultant and also owns a media production business, explains their market-oriented approach:

> When we started Al Kafala, we thought: we are all doing very well in our activities, professions and businesses, why not making it work in the same way for zakat? We have a lot of expertise, so one of our members, an architect designed and budgeted for the houses we are building for poor rural Muslims. If we have a new idea, we will determine its feasibility and implement it straight away. We have a result-oriented approach: if one project does not bring the expected results, we either change it or stop it altogether. It is really important to monitor projects to check whether money is used properly. Money, even the smallest donation, should not be wasted!

This emphasis on efficiency through a cost–benefits analysis of zakat projects reveals how spiritual and material interests were combined in the charitable practices of Al Kafala.

Similar to Al Kafala, the Islamic Welfare Society, started some ten years ago by a group of accountants who became friends at university, also collects donations through word of mouth, especially from Sri Lankan Muslims living and working abroad. Personal connections, managerial efficiency and accountability work towards fostering the trust of donors who need to be reassured that their contributions, zakat in particular, are directed entirely towards rightful recipients and hence fulfill religious obligations. Indeed, rumours of corruption and embezzlement that tarnished the reputation of some charitable organizations following the 2004 tsunami are one of the reasons that donors are weary of "systematic and planned" forms of giving.[17] A system of checks and references, often provided by local mosques or government employees, establishes the recipients' reputation. "We always check the credentials of everyone who approaches us for help," explained one of the members of the Islamic Welfare Society, "and when we can we interview them in person. In the past some people applied for and received studentships from many organizations, and made a good living from the grants, supporting the whole family with the money! Zakat is only given to Muslims, and so one has to make sure that the recipient prays at least five times a day. If you are sure of that, you can give, otherwise zakat doesn't count."

There are different opinions as to whether zakat should be given in kind – from food and clothing, to buying a sewing machine and building a house – or as a cash transfer. For instance, Al Kafala members maintain that by providing adequate sanitation, digging wells or building houses they make sure that recipients "do not squander" the help they receive. The Islamic Welfare Society, on the contrary, takes the position that zakat constitutes a set 2.5 percent of one's wealth that in fact belongs, as property, to those who are entitled to receive it. That is, the person who has enough financial means (*nisab*) to fulfil the obligation to give is simply entrusted by God to look after zakat on behalf of the future rightful recipients. Therefore donors cannot put any conditions to the use of zakat because the money is not their own. Zakat, then, should be given only as cash, and it is the responsibility of the donor to make sure, beforehand and discreetly, that they are "good Muslims and not drunkards or addicts." Here, zakat is not just an obligation of the nisab, but the right (*haqq*) of the recipients to collect what is already theirs, making failure to give zakat the equivalent of stealing (cf. Retsikas 2014).

Differences notwithstanding, though, these organizations, whose members are often close to the Islamic reformism of groups such as Tablighi Jamaʾat and Jamaʾat Islam, reframe both zakat and sadaqa as instruments of individual self-improvement and community development. In these circles, everyone agrees that zakat should enable the poor to "help themselves," so that the following year they would not need help any longer, and eventually will be able to give zakat themselves. "In general, when Muslims see someone in need and distress, they will give immediately, if they can. It is a very emotional response", according to a stockbroker involved in a Mosque zakat committee, "but giving small amounts of money to lots of people does not make any difference. You need to give enough to change, to improve people's lives for good." The founder of an Islamic women's organization invoked the times of the Prophet Muhammad and the first four Caliphs as exemplary of the virtues of centralized collection and distribution of zakat:

> In those times it was used effectively and poverty was soon eradicated, eventually there was no need for zakat any more. The spirit of zakat is that it should be given to improve people's lives, so that in a year or two they will be in a position to give zakat.

Other members or donors of these new charitable groups extend the notion of *sadaqa jariya* (continuous charity) to zakat. The director of a company that provides training on Islamic business and finance explains:

> Just giving zakat, without thinking about how it might be used and by whom – for example by giving cash outside your house during Ramadan – is like discharging an obligation. Not giving zakat if you have nisab is a sin, so giving in this way does not give you *sawab* [spiritual merit]. But if you give zakat to someone whose life improves, comes out of poverty, than this gives you continuous sawab, even after your death. In the past people, especially if they worked abroad in the Gulf, believed that you received merits in the afterlife only by building a mosque or giving money to a madrasa, but more sawab comes from helping others to a better life.

Whether the effect of zakat or sadaqa, the circulation of resources enabled by organized forms of charity is envisaged as a transformative act that should elicit, ideally, specific moral and practical dispositions. It reinforces and supports community and religious life, and, in the meantime, renders charitable donations anonymous, thus helping donors to resist the temptation to aggrandize their status through the public display of largesse.[18] The practices promoted by these charitable or religious organizations and committees underscore an apparent shift in the understanding of the role of Islamic charity. Almsgiving – an act of worship which purifies and accumulates merits to givers or an expression of pious concern for (a degree of) social justice – is turned into a religious pedagogy directed towards stimulating spiritual and material transformations in poor Muslims' lives. Recipients of zakat and sadaqa are no longer imagined as beggars queuing outside middle-class houses, nameless bodies enabling the exercise of religious obligations. Individually selected, scrutinized and assessed by organizations standing for an anonymized body of givers, recipients become the object of care and intervention. The logic and discourse of the market are mobilized here to rationalize almsgiving, underpinning the production of what Farzana Haniffa defines as a merit economy (this volume). To maximize spiritual merits, givers should engage in a careful cost–benefit analysis of their charitable deeds; recipients should carefully invest charity into activities directed towards securing their livelihood and, simultaneously, strengthen their religiosity. At both ends, then, charity is envisaged to require and foster degrees of spiritual and economic calculation and entrepreneurship.

The influence of various strands of Islamic reformism – whose orientation is for more engaged and systematic forms of charity in the name of piety, as well as community strengthening and self-reliance in the face of Sinhala Buddhist xenophobia – in the production of ethics of individual and collective responsibility of givers and recipients alike is evident. The Friday *khutbah* (sermon) and pamphlets one can buy in shops near mosques are no longer the only means through which these ideas and practices are circulated. All the main religious organizations have websites that stream the recorded sermons of popular preachers, and reproduce the speeches and *fatwas* of religious scholars from the Sri Lankan diaspora, as well as from Muslim-majority countries, most commonly from Egypt, Saudi Arabia, Indonesia and Malaysia. The English-speaking Muslim middle class thus accesses Islamic websites directed at a global audience – widely consulted especially about the calculation of zakat – through which notions of Islamic charity as a means to engender development gain local purchase.

The global reach of organizations such as Jama'at-e-Islami and Tablighi Jama'at, as well as access to web-based sources of advice on religious matters, enable middle-class Muslims in Colombo to participate in debates resonating across the Muslim world. Unsurprisingly, then, the novel charitable practices emerging in Colombo echo transformations in Egypt and Indonesia (Atia 2013; Fauzia 2013). However, in Colombo we can also discern the effects of the circulation of practices and discourses brought to the island by the scores of international NGOs participating in relief efforts and reconstruction, as well as of reflections on the negative legacy of the tsunami emergency, especially the lack of coordination between relief agencies leading to substantial waste of money and resources. A *systematic* approach to charity built around notions of bureaucratic efficiency and economic efficacy, as well as the discourse of charity-as-development itself, have become currency in charitable organizations across the Sri Lankan ethnic and religious spectrum, as well as in many private companies' corporate social responsibility (CSR) programs (Osella, Stirrat and Widger 2015). Through their CSR enterprises, Muslim-owned companies as well as a number of Muslim and Islamic charities have provided emergency relief and long-term rehabilitation to Muslims displaced by the civil war in the north of Sri Lanka, acting either independently or alongside government bodies (Widger 2015).

A focus on the (material and spiritual) virtues of more engaged forms of charity is also couched in widespread concerns about what H. S. Ismail, the founder of Baithulmal, called "the shame of beggary." Beggars are increasingly seen as a nuisance, bothering respectable households with their incessant demands and giving the community a bad name. The problem, according to some members of the urban Muslim middle class, is that the obligation to give zakat and the merit accruing from sadaqa are such that much money is given away, making the poor dependent on charity. A young investment banker working for an Islamic bank recounts that

> During the month of Ramadan people will start queuing outside my house from 4am, and I have to give everyone small amounts of money. Also I have to listen to all the stories that they say to claim help. In my village, where my sister and parents live, is even worse because everyone knows that you can give. You cannot turn people away during Ramadan, and often you end up giving out more than your share of zakat. In fact, every year I have to send part of my zakat to my sister so that she can give to everyone.

Some argued that this system is open to abuse: "Lots of cheating is taking place. Any Tamil speaker can put a skullcap on his head and go around to Muslim houses in places where he is not known, and ask for money. He can make 5000 rupees or more per day!" Others bemoaned the queues of beggars outside mosques or prowling the streets from shop to shop asking for charity. "It has become a profession for many", the same founder of an Islamic women's organization encountered earlier explained, "and you can make a good living out of it. Charity should not create dependency, but help people to become self-sufficient. When women come to us begging for money, we tell them to go home and pray. Help will come to them."

The debates between members and donors of various organizations devoted to the collection of Muslim charity reveal an impetus toward individual and collective responsibilization, a form of governmentality which Nicholas Rose (1999) has identified as a characteristic of advanced liberalism, framed as much by nineteenth century colonial discourses about the idleness of the (non-working) poor and the moral value of work (see, e.g., Ashcraft 1996: 48), as in neoliberal notions of the entrepreneurial self (Lazzarato 2012). These different strands converge with Islamic reformist orthopraxis to produce forms of religious engagement in public and private life resonating with what Mona Atia (2013) aptly glossed as pious neoliberalism. The self-ascribed pastoral power of Muslim and Islamic charities, to use Foucault's words, is here intensified, institutionalized and transformed into an art of governing the poor, shaping them into self-disciplined economic *and* religious subjects (Foucault 1978; see also Agamben 1998).

Charity as Investment and Insurance

Moving from the circle of middle-class professionals and entrepreneurs animating emerging charitable organizations, to the world of traders and businessmen in the crowded streets of the Pettah bazaar in downtown Colombo, we find that encouragements to adopt more (religiously and socially) engaged forms of giving are mediated by the complexity and hazards of everyday practice. Only some of the shopkeepers I encountered were hostile to organized forms of charitable giving, citing lack of trust and endemic corruption as the main reason for their stance. The vast majority shared the view that almsgiving should foster long-term economic development and discourage dependency. This is perhaps unsurprising given that many of the men I talked to were either close to Islamic reformist organizations, Tablighi Jama'at in particular, or belonged to Muslim communities (mainly Memon and Bohra) with established traditions of organized giving to support community welfare. And yet, although these men did respond to the fundraising appeals of Muslim charitable organizations, they continued to distribute a substantial part of their donations in person. The cohabitation of different practices reveals a sharper distinction being drawn here between the scope of zakat and sadaqa, which in the practices of organized charity are often conflated for the sake of development intervention. It also indicates that Pettah traders and shopkeepers neither reduce all direct demands for financial help to acts of "beggary" or condemn them as shameful.

Qur'anic injunctions concerning who is entitled to receive zakat notwithstanding, in the Pettah Bazaar the distribution of zakat is embedded in degrees of responsibility towards dependants spreading outwards from the family. Abdul Azeez, a forty-year-old owner of three textile shops, echoed what others told me:

> First I give zakat to poor people within the family, both my own and wife's side, then to my employees because wages in the bazaar are low. I help them to pay rent and bills,

and also when they have big expenses such as a marriage. I was born in Colombo, but my father comes from a village [north of the capital]. He always gave zakat to some families there, and I continue to do the same, they rely on me. And there are people who come to my shop to ask for help, especially for medical expenses. When they come I ask for proof of their background and needs, such as a letter of recommendation from their mosque or the bill from the hospital. If the case is genuine, I pay directly the hospital, but if the bill is very big I also direct them to some of my friends in the Pettah. Once I calculate the amount of my zakat, I give some money to the mosque's Ramadan fund, maybe 10 percent of the total. I use most of the balance during Ramadan because most of the demands come during this month, but keep a portion in a separate account to give throughout the year.

Sadaqa, free from the restrictions imposed on zakat, does not require the same degree of calculation and planning, and what counts here is the intention (*niyya*) of the giver. "Sadaqa is not limited in scope and is voluntary, so you get merits for giving it," explains Jafar Farook, the owner of a modern glass shop and Emir of Pettah mosque:

Zakat is a must, so you don't get rewards, but it is a sin if you don't give it. Anyone can give sadaqa, and you can give anything, even 1 rupee or helping someone with your time as long as you have sadaqa in your mind. If you use sadaqa to build something – a well, a mosque and so on – that will bring merits to you for a long time, even after your death. It is sadaqa jariya. If I give 100 000 rupees as zakat, I will give twice that amount as sadaqa because there is no target to reach.

Jafar Farook, like many others in Pettah, argued that while zakat is "for the poor", sadaqa goes instead to those who ask for alms on the doorstep of shops or outside mosques.

The economy of merits that undergirds almsgiving produces different tangible material benefits. Pettah respondents described zakat as an insurance on property and business: "If you give it, your business will be protected, but if you don't it will be destroyed, you will lose everything, even your health will be affected." Indeed they narrated plenty of stories of businesses that failed or prospered according to whether the owners fulfilled their obligation to give or not. Sadaqa, on the contrary, was considered to be akin to an investment that leads to immediate material returns: what is given comes back increased manifold. So, when a trader or shopkeeper comes out of the mosque on a day he is doing some important deal, he will give plenty to beggars to ensure a successful outcome, knowing that money will return multiplied. Although many acknowledged the tension between, on the one hand, the desire to give charity to beggars to forward one's chances in a competitive market, and, on the other, the "mire of beggary" their actions help to reproduce, in Pettah Bazaar the impulse to give cannot be subsumed or morphed entirely into projects of community *upliftment* (a South Asian idiom for the socioeconomic enhancement of low status communities) in that it remains central to donors' economic success and capital accumulation. So, the most common practice is to continue responding to demands from relatives, unrelated people – not only beggars, but also those unable to meet expenses for medical emergencies, life-cycle rituals, education expenses or payment of utilities bills – as well as dependents, and to support religious institutions, whilst giving a proportion of the donations to various (religious and non-religious) charitable organizations. Here the boundaries between charitable giving and patronage are indeed porous, and in any case, as one bazaar trader put it, "I just don't like someone else giving away my money!"

Conclusion

In Colombo, Muslim charity, various modalities of capital accumulation and political assertion have been deeply intertwined at least since the late nineteenth century, well before the implementation of neoliberal reforms (cf. Rajak 2011; Muehlebach 2012). During the late British colonial period, various forms of giving became the means through which a Colombo-based elite fraction of the Muslim middle class sought to assert and substantiate claims to status, and to support economic interests, political ambitions and projects of community building. Establishing a waqf to provide for one's own plantation workers, giving zakat to one's employees and clients, the publicity derived from public displays of philanthropic largesse or, nowadays, CSR projects distributing medicines at subsidized prices (Widger 2015) have all been instances through which charity mirrors and sustain donors' economic practice by securing allegiance of employees or the creation of new markets for one's products. Indeed, recipients' interrogations testify if not to open distrust of donors' motivations and sincerity then at least to the possible instrumentality of apparently pious acts. Simultaneously, giving practices remake recipients of charity as market actors molded, either implicitly or explicitly, to the economic interests of donors. Whilst charity given to plantation workers and bazaar employees embedded labor relations in the logic and politics of patronage, provision of subsidized medicines transforms the urban poor into modern consumers.

This is not a one-way traffic. Reading waqf deeds, often drawn towards the end of the grantors' life, suggests that piety, the acquisition of spiritual merits and a concern with the afterlife were seldom eclipsed by more mundane preoccupation or interests (cf. Osella and Osella 2009). Wealthy Colombo businessmen such as Sir Mohamed Macan Markar and N. D. H. Abdul Caffoor were described as "characterized by piety" and "of a charitable and religious disposition" (Ali 1987: 324). They are remembered for their piety as much as for their wealth. Ameer Ali has argued that in colonial and postcolonial Sri Lanka the desire to fulfil the religious injunction to give drove Muslims "to strive hard and accumulate the means with which to do so... instead of killing the desire to accumulate...actually worked in reverse to encourage accumulation (2007: 331). This certainly resonates with my respondents' sensibilities, as many of them reminded me, "a poor Muslim cannot be a good Muslim." A degree of economic prosperity not only enables people to objectify their piety, but in doing so it also allows for the accumulation of merits, producing in turn an actual economy of merits (Haniffa, Chapter 5). Giving during Ramadan, for instance, multiplies the merits one accrues; the notion of sadaqa jariya (continual charity) suggests that particular meritorious acts of charity will produce merits even after the donor's death. Piety, that is, seldom shies away from quantification, calculation and differential accumulation.

But there is another aspect of charitable giving that, by unsettling apparent affinities between the logic underpinning organized forms of charity and neoliberal capitalism, reveals a subtle and enduring relation between charity and economic action. We have seen in the bazaar that "traditional" ways of giving zakat and sadaqa either protect or multiply donors' business returns, that is, acts of charity are a means through which risk can be managed and contained, and chances of success increased. In a recent article analyzing post-2008 crisis financial derivative markets, LiPuma and Lee consider representations of "the economic" that are produced and taken up by market players (see also Callon 1998). These illusive representations move actors to believe "as an article of faith that a market is a bounded, complete economic space in which prizes are always the outcome of transparent...communication among rational decision makers" (2012: 306), a belief that in financial markets is amplified by "quasimagical [sic] reverence" for mathematical models and statistics. For LiPuma and Lee, the illusion here is not simply a misrepresentation of the sociality of the market, but "a real relation of its production" (ibid.). Performativity, that is, has generative powers akin to those of ritual action. In other words, the virtualization of market exchange through the deployment of sophisticated technical devices entails and calls for an aesthetic of enchantment normally associated by Weberian sociology to the worldview of religion (see also MacKenzie 2008). From this perspective, mathematical models such as the notorious Black–Scholes formula are endowed with a quasimagical power to minimize risk and maximize profit that is not so far removed from the effects attributed in the bazaar to (individual and spontaneous) daily acts of almsgiving. Significantly, then, we discern a degree of continuity in the ways piety, religious duties, humanitarian concerns, pragmatic self-interest, market competition and capital accumulation might be brought together in the everyday practices and orientations of Muslims in Sri Lanka, although the modalities and expression of such an assemblage might take historically specific configurations (see, e.g., Hosseini 2003).

Differently from H. S. Ismail's times, though, today charitable concerns for the Muslim poor are no longer simply a response to nation building or emerging Sinhala nationalism. The conflation of poverty into beggary and a discourse framing charity as a means "to help the poor to help themselves" has turned entrepreneurship into a moral duty and, consequently, failure to improve oneself becomes the symptom of wider moral shortcomings (see Elyachar 2005; Osella & Osella 2009; Rudnyckyj 2010). Charity, then, has taken up the explicit pedagogical scope of transforming not only spiritual and material well-being, but also the cultural and social dispositions of recipients.[19] This is accompanied by an emphasis on the anonymity of giving that, by delegating the distribution of charity to organizations, seeks either to rescind charity from long-term social obligations or to deny "beggars" the power to elicit donations (Appadurai 1990; Osella and Osella 1996; Staples 2007).

Unsurprisingly, we have seen that a penchant for turning organized charity into a means for fostering both religious piety and an entrepreneurial spirit amongst the urban and rural poor has a particular purchase amongst young professionals and MBA-educated businessmen, that is, those who participate more enthusiastically in, and have benefitted more from, the liberalization of the Sri Lankan economy. The most entrepreneurial fraction of the Colombo Muslim middle class has shared in and contributed to the apparent economic boom engendered by market liberalization in the aftermath of the civil war – from export-oriented production and trade to retail and real estate developments (Haniffa, Chapter 5). In a brave new world of economic opportunities and expansive consumption that has seen Sri Lanka being awarded the status of middle-income country, emerging forms of organized religious giving practised by the Muslim middle class might resonate, then, with the pious neoliberalism of activists, volunteers and donors animating Cairo's buoyant charity scene (Atia 2013). And yet, unlike in Cairo, the orientations and practices of professionals and entrepreneurs who support or run charitable organizations and zakat committees, and those of Pettah bazaar traders who continue to give alms every day to beggars, cannot be easily plotted on a traditional/modern or reformist/non-reformist grid. All providers of zakat and sadaqa participate in a highly competitive economy that, since liberalization in 1977, has had several periods of expansion and contraction; and the reach of Islamic reformism cuts across different fractions of the middle class.

Reproducing dependency, political ambition, competition for status and patronage are some of the apparent shortcomings of individual forms of giving (Osella, Stirrat and Widger 2015; Widger 2016). The endless drawbacks marring everyday forms of charity and philanthropy would lend support, then, to those Muslims in Colombo who tirelessly argue that charity can become a means for (religious and material) development only when it is anonymous, organized, planned, coordinated and administered efficiently. And yet, the latter more often than not fails to live up to its promises: donations are not enough to complete projects, and follow-up monitoring and support remain slight. The pedagogical intents of organized charity, then, are mediated and affected by shortcomings and contradictions in their interventions. Eventually, though, whether the giver of zakat or sadaqa is moved by humanitarian concerns, religious piety, economic self-interest, political calculation or indeed a combination of these motivations might make little difference to the "poor and needy" who have to rely on the help of others to make ends meet or to deal with the unpredictable contingencies of everyday life. In other words, whilst it is far-fetched to suggest that neoliberal subjectivities engendered by novel forms of charity might be explicitly resisted by donors or recipients, the pedagogy of piety and entrepreneurship promoted by contemporary Muslim or Islamic charitable organizations might fall short of its intent of inculcating radical transformations in Colombo Muslims' life-worlds.

Notes

A big thank you to Jock Stirrat and Humeira Iqtidar for their comments on earlier drafts. Many thanks also to Farzana Haniffa, who provided me with many of the initial contacts for my interviews, and with whom I discussed extensively the issues at hand. Without her help, advice and encouragement this research would not have been possible. This research was carried out in collaboration with the Centre for Poverty Analysis (CEPA), Colombo, and was supported by a generous grant from ESRC/DfID (grant no. ES/I033890/1) for which I am grateful.

1 This reformist organization became active in Sri Lanka in the early 1950s. For a discussion of the emergence and role of Islamic reformism in Sri Lanka, see Nuhman 2007; Haniffa 2008 and McGilvray 2008, 2011.
2 Baithulmal is from the Arabic Bayt al-Maal ("house of wealth/money"), an institution in the early Caliphate devoted to collection of taxes and distribution of zakat.
3 See www.baithulmal.com/home.html.
4 Zakat literally means "to be clear, to grow, to increase".
5 Latief's (2010) study of the rise of Islamic charitable hospitals in Indonesia, for instance, discusses the revitalization of *zakat* and other charitable practices to sustain medical assistance to the poor, as well as to provide services to the middle class (see also Clark 2004).
6 Unlike zakat and sadaqa, charitable endowments/trusts (awqaf; sing. waqf) have been studied extensively. Not only did awqaf sustain religious institutions and centres of learning (see, e.g., Metcalf 1978; Zaman 2002; Sikand 2005; Singer 2008), but they also provided resources for public services (water, sanitation and health, for instance) and support for the poor (Sabra 2000; Singer 2012). The extensive use of awqaf in the Ottoman Empire has led some historians to characterize it as a "welfare society" (Singer 2008). Importantly, these characterizations attend as much to economic calculation and political expediency as to religious piety (see, e.g., Kozlowski 1985; Baer 1997; Sabra 2000; Kuran 2001; Bonner et al. 2003; Lev 2007; Singer 2008).
7 See, for instance, Kozlowski 1985; Haynes 1987; Powers 1989; White 1991; Caplan 1998; Joshi 2001; Sharma 2001; Palsetia 2005; Birla 2009; cf. Bornstein 2012.

8 Both Ordinances were derived from legislation introduced in British India (Mahroof 1985).
9 The former advocated an exclusive "Moor" identity that excluded Indian and Malay Muslims; the latter promoted a community inclusive of all Muslims, regardless of ethnic origin (McGilvray 1998).
10 Sir Macan Markar was another famous philanthropist. Together with his brother, he established a waqf to support the Bahjathul Ibrahimiya Arabic College founded in 1892 by his mother. He also funded three endowments for the Islamic education of boys and girls.
11 "Leaders of these two wealthy families," McGilvray writes, "also vied jealously for British knighthoods, litigated over control of the Colombo Maradana mosque, and cultivated rival Sufi brotherhoods, with Macan Markar heading the Sri Lankan Shazuliya order and Abdul Caffoor leading the Qadiriyya order" (1998: 452).
12 For instance, in the building of Zahira College – a project seeking to appropriate and domesticate modern English-medium education hitherto provided by Christian schools – converged diverse and overlapping orientations: those of British colonial modernity, of the Islamic modernism of the north Indian Aligarh movement, and of the Egyptian pan-Islamism brought by Arabi Pasha during his long exile in Ceylon (Jayawardena 1970, 2002).
13 With the exception of Zahira College, which after a brief period under government control regained semi-independent status.
14 One of his descendants recounted that after independence Ebrahim Lebbe Marrikkar refused to pay taxes to the government because he argued that he was already giving lots of money as zakat. He was taken to court and eventually lost the case.
15 One of the first actions of Sri Lanka Freedom Party's Prime Minister S. W. R. D. Bandaranaike was the introduction of the Official Language Act, otherwise known as the "Sinhala Only" (Rowell 2009). The majority of Sri Lanka Muslims are Tamil speakers.
16 An umbrella organization bringing together Sri Lankan Muslim NGOs and other civil society organizations.
17 Concerned with becoming embroiled in accusations of corruption and mismanagement, many Colombo mosques have not taken up calls from the All Ceylon Jamiyyathul Ulama (a religious body representing Sri Lanka's Islamic scholars) to constitute local zakat committees. The latter have been more successful amongst east coast Muslim communities.
18 Although most respondents explained this by citing from the New Testament, "The left hand doesn't not know what the right hand is doing" (Matthew 6:3), they referred to the following passage from the Qur'an: "If you give alms openly, it is well, and if you hide it and give it to the poor, it is better for you; and this will do away with some of your evil deeds; and Allah is aware of what you do" (2: 271).
19 This is a major preoccupation in nineteenth century British philanthropy (Himmelfarb 1991), as well as in contemporary development philanthropy (Stirrat 2008).

References

Agamben, G. 1998. *Homo Sacer: Sovereignty and Bare life*. Stanford, CA: Stanford University Press.

Ali, A. 1981. "The 1915 Racial Riots in Ceylon (Sri Lanka): A Reappraisal of its Causes." *South Asia: Journal of South Asian Studies* 4(2): 1–20.

1987. "Muslims and Capitalism in British Ceylon (Sri Lanka): The Colonial Image and Community's Behaviour." *Journal Institute of Muslim Minority Affairs* 8(2): 311–344.

2014. "Political Buddhism, Islamic Orthodoxy and Open Economy: The Toxic Triad in Sinhalese–Muslim Relations in Sri Lanka." *Journal of Asian and African Studies* 49(3): 298–314.

Appadurai, A. 1990. "Topographies of the Self: Praise and Emotion in Hindu India." In *Language and the Politics of Emotion*, edited by A. C. Lutz and L. Abu-Lughod, 92–112. Cambridge: Cambridge University Press.

Ashcraft, R. 1996 [2014]. "Lockean Ideas, Poverty, and the Development of Liberal Political Theory." In *Early Modern Conceptions of Property*, edited by J. Brewer and S. Staves, 43–61. London: Routledge.

Atia, M. A. 2013. *Building a House in Heaven: Islamic Charity in Neoliberal Egypt.* Minneapolis: University of Minnesota Press.

Baer, G. 1997. "The Waqf as a Prop for the Social System (Sixteenth-Twentieth Centuries)." *Islamic Law and Society* 4: 264–297.

Bashear, S. 1993. "On the Origins and Development of the Meaning of zakāt in Early Islam." *Arabica* 40(1): 84–113.

Bayat, A. 2007. *Making Islam Democratic: Social Movements and the Post-Islamist Turn.* Stanford, CA: Stanford University Press.

Benthall, J. 1999. "Financial Worship: The Quranic Injunction to Almsgiving." *Journal of the Royal Anthropological Institute* 5(1): 27–42.

Birla, R. 2009. *Stages of Capital: Law, Culture, and Market Governance in Late Colonial India.* Durham, NC: Duke University Press.

Bonner, M., E. Mine, and A. Singer (eds.). 2003. *Poverty and Charity in Middle Eastern Contexts.* Albany: State University of New York Press.

Bornstein, E. 2012. *Disquieting Gifts: Humanitarianism in New Delhi.* Stanford, CA: Stanford University Press.

Callon, M. (ed.). 1998. *The Laws of the Markets.* Oxford: Blackwell.

Caplan, L. 1998. "Gifting and Receiving: Anglo-Indian Charity and Its Beneficiaries in Madras." *Contributions to Indian Sociology* 32(2): 409–431.

Clark, J. A. 2004. *Islam, Charity, and Activism: Middle-class Networks and Social Welfare in Egypt, Jordan, and Yemen.* Bloomington: Indiana University Press.

Dean, H., and Z. Khan. 1997. "Muslim Perspectives on Welfare." *Journal of Social Policy* 26(2): 193–209.

Deeb, L. 2006. *An Enchanted Modern: Gender and Public Piety in Shi'i Lebanon.* Princeton, NJ: Princeton University Press.

Elyachar, J. 2005. *Markets of Dispossession: NGOs, Economic Development, and the State in Cairo.* Durham, NC: Duke University Press.

Fauzia, A. 2013. *Faith and the State: A History of Islamic Philanthropy in Indonesia.* Leiden: Brill.

Foucault, M. 2000 (1978). "'*Omnes et Singulatim*': Toward a Critique of Political Reason." In *Power: Essential Works of Michel Foucault, 1954–1984*, Vol. 3, edited by James D. Faubion, 298–325. New York: The New Press.

Haniffa, F. 2008. "Piety as Politics amongst Muslim Women in Contemporary Sri Lanka." *Modern Asian Studies* 42(2–3): 347–375.

2009. "Muslims in Sri Lanka: Political Choices of a Minority." Living on the Margins: Minorities in South Asia. EURASIA-Net, Kathmandu, Nepal. www.eurac.edu/en/research/institutes/imr/Documents/EURASIA-Net_Deliverable_18_materials_NGOs_final_colored_cover.pdf (Accessed 12 December 2013).

Haynes, D. E. 1987. "From Tribute to Philanthropy: The Politics of Gift-Giving in a Western Indian City." *The Journal of Asian Studies* 46(2): 339–360.

Himmelfarb, G. 1991. *Poverty and Compassion: The Moral Imagination of the Late Victorians*. New York: Alfred A. Knopf.

Hosseini, H. 2003. "Understanding the Market Mechanism Before Adam Smith: Economic Thought in Medieval Islam." In *Medieval Islamic Economic Thought: Filling the "Great Gap" in European Economics*, edited by S. M. Ghazanfar, 88–107. London: RoutledgeCurzon.

Ismail, H. S. 1970. "Muslims and Social Welfare Work." In *Moors' Islamic Cultural Home: The First Twenty-One Years*, 67–69. Colombo: Moors' Islamic Cultural Home.

Jayawardena, K. 1970. "Economic and Political Factors in the 1915 Riots." *The Journal of Asian Studies* 29(2): 223–233.

2002. *Nobodies to Somebodies: The Rise of the Colonial Bourgeoisie in Sri Lanka*. London: Zed Books.

Joshi, S. 2001. *Fractured Modernity: Making of a Middle Class in Colonial North India*. New Delhi: Oxford University Press.

Karaman, O. 2013. "Urban Neoliberalism with Islamic Characteristics." *Urban Studies* 50(16): 3412–3427.

Kochuyt, T. 2009. "God, Gifts and Poor People: On Charity in Islam." *Social Compass* 56(1): 98–116.

Kozlowski, G. C. 1985. *Muslim Endowment and Society in British India*. Cambridge: Cambridge University Press.

Kuran, T. 1986. "The Economic System in Contemporary Islamic Thought: Interpretation and Assessment." *International Journal of Middle East Studies* 18(2): 135–164.

2001. "The Provision of Public Goods under Islamic Law: Origins, Impact, and Limitations of the Waqf System." *Law and Society Review* 35(4): 841–898.

2003. "Islamic Redistribution through Zakat: Historical Record and Modern Realities." In *Poverty and Charity in Middle Eastern Contexts*, edited by M. Bonner, M. Ener, and A. Singer, 275–293. Albany: State University of New York Press.

2004. *Islam and Mammon: The Economic Predicaments of Islamism*. Princeton, NJ: Princeton University Press.

Latief, H. 2010. "Health Provision for the Poor: Islamic Aid and the Rise of Charitable Clinics in Indonesia." *South East Asia Research* 18(3): 503–553.

Lazzarato, M. 2012. *The Making of the Indebted Man: Essay on the Neoliberal Condition*. Los Angeles: Semiotext(e).

Lev, Y. 2007. "The Ethics and Practice of Islamic Medieval Charity." *History Compass* 5(2): 603–618.

LiPuma, E., and B. Lee. 2012. "A Social Approach to the Financial Derivatives Markets." *South Atlantic Quarterly* 111(2): 289–316.

MacKenzie, D. 2008. *An Engine, Not a Camera: How Financial Models Shape Markets*. Cambridge, MA: MIT Press.

Mahroof, M. M. M. 1985. "The Enactment of 'wakf' Legislation in Sri Lanka: The Law in Context." *Journal of the Institute of Muslim Minority Affairs* 6(2): 283–294.

Mandaville, J. E. 1979. "Usurious Piety: The Cash waqf Controversy in the Ottoman Empire." *International Journal of Middle East Studies* 10 (3): 289–308.

Maurer, B. 2005. *Mutual Life, Limited: Islamic Banking, Alternative Currencies, Lateral Reason*. Princeton, NJ: Princeton University Press.

May, S. 2013. "Political Piety: The Politicization of Zakat." *Middle East Critique* 22 (2): 149–164.

McGilvray, D. B. 1998. "Arabs, Moors and Muslims: Sri Lankan Muslim Ethnicity in Regional Perspective". *Contributions to Indian Sociology, 32*(2): 433–483.

2008. *Crucible of Conflict: Tamil and Muslim Society on the East Coast of Sri Lanka*. Durham, NC: Duke University Press.

2011. "Sri Lankan Muslims: Between Ethno-nationalism and the Global Ummah." *Nations and Nationalism* 17(1): 45–64.

Metcalf, B. 1978. "The Madrasa at Deoband: A Model for Religious Education in Modern India." *Modern Asian Studies* 12(1): 111–134.

Mohamed Sameer Bin Haji Ismail Effendi. 1982. *Personages of the Past: Moors, Malays, and Other Muslims of the Past of Sri Lanka*. Colombo: Moors' Islamic Cultural Home.

Muehlebach, A. 2012. *The Moral Neoliberal: Welfare and Citizenship in Italy*. Chicago: University of Chicago Press.

Nuhman, M. A. 2007. "Sri Lankan Muslims: Ethnic Identity within Cultural Diversity." Colombo: International Centre for Ethnic Studies Colombo.

Osella, F., and Osella, C. 1996. "Articulation of Physical and Social Bodies in Kerala." *Contributions to Indian Sociology* 30(1): 37–68.

2008. "Islamism and Social Reform in Kerala, South India." *Modern Asian Studies* 42(2–3): 317–346.

2009. "Muslim Entrepreneurs in Public Life between India and the Gulf: Making Good and Doing Good." *Journal of the Royal Anthropological Institute* 15(s1): S202–S221.

Osella, F., R. Stirrat, and T. Widger. 2015. "Charity, Philanthropy and Development in Colombo, Sri Lanka." In *New Philanthropy and Social Justice: Debating the Conceptual and Policy Discourse*, edited by B. Morvaridi, 137–156. Bristol, UK: Policy Press.

Palsetia, J. S. 2005. "Merchant Charity and Public Identity Formation in Colonial India: The Case of Jamsetjee Jejeebhoy." *Journal of Asian and African Studies* 40(3): 197–217.

Powers, D. S. 1989."Orientalism, Colonialism, and Legal History: The Attack on Muslim Family Endowments in Algeria and India." *Comparative Studies in Society and History* 31(3): 535–571

Rajak, D. 2011. *In Good Company: An Anatomy of Corporate Social Responsibility*. Stanford, CA: Stanford University Press.

Ramanathan, P. 1916. *Riots and Martial Law in Ceylon, 1915*. London: St. Martin's Press.

Reda, A. 2014. "Trading with Allah: An Examination of Islamic Scripture in Relation to Markets." *Journal of Markets & Morality* 16(2): 441–462.

Retsikas, K. 2014. "Reconceptualising Zakat in Indonesia." *Indonesia and the Malay World*" 42(124): 337–357.

Rodinson, M. 1978. *Islam and Capitalism*. Austin: University of Texas Press.

Rose, N. 1999. *Powers of Freedom: Reframing Political Thought*. Cambridge: Cambridge University Press.

Rowell, G. 2009. "Ceylon's Kristallnacht: A Reassessment of the Pogrom of 1915." *Modern Asian Studies* 43(3): 619–648.

Rudnyckyj, D. 2010. *Spiritual Economies: Islam, Globalization, and the Afterlife of Development*. Ithaca, NY: Cornell University Press.

Sabra, A. 2000. *Poverty and Charity in Medieval Islam: Mamluk Egypt, 1250–1517*. Cambridge: Cambridge University Press.

Schwittay, A. 2014. *New Media and International Development: Representation and Affect in Microfinance*. London: Routledge.

Scott, J. C. 1987. "Resistance without Protest and without Organization: Peasant Opposition to the Islamic Zakat and the Christian Tithe." *Comparative Studies in Society and History* 29(3): 417–452.

Sharma, S. 2001. *Famine, Philanthropy and the Colonial State*. Delhi: Oxford University Press.

Sikand, Y. 2005. *Bastions of the Believers: Madrasas and Islamic Education in India*. Delhi: Penguin Books India.

Singer, A. 2008. *Charity in Islamic Societies*. Cambridge: Cambridge University Press.

2012. *Constructing Ottoman Beneficence: An Imperial Soup Kitchen in Jerusalem*. Albany: State University of New York Press.

Soares, B. F. 2005. *Islam and the Prayer Economy: History and Authority in a Malian Town*. Edinburgh: Edinburgh University Press.

Staples, James. 2007. *Peculiar People, Amazing Lives. Leprosy, Social Exclusion and Community-Making in South India*. Delhi: Orient Longman.

Stirrat, R. L. 2008. "Mercenaries, Missionaries and Misfits: Representations of Development Personnel." *Critique of Anthropology* 28(4): 406–425.

Sullivan, D. J. 1994. *Private Voluntary Organizations in Egypt: Islamic Development, Private Initiative, and State Control*. Gainesville: University Press of Florida.

Tripp, C. 2006. *Islam and the Moral Economy: The Challenge of Capitalism*. Cambridge: Cambridge University Press.

Van Hoven, E. 1996. "Local Tradition or Islamic Precept? The Notion of zakāt in Wuli (Eastern Senegal)." *Cahiers d'Études Africaines* 36(144): 703–722.

Werbner, P. 2003. *Pilgrims of Love: The Anthropology of a Global Sufi Cult*. Bloomington: Indiana University Press.

White, D. L. 1991. "From Crisis to Community Definition: The Dynamics of Eighteenth-Century Parsi Philanthropy." *Modern Asian Studies* 25(2): 303–320.

Widger, T. 2016. "Philanthronationalism: Junctures at the Business-Charity Nexus in Post-war Sri Lanka." *Development and Change* 47(1): 29–50.

Wiktorowicz, Q. 2001. The Management of Islamic Activism: Salafis, the Muslim Brotherhood, and State Power in Jordan. Albany: State University of New York Press.

Zaman, M. Q. 2002. *The Ulama in Contemporary Islam: Custodians of Change*. Princeton, NJ: Princeton University Press.

11 "For God and the Country": Agricultural Migrations and their Moralities in South India

V. J. Varghese, University of Hyderabad

Migration and the consequent expansion of agriculture to previously untamed areas has been one of the defining features of Kerala's economic modernity.[1] Entangled in the intertwined history of colonialism, capital and native agency, mobilizing a new discourse of development that broke radically with the existing notions of land management, it not only led to the conversion of vast areas of forests, hills and "wastelands" into arable land and the emergence of capitalist agriculture, but also provided the local Syrian Christian community with a new identity as oriented towards progress and development. As *purogamana karshakar* (forward-looking peasants) and productive citizens committed to national development, the community claimed a particular affinity to and wielded an authority over Kerala's modernity. In this chapter I will consider the migration of Syrian Christian peasants from the cultivated plains of rural Travancore to the pristine and sparsely inhabited mountain forests of Malabar. Starting in the early decades of the twentieth century and continuing well into the 1960s, this migration picked up in the 1940s. Over more than forty years, tens of thousands of Christian migrants colonized huge tracts of fallow land, turning hills and forests into highly profitable farms and plantations. I will argue that the Syrian Christian Church was directly involved in this modernist enterprise of turning "empty" environments into sites of human activity, production and development. It did so not only by offering a theological rationale for land reclamation and its hegemonic developmentalist ideology, but also by leading the political struggle of the laity to protect its arduously won material world in Malabar from state interventions. During the expansive colonization of a space described as "lost" and largely heathen by its leadership, the Church provided a particular orientation towards modern entrepreneurship and capital accumulation by expounding and sanctifying a new conduit for social and spatial mobility, with land and hard work at its heart. I will also suggest that in this engagement with the modern economic sphere, the Church and its narratives did not stick to any single line of reasoning. It straddled theological, nationalist, economic, ethical and humanitarian rationalities with ease and careful calibration, moving freely between the spiritual and the material with claims of morality and citizenship and building bridges with "anti-religious" communist ideology. By demonstrating the role of the Church in fostering and eventually defending modern forms of capital accumulation, the chapter complicates teleologies of the modern that prophesied the progressive withering away of religion as a result of expansive political and economic rationalities. What we find here is that the Church, through its theology and organization, produced a specific rationality in support of land colonization and expansion, as well as the modernization of agriculture. At the same time, it displayed substantial political acumen by mobilizing its contextual reasoning and imaginative maneuvering against state regulations and interventions.

Modernity, Agriculture and the Syrian Christians

The material transformations engendered by colonial modernity on the Malabar Coast in south-west India hinged on the development of a plantation economy accompanied by substantial land colonization. New spaces were opened up for individual initiatives and entrepreneurship as a means to reap the benefits of an expanding global market. The unprecedented economic turmoil in the region, resulting from a shift to commercial agriculture at the cost of food crop production, coupled with explosive population growth drove the princely state of Travancore towards a new development model based on colonial regimes of land use that engendered sustained waves of agrarian migration (Varghese 2009). The Syrian Christian community – which had lost its main economic niches as traders and local militia, as a result of the demilitarization of the native state of Travancore and the British commercial monopoly – led this transition by turning to the cultivation of fallow land through shrewd entrepreneurship, sheer hard work and spirit of adventure (Bayly 1989; Baak 1997; Varghese 2007). In a new sociopolitical imaginary in which the expansion of agricultural production became the main means to achieving the twin goals of modernization and progress, migration to hitherto uncultivated hills and mountain ranges was advocated and adopted in earnest as a solution for food scarcity, economic crises and population growth. From the early twentieth century through the 1960s, the development and modernization of agriculture through migration hardly took notice of either ecological issues concerning the destruction of forests, or the dispossession of the original tribal inhabitants of reclaimed lands. Between 1930 and 1970, at the peak of migration from south Kerala to Malabar, for instance, around 2000 square kilometers of forest were cleared in Malabar (Varghese 2006).[2] As the forests of Malabar were transformed into rich agricultural settlements, the Syrian Christian peasant-settlers became a "national asset" (Sivaswamy et al. 1945: 3), whose fearless and entrepreneurial spirit stood for modernity and (capitalist) development (Varghese 2006).

Before the migrations to Malabar, the Syrian Christian community was predominantly concentrated in the geographical area south of the river

Bharathapuzha, in the erstwhile Cochin and Travancore princely states, roughly covering the regions of the present-day central and southern Kerala.[3] Though there are claims to conversion at the hand of Thomas the Apostle, it is certain that the Malabar Coast had a Christian community from at least the fourth century AD onwards, with sustained arrival of East Syrian Chaldean Christian spice traders (Dempsey 2001). The total population of the community during the sixteenth and seventeenth centuries is estimated to have been between 70,000 and 150,000 souls. By 1901, the total number of Christians rose to 697,387 in Travancore (23.6 percent of the total), of which 451,570 were Syrian Christians, whereas the respective numbers for Cochin were 198,239 (24 percent of the total) and 119,018 (Aiya 1906: 135; Menon 1911: 292). The Christian population in Travancore increased considerably throughout the first half of the twentieth century, rising to 1,960,207 (32.29 percent of the total) in 1941, of which more than three-fourths were Syrian Christians, registering an overall growth of 181 percent between 1901 and 1941.[4] By 1951, the total number of Christians in Travancore-Cochin had reached 2,968,030 (31.98 percent of the total).[5] Malabar, the northern area of present-day Kerala, had just 53,017 Christians in 1921, who were mostly non-Syrians. The number reached 77, 895 by 1941 and surged suddenly to 153,956 by 1951, owing to the steady flow of Syrian Christian peasant migrants from Travancore.[6] As the result of their engagement with land and commercial agriculture, the Syrian Christian community reached the interiors of Malabar and Travancore, a process of ruralization that transformed its original urban and coastal patterns of residence and livelihood (Varghese 2007).[7] Driven by compelling economic circumstances and the promises of a market-driven colonial economy, the Syrian Christian community took inspiration from colonial plantations and the model of land use they represented to transform the fallow hills, forests and wastelands of Kerala into producing fields. The achievements that changed community's economic fortunes, though, came at enormous personal costs. In the early years of land colonization, Syrian Christian migrants had to battle with a hostile environment in which wild animals and malaria claimed endless lives. The ostensible single-minded determination, remarkable ability, sheer hard work and ceaseless courage of the Syrian Christian peasant-entrepreneurs turned them into national heroes whose sacrifices presumably brought benefits not only to themselves but also to Kerala as a whole (Varghese 2009). They were thus endowed with a distinctive moral authority in Kerala's developmentalist imagination, as a productive and industrious community committed to the nation's progress, to be emulated by other (Christian and non-Christian) groups. On the strength of such a position, Syrian Christians were able to protect and defend their economic interests and resources, eventually foiling state attempts to reinstate alienated tribal land (Devika and Varghese 2011).

Redeeming the Landscape: A Theology for Land Colonization

The Syrian Christian Church reached the interiors of Malabar with the migrant settlers.[8] In the wilderness of fallow lands, the Church, an apparently redundant traditional institution, performed the very modern role of supporting the development of capitalist agriculture.[9] In its mission to reclaim a "lost world," the narratives of the Syrian Christian Church – shared by ecclesiastics and laity alike – defined the enterprise of land colonization in a cogent Christian vocabulary.[10] Indeed, the deployment of Christian theologies to shore up the practices of industrial capitalism and development has long been part of Western modernity (see, e.g., Thompson 1963; Weber 1992); in the case of imperial Britain, it also provided justifications for ideologies of improvement in the field of agriculture (Drayton 2005).[11] The British imagination posited earth as "the fountain and mother of all riches and abundance of the world"[12], envisioning agriculture and other projects of transformation of the natural environment as a sacred mission aimed at a restoring the lost "garden of Eden" to its original splendor and abundance (Drayton 2005). Divinely created to be nature's Sovereign, after the Fall, Adam becomes the toiler "charged with perfecting the fallen world with his skill and labour" (Drayton 2005: 50). Agriculture here becomes an art that could lead humankind back to the original communion with God. "Guided by science and revealed by religion," transformations of the environment engendered by agriculture became sacralized, thus justifying "the violence and coercion involved" (Drayton 2005: 54).

Such an imagination – arguably making its way to Travancore through European Christian missionaries, many of whom were cultivating interests in plantations, commerce and industry (Jeffrey 1976: 119; Kooiman 1989: 126) – found vernacular afterlife in the narratives of the Syrian Christian community. Migration and the clearing of virgin forests and landscapes were narrativized as a divinely revealed and guided mission, akin to the exodus of the Israelites from Egypt to Palestine: a migration from the land of persecution to that of milk and honey. Recollecting the divine planning behind the Syrian Christian migration to Malabar, the first bishop of the diocese of Taellicherry in Malabar, Mar Sebastian Vallopilly, describes the migrants as the dear children of God, the "new Israelites" (Vallopilly 1999: 286), and his own journey into Malabar was illustrated as the "Story of an Exodus".[13] Sebastian Vallopilly's pastoral leadership of Syro-Malabar/Syrian Catholic migrants has also been remembered with reference to the Biblical Exodus, as the Moses of Malabar who led "the migrants to a country of blessings".[14] Mar Joseph Valiyamattom, who followed Mar Vallopilly in the Tellicherry diocese, found analogies between his predecessor and the biblical Joshua who "helped the Israelites to settle down in Canaan and grow as a people."[15]

The "exodus to Malabar," like the biblical Exodus, was portrayed as a miraculous escape from the slavery of oppression and poverty to the promised land (Pazheparambil 1978; Karimattom et al. 2004). Under the repressive Dewan C. P. Ramaswami Aiyar's regime and suffering from the effects of a stagnant economy, 1930s and 1940s Travancore was construed as the land of bondage which the "new Israelites" were longing to leave. Unlike the biblical Canaan, though, the Syrian Christians' promised land of milk and honey was not readily available: it had to be forged through migrants' efforts. Malabar is the promised land in the sense that God had endowed it with natural resources that could be converted into a Canaan through human effort and ingenuity. Whilst Canaan might be deferred for want of human efforts, God would stand with his chosen people in actualizing it.[16]

These narratives – produced by Church and laity alike in the form of autobiographies, memories and articles appearing in popular religious publications – have a wide discursive scope, in which migration becomes part and parcel of human history as a divinely endorsed human duty and mission (see, e.g., Pinakkatt 1964: 9). As the earth is God's gift to all of humanity, it is the "birth right of all born human beings to live and thrive" on it (Nedumkunnam 1967: 11). Accordingly, "those who are keeping the earth without cultivating are sinners, leaving the society starving. God never want people to be famished. And He doesn't want the fertile soil to be left uncultivated causing human starvation and death" (Nedumkunnam 1967: 12). The earth is described as "capable of providing us with everything we want", gifted to man by the Lord, for which man should be eternally grateful and make use of it imaginatively (M. M. F., C. M. I. 1964, *Girideepam* 1966). Creation is here alluded to as incomplete, God leaving humankind with the responsibility of "completing the act of creation" (*Girideepam 1966*: 3). Human beings are invested with the divine duty of discovering and tapping nature's resources to perfect creation as desired by God. Failing to discharge such a divine obligation is not only "against the law of nature" and hence "a dereliction of duty", but also a "punishable act" (*Girideepam 1966*: 3). Fr. Joseph Vadakkan, who championed the cause of the migrant settlers, for instance, points out that the very existence of wild forests "full of woods, thickets, prickles and cobras" epitomizes the incompleteness of creation:[17]

> God is love. Love is lively and dynamic. When the holy mind of God moved, the world was created. In the beginning this world was incomplete. It was full of woods, thickets, prickles and cobras. God's heart then beats for reforming this particular world. God created man in his own image and likeness because of such a love. He was carved out to [to make things] move and write [things anew]. For making the imperfect world beautiful and affluent God showered skills and dexterity on man. He has given to man the genius and capability to make wild forests into paradise.[18]

Fr. Vadakkan is unequivocal that the clearing away of forests is a universal historical duty of all god-fearing men: "[T]he soil covered with woods and thickets will only produce thorns," and hence it was advocated that that "not even a needle-space of soil is left in our custody uncultivated like a dead desert" (M. M. F. 1964: 20).

These Syrian Christian narratives first appeared in Church-based publications like *Girideepam* (mouthpiece of the Tellicherry Syro-Malabar Catholic diocese) and *Sathyadeepam* (the publication of the Syro-Malabar Catholic community, established in 1927 and today drawing more than a million readers). They acquired wider purchase by being reproduced in parish-based publications, migrant memories and newspaper articles, particularly those printed in the *Deepika* daily (belonging to Syro-Malabar Catholic publishers, it started publication in 1887 and for long it was the most read vernacular newspaper in Kerala). We can discern here a decisively anthropocentric view of the universe, which invests human beings – God's best creation – with the duty of executing the divine plan in the world, in its foreordained march to perfection. Since God wanted man to "be fruitful and multiply", it is his responsibility to occupy "empty and void" space and "replenish and subdue it" to accomplish the mission to lead the "half-perfect" world into perfection (M. M. F. 1964: 20). Such a worldview did not permit restrictions upon the occupation of territory in God's earthly kingdom. A boundless earth is said to be at man's disposal, because "it is not God but man who had laid boundary lines in the resourceful earth created by God for the use of all human beings" (Vallopilly 1965: 3). Here the Christian obligation of conquering the earth and to transform it through agriculture overlaps with the patriotic responsibility of the migrants, a duty encapsulated in *Girideepam*'s famous injunction: "For God and the country."[19] This represents a shift in the self-representation of Travancore Syrian Christians, from a persecuted community during the colonial period to a community committed to post-independence Nehruvian nationalist reconstruction, wherein the postcolonial nation and Syrian Christian migrants share the common destinies of development and well-being. Toiling the soil through hard work is revealed as the appropriate means for fulfilling this dual obligation incumbent on the citizen-believer. This ensures not only the family's welfare, but also food and well-being to fellow humans and the nation as a whole (*Girideepam 1966*). Migration to undeveloped regions is invoked as a solution to their apparent backwardness, redeeming them to a modern work ethic and, consequently, restoring them to their glory (Nedumkunnam 1967). Nedumkunnam underlines the need for "erecting memorials" for such "brave *nationalists*", who, with their "adventurous spirit, unfailing enthusiasm and anticipation of a good future", turned the destiny of the land, transforming the forest ranges of Malabar into "pleasant gold-yielding gardens" at the cost of "enormous blood and sweat" (Nedumkunnam 1967).

The glorification of divinely ordained and nationalist development coincides with the critiques of the unpatriotic and irrational, obstructive attitudes of local political actors and institutions who sought to thwart the patriotic efforts of the divinely chosen. The Congress government in Kerala through most of the 1960s and the Nairs, the high status Hindu community who allegedly instigated the government against the Christian migrants, were lambasted for thwarting the Indian state's efforts to increase food crop production and save the nation from hunger. Thomas Pazheparambil, the first Vicar-General of Tellicherry diocese, bemoaned that had the migrants received adequate support from their "own government" they would have "produced food crops and dollar crops in an astonishing manner and ma[d]e this country more prosperous" (Pazheparambil 1964). In the context of various eviction attempts in the 1960s,[20] there was a reassertion of the patriotic dimension of migration, urging the Kerala state to promote migrants' settlement within and outside the state and country (Nedumkunnam 1967). At the same time, Syrian Christian narratives also place the agency of hardworking (Christian) citizens – those who rationally and conscientiously exploit the riches provided by God – at the centre of this divinely ordained transformation. By underscoring the arduous labor of those who migrated into Malabar to transform a "spacious and void" region into a garden of prosperity and plenty, the Church endorsed settlers' claims over the creation of a modern Malabar. This was accompanied by a strong censure of laziness and indolence, violations of God's commandment, causing "malice to the family and the community...increasing the number of beggars in their own country." Those who do not work hard to cultivate the land said to have "to give explanation to God" (*Girideepam 1966*; Nedumkunnam 1967). The migrant community is thus imagined as called upon by God to disperse to remote destinations with a "divine aim."[21] Apart from completing the act of Creation, "heathen Malabar was seen by Syrian Christian groups as a missionary frontier for spreading the gospel."[22]

Beyond Salvation: The Church and the Anti-eviction Movement

Alongside developing a theological discourse which legitimized the enterprise of migration and land colonization as a divine mission incumbent on believers, throughout the 1960s the Malabar Syrian Christian Church deployed its expanded pastoral role to organize migrants' resistance against threats of evection from the land that they had cleared and cultivated. Michael Foucault has argued that the emergence of a (European) modern secular state – endowed with the avowed task of ensuring deliverance in this world via rational-scientific means – would lead to a progressive withering away of the salvation-oriented pastoral power of the Church (Foucault 1982). In Kerala, the Syrian Christian church responded to the policies of the postcolonial developmental state by combining its traditional pastoral responsibilities directed towards ensuring the eventual salvation of its flock, with an orientation towards ensuring the wellbeing and *upliftment* of thc faithful in this world.[23] The involvement of the Church in the anti-eviction struggles in Malabar came at a time when the promised land of Canaan arduously built since the 1930s was threatened by state interventions. By the 1960s, novel political configurations and alliances between different communities and castes in Kerala and burgeoning environmental concerns resulted in the articulation of a strong critique against a development enterprise hitherto hinging on a model of land colonization that led to the extensive destruction of forests, the dispossession of aboriginal inhabitants and, more importantly, appeared to favor Christian communities over the Hindu majority population (upper-caste Nairs, in particular). The latter's interests and concerns, allegedly represented by the Indian National Congress–led coalition governing Kerala at the time, resulted in accusations of land encroachment against Christian settlers and calls for the return of colonized land to the state, its redistribution to the original owners, and the implementation of environmental conservation policies (Varghese 2006). This resulted in the mobilization of the Syrian Christian migrants and settlers who rallied around the Church, and a leadership handpicked by the latter, to protect their material interests in the right to remain on the land they had reclaimed from the "wilderness." The pastoral power of the church and its involvement in the campaigns against land evictions lent a particular moral legitimacy to the struggle.

It was during the early 1960s with the Ayyappankovil anti-eviction movement in the erstwhile Travancore that the struggle against eviction gathered momentum. The movement, which provided the normative idioms and leadership to the subsequent struggles elsewhere in the state, was headed by two unlikely partners: A. K. Gopalan (AKG), a firebrand communist leader who had organized landless cultivators in a successful campaign for land distribution, and Fr. Vadakkan, a priest who had become a leader of *vimochana samaram*, the liberation struggle against the first communist government elected in 1957 in Kerala.[24] Around 1,700 families with 10,000 members occupying about 8,000 acres of land were evicted from Ayyappankovil in May 1961 to make room for the construction of a hydroelectric dam (Gopalan 1975: 84). According to Fr. Vadakkan, more than 2,000 families were "monstrously driven out" at the peak of the monsoon rains (Vadakkan 1974: 142). Fr. Vadakkan was appalled by the brutality of a government that had come to power as a result of the bloody liberation struggle in which thousands of those who were being evicted had themselves participated. He was quite certain that the Ayyappankovil had been orchestrated by a group of *vimochana samaram* leaders who used their political clout to appropriate thousands upon thousands of acres of plantations for themselves (Vadakkan 1974: 143). Though Fr. Vadakkan had led the struggle against evictions, the Church hierarchy in south Kerala maintained distance from the movement to preserve the solidarity between high-caste Hindus and Christians established during the anti-communist liberation struggle.[25] In another instance in Travancore itself, to protect forests from encroachers, more than 4,000 families were evicted from Churuli-Keerithode in 1963–1964 (Gopalan 1975: 326). AKG, who had joined both struggles by starting a fast-unto-death protest, lambasted the "bourgeois newspapers" who were justifying government action as a necessary move to promote forest conservation. He argued that environmental protection could not be enforced by "annihilating people", a view shared by Fr. Vadakkan (Gopalan 1975: 327).[26]

Unlike the south of the state, the north Kerala Syro-Malabar Church in Tellicherry took a prominent role in organizing the movement against evictions in its diocese. Regardless of the mainstream Syrian Church leadership's open hostility against Fr. Vadakkan's untoward alliance with the communist AKG at Amaravathi, in Tellicherry the diocese and its bishop had no hesitations in seeking the intervention of the Christian priest who had joined forces with the "anti-Christ," the Communists. This "unholy" alliance of the Church with the Communists in defense of the interests of its migrant congregation produced significant fissures in the structures of thought of the Church and its laity, which had hitherto regarded the Communists as downright enemies, engendering a form of vernacular *complexio oppositorum*.[27]

In 1961 Kottiyoor, in Malabar, became a trouble spot. It was rumored that the leader of the powerful Nair Service Society (NSS), Mannath Padmanabhan, had ostensibly acquired the land belonging to Kottiyoor *devaswam* (Hindu temple) through a "super-lease" (*melcharth*, a lease over and above an already existing lease), at a time when the temple trustees had already leased out 30,000 acres of temple-owned land – mainly forests – to the land-hungry Syrian Christian migrants. The latter had cleared the forest and turned the land to cultivation (Vallopilly 1999: 350). Apparently at the behest of Mannath Padmanabhan, the government and the Devaswam (temple-affairs) minister planned to evict all the Syrian Christian "encroachers" on the devaswam land in order to transfer it to the NSS on a ninety-nine-year lease.[28] When the initial protests of the migrants and the Communist-led "Karshaka Sangham" (peasant union) failed to bear fruit, and in response to the arrival of a large contingent of the infamous Malabar Special Police (MSP)[29] to support the evictions, Mar Vallopilly and the Church entered the scene to organize the resistance.[30] The bishop sent his trusted secretary to Kottiyoor parish as its vicar to mobilize people, and at the same time enlisted support from all possible quarters, including that of the "notorious" Fr. Vadakkan and B. Wellington, the Socialist leader who had championed the cause of peasants and workers and allied with the Communists in parliamentary politics. With the arrival of these two, the campaign against the impending eviction heated up with countless protest meetings and marches organized in Kottiyoor and other adjacent migrant areas. Settlers pledged not to leave their land under any circumstances. Wellington, along with other leaders mobilized by the Church – Fr. Jacob Chirayath, Fr. Vettikatt and Thuruthiyil Scaria – led the Kottiyoor *jatha*, a march to the state capital Trivandrum that took forty-six days to reach its destinations, after covering more than 400 miles by foot and generating significant popular support (Varghese 2006: 241–245). Subsequently, on 12 February 1962, Wellington started a fast-unto-death at Kelakam (a town in near the eviction area) that lasted for twenty-one days. Facing growing protests from a community that had traditionally supported the party and fearing that the Communists would "make use of the situation", the ruling Congress party was forced to constitute a committee of five members of the legislative assembly to enquire into the issue and find a possible solution.[31] In the ensuing negotiations, the migrant community was represented primarily by the Church leadership – the bishop did not compromise even on a single inch of land the migrants held (Vallopilly 1999: 353).[32]

In 1961 the migrant settlers of Pulpally, another prominent migrant area in Malabar, faced the threat of eviction from 15,000 acres of temple land they had been accused by an Hindu militant organization, the Rashtriya Swayamsevak Sangh (RSS), of having encroached upon illegally. Once more, the Church organized the laity and stood firm; the government eventually gave up the eviction plans. Whilst other locations in Malabar such as Ambalavayal, Kakkadavu and Gudallur witnessed similar struggles,[33] it was in Shimoga, a district in the neighbouring Karnataka state, that migrant settlers were actually evicted. The Church had been instrumental in inviting migrants from Malabar to move to Shimoga with the prospect of a bright future with "thousands and thousands of acres of land awaiting hardworking hands" (Kunnel 1965a; Nechikkatt 1966). On 10 May 1966, around 600 migrant families who had migrated to Shimoga stood accused of having occupied reserved forests and were evicted by the Karnataka government, regardless of pressures from the migrant community and their political representatives.[34] More than 4,000 people were made landless and homeless at a stroke, forced to move in temporary tents in a plot of land made available by a local activist woman. Before being moved to the next "promised land," these refugees lived for seventy-nine days in precarious conditions in the camp, under Church management headed by Fr. Joseph Kunnel and Fr. Joseph Mannur. The 240 families who were completely landless were later rehabilitated in Chandanakkampara, where the Church purchased 500 acres of land and established the Shimoga Colony.

As well as asserting migrants' right to belonging in the regions where they had settled, these struggles allowed the Church to consolidate its undisputed pastoral power over its laity. By mobilizing the theology of divinely ordained human destiny to address the dire predicament of its constituency, the Church emerged as the sole and obvious representative of the interests of the migrant community. The participation of the Church lent an ethical principle of (divinely ordained) justice to the struggle;[35] Mar Vallopilly became known as the real leader of this "moral struggle."[36] More importantly, the Church and its laity received the support of the Communist party and its labour organizations, whom they had fought bitterly in previous years, during the liberation struggle. A. K. Gopalan, the communist leader who had joined anti-eviction protests in south Kerala, became actively involved in the Kottiyoor movement; he led, for instance, a jeep *juthu* (procession) to Trivandrum to campaign and draw public support for the migrant settlers. The general secretary of the Communist Party, E. M. S. Namboodiripad (EMS), and the communist-led Karshaka Sangham in the Kannur district of Malabar, actively supported the Syrian Christian migrants under threat of eviction. *Krishikkaran*, the mouthpiece of Kerala State Karshaka Sangham, warned those who argued for forest conservation and protection of temple land from trespassers to desist from making claims on land in the possession of tenants. The magazine criticized the anti-migrant and pro-eviction stance of the Nair Service Society and the Congress leader Kelappan, suggesting that the latters' actions were "not in spirit of *survodaya* [progress for all] but [upper caste] *gharvodaya* [arrogance]."[37] B. Wellington – leader of the Karshaka Thozhilali Party (KTP; Kerala Workers Party), which he had founded with Fr. Joseph Vadakkan[38] – was one of the few politicians who visited the Shimoga evictees to offer support. When the communist leader EMS was reelected in 1967 as Chief Minister, he allotted 50 rupees to each evicted family, also sanctioning a post office and a government hospital at Chandanakkamppara, where the families had been moved (Kunnel 1998: 78). AKG, on his part, threw himself into the agitation against the evictions at Gudalloor[39] speaking at many migrant protest meetings, visiting the fasting Fr. Vadakkan, and meeting the district Collector to find a positive outcome to the protest.[40] The participation in and support of the Communist Party for the protests in both south Kerala and Malabar – with AKG in the forefront, regardless of serious reservations from his own party – led the Syrian Christian community to redefine its historical political allegiance to the Indian National Congress. Syrian Christian migrants realized that *their* political party had not only failed to support them, but also actively advocated police-led eviction attempts. As a result, the Tellicherry diocese informally advised its laity not to vote for the Congress candidate in the parliament election of the early 1960s, thus going against its bishops who had directed people "not to vote for the Communists". Standing in the parliamentary constituency of Kasaragod in the Kannur district of Malabar, AKG, with the support of Christian voters, won the election with a thumping majority (Kunnel 1998: 36–38). Fr. Vadakkan summarized the new political climate among Malabar Syrian Christians: "there is nothing wrong in enlisting the support of the Communists for doing virtuous things" (Vadakkan 1974: 147).[41]

The anti-eviction struggle provoked a similar soul searching amongst the communist movement. AKG – who had pushed the Communist Party to take a leadership role in migrants' protests at Amaravathi, Kottiyoor and other places – argued that the Amaravathi struggle had punched holes in the "iron curtain" erected by the mainstream Church to separate poor Christian cultivators from the communist movement. He was hopeful that the unity established between Christian and non-Christian peasants in Amaravathi and Kottiyoor would lead to the eventual withering away of mistrust and ideological differences.[42] At the same time, both the Syrian Church and the Communist Party had to respond to accusations that they had been supporting narrow and divisive community interests and politics. The communists countered this by underscoring the wider secular agenda of the protest, which sought to defend the livelihoods of peasant cultivators. They highlighted the class dimension of the struggle, in which they were championing the cause of tenants against the landlords, driven unambiguously by secular political motives (Keraleeyan 1997: 182–183). The Church, for its part, articulated a two-pronged explanation. Recognizing that most of the migrant settlers under threat of evictions were Christian, it argued that communities resentful of Christians' economic success had conspired to orchestrate the evictions.[43] At the same time, the Church defined its role in the protests as being driven by wider humanitarian considerations that were secular in nature. Thus, while the communists found justifications for their brand of *Complexio oppositorum* in the language of class, the imaginative and contextual deployment of notions of humanitarianism allowed the Church to join forces with its hitherto political and ideological foes.

Countering Family Planning as a Development Option

Faith in a development model hinging on the full exploitation of natural resources (land, in particular) coupled with appropriate use of human resources and modern technologies spilled over to other terrains of conflict. Most importantly in post-independence Kerala, it informed the opposition of the Church and of the Communist Party to family planning through artificial birth control which, in the 1950s and 1960s, was proposed as a solution to Kerala's (and India's) escalating developmental crisis.[44] As the leading proponents of the land-and-labour development model, they refuted the wisdom of promoting birth control as a means to ensure socioeconomic development, but eventually implicitly endorsed it.

The Church argued, on the one hand, that it would be sinful to use God-given reproductive capacities just for selfish carnal pleasures, contravening the divine injunction to control birth only through natural means (Matheckal 1955: 9).[45] Artificial birth control was censured as a sin in that it promoted sensual pleasures while preventing reproductive sexual functions of fulfilling God's creation (Paul 1961: 4). In 1961, the bishop of Varapuzha declared birth control the "biggest destructive movement of modern times", destroying the holiness of marriage and disrupting conjugal life, a misguided attempt to create well-being against the commands of the Creator, and hence to be forbidden to all – Hindus, Muslims and Christians alike – who believe in the existence of God.[46] Any policy of birth control or sterilization, the Church argued, would turn wives into prostitutes, the holy family would become a house of harlots and love would be reduced to sexual pleasure (Palathumpad 1964: 4). The evil of birth control could not be the solution to the evil of poverty and unemployment in Kerala.[47] Moreover, the imposition of artificial birth control would undermine the "self-determination capacity of human beings", generating a "sense of helplessness and defeat" (Mampilly 1963: 10). The Church not only invoked Indian culture and traditions to add a nativist and patriotic flavor to its criticism (Sathyadeepam 1956: 6), but also went as far as praising Communist China and the Soviet Union for considering "a mouth to be fed as two hands capable to work" and that "two working hands can feed four mouths" (Sathyadeepam 1962: 6).

As the campaign for birth control gained ground in the state, a weary Church rearticulated its criticism by suggesting that it was not against "family planning" as such, but only opposed artificial birth prevention (Sathyadeepam 1959: 6).[48] It could support family planning conducted in accordance with God's laws, that is, through self-restraint and the "system of safe period" (Hillariyon 1967: 3, *Sathyadeepam 1968*: 6). While the church continued to appeal to the Christian notion of "Divine Care,"[49] it sought alternatives, arguing that the only solution to the economic and social problems engendered by population growth was to make use of the thousands upon thousands of acres of virgin land that were still available for colonization and cultivation (Palathumpad 1964; Pulikkodan 1965: 22). In a pastoral article published in *Sathyadeepam* in 1965, Mar Vallopilly, the most vocal supporter of this policy, called for migration to and the occupation of all available land to resolve the population problem, citing the case of Syrian Christian migration in search of cultivable land to Malabar as a case of "Divine Care" (Vallopilly 1965: 3). He referred to Acharya Vinoba Bave – considered by many to be Gandhi's spiritual successor – whose critique of birth control had been reported by the Church press. Acharya had reportedly said: "Give earth to those who cultivate. The earth is everyone's. Everyone is God's. Hence earth is under the ownership of God... Nobody should worry about the growth of population supposedly beyond earth's capacity. The earth can put up with that are created on it. The creator of earth also knows it."[50] Forests and animals should not privileged over human beings, and migration should be promoted to resolve food crises (Kunnel 1965: 21–22).

Family planning was a problematic policy for the Communists too, for they favored a developmental model hinging on the rational and planned exploitation of all available human and natural resources through agricultural expansion, industrialization and modernization. The Kerala Communists' call for distribution of land to the tillers went alongside demands for the allocation to landless farmers and agricultural labourers of "cultivable fallows" and forests owned both by the government and landlords.[51] Writing in 1959 in the Communist weekly *Navayugam*, Athirungal Prabhakaran strongly recommended making use of all swamps along with forestlands for food crop cultivation as a long-term plan for state's economic development. His suggestion was to convert the whole "outer forest" of Kerala into rubber plantations, which would retain all the ecological features of forests whilst simultaneously producing enormous wealth and generating employment (Prabhakaran 1959). The Communist Party denounced the Congress-led government for blocking the occupation "of the five lakhs [500,000] acres of odd cultivable land in Kerala" at a time when it was implementing the "Grow More Food Programme" directed at reducing food shortage in the state.[52] The Communist leader E. M. S. Namboodiripad went further to underscore the inherent contradictions in the Congress Party's development policies in Kerala. He argued that on the one hand Congress politicians evoked Nehru's words to describe modern infrastructures – dams, power stations, factories and more – as "temples of national development" capable of securing decent livelihoods and well-being for all, but on the other they promoted family planning as the only means to resolve severe food scarcity in the state (Namboodiripad 1954). The latter, EMS argued, was not the outcome of either overpopulation or "any inherent trouble of farmers and land of our country, instead of [Congress] reluctance to adopt actual land reforms."[53] Communist critiques of family planning were accompanied by agitations in support of those "poor farmers who fought with wild elephant and malaria, cleared the forest, confronted the oppression and robbery of forest officials and affluent forest bandits and produced food grain" in areas such as Amaravathi, Churuli-Keerithode and Kottiyoor (Madhavan Pilla 1956; Gopalan 1975: 57–60). Under the leadership of AKG and supported by Fr. Vadakkan, the "surplus-land struggle" that developed in the early 1970s eventually forced the government to confiscate fallow/spare land in the hands of former feudal landlords and institutions for allocation to the landless poor, underscoring the centrality of farmers and land in the Communist development strategies (Vadakkan 1974: 260–274; Gopalan 1975: 187–272).[54]

Conclusion

What is apparent in the foregoing story is the political positioning of the Church in providing theological justifications to entrepreneurship, hard work and capital accumulation, mobilizing successfully against evictions to ensure the security of its lay constituency, and opposing an emerging developmental imaginary constituted around policies of family planning. This was done by effortlessly straddling modernist rationalities and theological reasoning, combining the religious and secular with ease. One way of explaining this apparent contradiction could be via Ranajit Guha's argument concerning the failure of colonialism to veer entirely traditional societies in the direction of "Western modernity" (Guha 1988; Guha 1997: 97–98;). Consequently, Guha argues, "vast areas in the life and consciousness" escaped the hegemony of capital, even as the changes beckoned by colonial modernity remained significant. Instead of pathologizing Indian modernity as either an incomplete or failed project, I would rather draw attention to the multiple sites where modern capital and entrepreneurship allowed the colonized to reinvent religion as a means to engage critically with political and economic processes of transformation engendered by modernity. Whilst modern forms of production and capital accumulation are seen as endowed with the divine mission of fulfilling God's plans for humankind, God's will became a means to oppose modernist modalities of planning and intervention such as those embodied in family planning state policies. In this vernacular expression of a theological tradition – *Complexio oppositorum* – in which contradictory opposites are kept in productive tension without any apparent resolution, the extraordinary becomes possible.

Far from engendering a homogeneous time wherein religious rationality withered away under the weight of colonial modernity and capitalism, the theological rationality produced by the Syrian Christian Church combined a (secular) humanitarian obligation to eradicate poverty with a Christian deontology focused on the ethical virtue of hard work to sanction and advance modern forms of capital accumulation and production. The Church also played a significant role in the making of a Syrian Christian political society around the struggles of the settlers to remain in the reclaimed spaces and ensure legal rights for the land they (often illegally) occupied. Resonating with John Locke's formulation, the Church narratives reiterated the principle that God provided man with all riches in common and once the conscientious and industrious man subdue the earth with his labour, the "subdued, tilled and sowed" land became "his *Property*" (Locke 1960: 290–291). Such an ethics of individual entrepreneurship, private property and capital accumulation underpinned Syrian Christian political mobilizations endorsed and facilitated by the Church. In doing so, the Syrian Christian Church repudiated the nativist claims of upper-caste Hindu communities for whom, as recounted in the famous *Keralolpathi* myth, "Kerala was created by Lord Parasurama for Brahmins" and as a result "the major portion of land is in the hand of devaswams (temple trusts) and brahmaswams (Brahmin trusts)." Portraying the myth as justifying an action "against the justice of God done in the name of God" (Nedumkunnam 1967), Syrian Christians claimed equal participation and belonging to modern Kerala. However, the theology of deliverance from poverty and hunger through hard work and human ingenuity exercised towards the colonization of fallow land hinges on the extensive and progressive marginalization of aboriginal hunter-gatherer populations who, as consequence of migration and settlement, lost access to natural resources and were themselves driven to hunger.

What stands out in the Syrian Christian narratives of migration and land colonization is the articulation of a subjecthood yielding to divine will, undertaking a virtuous path of geographical and social mobility against all odds. Hard work, self-sacrifice, ruthlessness, shrewdness and entrepreneurship are community qualities that in popular Malayalee imagination have conjured an image of the Syrian Christians as staunch capitalists and innovators. This is a pioneering frontier spirit that in recent years has sustained the community in their ceaseless search for novel promised lands through transnational migrations to the Gulf countries of the Middle East, North America, Australia and Europe.

Notes

1 The state of Kerala was formed in 1956 by merging the three predominantly Malayalam speaking regions in the south-western coast of India, namely Travancore, Cochin and Malabar. Malabar was a district in the Madras presidency of British India, while Travancore and Cochin were princely states under native kings during the colonial time.

2 The mountain district of Wayanad in Malabar today has the highest proportion of migrant settlers amongst its population, alongside the highest proportion of deforestation and highest amount of tribal land alienation in the state of Kerala.

3 The Syrian Christians of Kerala trace their origin back to the evangelization of the Apostle St Thomas and described originally themselves as Nazranis or St Thomas Christians. The appellation Syrian Christian was given by the Dutch missionaries to differentiate them from the Latin Christians, who were converts to Roman Catholicism and date from the Portuguese time onwards. The Syrian Christians followed the Syrian liturgy due to their ecclesiastical commune with the East Syrian Patriarchate. They engaged in mercantile activities, agriculture and territorial soldiering before the advent of colonialism and enjoyed a high social status in the traditional, caste-based socio-moral order. A community that was free of internal divisions prior to colonial missionary activities, the Syrian Christians are at present divided into many denominations and affiliated to Catholic and non-Catholic sects such as the Syro-Malabar, Syrian-Orthodox, Orthodox-Syrian, Malanakara Syrian, Marthoma Syrian and others (Jeffrey 1976; Mundadan 1984; Zacharia 1994).

4 Census of India, 1941, Vol. XXV, Travancore Part II, Tables (Trivandrum: Government of Travancore, 1942).

5 Census of India, 1951, Vol. XIII, Travancore-Cochin Part II, Tables (New Delhi: Government of India, 1953).

6 Of the total, 88,275 were born in Travancore-Cochin area and as many as 78,148 in rural Malabar (Census Handbook 1951, Malabar District, pp. 246–249).

7 In Kerala as a whole, the proportion of Christians living in rural areas increased from 1,352 per 10,000 in 1901 to 2,149 in 1961, whereas there was a decline in urban areas from 2320 in 1931 to 1970 in 1961 (Census of India 1961, Vol. VII, Kerala, Part A, General Report, Table 9.3, pp. 400–401).

8 Approximately over 200,000 Syrian Christians, mostly small and marginal peasants, migrated to Malabar from Travancore between 1920 and 1970. The numerically strong Syro-Malabar Catholic rite is referred to as Syrian Christians unless specified otherwise throughout this chapter.

9 Attempts to understand India's modernity until recently have defined "religion" as a premodern/pre-political category (Guha 1997)

10 Malabar was seen by the Syrian Catholic (Syro-Malabar) leadership as a region stolen from them by the Portuguese invaders, who forced native Christians to convert to and adopt the practices of Latin Catholicism. The Syrian migration to Malabar was an attempt at repossessing a precolonial lost world (Pazheparambil 1978: 167).

11 Drayton argues that the ideology of agrarian improvement as it arose in modern England had variously drawn support from Christian Providentialism, patriotism and individualism.

12 Lewis Roberts, *The Merchant's Map of Commerce* (1638), quoted in Drayton (2005: 56).

13 The illustrated story of Bishop Sebastian Vallopilly, titled "Story of an Exodus" (Karimattom et al. 2004).

14 Mar Joseph Pallikkaparambil in Karimattom et al. 2004: cover page, 3–4; preface by Mar Joseph Pallikkaparambil to Valavoor 1995.

15 Mar George Valiyamattom, preface to Karimattom et al. 2004: cover page, 2.

16 The parallels between the two exoduses are forcefully drawn in "Purappadu" in *St. Joseph's Church Chempanoda- Golden Jubilee Souvenir*, pp. 33–69.

17 Fr. Joseph Vadakkan was the firebrand Syrian Catholic priest who played a lead role in the "liberation struggle" that ousted the first elected Communist government in Kerala. He later allied with the Communists for protecting the migrant peasant settlers (Vadakkan 1974; Varghese 2006).

18 Fr. Vadakkan, "Mattam Vithacha Van Kutiyettam", *St. Joseph's Church Vayattuparambu Smaranika* (Vayattuparambu: St. Joseph's Church, 1986), pp. 54–55.

19 *Girideepam*'s epigraph, "Daivathinum Rajyathinum Vendi", which was inscribed on the cover page along with the title of the magazine. The Tellicherry diocese, constituted by the Holy See in 1953 in response to the demands of the Syrian Christian migrant settlers, started publishing *Girideepam* from the early 1960s, at a time when migration and land colonialization as a development model began to be questioned and eviction attempts gathered momentum. The circulation was predominantly through the parish networks and the magazine have been underscoring the righteous role of the migrant settler in Malabar.

20 The reasons for the eviction threats in and around Kerala in the 1960s included the stated aims of recovering forestland, building hydroelectric projects and dams, saving forests from further depletion, reinstating "illegally occupied" temple-lands and rehabilitating Tamil refugees from Sri Lanka.

21 Rev. A. T. Zachariah, "Samaryayile Suvishesha Sakshyam", *Malabar Jubilee – Maha Jubilee Smaranika* 1950–2000: 58–62.

22 Kallidukkil 1949: 16–17; Pazheparambil 1978: 163–164; see the article by Rev. A. T. Zachariah, the interview with Rev. J. Joseph entitled "Suvishesham Malabarinte Mannilekku", "Yathrageetham" (farewell song) and the Message by Geevarghese Mar Theodosius, all in *Malabar Jubilee Maha Jubilee*, pp. 58–62, 46–52, 74. Also

see the description by Fr. V. I. Thomas (the Vicar General of Malabar diocese) in Mammen 1992: 89–96.

23 The development initiatives being run by various churches in Kerala is a case in point, though the understanding of development remains "elitist" (Lemercinier and Houtart 1974).

24 The *vimochana samaram* (1958–1959), launched by a majoritarian front against land reforms and educational policy initiated by the Communist government, resulted in the dismissal of the government in 1959. The land reforms subsequently implemented were less radical than were originally proposed in the Land Reforms bill of 1957. Though it ended the feudal system and upheld the rights of tenants, cash crop plantations were exempted from its purview and the promise of "land to the tillers" could be only partially achieved (Oommen 1971).

25 Vadakkan writes that many selfish associates of Mannam, many Christian elites, Christian bishops and Religious Societies were said to have targeted the lush eastern hills to make estates, for amassing wealth (Vadakkan 1974: 145–146).

26 For a detailed discussion, see Varghese (2006).

27 *Complexio oppositorum* is a concept engaged by Carl Schmitt to explain the ability exhibited by Catholicism to hold opposites, in its sway often neutralizing the apparent dualism. It engineers ways to diffuse particularly political contradictions by embracing them under a higher/universal authority (Schmitt 1985).

28 According to Mar Vallopilly by 1960 around a thousand families migrated to Kottiyoor (Vallopilly 1999: 351). But according to AKG and Fr. Vadakkan, around 5,000 families had settled in the contested land (Vadakkan 1974: 149; Gopalan 1975: 76).

29 Formed during the Malabar rebellion of 1921 by the Mappilas to suppress it, MSP earned notoriety as an emblem of colonial oppression. Becoming a paramilitary unit of the Kerala State Police after the formation of the state, MSP even today symbolizes ruthlessness in dealing with internal disturbances.

30 While Vallopilly could see 500 MSP men camping in Kottiyoor, for Valavoor and Vadakkan it was 2000 (Vadakkan 1974: 149; Valavoor 1995: 116; Vallopilly 1999: 351).

31 The members of the committee were K. M. George, T. O. Bava, N. S. Krishnapilla, T. A. Thomman and P. Gopalan. M. C. Xavier, "Kottiyoor Kutiyetta Charithram", p. 20 and Joseph 1991: 434.

32 Mar Vallopilly in the migrant ruminations of Kottiyoor, as a result, is "the real shepherd who understood the condition of the Kottiyoor peasant" and "the spiritual father who identified with the agonies of the farmers." T. S. Scaria Thuruthiyil, "Kottiyoor Kutiyettam Ormakalil", in *St. Sebastian's Church Kottiyoor Dedication of Newly Built Church Souvenir*, pp. 66–69.

33 For a detailed discussion, see Varghese 2006: 240–255.

34 A contingent of 500 army personnel (2000, according to Fr. Kunnel) cleared everyone who sat on hunger strike against the impending eviction, "set the houses ablaze, destroyed the cultivation and crops, pulled everybody assembled in the church and convent out and set them to fire" (Kunnel 1998: 60; Vallopilly 1999: 357).

35 Mar Vallopilly always foregrounds the injustice entailed in eviction attempts. For him, the land in the possession of the migrants, once dominated by malaria and wild animals and terrifying the natives, was claimed by various interest groups once

they were converted into gold-yielding gardens at the cost of assiduous hard work. The *janmis* who sold out their lands at cheap prices began to regret their decision by seeing the opulent agricultural tracts that were once abandoned landscapes. See Rt. Rev. Dr. Sebastian Vallopilly, "Malabarile Kutiyettathinte Kadha", in *Suvarna Jubilee Smaranika 1992–Kulathuvayal St. George Forane Church.*

36 Mar Vallopilly is called in some instances the "Kutiyettakkarude Samara Nayakan" (leader of migrants' struggles) precisely because of his role as a leader in the anti-eviction struggles of the Malabar migrants. See "Mar Sebastian Vallopilly: Kutiyettakkarude Samara Nayakan", in *Girideepam Methranabhisheka Pathippu*, May 1981, pp. 74–76.

37 K. A. Keraleeyan, "Kaivasavakasavum Kollayum", in *Keraleeyante Leghanangal*, pp. 178–185. The editorial ridiculed *Mathrubhumi* daily for branding the migrant tenants as "encroachers" into the temple land, raising the question, "how can about 25000 people in 5000 families live and cultivate vast areas of land owned by the temple, for about twenty years, without the knowledge of the temple trustees?"

38 Founded in 1962, the KTP contested the Kerala election of 1967 as part of a United Front led by the Communist Party; its general secretary B. Wellington became the health minister in the EMS ministry of 1967–1969.

39 Gudalloor, part of the adjoining state of Tamil Nadu, witnessed protests from the 1960s to the 1980s against eviction, when the government there sought to evict migrant settlers for rehabilitating Tamil refugees from Sri Lanka.

40 C. Bhaskaran (ed), *A. K. G. Album*, p. 72.

41 The anti-hero of the Church in the Christian mainland continued to be a reverential figure to the Malabar church and its people. When Fr. Vadakkan was later excommunicated from the priesthood by the Church, for his alleged Communist links and for publically defying the Church policies, the migrant community at Kottiyoor organized a grand reception for its "hero" against the decision of the mainland Church leadership. The Malabar church utilized the services of Fr. Vadakkan even after the excommunication and continued to hold him in reverence. See *St. Sebastian's Church Kottiyoor Dedication of Newly Built Church Souvenir* and Jose Poovannikunnel (ed.), *Kutiyetta Janathayude Pithavu.*

42 A. K. Gopalan, "Anubhava Padangal", *Navayugam*, 9 September 1961, reported with the title "Irumbu Mara Neekkan Amaravathi Sahayichuvennu A.K. Gopalan", *Malayala Manorama*, 30 September 1961.

43 The church, in addition, often divulged the "communal element" behind the government's decision to evict, which was in contrast with their own "humane" and of course "secular intentions". To them Kottiyoor was a handiwork of NSS; Pulpally by RSS, Devi Seva Sangham and Vishva Hindu Parishath; and in Shimoga the RSS and the regional chauvinists.

44 Family planning was mooted in the context of excessive population growth in Kerala. It also represented Kerala's resolve to build a subnational developmental identity and to assert its self-made difference from other states. For a detailed discussion, see Devika (2002).

45 *Sathayadeepam* compared birth control to cholera, plague and suicide, dangerous evils the whole humanity should fear and fight against. See "Chodichal Parayam", *Sathyadeepam*, 2 May 1956, p. 9.

46 Speech of the bishop of Varapuzha, Most. Rev. Joseph Attippetti, reported in *Sathyadeepam*, 20 December 1961, p. 6.

47 "Chodichal Parayam", *Sathyadeepam*, 6 June 1956, p. 4.
48 Editorial notes, "Janana Niyandranathe Sambhandichu", *Sathyadeepam*, 30 December 1959, p. 6.
49 Most Rev. Joseph Attippetti, "Janana Niyandranam", *Sathyadeepam*, 20 December 1961, p. 6; editorial, "Janasanghya Vardhanavum Janana Niyandhranavum", *Sathyadeepam*, 8 October 1958, p. 6; editorial, "Janasanghyayecholli Vevalathippedendannu", *Sathyadeepam*, 18 March 1959, p. 6 and Mampilly (1963: 4).
50 "Vidyabhyasatheyum Kudumba Samvidhanatheyum Patti Acharya Vinoba", *Sathyadeepam*, 8 May 1957, p. 7.
51 V. P. Nair, "Vichithramaya Kudumbasoothranam", *Navayugam* 4(12), 4 September 1954, pp. 7–10. This has been the position of the Communists right from the 1930s, when they entered the political scene through peasant movements in Kerala.
52 See A. K. Gopalan, *Manninuventi*, pp. 33–41 and the report "Bhoomikku Vendiyulla Samaram", *Navayugam* 9(42), 27 March 1954, pp. 15–17. See, for instance, the resolution of the state meeting of the Communist Party held at Thrissur in 1956, where agrarian reforms and distribution of fallow and forest lands to the landless figure as two major items; "Puthiya Keralam Paduthuyarthan Communist Partiyude Nirdesangal", *Navayugam* 3(6–7), 14 July 1956, pp. 18–28.
53 Arguably, this position was also informed by a Communist self-projection as adhering to the essential moralities of family life, as against claims of ethical anarchy and bankruptcy with regard to family, sex and position of women (Damodaran 1953).
54 Eventually, the Communist Party had to come to terms with the slow pace of industrialization and land reclamation, and so embraced family planning as an effective means for Kerala's development (Devika 2002).

References

Aiya, V. N. 1906 [1999]. *Travancore State Manual*, Vol. 1. Trivandrum, Kerala Gazetteers.

Baak, P. E. 1997. *Plantation Production and Political Power: Plantation Development in South-West India in a Long-Term Historical Perspective, 1743–1963*. New Delhi: Oxford University Press.

Bayly, S. 1989 [1992]. *Saints, Goddesses and Kings: Muslims and Christians in South Indian Society, 1700–1900*. Cambridge: Cambridge University Press.

Damodaran, K. 1953. "Marxisavum Kudumba Jeevithavum." *Navayugam* annual issue: 117–127.

Dempsey, C. G. 2001. *Kerala Christian Sainthood: Collisions of Culture and Worldview in South India*. New Delhi: Oxford University Press.

Devika, J. 2002. "Domesticating Malayalees: Family Planning, The Nation and Home-Centred Anxieties in Mid-20th Century Keralam." CDS Working Paper 340. Trivandrum: Centre for Development Studies.

Devika, J., and V. J. Varghese. 2011. "To Survive or Flourish? Minority Rights and Syrian Christian Community Assertions in the 20th Century Travancore/Kerala." *History and Sociology of South Asia* 5(2): 103–128.

Drayton, R. 2005. *Nature's Government: Science, Imperial Britain, and the 'Improvement' of the World*. New Delhi: Orient Longman.

Foucault, M. 1982 [1986]. "Afterword: The Subject and Power." In *Michel Foucault: Beyond Structuralism and Hermeneutics*, edited by Hubert L. Dreyfus and Paul Rabinow, 206–226. Sussex, UK: Harvester Press.

George, T. K., and P. K. M. Tharakan. 1986. "Penetration of Capital into a Traditional Economy: The Case of Tea Plantations in Kerala, 1880–1950." *Studies in History* 2(2): 199–229.

Girideepam. 1966. "Viyarppinte Phalam" (editorial), *Girideepam* 5(9): March.

Gopalan, A. K. 1975 [1986]. *Manninuventi*. Trivandrum: Chintha Publications.

Guha, R. 1988. "On Some Aspects of the Historiography of Colonial India." In *Selected Subaltern Studies*, edited by Guha R and G. C. Spivak, 37–44. New Delhi: Oxford University Press.

1997. *Dominance without Hegemony: History and Power in Colonial India*. Cambridge, MA: Harvard University Press.

Hillariyon, Fr. J. 1967. "Niyandranamo Nirodhanamo?" *Sathyadeepam*, 6 September.

Jeffrey, R. 1976 [1994]. *The Decline of Nair Dominance; Society and Politics in Travancore: 1847–1908*. Delhi: Manohar.

Joseph, K. 1991. *Konippadikal*. Kozhikkode: Boby Books.

Kallidukkil, J. V. 1949 [1983]. *Kerala Suriyani Reethum Malabar Kutiyettavum*. Tellicherry: Vimala Press.

Karimattom, M., Devassy and Benny. 2004. *Oru Purappadinte Katha*. Tellicherry: Director Bible Apostolate.

Keraleeyan, K. A. 1997. *Keraleeyante Leghanangal*. Kozhikode: Keraleeyan Smaraka Samithi.

Kooiman, D. 1989. *Conversion and Social Equality in India: The London Missionary Society in South Travancore in the 19th Century*. New Delhi: Manohar.

Kunnel, Fr. J. 1965. "Anthar Samsthana Kutiyettam Oru Adiyanthira Aavasyam." *Girideepam* 5(6): 31.

Kunnel, Fr. J.. 1965a. "Shimogaye Parichayappeduka." *Girideepam* 5(5): 17–18.

1998. *Kutiyettakkarodoppam*. Kozhikkode: CMI St. Thomas Province.

Lemercinier, G., and F. Houtart. 1974. *The Church and Development in Kerala: Analysis of Developmental Activities of the Roman Catholic Church*. Kochi: Pastoral Orientation Centre.

Locke, J. 1960 [1988]. *Two Treatises of Government.*, edited by Peter Laslett. Cambridge: Cambridge University Press.

M. M. F, C. M. I. 1964. "Kutikayattam." *Girideepam* 3(12): 20.

Madhavan Pilla, P. P. R. 1956. "Thiru-Kochiyile Vanam Krishikkarude Samaram Oru Puthiya Ghattathil." *Navayugam* 3(6–8): 18–21.

Malabar Jubilee. 2000. *Mahajubliee Smaranika*. Calicut: Malankara Marthoma Suriyani Sabha, Malabar Diocese.

Mammen, K. V. 1992. *Malamkara Sabha Malabaril*. Kottayam: Kottackal Publishers.

Mampilly, S. G. 1963. "Prakriti Virudhamaya Janana Niyandrana Nayam." *Sathyadeepam*, April 3.

Matheckal, Fr. J. 1955. "Vaivahika Jeevitham." *Sathyadeepam*, May 4.

Menon, C. A. 1911 [1995]. *The Cochin State Manual*. Trivandrum: Kerala Gazetteers, 1995.

Mundadan, A. M. 1984. *History of Christianity in India*, Vol. 1. Bangalore: Theological Publications.

Nair, V. P. 1954. "Vichithramaya Kudumbasoothranam." *Navayugam* 4(12): 7–10.

Namboodiripad, E. M. S. 1954. "Kudumbasoothranam: Bhashya Prasna Pariharathinulla Papparaya Mudravakyam." Reprinted in *EMSinte Sampoorna Kritikal* 24: 85–100. Trivandrum: Chintha Publications.

Nechikkatt. 1966. "Mysore: Kuthichuyarunna Shimoga Colonikal." *Girideepam* 5(10): 7–9, 27.

Nedumkunnam, M. O. J. 1967. "Kutiyettam Chila Chinthakal." *Girideepam* 6(8): 11–13.

Oommen, M. A. 1971. *Land Reforms and Socio-economic Change in Kerala*. Madras: Christian Literature Society.

Palathumpad, G. 1964. "Krithrima Janana Niyandranavum Sambathika Samoohika Prasnangalum." *Sathyadeepam*, September 30.

Paul, C. K. 1961. "Janana Niyandranam." *Sathyadeepam* October 4: 4–5, 9.

Pazheparambil, T. 1964. "South Canara–Coorg Kutiyettam Thutarunnu." *Girideepam* 3(10): 13, 9.

1978. *Swapna Bhoomiyil*. Muvattupuzha: Mar Mathews Press.

Pinakkatt, S. 1964. "Brazil Kutiyettam." *Girideepam* 3(10): 9–10.

Poovannikunnel, J. (ed.). 1995. *Kutiyetta Janathayude Pithavu*. Thalassery: Catechetical Centre.

Prabhakaran, A. 1959. "Nammude Vanasambathu Engane Vardhippikkam." *Navayugam* 8(36): 23–24, 37–38.

Pulikkodan, Fr. J. 1965. "Catholikkarum Janana Nirodhanavum." *Girideepam* 5(3): 21–25.

Raman, R. K. 1997. "Global Capital and Peripheral Labour: Political Economy of Tea Plantations in Southern India *c*. 1850–1950." PhD diss., University of Kerala, Trivandrum: Centre for Development Studies.

Sathyadeepam. 1956. "Bharathavum Kudumba Samvidhanavum" (editorial), April 18.

1959. "Janana Niyandranathe Sambhandichu" (editorial), December 30.

1962. "Janana Niyandranathinte Chila Yadhartha Vasangal" (editorial), August 22.

1968. "Janana Niyandranathil Krithrimopadhikal Sweekaryamalla" (editorial), August 21.

Schmitt, Carl. 1985. *Political Theology: Four Chapters on the Concept of Sovereignty*, trans. George Schwab. Cambridge, MA: MIT Press.

Sivaswamy, K. G. T. S. Shastry, T. D. Nair, T. S. Nair, P. A. Narayanan, C. V. Narayana Aiyar, and Atzorri. 1945. *The Exodus from Travancore to Malabar Jungles*. Coimbatore: Servindia Kerala Relief Centre.

Thompson, E. P. 1963 [1980]. *The Making of the English Working Class*. London: Penguin.

Vadakkan, Fr. J. 1974. *Ente Kuthippum Kithappum*. Kottayam: Newman Publishers.

Valavoor, Z. 1995. *Malabarinoru Moses (A Moses for Malabar)*. Kottayam: Author.

Vallopilly, Mar, S. 1965. "Krithrima Janana Niyandranam Thikachum Asweekaryam." *Sathyadeepam*, July 28.

Vallopilly, Mar, S.. 1999. *Daivam Nammotukoode*. Thalassery: Author.

Varghese, T. C. 1970. *Agrarian Change and Economic Consequences: Land tenures in Kerala 1850–1960*. Bombay: Allied Publishers.

Varghese, V. J. 2006. "Memory as History: A Study of Peasant Migration in Kerala from Travancore to Malabar, 1920–1970." Unpublished PhD Diss., submitted to the University of Hyderabad.

2007. "The Alluring Music of Labour: Modernity, Migrations and Recreation of the Syrian Christian Community." *Tapasam* 2(3/4): 501–538.
2009. "Land, Labour and Migrations: Understanding Kerala's Economic Modernity." CDS Working Paper 420. Trivandrum: Centre for Development Studies.
Weber, M. 1992 [1930]. *The Protestant Ethic and the Spirit of Capitalism*. London: Routledge.
Zacharia, S. 1994. *Udaymperor Sunhadosinte Kanonakal*. Edamattam: Indian Institute of Christian Studies.

12 "The Globalization of Indifference": On Pope Francis, Migration and Global Acedia

Valentina Napolitano, University of Toronto

> The perfect life coincides with the legibility of the world, sin with the impossibility of reading it.
>
> Giorgio Agamben

> It was not enough to proclaim poverty to make Western capitalism's forms of living conditional on Christianity: it was necessary to practice poverty, to nourish it, as a revolution.[1]
>
> Toni Negri

In the long history of the papacy, Francis is the first pope from the Americas. On the night of his election, he referred to himself as the new bishop of Rome, wittily suggesting that "it seems my brother Cardinals have gone almost to the ends of the earth to get him."[2] Since the beginning of his papacy, Pope Francis has brought attention to the geographical margins of the Catholic Church in relation to the historical centrality of Rome's Catholic Curia. At the same time, his public rhetoric and actions seek to put those whom he sees as socially marginalized (undocumented immigrants, the poor, those living in the deprived peripheries of cities, those with disabilities and others) at the centre of an internal renewal of the Catholic Church. By envisioning an evangelization from the (geographical and social) fringes, he has sent a warning to the heart of the Roman Catholic Church and the Curia Romana: that a worldwide renewal of Catholicism can be engendered only by placing people who are marginal at the evangelical centre of the Church and by curbing the self-referentiality and thirst for power of the Roman Curia.

As the first non-European pope and standing for those, like himself, who are from the "ends of the earth", he gives visibility to concerns about poverty and inequality, which have a long and controversial history in the Catholic Church. With the choice of his papal name, Francis has drawn inspiration not only from his own religious order, the Society ("Company") of Jesus, but also from the strength of the theological stances and historical experiences of the cenobic orders (which, especially the Franciscans, stress communal monastic life) within the Catholic Church. The decision to celebrate an open daily mass, repeated breaches of papal public protocols (or papal liturgy), the choice to live in the modest Hostel of Domus Santa Marta (close to the Vatican, but outside its perimeters) instead of the papal apartments in the Vatican and the masterminding of an extraordinary synod on the family in autumn 2015 via an innovative system of parish-led consultations have been interpreted by media pundits as a challenge to a too-powerful Roman Curia.[3] This has also been read as a confrontation over the administrative office of the pope (which happened with Benedict XVI too, and some argue brought on his resignation in 2013). Most importantly, though, Francis is advancing an explicit critique of poverty based on particular theological understandings on property and proper ways of living a life (*modus vivendi*). Unlike his predecessor, Benedict XVI, Pope Francis is not interested in promoting a Catholic faith based on truth and moral duty against relativism and secularization of European societies, but on a renewed evangelization that places the socially marginal at the ethical centre of the Catholic Church.[4]

Reflecting on the apparent momentous changes taking place in the Catholic Church, in this chapter I develop two interconnected arguments. First, in light of Francis's reading of the shortcomings of capitalism and the "culture of indifference" it produces, I explore aspects of the evangelization of a group of Catholic Latin American migrants who converge around the Latin American Mission in Rome. Here the clergy promotes a Catholic catechesis that represents migrants as enduring a life of sacrifices, away for years on a stretch from their families and kin back home. In a context in which their labour rights – especially if undocumented immigrants – are often curtailed by the current Italian legislation on immigration, those migrants attending the Latin American Mission may try to play with the gaze of Catholic clerics. Some not only hope for godly protection, but also believe that by making themselves visible to the clergy as suffering migrants in need they will gain some privileged access to welfare resources that the Catholic Church provides. However, I also underscore the fact that migrants live complex lives and also seek a partial invisibility, keeping part of their lives away from the scrutiny of the Church and the state.

Second, I illustrate Pope Francis's critique of the "globalization of indifference" and anesthesia of the heart engendered by capitalism through his interventions on poverty and, in particular, on undocumented immigration. Francis's understanding of migration is a redefinition of an already existing position within the Catholic Church on the dignity of migrant life and the right to family reunification. He frames this within structures of global inequality – the outcome, that is, of capitalism's ethical failures. Likewise, his understanding of poverty builds on previous papal critiques of labour's exploitation and the individualism and moral relativism fostered by capitalism – yet he introduces a novel analysis of causes and outcomes. If capitalism has exacerbated inequalities among people and unequal geographies of distribution and mobility, its shortcomings manifest themselves as a sinful incapacity to see the suffering of others that, in turn, feeds into a progressive "globalization of indifference".

With these premises I will then argue that Francis's critique of capitalism's insensitivity to the suffering of people experiencing conditions of social marginality arches back to historical debates on the nature of Catholic monastic ethical regimes and, in particular, the sin of acedia (from the Greek *akēdia*, without care). Acedia refers here to a global incapacity to see and experience the world correctly, and I use this concept to underscore the bodily (theologically referred as "incarnated") tension between visibility and invisibility, which inform relationships between the Catholic Church and transnational migrants. That is, the *politics of visibility* championed by the pope, and the part of the Catholic Church that he represents, seek to reveal and turn into a public concern the (individual and collective) suffering of migrants, hitherto willfully concealed from mainstream society.

Yet, some migrants might embrace strategies that obscure the transparency of their lives, allowing them to live a *viveza criolla* (having a double life, as for instance, having sexual partners out of wedlock). My aim, then, is to understand Pope Francis's denunciation of a "globalization of indifference" in the light of monastic debates on the nature of attention, as well as of migrant strategies producing contextually different degrees of visibility or invisibility. Hence I focus on an intersection of religion and the market as an "heterogeneous assemblage" of forces (see the introduction to this volume) animated by theological underpinnings to embodied practices of visibility, invisibility, accumulation and loss, and their possible ethical reorientations. In this light, the anthropological study of contemporary Catholic, ethical personhood benefits from an analytic lens into a pre-Reformation Christianity, an angle underexplored in the burgeoning field of the Anthropology of Christianity.

Migrants and Missions

The notion of brotherly love is central to Pope Francis's engagement with immigration and a critique of capitalism and inequality. His interventions criticize the seduction of the gains of capitalism, underscoring the need to produce an ethical response to the inequalities it has exacerbated. Citing the parable of the Good Samaritan, Francis has argued that when we look away from "our brother half dead on the side of the road", we abdicate our ethical responsibilities.[5] By becoming indifferent and numbed to the suffering of others, we no longer care for them. Arriving in his first visit to Lampedusa in 2013 – the landing point for many migrant boats crossing from North Africa and site of countless tragic deaths, and chosen as the destination for his first extramural trip as a newly elected pope – Francis said:

> The culture of comfort, which makes us think only of ourselves, makes us insensitive to the cries of other people, makes us live in soap bubbles which, however lovely, are insubstantial; they offer a fleeting and empty illusion which results in indifference to others; indeed, it even leads to the globalization of indifference. In this globalized world, we have fallen into the globalization of indifference. We have become used to the suffering of others: it doesn't affect me; it doesn't concern me; it's none of my business![6]

With an increasing number of people dying while trying to reach its shores, the Italian island of Lampedusa has become an index in the media of a Mediterranean deathscape, the inevitable outcome of European Union politics on undocumented migration and asylum seeking to bolster a fortress Europe defined along colonial and postcolonial racial lines.[7] European borders act as governmental regimes that reclassify the space and practices that they entail (Green 2013: 349), while they also engender and spatially distribute racialized (immigrant) deaths and evolve around particular spectacles and mediatic modes (De Genova 2012; Albahari 2015).

Pope Francis and other critics in the Catholic Church (for instance Migrantes, a pastoral association of the Italian Bishop's Conference) have raised their voices against such a Mediterranean deathscape while Italian politicians and the government have launch a first military-humanitarian intervention called *Mare Nostrum* (2013–2014). In an uncanny and literal evocation of the Roman empire's control over the Mediterranean, this operation deployed Italian navy patrols along the coastal areas of southern Italy to rescue stranded migrant boats and clamp down on so-called human traffickers. By 2014 Operation Triton, a wider European Union (EU), still militarized operation of sea border control conducted by Frontex (the EU border security agency) had been launched. While the southern Mediterranean Sea has turned into a haunting graveyard, in Italy – as in other parts of the EU – debates on immigration and its governance are marred by heated political controversy.

In Italy, reforms of immigration legislation since the mid-1980s continue to privilege *ius sanguinis* over *ius solis*. For non-EU immigrants the path of obtaining and renewing a residency permit, and eventually acquiring citizenship, is arduous and ridden with difficulties.[8] It is within this landscape of contradictory and contingent legislation that Catholic Missions work with non-EU documented and undocumented immigrants in Rome, mostly from the Philippines and Latin America. In Italy, though, ethical and moral debates concerning immigration that involve and mobilize Church, state, political parties and civil society cannot be seen in isolation from the global role of the Catholic Church. At the same time, Pope Francis's current interventions, about the Mediterranean, but also on the erection of "walls" worldwide, not only draw from and emerge in dialogue with his predecessors' politics and theologies, but also underscore successive popes' power of influence in modern Italian and world politics.[9] Francis might be the pope from the "end" of the world, but he embodies the foundation of the Church as a global institution.

I have argued elsewhere that we need to understand Catholic Latin American migration in Rome as a part of a wider process that I have called the Atlantic Return, rooted in dynamics and anxieties generated by the Catholic conversion of the New World in the sixteenth century. The experiences and histories in Rome of priests, nuns and laity from the Americas challenge a Eurocentric Roman Catholic identity. Their experiences and devotions, inflected as they are by specific national trajectories and histories, are testimony to the multiple modalities of being Catholic, which inform gender, labour and sexuality at the heart of Roman Catholicism in Europe. This plurality of practices and orientations opposes the collective, singular call for pan-American unity of the Catholic faith promoted by Vatican pastoral teaching. In that sense, the Americas reorient Europe (Napolitano 2016). Moreover, some Latin American clergy narratives show that this return also strengthens a conservative core present in the Roman Catholic curia, which perceives a challenge, a reaction against the pluralization of modes of being Catholic emerging through migration (ibid.). Hence the intersection between Catholicism and transnational migration is a field of tension between "progressive" and "conservative" wings of the Church in Rome. Pope Francis is part of this Atlantic Return too and to explore his theology of poverty and "globalization of indifference", we need to think him also as an index of this Atlantic Return – almost a "too-good-example" of it (Kaell, 2016).

The majority of Latin American migrants attending the Latin American Mission in Rome are single women working in the care industry as *badanti.*[10] Men are present too, but in smaller numbers[11] ; it is those who are unable to find work in the construction industry who find work in the care of the elderly. The physical structure of the church provides a space where migrants can meet and access jobs offered by Roman families looking for *badanti*, house cleaners, caregivers for the elderly or child minders. In a way, the headquarters of the Mission – located in the parish of Santa Maria della Luce, in the central Roman neighbourhood of Trastevere – acts as a job centre.

Migrants' invisibility is a concern for Catholic evangelization. Immigrants are engaged by the Scalabrian priests,[12] who coordinate the Latin American Mission in Rome, as providers of services in which the immaterial labour of love is central. This is a niche in the caring industry, where (mainly female) immigrants work in the intimate spaces of Italian family life, especially to look after the elderly. The priests are vocal against the abuses that more often than not weigh on the badanti"s work; *lavoro nero* (illicit economy) is chided not because the income of the immigrant is not taxed, but because it comes with no statutory benefits for the workers.

Both female and male migrants, especially "living-in" badanti who are normally allowed time off only on Thursday afternoons and Sundays, frequently argue that they are, and feel, invisible, excluded from wider Italian society. Women in particular feel they are not as well dressed as many Roman women, and complain that they are invisible to (well-mannered) Italian men.[13] Yet invisibility may not be always and exclusively produced by Italian society's unwillingness to "see" the marginal (at times "de-sexualized") migrant Other. It can also be a way to make oneself less visible to the state. Hence a priestly calling to a particular devotional and suffering identity for Catholic Latin American migrants makes sense in light of a specific historical conjuncture for the larger Catholic Church on the promotion of the New Evangelization, this same call is challenged by local practices. Making oneself more or less visible can be a strategy to negotiate particular interpellations (as calling into being a particular from of migrant subjectivity and personhood)[14] by the priests and nuns to obtain better access to resources (employment placements, food supply and small cash sums that the priests in charge of the Mission can sometime give out to help in particular cases).

Latin American migrants attending the Catholic mission can also play up an image of suffering to negotiate better working conditions and wages.[15] This is sometime acted out by those who claim either to have just arrived in Rome, or to have suffered a particular personal setback, an unexpected loss of employment. Some would claim to be willing to work as live-in caregivers, but once they are offered the job through the Church, they then ask to renegotiate working conditions, often refusing to live full-time with the employer. These negotiations bring together or mediate interests that, at best, run parallel to each other: the Church whose mission is to look after the spiritual and practical welfare of immigrants; prospective employers who turn to the Church to find trustworthy household help; and the migrants themselves, who are looking for work in a rather precarious and exploitative labour market. Bringing together prospective employers and employees and managing the expectations of each is a source of constant anxiety for the priests in the Mission. They often feel that migrants cannot be trusted to fulfil the expectations of families looking for domestic help – suddenly demanding better working conditions or leaving their job without any warning and, in doing so, ruining the reputation of the parish. Nonetheless, the Mission priests are extremely critical of those families who unashamedly target migrants as a source of cheap and unprotected domestic labour.

At stake in the complex negotiations among clergy, migrants and prospective employers are strategies of simultaneous concealment and foregrounding of different migrant subjectivities, and of their public representation and display. The Latin American Mission becomes the stage for playing out complex dramas and personae. Take, for instance, Santa Maria in Via, a twelfth-century basilica close to the famous Trevi Fountain, in the heart of Rome. Together with a network of seventeen other parishes, this church was selected by the Vicariate of Rome as the main centre for the Ecuadorian Catholic migrant community in the capital. The Latin American Mission network, established in 2003 by the dioceses of Rome after a recommendation of John Paul II, provides a space for different Latin American and Caribbean communities to meet regularly, organize activities and gather around the celebrations of particular national patron saints throughout the year. Over time, the Ecuadorian Catholic community has been led by different Ecuadorian priests, mostly diocesans sent to Rome for educational training at different pontifical universities in the capital.

Regular meetings are held on Sunday afternoons in the refectory of the Church, after the celebration of the Spanish mass, for a group of normally around thirty Ecuadorian immigrants, mostly single women working in the care industry. These meetings include an evangelization session (reading out a selection from the New or Old Testament or collective reflections on the passages read by the priest during the mass). This is followed by an hour or so dedicated to fostering fellowship (accompanied by provision of non-alcoholic beverages and light snacks), when events in connection to national and religious festivities may be planned. Concrete support and help are also extended, from organizing collections of funds to repatriate the body of a deceased migrant, to exchanging clothes or sharing information about jobs in Italian families. Evangelization taking place in Santa Maria in Via – and in the Latin American Mission at large – starts from the premise that (Catholic) Latin America is *el continente de la esperanza* (the continent of hope), and that Catholic faith is what unites immigrants, making them siblings (*lo que nos hermana*). However, creating brotherhood, making people siblings, is an ongoing process, often rife with conflicts that are not only personal but also the outcome of regional differences in the country of origin and the unspoken racial and class categories that are reproduced in the immigrant community in Rome.[16]

In a meeting in May 2006, for instance, the then-Ecuadorian ambassador, Francisco Salazar Alvarado, participated in the Sunday meeting to celebrate and remember the one hundredth anniversary of the miracle of the Ecuadorian *Virgen Dolorosa*, or *Virgen de los Ojos*. The story goes that a representation of the *Virgen Dolorosa* or *Nuestra Señora de los Dolores*[17] hanging in the San Gabriel's Jesuit convent of Quito, was a site of a miraculous manifestation. On 20 April 1906, in the presence of a group of young devotees, the Virgin started to move her eyes, *opening and closing her eyelids*. In response to this divine manifestation, so the story goes, the youth and the priest immediately gathered in prayer, and later the miracle was interpreted by the church as a sign that Ecuadorian youth carried the awe and the purity of Catholics as national subjects.

In Ecuador, as in many Latin American countries, the early part of the twentieth century was a period of confrontation between state and Church over the definition of the role and powers of the Catholic Church in public life. The newly formed Ecuadorian state and republic was championing secular-liberal values that the Church perceived as anticlerical in nature. Curtailing the public display of the glory of the Catholic Church de facto promoted a privatization of Catholic faith. In the midst of such an intense and acrimonious confrontation, the miraculous protection of Catholic youth extended by the *Virgen Dolorosa* became a rallying call to defend and foster Catholic education in Ecuador. Pope Pius XII coronated this Virgin in 1956 and in 1985 John Paul II made her the patron of education.[18]

Some hundred years after the manifestation, in a gathering at the back of the church of Santa Maria in Via on a rainy Sunday afternoon, the ambassador addressed a group of gathered Ecuadorian migrants:

> We need to get back to the Virgin de los Ojos, to recover the values that have been lost, to get back to a moral principle, what is good and what is bad. With her eyes the virgin signals us, she warns us to strengthen the family – as the Vatican tells us. We need an education, and Catholic educations to recoup her strength [of the Virgin]...Education is the only thing that can save us, not only the prayer but also the actions as we are all responsible of the Church taking the responsibility to fulfil our obligations (*nuestro deber*). And also as migrants, as it was one hundred years ago, we need to fight for the education and the strengthening of the Church (*la fortaleza de al Iglesia*). Her eyes always see us...

Calls to mobilize Catholic Latin American migrants as the new evangelizers in a Catholic Europe threatened by secularism and anticlericalism, and their representation as the strength of the Church, are well-rehearsed themes in these missionary fora in Rome. However, there are multiple ways in which Latin American migrants see and live this imagined Catholicism vis-à-vis a perceived secularization happening in Europe. I want to pursue here an angle on this image of the Virgen Dolorosa and the connection that the Church has made between the purity of the Ecuadorian children and the aspired purity of Ecuadorian immigrants in Rome, the geopolitical centre of Catholicism. A complex nexus of faith, histories, revelations and concealments connects the catechesis with the everyday life of migrants. Let me explain further the ambiguity of this nexus between modalities of visibility, invisibility and immigration.

A few weeks before the meeting attended by the Ecuadorian ambassador, the congregation had collected donations to repatriate the dead body of a well-known and very active Ecuadorian migrant who had been run over by a bus while crossing the road. Marta, the lay leader of the group at the time, explained to the congregation that she had been killed by *un apuro* (a rush): the deceased was rushing to get to her next cleaning job in time. The constant running and lack of time was killing people like her. In the congested roads of Rome, public transport can be very slow, and low-paid migrants need more than one job – often in different parts of the city – to be able to save enough money to send remittances back home. The bus driver had not "seen" her while she was crossing and "did not even stop". Marta's account ended with words often repeated by Ecuadorian migrants in Rome: we need to "trabajar como negro para vivir como blanco" (work as a black [that is, work very hard] person, to live as a white person).

To many Ecuadorian migrants – the majority of them women – attending the Latin American Mission, time seems to either stretch or contract with equal ease. The woman who had died in the bus accident – and whose two children live with relatives in Ecuador – was killed because she was running late; she didn't have enough time to move between jobs. Migrant women are under extreme pressure to increase their working schedule. One badly paid job as a badante alone is not enough either to meet Rome's costs of living or to send enough remittances to support children and family left in Ecuador. But for these women time can also be painfully slow.

Magda, a Peruvian migrant in her mid-forties with two grown children living in the outskirts of Lima, recalls that she had lived for more than two years as the only carer of an elder Italian lady who was totally housebound. Magda was living with her in a third floor flat, "taking care also of the plants". She remembers that she stared at the clock in the kitchen the whole time: "I felt", she said, that "I was going mad with boredom." The *nonita* (endearing diminutive for grandmother) used to ask her to put on the coffee just before going out for her (half) free day on Thursday afternoon, a ruse for delaying her leaving the house. Although she no longer worked there after the lady passed away, she recalled the painful stretching of time in that flat. She had even approached the Mission priest for advice on how to endure such a slow pace of life, when time would not pass. The priest told her that it was a sacrifice, in the same way as the Virgin Mary had seen her child slowing dying on the cross. For the priest the badante's work was a form of sacrificial and sanctifying labour. Migration is hardly conceived by priests as an emancipatory, female choice, but more as a sacrificial act endured in the name of a family and children left back home. However, Magda was still terribly bored and remembered she felt like crying all the time, confessing to the priest later that his words did not help her to alter the slow pace of her working days.

If migrants' time is experienced as extending and compressing in multiple ways, the language of the Catholic Church often stresses the "endurance" necessary to cope and to remain a reliable support for the Italian elderly left in the care of immigrant badanti. Needless to say, this sacrificial rhetoric functions towards a reproduction of labour much needed in Italian society, where demographic changes, residential patterns, as well as an increasing female presence in the labour market contribute to a reduced possibility to care for the elderly people by family members. Hence everyday practices of immigrant labour working in the caring sector entail subtle strategies and techniques to cope with the rhythms of living and to fit in the intimate routines of their employers' time. Many of these women feel that while they become hypervisible in the domestic spaces where they work, they remain invisible in public places. In some circumstances, some of them may actively try to foster invisibility to escape the attentions of immigration officials or police, and yet they might also make themselves visible as a migrant in need to procure charitable aid from the clergy.

The contextual and tactical deployment of modalities of (partial) visibility is the expression of what Latin American migrants call in different (but somehow always derogatory) ways, a *viveza criolla.* This is the term used among migrants to define a way of living in which one's predicaments are regularly presented as much worse than they actually are. This might take many forms, from claiming to have arrived in Italy recently while in fact having been in the country for a considerable length of time to approaching the church for financial help to make up for loss of money or goods stolen in fictional thefts. These apparently mendacious stories help migrants to get access to small amounts of money and to receive food and groceries from the parish, or to find quickly a badante job in an Italian family. Viveza criolla is also used to describe those migrant men who court or have relations with women without disclosing their married status, or the existence of a wife and children back home. The cunning practices of the streetwise migrant-trickster, then, undermine a current Catholic Church rhetoric that represents migrants solely as "passive" suffering victims of exploitation, moved by the pious wish of family reunification. There is far more "shrewdness" in the lives of Catholic migrants than the Catholic Church and its clergy are prepared to openly acknowledge.

Pope Francis and the "Globalization of Indifference"

The politics informing the articulation of practices of visibility amongst (Latin American) immigrants in Italy are complex and contradictory. They are as much the outcome of an immigration legislative language (which makes the process of acquiring citizenship cumbersome for non-EU immigrants) as they are about a discourse of the Catholic Church, which supports undocumented migrants in their path toward legalization of their status and improved working conditions. The Church's pastoral teaching toward migrants pivots around carefully enduring the difficulties of migration in a path of suffering for migrants – with a teleological horizon in migrants' family reunification. Caring for others is also highlighted as a central practice that enables the constitution of the Latin American Mission as a "home" for the migrants, a sacred space for extending mutual support and to receive God's care. From the priests' perspective, divine care will extend back into the workplace, to the intimacy of the employers' life. If the gift and duty of care makes for both good Catholic subjects and disciplined workers, what does it mean to be "uncaring" in this Catholic and migrant domain? Does uncaring thrive on invisibility? To understand the intersection between the Catholic Church and transnational migration we need to consider the broader politics and strategies of visibility at stake.

Pope Francis's condemnation of global poverty, and his stress on the importance of the dispossessed and those who are perceived to be at the margins of society, is located in a long tradition of Catholic thought and action on the relation among labour, charitable love and the economy. There is a wealth of interventions on and interpretations of the social teaching of the Catholic Church, starting from Pope Leo XIII's encyclical *Rerum Novarum* (1891). In this influential encyclical, the pope articulated a wider theological understanding of poverty not as a sin, but as a condition of life from which the whole of humanity should be eventually relieved. And yet, the encyclical also suggested that if the poor could draw sustenance from a strong Catholic faith, they could endure poverty with dignity. In a condition of divine–human exchange, this theology underscored that by drawing from the example of Christ's poverty, humanity at large could become richer. Jesus' sacrifice and his redemption of human sin can engender a brotherly, human love, and yet still be an expression of a divine or transcendental presence.

It is in John XXIII's encyclical *Mater et Magistra* (1961) that poverty is conceived for the first time as the outcome of unequal distribution of wealth and exploitation of labour resulting from global relations between developed and underdeveloped nations. Some years later, in one of the four Apostolic Constitutions of the Second Vatican Council, *Gaudiem et Spes* (1963–1978), poverty does not relate solely to unequal distribution of wealth between nations. Here the causes of global poverty are attributed to lack of freedom, breaches of human rights and violations of the dignity of labour. Reflecting the emergence of novel political sensibilities, in a later encyclical, *Populorum Progressio* (1967), Paul VI (1963–1978) went even further by calling for a reduction of global poverty via the fostering of economic growth in underdeveloped countries. By then, for the Church, the alleviation from poverty not only consolidated individual dignity, but also represented a collective recognition of a fundamental human right.

It is under the leadership of John Paul II (1978–2005) – who was highly critical of communist and socialist ideologies of social redistribution and equality – that poverty becomes the consequence of individual attachment to "selfish wealth".[19] Poverty is framed here as an impoverishment of, and constraint on human existence and moral life. For John Paul II it is not the nature of private property that is under question, but the evils of "*socialismo reale*" (actual socialism).[20] Poverty should be lessened through a renewal of forms of subsidiarity – whereby the family and the Church engender the cultivation of individual moral virtues – and charitable love.[21] Eventually, under Benedict XVI's papacy (2005–2013) – and in the context of growing concerns about globalization, structural adjustments and policies of economic liberalization – debates on poverty within the Catholic hierarchy returned to a critique of capital accumulation, consumerism and global inequality. For Benedict that is a "scandal of glaring inequalities" (Benedict XVI, 2009).

Whilst we can discern, then, a degree of continuity in modern Catholic theologies concerning the nature of wealth and its accumulation, Pope Francis is adding novel nuances to the debate. Take for instance his first papal exhortation, *Evangeli Gaudiuum* (2013), in which he argues that

> Human beings are themselves considered consumer goods to be used and then discarded. We have created a "throw away" culture, which is now spreading. It is no longer simply about exploitation and oppression, but something new. Exclusion ultimately has to do with what it means to be a part of the society in which we live; those excluded are no longer society's underside or its fringes or its disenfranchised – they are no longer even a part of it. The excluded are not the "exploited", but the outcast, the "leftovers". In this context, some people continue to defend trickle-down theories which assume that economic growth, encouraged by a free market, will inevitably succeed in bringing about greater justice and inclusiveness in the world [.…] to sustain a lifestyle which excludes others, or to sustain enthusiasm for that selfish ideal, a globalization of indifference has developed. Almost without being aware of it, we end up being incapable of feeling compassion at the outcry of the poor, weeping for other people's pain, and feeling a need to help them, as though all this were someone else's responsibility and not our own.[22]

Focusing on the moral shortcomings produced by an uncaring culture of greed, Francis brings attention to those who have become the disposable jetsam and flotsam of free market capitalism, and its economy (and ontology) of waste. The poor have been turned into non-persons, to use Gustavo Gutiérrez's (1983) words, that is, people who are deemed insignificant or invisible in a terrain whose distribution remains variable: a certain type of economic affluence has made some (poor) people invisible, while others have become stuck in their responsiveness to the world.[23]

Francis's position on poverty arches back to the thinking of a group of Jesuit scholars which includes Michel de Certeau (1925–1986),[24] Karl Rahner (1904–1984), Henri de Lubac (1896–1991) and the Argentinean Juan Carlos Scannone (b. 1931). Denouncing the "narcissistic and authoritarian elitism"[25] of a part of the Church – a critique borrowed from Henri de Lubac's account of the historical importance of the clergy's poverty – Francis has underscored two contradictory orientations of the Catholic Church. One part of the Church is oriented towards the wider world and celebrates the glory of God through evangelization; another part of this same Church may suffer the sin of "spiritual worldliness", whereby the clergy becomes inward looking and self-referential. For Lubac and Francis there is a potential for corruption in this latter expression, which is perceived as too anthropocentric, too focused on an earthly, mundane glory. For Francis, in particular, this Church's self-referential focus on human and personal glory precludes living the mystery and divine glory encapsulated in the experience of poverty. And poverty, also following the inspiration of Juan Carlos Scannone, becomes one of the main hinges of Francis's evangelization.[26]

Pope Francis's critique of the "globalization of indifference" goes alongside a "globalization of solidarity" centred on the everyday lives of the poor that Scannone theorized in the late 1990s, when Pope Francis (as Jorge Mario Bergoglio) was the Archbishop of Buenos Aires.[27] The poor show a *vivens homo* that can be a real alternative and renewed way to live the presence of God in the world.[28] Moreover, a critique of the "globalization of indifference" cuts across lay and clerical domains, for indifference is not a sin exclusive to the secular world.

Pope Francis's focus on *inequalities* of distribution of wealth, rather than the relief of poverty as such, envisages a Catholic ethics hinging on the critique of the sin of inequality. As explained earlier, Pope Francis's call to see all people in the world who are marginal in their society as the core of the Catholic Church has a genealogy into a twentieth-century theology that rethinks the role of the poor in Latin America indeed as motors of divine and human history. In this perspective, Latin American poor are viewed as the theologically renewed heart of the Church. Doctrinally, a (poor) Latin American Catholic subject is critically inserted at the heart of a global reanimation of the Roman Catholic Church. This is a reanimation, a renewed articulation of a vector of affects moving in two directions. One is from within its Roman core (as the part of the Church that Pope Francis champions from Rome); the other is an outside movement directed inward (renewing the same Vatican curial core from the perspective of the Latin American poor).

Catholic Latin American migrants in Rome, from *el continente de la esperanza*, often perceive themselves as invisible to the larger Italian society, and yet in Francis theology they constitute an imagined embodied hope for the renewal of the Catholic Church's centre. Theological subjects, though, do not always coincide with ethnographic subjects; everyday practices and politics concerning the visibility/invisibility of immigrants are ridden with tensions. Migrants attending the Latin American Catholic Mission in Rome play with their being seen in certain ways, not always to their disadvantage. They are part of economies of care, often enwalled and out of view, yet they are also the producers and the consumers of a thriving migrant entertainment industry in the capital around Latin American music and sport celebrations. During these events food and other goods are sold without the control of municipal authorities, and often alcohol flows easily, demonstrating, in the eyes of the local Italian population, the "incivility" of migrants (Napolitano 2016). Hence migrants in these contexts may not always want to be visible to state authorities, nor are they the "suffering subjects" that much of Catholic mission's catechesis portrays them to be. Subjective migrant practices reveal a degree of ambivalence that exceeds the practices of visibility enforced by the state (Mezzadra 2010). Yet, this ambiguity, I argue, should also be understood through a political theology informed, in the case of migration and return missions, by a long durée of (Catholic) histories (Napolitano 2016).

Moreover, narratives crop up of Latin American men being in sexual relationships in Rome without disclosing the existence of a family back home. Some women attending the Latin American Mission talk about the tricks of certain men, taking advantage of lonely women. Women, however, also talk about other, predatory, women who go after men they know are married back home, creating incurable cleavages. So if gendered betrayal may be de facto heightened in this context of migration, out-of-wedlock relations are actively "hidden" from view by migrants vis-à-vis a Church that visibilizes "good," family-devoted Catholics and suffering migrants.

If Pope Francis calls for a new visibility of the suffering migrant, there is more agency to migrants and migrant modes of living than acknowledged by everyday practices of Catholic catechesis towards migration. In fact, a tension between visibility and invisibility is at the core of a long theological reflection on a particular sin in Catholic practice, the sin of acedia.

On Global Acedia

There is a final connection I want to draw in the remainder of the chapter between poverty, social marginality – both experienced by many undocumented migrants in Italy – and Pope Francis's theological critique of capitalism as an embodied sin.

While in Weber's classic analysis faith is expressed as a received vocation in the world, where human actions become a mere orientation, a tool of God in the world, and capitalism an index of God's right orientation in it, Pope Francis stresses instead a world and its economic system as God's vessel – not the Lord's paramount expression. For Catholicism the incarnation of God in the human world is a central principle, and this principle has, of course, a long and nuanced history of calibrations in the trajectory of Catholic pre- and post-Reformation theologies.

In light of an anthropological exploration of possible presences of past histories and Catholic *modus vivendi*, I propose a reading of Pope Francis's interventions on current poverty as a combination of these pre- and post-Reformation theological sensibilities.[29] More specifically, I wish to address Pope Francis's call against a "globalization of indifference" through a pre-Reformation reading of the sin of acedia, and post-Reformation theological elaborations on the centrality of brotherly love. Acedia, in some of its medieval understandings, is an embodied incapacity to see or to respond to the world. It resonates, I argue, with Francis's critique of indifference to global suffering, an embodied sinful disposition that underscores deficiencies of brotherly love and a lack of equal relations of exchange under contemporary capitalism.

Acedia is a multifaceted affect with a complex history. Broadly speaking, up to the twelfth century it related to a monastic world and to a temporal and spatial lack of response in practices of God's devotion. From the thirteenth century onwards, acedia began to index a neglect of religious duties, which resonates with modern and contemporary understandings. In the writings of Alcuin (799–800), a Yorkshire scholar,[30] acedia is portrayed as a monastic shortcoming of "spiritual dryness", akin, to some extent, to *tristitia* (a multifaceted affect understood as sadness and depression) (Wenzel 1966: 92). In the writings of St. Pier Damiani (1007–1072), an Italian Doctor of the Church,[31] acedia is a habit that hinders the *principalia vitia*, the rules of monastic life.

Acedia then should be "attacked," with precise instructions on how to change bodily practices such as prayers, nocturnal sleeps and physical work. In Damiani's reading, acedia is translated and manifested in the "heaviness of the eyelids" (ibid: 83), a common problem for many monks, often strongly condemned by abbots. In early monastic writings, then, acedia is an embodied state that not only denotes a lack of awareness to the world, but is also a form of being in the world that requires rectification via renewed application in daily routines. But even in the words of the fourth-century Evagrius of Pontius (345–399 AD) – a Christian ascetic who lived in Egypt and Constantinople[32] –acedia is discussed as a faulty affective response to the world, rather than an interior quality of the spirit, which is a quality that acedia will acquire later:

> The one afflicted with acedia yawns a lot and readily drifts off into sleep; he rubs his eyes and stretches his arms; turning his eyes away from the book, he stares at the wall and again goes back to reading for awhile; leafing through the pages, he looks curiously for the end of the texts, he counts the folios and calculates the number of gatherings. Later, he closes the book and puts it under his head and falls asleep, but not a very deep sleep. (Agamben 2013: 27)

It is only later, from the Fourth Lateran Council (1215–1216) and the establishment of scholastic theology, that acedia begins to matter to life outside the monastery. Within an emerging confessional and penitent regime of Christian living in the world, acedia then begins to connect to a sense of sadness (*tristitia*) and torpor and it begins to be "laicized" as a vice. From a monastic affect of spiritual dryness, acedia extends to a Christian layman's neglect of duties.

In contemporary times, psychoanalysts have read an increasingly "interiorized" understanding of acedia as a root of modern melancholia and boredom (Phillips 1994). However, I would like to stay with a fourth-century monastic and ascetic understanding of *acedia as a relation-to-the world* rather than an inward sin. In this early definition, acedia is a habit of (in)attention and an incapacity of relating to the world, rather than a failure of internalization of Christian moral principles. Pope Francis's evocation of Franciscan roots of poverty and his critique of capitalism as a globalization of indifference should be read, I suggest, alongside these different aspects of acedia: both an inward-felt sin and an incapacity to see God's manifestations and take action in the world to rectify it. The habit, or better the sin, of not seeing the world as it stands, to have the eyelids closed to the world (as God's creation), is very much with us and for Pope Francis it is ingrained in capitalism, a distorted form of *oekinomia.*[33]

In the Catholic theology that Pope Francis champions, capitalism has produced an affective and (un)ethical response to the world that has desensitized people to God's presence and has brought them to not see the suffering and presence of the Other (as an embodiment of the divine presence). I suggest then that Pope Francis directs a powerful critique against a form of alienation from sociality induced by acedia that rests on a long history of ethical and affective Church teaching on forms of living in the world and human responses to God's presence.[34]

As with early monks suffering from acedia, the global acedia of capitalism requires to be "attacked" with work, to awaken from a state of torpor – in Francis's understanding, awakening and "seeing" the reality of multiple and equally existing forms of living. Returning to Evagrius of Pontius, his cure for acedia consisted in an array of bodily dispositions, practices of *memorias mortis* (remembering the dead) and midnight prayers, so much so that an historical interpretation reads, "...the baffling array of acedia's signs stems from underlying social strain between the institutionally supported goals of a society and the capacities of its members to achieve them" (Crislip 2005: 169).

Pope Francis's take on current global poverty as an effect of a "globalization of indifference" is in subtle continuity with some of these early monastic understandings. What I have called here global acedia, then, is an index that articulates the current, failing global political economy with a longstanding sinful practice of misguided (ethical) attention: an oekonomia based on an (un)ethical practice of uncaring and invisibility. This conjuncture impels, for Francis and the Church he stands for, a call for different forms of living together, as well as different forms of seeing. To combat the *acedia* of global capitalism (and the politics of undocumented migration and poverty it has produced) requires, in Francis's eyes, a (political) transformation of *modus vivendi* – a different ethical practice of seeing and responding to the world as it stands. Yet, I have argued that there is a tension between visibility and invisibility that runs through Catholic Church pastoral practices towards transnational (mainly undocumented) migration, which problematizes Francis's position.

If migrants and their suffering should be seen, cared for and acknowledged by society at large, some migrants do not want to be in full view – not only when their public behavior may be read as "uncivil," but also while seeking out-of-wedlock relations in Rome. Hence, migrants strategically play with different forms of visibility and invisibility, as they go about shaping their lives in different forms, not always embraced by a Catholic catechesis. For some their *viveza criolla* is strategically hidden from view, for it not only stands in the way of being a good Catholic but is also a navigation into a complex, transnational, contingent and sexualized modus vivendi emerging out of particular market conditions and state regimes.

A "poor" Catholic theological subject and the visibility/invisibility of transnational migrants' tactics and strategies are informed by market forces, papal positions on the social doctrine of the Church, as well as hope for an embodied reorientation of ethical practices. If acedia and "the globalization of indifference" both entail particular dispositions towards the distractions of materialism, the perspective onto the intersection of religion, transnational migration and market forces, that I have offered here, articulates everyday practices, reorientations of sin, and the theological underpinnings that are part, not beyond, of multiple, coexisting modus vivendi.

Notes

1 Author's translation from Italian: "Non bastava tuttavia proclamare la povertà, per subordinare al cristianesimo le forme di vita dell'Occidente capitalista: occorreva praticare la povertà, nutrirla, come una rivoluzione" (Negri 2013).

2 www.news.va/en/news/pope-francis-his-first-words.

3 For the final 2015 Report drawn by the Synod of the Bishops see www.vatican.va/roman_curia/synod/documents/rc_synod_doc_20151026_relazione-finale-xiv-assemblea_en.html.

4 As I discuss further, this is not to say that Benedict XVI was oblivious during his papacy to issues of poverty and marginality, but that those issues are much more central to Pope Francis's current mobilization of the Church.

5 Pope Francis, Homily in Lampedusa on 8 July 2013, http://w2.vatican.va/content/francesco/en/homilies/2013/documents/papa-francesco_20130708_omelia-lampedusa.html.

6 Ibid.

7 Please note that this article analyzes political conjunctures within a period until winter 2015.

8 The still-enforced 2002 Bossi–Fini law requires non-EU immigrants seeking labour and residency in Italy to hold, within eight months from the entry in Italy, a *contratto di soggiorno*, that is, an employment guarantee offered by an Italian

resident employee or firm. In other words, acquisition of residency rights is directly connected to proof and renewal of a labour contract with an Italian employer. Acquisition of citizenship is connected to the capacity to demonstrate continuous contracts of employment and residency over a period of ten years.

9 See Pope Francis's intervention on a prospective US/Mexican wall's construction by potential US presidential Republican nominee Donald Trump: www.bbc.com/news/election-us-2016-35607597.

10 This is a legal term used to define those who care for older or impaired people. The majority of *badanti* in Italy are women and immigrant labour, and they often live in the houses of those they care for.

11 As of 2012, Latin American immigration constituted 7.7 percent of all the immigration in Italy for an overall more than 350,000 people clustered in and around major urban centres such as Genoa, Milan and Rome. The fieldwork through which my research developed was carried out over repeated trips between 2005 and 2012. The core of my research was originally the Latin American Mission, but by the end of my fieldwork the research also involved clergy who were not connected to this group.

12 The Scalabrinian order was founded in 1895 by the Italian Giovanni Battista Scalabrini originally to care for poor Italian migrants migrating to North America at the turn of the twentieth century. It now has Fathers working around the world, but especially in the Philippines, Australia and in the Americas. It is the only order within the Catholic Church exclusively dedicated to the care of migrants.

13 Immigrants may gather for entertainment in Latin American restaurants or, on Sundays, in a few bars across the capital. There is, of course, an entertainment industry thriving among different national clusters, and championed by a proliferation of different civic migrant associations in Rome.

14 I use the word interpellation in an Althusserian sense via Povinelli's work on the limits of the liberal state's politics of minority recognition. That is the idea that minority identities within state discourse are shaped by the means through which different minority subjects are called to participate and partake of particular legal rights and duties (Povinelli 2002, 2006).

15 For different analytical and ethnographic engagements with gendered transnational migration, suffering and labor markets, see Mahdavi (2011); Sayad (2004); Napolitano Quayson (2005); Keough (2006).

16 Historically Latin American Catholicism has been fractured by antagonisms between the Church and (often anti-clerical) liberal-informed Latin American nations/states. Contemporary spaces within the Latin American Mission at times re-narrativize these pasts.

17 This is a representation of the Virgin drawn with her heart struck by seven bodkins, her left hand pierced by three nails from Jesus' cross, and the right holding a crown.

18 A Virgin coronation is a canonical act by a pope, supported by a papal bull, wherein the Roman Catholic Church recognizes an image of the Virgin Mary under a specific name being venerated in a certain locality.

19 John Paul II, *Solicitudo Rei Socialis* (1987).

20 John Paul II, *Centesimus Annus* (1991).

21 Ibid.

22 http://w2.vatican.va/content/francesco/en/apost_exhortations/documents/papa-francesco_esortazionc-ap_20131124_evangelii-gaudium.html.

23 Again in the words of Francis: "The culture of prosperity deadens us; we are thrilled if the market offers us something new to purchase. In the meantime all those lives stunted for lack of opportunity seem a mere spectacle; they fail to move us" (Francis 2013, *Evangelii Gaudium*).

24 Pope Francis draws on the early work of Michel de Certeau on the mystics Peter Faber (1506–1546) – the contemporary of Francis Xavier, the co-founder with Ignacio de Loyola of the Society of Jesus – and Jean- Joseph Surin (1600–1665). De Certeau defines Faber as "the reformed priest" who brought together mystical experiences and new forms of missionary work for the expansion of the Church. Rather that reading mysticism as an inner space, de Certeau interprets it as a practice that breaks with existing rhetoric and regimes of intelligibility. This mystic embodies the presence of the Other, the outsider or stranger who deploys his Otherness to challenge systems of power and thought. De Certeau's analysis of the productiveness of the social Other (of which mystics are examples) has inspired Pope Francis's present formulation of the centrality of those who are deemed marginal to society, not only for the renewal of the Catholic Church but also to engender global transformations.

25 *Evangelii Gaudium*, p. 76.

26 Juan Carlos Scannone is an Argentinian Jesuit theologian contemporary and friend of Francis who has had great influence on the Pope's words and actions. Scannone's reflections constitute a radical rethinking of the poor and the centrality of a theology of the poor to the New Evangelization. For Scannone the *irrupción de los pobres* (emergence of the poor) in Latin America is both a message of God incarnated in the flesh of Jesus (with his aliveness in the condition of the poor) and a human historical conjuncture that impels a rethinking of ethical imperatives. Instead of rehearsing a celebration of the *Gloria Dei* (the symbolic and the hierophantic tradition of the Church's teaching) the poor are theologically and historically a new *form of presence* in a global society that needs alternatives to the self-referential and aggrandizing power of the Catholic Church. The poor – and paying attention to them as subjects of theological as well as sociological transformation – embody a possibility for a profound and much needed rejuvenation of the Catholic Church (Perine and Scannone 1993: 129).

27 Juan Carlos Scannone's words are reminiscent of his dialectic formation: "In this way, it will be possible to correct the *ideology* of globalization, and to take on, in turns, its effects within a logic of an *ethical and historical alternative* more in tune with thc understanding of humans pertaining to the Gospel and with the evangelical preferential option for the poor. This in line with the *seeds of new life* that is already developing in the history of the *Spirit of Life*" (my translation, original emphasis, Scannone 1999: 290).

28 Perine and Scannone 1993: 139–140.

29 Jane Schneider has argued that the late medieval pastoralist and animistic preoccupation with equity and reciprocities (between men and the spirits of the land) with the Reformation and counter-Reformation "lost ground to ideas of generalized, abstract love for everyone in the widening community of faith" (1990: 34). From then on a Christian salvationist and universal ethics of human love emerged – based

on divine sacrifice and redemption of human sin. However, Schneider argues, preoccupations with a balanced exchange between people and spirits continued to be a concern of European peasants regardless of a focus on brotherly and abstract love promoted by the late mediaeval and then later counter-Reformation institutionalized Church (Schneider 1990: 45, 47). If part of a pre-Reformation sensibility had a strong concern for reciprocity and saw the presence of evil in bodily vices, post-Reformation concepts harboured sins in human misguided, interior dispositions. The point to keep in mind here is that anthropological readings help to see how and where past histories and tensions have precisely not gone, but instead are partially present in their residual and emergent formations.

30 Alcuin was a scholar and a poet who contributed to the introduction of Anglo-Saxon humanism into the tradition of the Roman Catholic Church, in particular via his teaching at the Court of Charlemagne during the 780s.

31 St Peter Damian was a cardinal, a Doctor of the Church and a central figure in the Gregorian Reform movement – which fought for the moral integrity and independence of the clergy. He became particularly well known for his interventions on the defense of celibacy versus clerical marriage (nicolaitism) and for a treaty on simony (the purchase of ecclesiastic office) and the validity of sacraments bestowed by simoniac clergy.

32 Evagrius of Pontius's surviving body of writings is not very extensive, but is crucially important for the development of mystical theology, especially among the Syrians and the Eastern Christians. His seminal work includes the *Monachikos* ("The Monastic Life") and a treatise "On the Eight Principal Vices".

33 This is a term in Giorgio Agamben's interpretation (retaken from Aristotle) that points to an economic theology, an immanent order of human and divine life that manages the *oikos* (the house) and reconciles the Trinity with the unity of a single, transcendental God.

34 I am glad to see also that this is not only a possible anthropological account, but a theological interpretation too. See here the work of Cardinal Walter Kasper on Francis, acedia and mercy (2015).

References

Agamben, Giorgio. 2013. *The Highest Poverty: Monastic Rules and Form-of-Life*. Translated by Adam Kotsko. Stanford, CA: Stanford University Press.

Albahari, Maurizio. 2015. *Crimes of Peace: Mediterranean Migrations at the World's Deadliest Border. Philadelphia: University of* Pennsylvania Press.

Benedict XVI. 2009. "Encyclical, Caritas in Veritate." www.vatican.va/holy_father/benedict_xvi/encyclicals/documents/hf_ben-xvi_enc_20090629_caritas-in-veritate_en.html.

Crislip, Andrew. 2005. "The Sin of Sloth or the Illness of the Demons? The Demon of Acedia in Early Christian Monasticism." *Harvard Theological Review* 98(2): 143–169.

De Genova, Nicholas. 2012. "Border, Scene and Obscene." In *A Companion to Border Studies*, edited by Hastings Donnan and Thomas. M. Wilson, 492–504. Oxford: Blackwell Wiley.

Francis. 2013. "Evagelii Gaudium." http://w2.vatican.va/content/francesco/en/apost_exhortations/documents/papa-francesco_esortazione-ap_20131124_evangelii-gaudium.html.
Green, Sarah. 2013. "Borders and the Relocation of Europe." *Annual Review of Anthropology* 42: 345–361.
Gutiérrez, Gustavo. 1983. *The Power of the Poor in History*. Maryknoll, NY: Orbis Books.
John Paul II. 1981. "Laborem Exercens." http://w2.vatican.va/content/john-paul-ii/en/encyclicals/documents/hf_jp-ii_enc_14091981_laborem-exercens.html.
1987. "Solicitudo Rei Socialis." www.vatican.va/holy_father/john_paul_ii/encyclicals/documents/hf_jp-ii_enc_30121987_sollicitudo-rei-socialis_en.html.
1991. "Centesimus Annus. www.vatican.va/holy_father/john_paul_ii/encyclicals/documents/hf_jp-ii_enc_01051991_centesimus-annus_en.html.
Kaell, Hillary. 2016. La Dolce Vita: Desires and Despairs of Latin American Migrants in Rome. Book review: http://marginalia.lareviewofbooks.org/la-dolce-vita-desires-despairs-latin-american-migrants-rome-hillary-kaell/
Kasper, Walter. 2015. *Papa Francesco: La rivoluzione della tenerezza e dell' amore. Radici teologiche e prospettive pastorali*. Brescia: Editrice Queriniana.
Keough, Leyla J. 2006. "Globalizing 'Postsocialism': Mobile Mothers and Neoliberalism and the Margins of Europe." *Anthropological Quarterly* 79(3): 431–461.
Leo XIII. 1891. "Rerum Novarum." www.vatican.va/holy_father/leo_xiii/encyclicals/documents/hf_l-xiii_enc_15051891_rerum-novarum_en.html.
Mahdavi, Pardis. 2011. *Gridlock: Labor, Migration, and Human Trafficking in Dubai*. Stanford, CA: Stanford University Press.
Mezzadra, Sergio. 2010. The Gaze of Autonomy. Capitalism, Migration and Social Struggle. In *UniNOMADE*: www.uninomade.org/the-gaze-of-autonomy-capitalism-migration-and-social-struggles/.
Napolitano, Valentina. 2016. *Migrant Hearts and the Atlantic Return: Transnationalism and the Challenge to the Roman Catholic Church*. New York: Fordham University Press.
Napolitano Quayson, Valentina. 2005. "Social Suffering and Embodied States of Male Transnational Migrancy in San Francisco, California." *Identities* 12(3): 335–362.
Negri, Toni. 2013. *L'Abdicazione del Padre Tedesco*. www.uninomade.org/abdicazione-del-papa-tedesco/.
Paul VI. 1965. "Gaudiem et Spes." www.vatican.va/archive/hist_councils/ii_vatican_council/documents/vat-ii_const_19651207_gaudium-et-spes_en.html.
1967. "Popularum Progressio." www.vatican.va/holy_father/paul_vi/encyclicals/documents/hf_p-vi_enc_26031967_populorum_en.html.
Perine, Marcelo, and Juan Carlos Scannone. 1993. *Irrupción del Pobre y Quehacer Filosófico: Hacia Una Nueva Racionalidad*. Buenos Aires: Editorial Bonum.
Phillips, Adam. 1994. *On Kissing, Tickling, and being Bored: Psychoanalytic Essays on the Unexamined Life*. Cambridge, MA: Harvard University Press.
Povinelli, Elizabeth. 2002. *The Cunning of Recognition: Indigenous Alterities and the Making of Australian Multiculturalism*. Durham, NC: Duke University Press.
2006. *The Empire of Love: Toward a Theory of Intimacy, Genealogy, and Carnality*. Durham, NC: Duke University Press.
Sayad, Abdelmalek. 2004. *The Suffering of the Immigrant*. Cambridge, MA: Polity Press.

Scannone, Juan Carlos (et alt.). 1999. *Argentina: Alternativas Frente a la Globalización: Pensamiento Social de la Iglesia en el Umbral del Tercer Milenio.* Buenos Aires: San Pablo.

Schneider, Jean. 1990. "Spirits and the Spirit of Capitalism." In *Religious Orthodoxy and Popular Faith in European Society*, edited by Ellen Badone, 24–54. Princeton, NJ: Princeton University Press.

Wenzel, Siegfried. 1966. "Acedia, 700–1200." *Traditio* 22: 73–102.

Index

www.ingramcontent.com/pod-product-compliance
Lightning Source LLC
LaVergne TN
LVHW011525200926
848484LV00001B/160
9781107186057